A SHORT HISTORY OF THE UNITED STATES NAVY

From a photogravure, copyrighted, 1896, by A. W. Elson & Co., Boston

U. S. S. CONSTITUTION

A SHORT HISTORY

OF THE

UNITED STATES NAVY

BY

GEORGE R. CLARK, Rear-Admiral, U. S. Navy, (Ret.)
WILLIAM O. STEVENS, PH.D., LITT.D.
CARROLL S. ALDEN, PH.D.
HERMAN F. KRAFFT, LL.B.

REVISED AND CONTINUED
BY
CARROLL S. ALDEN, PH.D.

WIPF & STOCK · Eugene, Oregon

Wipf and Stock Publishers
199 W 8th Ave, Suite 3
Eugene, OR 97401

A Short History of the United States Navy
By Alden, Carroll S. and Davis, Christopher R.
ISBN 13: 978-1-5326-1809-3
Publication date 2/17/2017
Previously published by Lippincott Company, 1910

PREFACE TO REVISED EDITION

Although each profession has its own history, of importance to those included in that profession, naval history has grown to wider significance. Mahan by his *Influence of Sea Power Upon History* revealed its far reaching relations, and obtained for it a recognition such as merited a place in every library.

A survey of the history of the United States Navy, especially that of the last quarter of a century, will show that the study has its value, not only for thrilling stories of heroism and devotion, but for an understanding of the forces shaping national progress. Thus, though it is peculiarly adapted to naval officers, it should have, in time, a real meaning for all students of American foreign relations.

This book, in its original form, was written seventeen years ago to meet the needs of the Naval Academy. And now, to meet similar needs, it is continued to the present year.

The period is one in which epoch-making events have occurred. The United States has had an increasingly important part in world affairs, especially in the World War and in the many problems resulting from unsettled conditions in the Mediterranean, the Caribbean, and the Far East. In carrying out the national policy, the navy has been called upon to take a leading rôle.

The number of officers and men has been reduced, but to compensate for the losses the navy has placed an increasing emphasis on the preparation for duty of its personnel, from ordinary seaman to rear-admiral, which is to be gained through both general and special education. The number of ships has also been reduced, but the remaining ships have been made more efficient. The Utopian day when the nation will no longer need a navy seems as far distant as that when it can dispense with all legislative bodies and courts.

Thanks are due to Rear-Admiral George R. Clark, U. S. Navy (Ret.); Captain Walter S. Anderson, U. S. Navy, and Professor Herman F. Krafft of the Naval Academy, for many helpful suggestions in the preparation of the last four chapters (the new part of the present edition); to several members of the Department of English of the Naval Academy for suggestions relating to the revision of the earlier chapters; and to Professor Charles L. Lewis, also of the Department of English, for reading the manuscript and the proof.

CARROLL S. ALDEN.

United States Naval Academy,
    April, 1927.

CONTENTS

CHAPTER		PAGE
	PREFACE	3
I.	THE NAVY IN THE REVOLUTION	9
II.	THE REVOLUTION (CONTINUED). THE CRUISES OF JOHN PAUL JONES	24
III.	THE BEGINNINGS OF A NEW NAVY AND THE WAR WITH FRANCE	42
IV.	THE WAR WITH TRIPOLI	61
V.	THE WAR WITH TRIPOLI (CONTINUED)	76
VI.	THE WAR OF 1812. CAUSES AND EARLY EVENTS	93
VII.	THE CAPTURES OF THE GUERRIÈRE AND THE MACEDONIAN	109
VIII.	A VICTORY AND A DEFEAT	126
IX.	THE SLOOP ACTIONS OF THE WAR	144
X.	THE BATTLE OF LAKE ERIE	161
XI.	THE CRUISE OF THE ESSEX	175
XII.	THE BATTLE OF LAKE CHAMPLAIN AND THE CONCLUSION OF THE WAR	189
XIII.	MINOR OPERATIONS	203
XIV.	THE MEXICAN WAR. PERRY'S EXPEDITION TO JAPAN	220
XV.	THE CIVIL WAR: THE FIRST YEAR	238
XVI.	THE BATTLE OF HAMPTON ROADS: THE DESTRUCTION OF THE CUMBERLAND AND THE CONGRESS	255
XVII.	THE BATTLE OF HAMPTON ROADS (CONTINUED): THE MONITOR AND THE MERRIMAC	273
XVIII.	OPERATIONS ON THE WESTERN RIVERS	288
XIX.	OPERATIONS ON THE LOWER MISSISSIPPI	310

Contents

XX.	THE BATTLE OF MOBILE BAY	330
XXI.	THE WAR ON ALBEMARLE SOUND	348
XXII.	ACTIONS IN FOREIGN WATERS	365
XXIII.	THE BLOCKADE AND THE END OF THE WAR	388
XXIV.	THE NAVY IN THE YEARS OF PEACE	406
XXV.	WAR WITH SPAIN : THE BATTLE OF MANILA BAY	426
XXVI.	THE WEST INDIAN CAMPAIGN	445
XXVII.	EMERGENCE OF THE UNITED STATES AS A WORLD POWER	462
XXVIII.	THE WORLD WAR	483
XXIX.	THE WORLD WAR (CONTINUED)	501
XXX.	THE NAVY AND AMERICAN FOREIGN POLICY	511
	AUTHORITIES	534
	INDEX	541

ILLUSTRATIONS

	PAGE
U. S. Ship-of-the-Line Columbus at Anchor	45
Frigate with her Sails loosed to dry	47
U. S. Sloop-of-War Albany under full Sail	49
U. S. S. Louisville	291
C. S. S. Tennessee	341

PLATES

U. S. S. Constitution	*Frontispiece*
Paul Jones	24
A 32-Pound Carronade	42
A 24-Pound Long Gun	42
Edward Preble	70
Stephen Decatur, Jr.	118
Oliver H. Perry	164
David Porter	176
Thomas Macdonough	190
George Bancroft	218
Delivery of the President's Letter	232
Andrew H. Foote	290
David G. Farragut	310
David D. Porter	388
Three Historic Ships Formerly at the Naval Academy	406
George Dewey	426
U.S.S. Palos in the Yangtze	462
Division of Battleships at Force Battle Practice	482
Capture of the U-58 by the Fanning	490
"The Return of the Mayflower"	486

Maps and Diagrams

Lake Champlain	16
Cruises of the Ranger and the Bonhomme Richard	28
The Bonhomme Richard and the Serapis	33
Scene of the War with France	55
The Barbary States	63
Harbor of Tripoli	79
The Constitution and the Guerrière	111
The United States and the Macedonian	120
The Constitution and the Java	128
The Chesapeake and the Shannon	138
The Frigate and the Sloop Actions of the War of 1812	145
The Lake Campaigns, 1812–1814	162
The Battle of Lake Erie	169
The Cruise of the Essex	181
The Battle of Lake Champlain	194
Japan	228
Battle of Port Royal	246
Hampton Roads	265
Transverse Section through Turret of Original Monitor	275
Operations on the Western Rivers	289
Island No. 10	300
Battle of Mobile Bay	333
Albemarle and Pamlico Sounds	349
Cushing's Launch and Torpedo	357
The Cruise of the Alabama	373
The Kearsarge and the Alabama	381
Second Attack on Fort Fisher	402
The Arctic Regions	417
Battles of Manila	438
The West Indian Campaign	448
America's Strategic Position in the Pacific	467

A SHORT HISTORY
OF THE
UNITED STATES NAVY

I

THE NAVY IN THE REVOLUTION

CAUSES OF NAVAL ACTIVITY IN THE COLONIES

THE Revolution, like most of the wars in which America has been engaged, was one in which the army did the greater part of the fighting, but also one in which sea power was a deciding factor. Great Britain had the most powerful navy of the time, against which no force in open battle could have escaped defeat. But she fought at a disadvantage against an enemy 3000 miles distant, easily hidden in the countless harbors and inlets of an extensive coast line. The colonists, on the other hand, were of the same stock as the English, even better inured to hardship, and ready to take desperate chances as they attacked merchantmen or isolated units of the Royal Navy.

As the Continental Army seemed to spring out of the soil, so the navy seemed to spring out of the sea. When, on June 12, 1775, a party of Maine Woodsmen, armed, for the most part, with pitchforks and axes, and fired by the news of the battle of Lexington, captured with a lumber sloop an armed British schooner off Machias, Me., O'Brien, their leader, quickly armed his sloop with the captured cannon and ammunition, and put to sea in quest of prizes. Without a commission, letter of marque, or legal authority of any sort, this freebooter captured several prizes and sent them to Machias. O'Brien's example was quickly followed by others. Our coasts soon swarmed with the privateers of New England, and those of Massachusetts were particularly successful.

The daring and success of these privateers so angered Admiral Graves, the commander of the British fleet on the coast, that he reduced to ashes the town of Falmouth (now Portland), Me., thus leaving the inhabitants shelterless at the beginning of the bleak New England winter. Smarting already under the wrongs that precipitated the war, the hardy coast dwellers of the new world, whose rights to fisheries and navigation had been curtailed by shortsighted acts of Parliament, hardly needed this act of Admiral Graves to spur them to building ships of war.

Other causes contributed to the beginning of a naval force along the Atlantic coast. The colonists, from their origin and environment, were naturally seafarers. Some of the New England Colonies even before the Revolution had made remarkable progress in ship-building, fishing, and commerce; they were thus not unprepared to furnish vessels and daring sailors. Then, too, the country, being new and largely agricultural, needed manufactured articles, clothing, and munitions of war; and these things had to be either captured from the enemy, or brought from European countries, at the risk of seizure by British men-of-war. In order to capture from English supply ships designed for Boston articles much needed by his troops, Washington, in the fall of 1775, fitted out several small vessels, manned by soldiers, under the command of army officers. Washington had the entire management of this fleet. One of these ships, the *Lee*, whose com-

The Marine Committee

mission, as well as that of her captain, John Manly, was signed by Washington, captured the *Nancy*, "an ordnance ship ... containing, besides a large mortar upon a new construction, several pieces of brass cannon, a large quantity of small arms and ammunition, with all manner of tools, utensils, and machines necessary for camps and artillery, in the greatest abundance. The loss of this ship was much resented in England."[1] Altogether Washington's fleet captured about thirty-five prizes.[2]

Thus not only the bitter feelings of resentment against tyranny, coupled in numerous instances with motives of personal gains from prize money, but also the needs of the Continental Army quickly gave birth to a heterogeneous collection of ships. This was composed partly of privateers, partly of vessels owned and commissioned by individual Colonies, and partly of vessels commissioned by Congress.

The Marine Committee

A letter from General Washington, reporting the burning of Falmouth, was read in Congress, November 1, 1775; and Congress acted promptly. The following day it voted $100,000 for a naval armament and appointed a committee to buy the ships. A few weeks later it appointed a second committee, which suggested a fleet of thirteen vessels ranging from 32 to 24 guns, to be ready by March, 1776, and recommended the appointment of a third committee to supervise their construction and equipment. The report was adopted by Congress. In the third committee, known as the Marine Committee, there were thirteen members, one for each colony. Its personnel was practically the same as that of the second committee.

---

[1] Dodsley's *Annual Register*, London, 1776, p. 147.
[2] Paullin, *The Navy of the American Revolution*, p. 65.

and included such men as Robert Morris, John Hancock, and Samuel Chase, a remarkable body of men, who worked with the greatest ardor and patriotism.

The Marine Committee administered our naval affairs from December, 1775, to December, 1779. It was the forerunner of our Navy Department, but its functions were far more complex. Like the Congress of its day, it exercised legislative, judicial, and executive powers, always, however, under the direction of that body; and the same weaknesses, the lack of an administrative head and of actual authority over the States, hampered the committee as they did Congress.

Some of the confusion with which the Marine Committee struggled is suggested by the fact that naval officers then, instead of being commissioned by the President with the consent of the Senate, might be appointed in any one of the following ways: by the Marine Committee itself, by its subordinate boards at Philadelphia and Boston, by any naval commander, by recruiting agents, by commissioners abroad, or even by local authorities in the several States. Further, besides building and equipping ships of war and directing their movements, the committee had to hold courts-martial, send abroad dispatches and diplomatic agents, and trade American produce for European munitions of war. Under such conditions it is remarkable that the committee accomplished as much as it did.

As the Marine Committee proved to be a clumsy administrative machine,[3] it was superseded in 1779 by a "Board of Admiralty," consisting of three commissioners and two members of Congress, which was in power until 1781. Finally, Robert Morris was appointed "Agent of Marine," and he managed very efficiently what was left

---

[3] Paullin, *The Navy of the American Revolution*, p. 182, ff.

The First Fleet

of the American Navy. By this time, Congress realized that an administrative department, especially in time of war, must be under one head.

THE FIRST AMERICAN FLEET

The first naval committee bought and fitted out two 24-gun frigates, the *Alfred* and the *Columbus*, and two brigs, the *Andrea Doria* and the *Cabot*, and supplied them with powder and muskets borrowed from the Pennsylvania Committee of Safety. On December 22, 1775, Congress organized the first "American fleet" by granting commissions to Esek Hopkins, commander-in-chief of the fleet; Dudley Saltonstall, captain of the *Alfred*; Abraham Whipple, captain of the *Columbus*; Nicholas Biddle, captain of the *Andrea Doria*; and John Burroughs Hopkins, captain of the *Cabot*. John Paul Jones headed a list of five first lieutenants commissioned at the same time.

By the end of January, 1776, the committee had added to this fleet the sloops *Providence* and *Hornet* and the schooners *Wasp* and *Fly*. For these first eight vessels of the navy the committee had spent $134,333. With this tiny force, the commander-in-chief was ordered to proceed directly to Chesapeake Bay to attack the British fleet of Lord Dunmore; then, if successful, he was to proceed to the Carolinas and attack the British force there, and thence he was to sail to Rhode Island and "attack, take, and destroy all the enemy's naval force that you may find there." This was the gigantic task of a fleet of eight vessels carrying 110 guns, and manned by landsmen or, at least, men without naval discipline. To oppose this force, the British had in American waters, or on the way hither, seventy-eight men-of-war mounting 2078 guns. In Commodore Hopkins' fleet, only forty guns threw shot of nine pounds or more in weight, while the seventy-eight British ships on this coast had at least 500 18-pounders and heavier guns. The orders of the Marine Committee to the commander-in-chief of the navy, Esek Hopkins, were therefore foredoomed to failure.

Perhaps Commodore Hopkins himself foresaw the futility of trying to adhere too strictly to his orders, for, instead of going to Chesapeake Bay, he proceeded to Nassau in the Bahamas, which he captured. After taking a large quantity of shot and shell, besides some eight cannon, fifteen mortars, and other munitions of war, he sailed northward with the Governor and Lieutenant-Governor as prisoners. As he neared his destination, Rhode Island, he came upon his Majesty's ship *Glasgow*, of 20 guns, Captain Tyringham Howe, which single-handed, inflicted considerable damage on Hopkins' fleet, and made good its escape. The loss of the British was four men; that of the Americans, twenty-four, among the latter two lieutenants.

This injury inflicted upon a fleet by a single vessel which escaped showed little tactical skill on the part of the officers of the American fleet. As Commodore Hopkins had, besides, disobeyed his orders, he was court-martialed and finally dismissed.

Commodore Hopkins was the only man to hold the rank "commander-in-chief of the navy." This title was later merged in that of the President of the United States. During the rest of the Revolutionary War, the only commissioned officers in the navy were captains and lieutenants; but Congress, evidently providing for the future, fixed the relative ranks of army and navy officers as follows: admiral equivalent to general, vice-admiral equivalent to lieutenant-general, rear-admiral to major-general, commodore to brigadier-general, captain of a ship of forty guns and upwards to colonel, captain of a ship of twenty

Arnold on Lake Champlain

to forty guns to lieutenant-colonel, captain of a ship of ten to twenty guns to major, and lieutenant in the navy to captain. This table, taken from the British regulations of those times, has, in the main, continued in force to our day.

IMPORTANT NAVAL EVENTS DURING THE REVOLUTION

From our standpoint it will hardly be profitable to follow all of the various actions fought by the little United States Navy during the Revolution. Paullin, in his *Navy of the American Revolution,* makes the total number of vessels under the Continental Congress forty-two. These were practically all annihilated before the end of the war; but the heroic struggles of this early navy were not without result. In considering them, we shall outline the work of Benedict Arnold on Lake Champlain, of Wickes, Conyngham, and especially Jones, in British waters, and of Biddle, Barry, and others on the American seaboard; and we shall not omit some mention of the State navies and the privateers, as well as of the assistance rendered by France.

THE FIRST BATTLE OF LAKE CHAMPLAIN

The possession of Lakes Champlain and George was felt early in the war to be of strategic importance. Not only did these lakes furnish an excellent waterway from Canada to the Colonies, but it was the design of the British that Carleton's army from Canada should rendezvous about Albany and thereby cut off all communications between the northern and southern Colonies. The American Army had invaded Canada in September, 1775, and during the following winter it had held Governor Guy Carleton shut up in Quebec. On the arrival of a

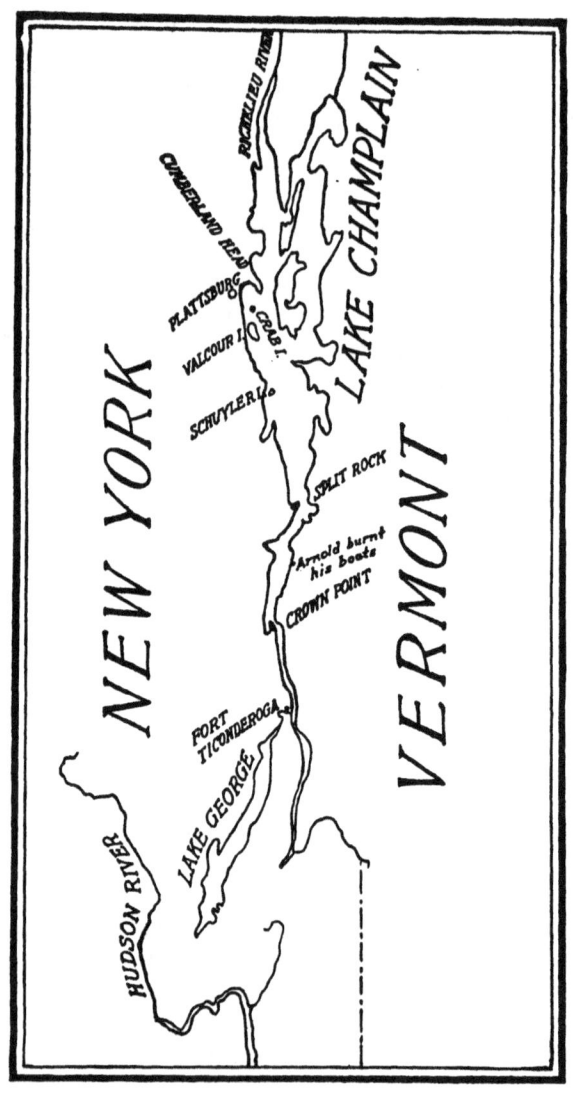

LAKE CHAMPLAIN

British fleet with reinforcements, the Americans retreated to Crown Point, where they arrived on July 3, 1776. Brigadier-General Benedict Arnold, who, earlier in his career as a West India merchant, had at times commanded his own ships, started immediately to build a fleet on the lakes in competition with the British. Late in July, he was appointed by Gates to the command of the naval forces on the lakes. By October, he was able to muster one sloop, three schooners, eight gondolas, and four galleys. These vessels mounted altogether ninety-four cannon, from 2-pounders to 18-pounders, and they were manned by 700 officers and men, according to Arnold, "a wretched motley crew; the marines the refuse of every regiment, and the seamen few of them ever wet with salt water." Arnold chose for his flagship one of the galleys, the *Congress*, a vessel of fifty-foot keel and of thirteen-foot beam, mounting one 18-pounder, one 12-pounder, and two 6-pounders.

But the British, with their greater resources in skilled seamen and in manufactured articles, won this race in building a fleet. Captain Charles Douglas, who had charge of the construction work of the enemy, had ready in twenty-eight days a full-rigged ship, the *Enterprise*, carrying eighteen 12-pounders. She had been begun at Quebec, and had been brought from the St. Lawrence up the Richelieu. The *Enterprise* was of 180 tons burden, and greatly exceeded in size and armament any of Arnold's fleet. Early in October, General Sir Guy Carleton, thanks to Captain Douglas' energy in ship-building, had under his command one ship, two schooners, one radeau (raft), one large gondola, twenty gunboats and four armed tenders. The British fleet in the St. Lawrence furnished Carleton with 700 experienced officers and seamen. The enemy also had a large detachment of savages under Major Thomas Carleton.

The first squadron battle to be fought by Americans, "a strife of pygmies for the prize of a continent," as Mahan styles it, was begun on October 11, 1776. Arnold was lying in wait for Carleton behind Valcour Island, not far from the site of a later battle of Lake Champlain (September 11, 1814), where the struggle was again for the control of this great waterway.

As the British van, coming down under a fair north wind, with full press of sail, passed the Americans before discovering Arnold's fleet, Carleton's heavier vessels had to beat back slowly to help his hard-pressed gunboats. The Americans fought desperately from eleven o'clock in the morning till five o'clock that afternoon. With the British attacking in front and the Indians occupying the shore in the rear, Arnold was indeed "between the devil and the deep sea." That night, however, under cover of the lake mist, he slipped through the British line toward Ticonderoga. The British gave chase, and on the two days following they continued the battle. Finally, Arnold beached his boats, and fought with desperate courage until his men had fired their gondolas and taken refuge in the woods. Most of Arnold's vessels were either captured or destroyed. In this battle the enemy captured 110 prisoners, among them being General Waterbury, the second in command. Arnold, with the rest of his men, made good his escape to Crown Point.

Although Arnold had lost his fleet, the delay which he thus forced on Carleton was of the greatest advantage to the Americans. "Never had any force," says Mahan, "big or small, lived to better purpose, or died more gloriously; for it had saved the lake for that year." The delay compelled Carleton to give up his plan of joining Howe to the south. When, next year, Burgoyne, renewing the attempt, invaded New York, he had not the aid which

Carleton could have relied on in 1776. Hence Arnold's work on the lakes opened the way for the surrender of Burgoyne at Saratoga.[4]

WICKES AND CONYNGHAM IN EUROPEAN WATERS

Nothing illustrates so completely the daring and enterprise of the Americans, save possibly the boldness of certain privateersmen, as the harrying of the British coast by Wickes, Conyngham, and Jones. In the fall of 1776, Captain Lambert Wickes, of the 16-gun brig *Reprisal*, while carrying Benjamin Franklin to France, captured two prizes. The next spring, the *Lexington* joined the *Reprisal*, and these two vessels captured about fifteen prizes. With these the cruisers returned to France; but, as the latter country was ostensibly at peace with England, the vessels were ordered to leave. After disposing of the prizes clandestinely to French merchants, the *Lexington* quickly refitted and sailed from Morlaix on September 18, 1777. She was captured shortly after by the *Alert*, and her officers and men were taken to Plymouth and thrown into Mill prison on a charge of high treason. Richard Dale, who later distinguished himself on the *Bonhomme Richard* under Jones, was one of these prisoners; but he made his escape a year later by boldly walking past the guards, dressed in a British uniform. On the insistence of the British, the *Reprisal* also left France; she foundered on her way home, off the Banks of Newfoundland, and, with the exception of one of the crew, all hands, including the brave Wickes, were lost.

The reckless daring and success of Captain Conyngham in harrying British commerce, strained almost to the breaking point the relations between England and France.

---

[4] Clowes, *Royal Navy*, iii, 368.

The American Commissioners at Paris, through an agent, had bought a cutter at Dover, and had then manned and equipped her at Dunkirk, naming her the *Surprise*. Congress, over the signature of John Hancock, as president, had issued blank commissions to the American Commissioners in France; it was such a commission, dated March 1, 1777, that Benjamin Franklin and Silas Deane, the commissioners, had filled out with the name of Gustavus Conyngham, authorizing him to sail in the *Surprise* as a captain of the American Navy. A great deal of difficulty was encountered in getting the *Surprise* out of Dunkirk. Captain Conyngham "took his arms out of his ship and said he should load it with merchandise for one of the ports in Norway. As this declaration was suspected, security was demanded. Two persons, Hodge and Allen, became responsible for him. Conyngham actually left the port of Dunkirk without arms, but he caused sailors, cannon, and ammunition to be sent out to him in the night, while he was in the road, off Dunkirk; and he shortly after took the English packet boat, *Prince of Orange*. As soon as this came to the knowledge of the French Government, Hodge, one of the securities, was arrested, and conducted to the Bastille. The packet boat was restored to the British Government without the form of process. After six weeks of confinement, Hodge was released." [5]

Shortly after this, Conyngham captured the Harwich packet and took it to a French port. This open violation of neutrality so enraged the British, that their ambassador threatened to leave France if Conyngham and his prize were not at once given up. The French Government imprisoned the captain and crew of the *Surprise*, and

---

[5] Sparks, *Diplomatic Correspondence*, i, 292, note (Franklin and Deane to the Committee of Foreign Affairs, May 25, 1777).

returned the vessel to her owners. But before England could enforce her demand for the delivery of Conyngham and his men to the sloops of war sent over for this purpose, the Americans, by some intrigue, had been released and sent to sea in another cutter, the *Revenge*, a vessel provided and equipped partly by the American Commissioners, and partly on private account. It seems probable that Hodge, a Philadelphia merchant, and perhaps some others, were pecuniarily interested, at least in the later cruises of this cutter.

The *Revenge* captured many prizes, and on two occasions boldly sailed in disguise into British ports and refitted. As Deane wrote to Robert Morris in August, 1777: "Conyngham's cruise effectually alarmed England, prevented the great fair at Chester, occasioned insurance to rise, and even deterred the English merchants from shipping goods in English bottoms at any rate, so that in a few weeks forty sail of French ships were loading in the Thames on freight—an instance never known before. . . . In a word, Conyngham, by his first and second bold expeditions, is become the terror of all the eastern coast of England and Scotland, and is more dreaded than Thurot [6] was in the late war."[7]

On a later cruise, Conyngham sent most of his prizes to Ferrol, Spain, and thus his depredations on British commerce embarrassed France and the American Commissioners less than former expeditions had done. In 1778, Captain Conyngham was captured, and while in prison he was treated with such severity, that Congress,

---

[6] A French corsair who did great damage in commerce-destroying expeditions against British shipping during the Seven Years War.

[7] Wharton, *Diplomatic Correspondence*, ii, 379–380 (Deane to Morris, Aug. 23, 1777).

in a resolution on July 17, of that year, protested against a treatment "contrary to all dictates of humanity and the practice of civilized nations."

NAVAL PRISONERS, PRIZES, AND THEIR EFFECTS ON NEUTRALITY

This matter of naval prisoners in England, combined with the violations of neutral rights committed by our vessels, was a great source of worry to the American Commissioners. These officials, having merely the status of private citizens in France, were treated by the French court with all civility, but they could not yet be openly received or recognized. Hence their work required the utmost tact and delicacy. That naval prisoners in England were treated with extreme harshness is admitted even by British authorities. This cruelty was undoubtedly due partly to the low conditions of prison systems in England, as indeed in other parts of Europe in the eighteenth century. One of the reasons for the cruises of American vessels in British waters was to capture Englishmen in retaliation for the treatment of Americans in Forton prison at Portsmouth, Mill prison at Plymouth, and the prison ship *Jersey* at Brooklyn.

"The British Government resisted the exchange of prisoners taken in European waters on three grounds: (1) This involved a recognition of belligerent rights in the insurgents. (2) The American prisoners could be kept out of harm's way in England; the same condition did not apply to British prisoners taken by American vessels, as long as France refused to permit such prisoners to be landed and imprisoned on her shores. (3) British seamen, being far more numerous than American, ex-

Neutrality of France and Spain 23

change would tell more favorably for the latter than for the former."[8]

To end their sufferings, some of these prisoners in England enlisted in the British Navy, or in whaling fleets, while others escaped from prison. Conyngham and sixty companions, in November, 1779, burrowed their way out of captivity, thus "committing treason through his Majesty's earth," as Conyngham remarked. It was long after the secret treaty between France and the United States was signed in February, 1778, before Franklin could persuade the English to take a more liberal view as regards exchanging prisoners. In fact, the first exchange was not effected till March, 1779. The Americans, before the treaty with France, had to confine their captives taken in British waters on shipboard, or let them go. After the treaty and after the breaking out of war between Spain and England in 1779, these men were imprisoned in France and Spain. So, likewise, the question of the disposition of prizes captured in European waters was a difficult one before the treaty. Many prizes were taken to France, where they were secretly sold, in spite of official orders commanding the American captains to leave port with their prizes. Indeed, it is very probable that, if hostilities between France and England had not for other causes broken out in 1778, the countries would have gone to war because of the connivance of the French at these breaches of neutrality.

---

[8] Wharton, *Diplomatic Correspondence*, ii, 724, note (Franklin, Lee, and Adams to the President of Congress, Sept. 17, 1778).

II

THE REVOLUTION (CONTINUED)—THE CRUISES OF JOHN PAUL JONES

Jones's Earlier Cruises

PAUL JONES'S early career during the Revolution may be briefly told. On May 10, 1776, he received the 12-gun brig *Providence* as his first independent command. On this vessel he carried troops and convoyed merchantmen, and so skilful was he in eluding the numerous British cruisers, that Congress promoted him in August to the full rank of captain, with orders to cruise for prizes along the Atlantic coast. In September, 1776, by a bold maneuver, he escaped from the 28-gun frigate *Solebay*. He later eluded the British frigate *Milford*, captured sixteen prizes, and destroyed other vessels. Some time after this, while in command of the *Alfred*, Captain Jones took the British brig *Mellish*, laden with military supplies. On the way home, he was again chased by the *Milford*, and as he was accompanied by a convoy of prizes, he skilfully lured the *Milford* away from them, under cover of night, so that they got safely to an American port, and then Jones, by superior seamanship, escaped from his pursuer.

Captain Jones, on June 14, 1777, was put in command of the new 18-gun ship *Ranger*, built at Portsmouth, N. H., and was ordered to France. What the motives were for sending him to foreign waters is not quite clear. His knowledge of British shores and his success in American waters were doubtless contributing factors. He was,

From the painting by Cecilia Beaux, copyrighted, 1906, by U. S. Naval Academy

PAUL JONES

moreover, looked upon by some of his colleagues as lukewarm to America, because he was a native of Scotland and had, from natural motives of generosity, been lenient to British prisoners.

It was true that he had been only about three years in America, and his ideas of liberty and the rights of man he had drawn from a brief association with the radicals of North Carolina and Virginia. But these radicals were no less than Willie Jones (son of the colonial agent of Lord Granville), Joseph Hewes, Patrick Henry, and Thomas Jefferson. What they taught certainly left a lasting impression.

Furthermore, the jealousy of the inactive Commodore Hopkins, who looked with eyes askance at the strenuous successes of his young subordinate, may have had some effect in sending Jones to a difficult task far from home waters. This feeling against him seems also to have existed in Congress, for on the reorganization of the Navy, October 10, 1776, thirteen men were promoted over his head. Some years later, in a letter to Robert Morris, Jones writes: " Rank, which opens the door to glory, is too near the heart of every man of true military feeling, to be given up in favor of any other man who has not, by the achievement of some brilliant action, or by known and superior abilities, merited such preference. If this be so, how must I have felt, since, by the second table of captains in the navy, adopted by Congress on the 10th of October, 1776, I was superseded in favor of thirteen persons, two of whom were my junior lieutenants at the beginning; the rest were only commissioned into the Continental Navy on that day; and if they had any superior ability, these were not then known, nor have since been proved. I am the eldest sea officer (except Captain Whipple) on the Journal, and under the commission of Congress, remaining in the service.''

Whatever the motives in sending him to Europe may have been, Jones started at once to prepare his ship for his long cruise. The selection of the commissioned and warrant officers of the *Ranger* was entrusted to a committee of three men—William Whipple, the New Hampshire member of the Marine Committee, John Langdon, Continental agent at Portsmouth, and John Paul Jones, the new commander of the vessel. This illustrates one of the various ways by which selections of this kind were made—surely not a bad way, inasmuch as it gave the man who was to command the vessel a voice in the choosing of the men who were to serve under him. The *Ranger* is said to have been the first vessel to fly the Stars and Stripes, then recently adopted.

Jones arrived at Nantes in December, 1777, and from there he sailed in February, 1778, for Quiberon Bay, to escort some American merchantmen. This was just about the time that the secret treaty was made between the United States and France. Jones, in his orders, had been warned to be very careful about the rights of the latter country as a neutral nation. Although Franklin was doing his utmost to have the United States recognized by France, thinking that this act would involve the French in trouble with the English, still any unwarranted breaches of neutrality might at the crucial moment spoil the plans of the American Commissioners at Paris. Captain Jones writes very proudly of the fact that, at Quiberon Bay, on February 14, 1778, the *Ranger* was the first American vessel to exchange salutes with a foreign nation. Jones sent a boat back and forth to the French flagship in his effort to get the French admiral to return gun for gun, but at length the American commander reluctantly consented to a salute of two guns less than his own. This incident shows Jones's pride in his adopted country; it also shows a willingness on the part

The Ranger and the Drake

of France to do a generous and overt act towards recognition of the new nation.

On April 10, 1778, Jones left Brest and sailed straight for the English coast. His first attempt was to set fire to the great quantity of shipping in the harbor of Whitehaven. Landing early on the morning of the 22d, he easily captured the forts. But, because of a hitch in his plans, the day was well advanced and the people were crowding to the shore in thousands before he reached the shipping. He had to content himself with setting fire to one ship, with the hope that the flames would spread to the 200 or more vessels in the harbor. The attempt was not successful, but its daring strongly impressed the British.

Shortly after these events, Jones stood over to the Scotch shore, where, with one boat and a very small party, he made a landing at St. Mary's Isle. The American captain did this with the purpose of capturing the Earl of Selkirk as a hostage for the better treatment of our prisoners in England. As this nobleman was not at home, the sailors contented themselves with the taking of the silverware of the castle, which Jones himself bought from his men and returned to the Countess of Selkirk with a chivalrous letter full of apologies.

The Ranger-Drake Battle

On the morning of the 24th of April, 1778, Jones appeared off Carrickfergus on the northeast coast of Ireland opposite Whitehaven, and lured out the British sloop of war *Drake*, 20 guns, which came to investigate the "suspicious stranger." Hails were exchanged, whereupon, says Jones, "the *Drake* being astern of the *Ranger*, I ordered the helm up and gave the first broadside. The action was warm, close, and obstinate. It lasted an hour and four minutes, when the enemy called for quarter; her fore and main topsail yards being both cut

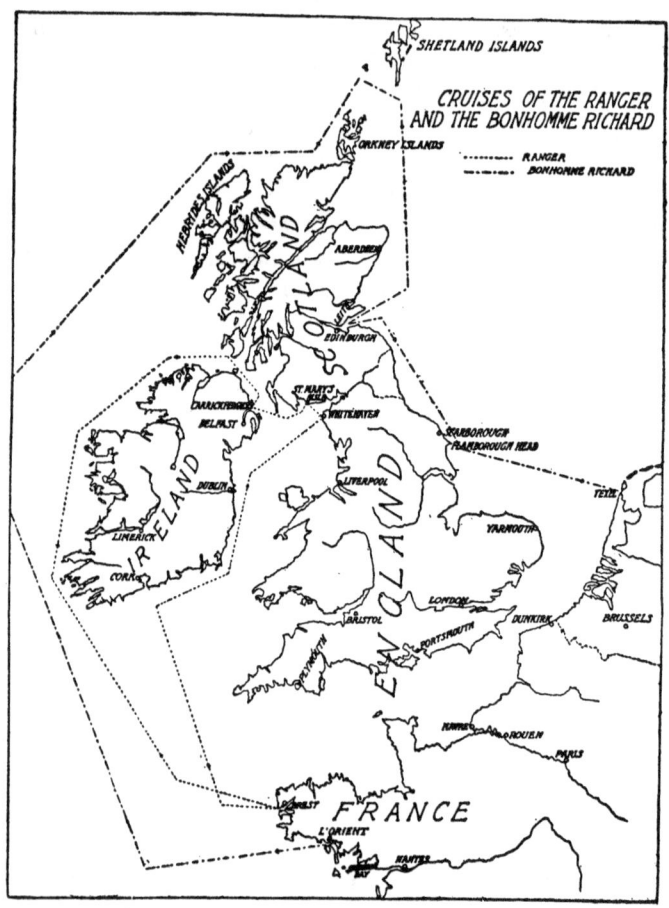

CRUISES OF THE RANGER AND THE BONHOMME RICHARD

away, and down on the cap; the topgallant yard and mizzen-gaff both hanging up and down along the mast; the second ensign which they had hoisted shot away, and

The War in Home Waters

hanging on the quarter-gallery in the water; the jib shot away, and hanging in the water; her sails and rigging entirely cut to pieces; her masts and yards all wounded, and her hull also very much galled. I lost only Lieutenant Wallingford and one seaman killed, and six wounded. The loss of the enemy in killed and wounded was far greater, . . . forty-two men. The captain and the lieutenant were among the wounded.''

It is fair to state that the *Drake*, though nominally the equal of the *Ranger*, was almost as unprepared for battle as the ill-starred *Chesapeake* in her encounter with the *Leopard*. The *Drake's* crew were new; her only officers were the captain, and a lieutenant who had come on board at the last moment as a volunteer; she had no gunner, no cartridges had been filled, and no preparations had been made for handling the powder.

Biddle and Barry in American Waters

While Jones was thus winning honors in British waters, the ships at home could accomplish little against the tremendous British Navy. But some of our captains, like Biddle and Barry, deserve mention for their heroic struggles in a losing game. On the 32-gun frigate *Randolph*, one of the thirteen frigates built by Congress, Captain Nicholas Biddle fought in West Indian waters the British 64-gun ship-of-the-line *Yarmouth*. After an hour's hard fighting, a shot from the *Yarmouth* exploded the *Randolph's* magazine and blew her to fragments. Of the latter's crew of 315 men only four were found alive.

In the *Lexington*, Captain John Barry captured, in April, 1776, the British sloop *Edward*. Barry was later promoted to the *Effingham*, but this vessel was destroyed in the Delaware. In the *Raleigh*, 32, Captain

Barry then fell in with the 50-gun ship *Experiment* and the frigate *Unicorn*, in September, 1778. He kept up a running fight for two days, and, when the wind died out, he finally beached his ship on the coast of Maine and escaped with his men. Some time before this, Captain Barry had, with twenty-seven men, boarded the British armed schooner *Alert* in the Delaware, capturing 116 men and officers, and sinking the schooner and two transports. Barry was one of the bravest naval officers of the Revolution; but he was, if anything, too daring, for it was useless for the American frigates to fight the powerful British ships-of-the-line. At the end of 1778, only four of the thirteen frigates were left.

The Battle Between the Bonhomme Richard and the Serapis

Meanwhile France and England had gone to war, and in 1779 Spain leagued herself with America against England. The joint fleets of France and Spain thereupon entered the Channel and even threatened a descent on the English coast.

Seemingly, France could now render effective aid to Paul Jones, yet he found great difficulty in persuading the French to give him a new command. The Minister of Marine, De Sartine, had promised him again and again specific ships, but the powerful aristocracy in the French Navy prevented De Sartine from fulfilling his promise to a foreigner, who was regarded by many as an adventurer. The impetuous Jones chafed under these repeated disappointments, and wrote many letters to Franklin, De Sartine, and even to the King. When, after five months of waiting, Jones's patience was exhausted, he went in person to the court and received the old hulk *Duras,* of 40 guns. He had learned the wisdom of one

Cruise of the Bonhomme Richard

of Franklin's adages in the latter's *Poor Richard's Almanac,* "If you would have your business done, go yourself; if not, send." In gratitude to his friend Franklin, Jones rechristened the *Duras* the *Bonhomme Richard.*

To this vessel were added four other ships: the *Alliance,* 36; the *Pallas,* 30; the *Cerf,* 18; and the *Vengeance,* 12. The new *Alliance,* the only American ship in the squadron, Congress had put in command of Pierre Landais, a Frenchman, in compliment to France. The squadron was hastily got ready at L'Orient. Some American prisoners, about 100, recently exchanged by England, gave Jones the nucleus of an American crew on the *Bonhomme Richard,* but otherwise the officers and crews were a motley and cosmopolitan assemblage, except those of the *Pallas* and the *Vengeance,* which were French. Indeed, the fact that Landais' crew were largely British may add some extenuating circumstances to the strange conduct of this "half crazy" officer during the battle. On the other hand, Richard Dale, Jones's first lieutenant, had unusual ability and did excellent service.

The relation of the American commodore to his squadron was peculiar. The representative of the French Minister of Marine, in giving Jones the squadron, had forced him to sign a paper, by which, instead of being the superior officer, he became only one of equal rank with his subordinates. This made the squadron a confederacy rather than a unit.

After repeated delays, Captain Jones finally set sail from L'Orient on August 14, 1779. He proceeded up the west coast of Ireland with the purpose of circumnavigating the British Isles. On August 26, the *Cerf* and two French privateers which had attached themselves to the squadron a few days before were separated in a gale, and never rejoined the fleet. On the cruise Jones took some ships as prizes and destroyed others; but he had considerable difficulty with his French captains, especially Landais, in regard to the disposal of prizes, and he could make no important move without much discussion with his colleagues. Indeed, Landais showed an insubordination that boded ill for the success of any concerted movement.

Having rounded the Orkneys, Jones intended to destroy the shipping at Leith, but was frustrated by the dilatory co-operation of the captains of the *Pallas* and the *Vengeance*. On September 23, at dawn, his lookout sighted a large ship rounding Flamborough Head. By noon it became apparent that a Baltic fleet of forty merchantmen, under convoy of two British men-of-war were heading northeast. The merchantmen, at the signal of danger, scattered in flight toward Scarborough. The warships, which were the *Serapis*, a new frigate of 50 guns, and the *Countess of Scarborough*, 20, under the command of Captain Pearson, then took a position between the Baltic fleet inshore and their enemy. Jones now stood for the *Serapis* and ordered his captains to form the line of battle, an order to which Landais paid no attention. Instead of maintaining his place behind the *Richard*, Landais, availing himself of the better sailing qualities of the *Alliance*, forged ahead to ascertain the power of the enemy. Then he went out of gun-shot and remained there until the battle began. Landais had already hailed Cottineau in the *Pallas*, saying that if the enemy had a ship of more than fifty guns their only course was to run away. This insubordinate and cowardly speech, uttered in the presence of the crews of both ships, shows what sort of officer Landais was.[1]

---

[1] Mahan. *Jones in the Revolution* (*Scribner's Magazine*. **xxiv.** 207.)

The Bonhomme Richard and the Serapis 33

At six P.M. the *Serapis* came about and steered westward with the *Scarborough* in her wake. Jones kept his vessel bows on toward the enemy to keep the British in the dark as to the number of his guns. His only hope was in a close encounter. Thus it was that, when at seven P.M. Jones came within range, the battle

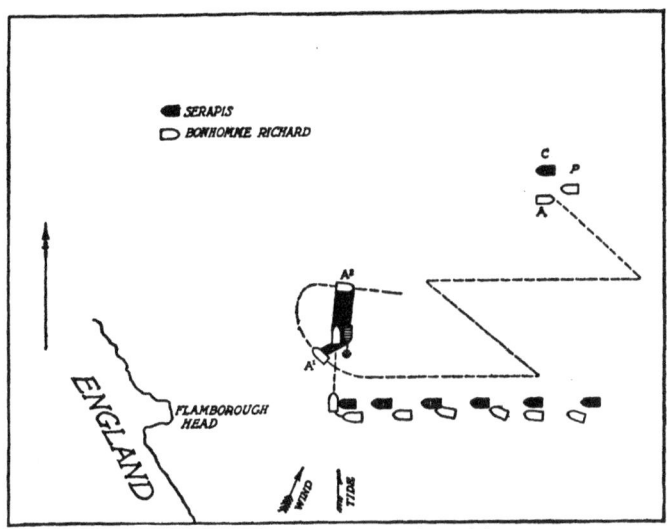

From Mahan's article in *Scribner's Magazine*, XXIV, 210, by permission

THE BONHOMME RICHARD AND THE SERAPIS

opened with both ships gradually running on parallel courses toward Flamborough Head. The wind at this time was southwest.

Jones answered Pearson's hail evasively, and immediately followed this up with a shot. At the very first exchange of broadsides, two of the three 18-pounders on the starboard side of the *Richard* burst, killing and wounding most of their crews and blowing up the deck above. These guns had to be entirely abandoned, leaving only the 12- and 9-pounders.

Of this stage of the battle Jones says in his report:[2]

"The battle, thus begun, was continued with unremitting fury. Every method was practised on both sides to gain an advantage, and rake each other; and I must confess that the enemy's ship, being much more manageable than the *Richard,* gained thereby several times an advantageous situation, in spite of my best endeavors to prevent it. As I had to deal with an enemy of greatly superior force, I was under the necessity of closing with him, to prevent the advantage which he had over me in point of maneuver. It was my intention to lay the *Richard* athwart the enemy's bow, but as that operation required great dexterity in the management of both sails and helm and some of our braces being shot away, it did not exactly succeed to my wishes. The enemy's bowsprit, however, came over the *Bonhomme Richard's* poop by the mizzenmast, and I made both ships fast together in that situation, which by the action of the wind on the enemy's sails, forced her stern close to the *Richard's* bow, so that the ships lay square alongside of each other, the yards being all entangled, and the cannon of each ship touching the opponent's side. When this position took place, it was eight o'clock, previous to which the *Richard* had received sundry 18-pound shots below the water, and leaked very much."

Although Jones had lashed the vessels together, the *Serapis'* crew were on the alert for any attempt at boarding. Pearson evidently recognized his great advantage in maneuvering, and at the moment of fouling had let go an anchor, hoping thus, by means of the tide and the wind, to wrench the vessels apart. But the ships held fast. As up to this stage of the battle the *Serapis*

---

[2]**Jones**'s report may be found in Stewart's *John Paul Jones Commemoration,* pp. 139, ff.

had fought only her port guns, the starboard lower ports were closed. Since now the close contact of the vessels prevented the opening of these ports, Pearson fired through them. So near to each other were the gun crews, that, according to Dale, the men had to run the rammers into the opponent's ports to load their pieces, and Pearson tells us that the muzzles of the guns touched the sides of the enemy's ship. During this part of the fight, the damage done to the American vessel by the more powerful 18-pounders of the enemy was terrible. Says Jones: "The rudder was entirely cut off the stern frame, and the transoms were almost wholly cut away. The timbers of the lower deck especially, from the main-mast to the stern, being greatly decayed with age, were mangled beyond any power of description."

In the course of this terrible pounding, Jones's battery of 12-pounders was entirely silenced and abandoned. In his report he continues:

"I had now only two pieces of cannon, 9-pounders, on the quarter-deck that were not silenced, and not one of the heavier cannon was fired during the rest of the action. The purser, Mr. Mease, who commanded the guns on the quarter-deck, being dangerously wounded in the head, I was obliged to fill his place, and with great difficulty rallied a few men, and shifted over one of the lee quarter-deck guns, so that we afterward played three pieces of 9-pounders upon the enemy. The tops alone seconded the fire of this little battery and held out bravely during the whole of the action; especially the main top, where Lieutenant Stack commanded. I directed the fire of one of the three cannon against the main-mast, with double-headed shot, while the other two were exceedingly well served with grape and canister shot to silence the enemy's musketry, and clear her decks, which was at last effected."

The condition of the *Richard* was becoming more and more desperate; her hold was filling with water and she was on fire in several places. The master-at-arms, who had charge of the prisoners in the *Richard's* hold, either thinking the old vessel was doomed, or inspired by treachery, had released them. The prisoners would naturally have joined battle against the crew of the *Richard*, assisting their countrymen in the *Serapis,* had not Dale shrewdly put them to work at the pumps, telling them that the enemy's plight was worse, and that their own safety depended on keeping the *Richard* afloat. Just before this, the gunner, in a state of panic, had loudly clamored for quarter, and was in the act of striking the colors, when Jones hurled his pistol at the fellow, breaking his skull. In the silence that followed, Pearson gave the order to board, but the men who attempted to carry out this command were quickly repelled. To Pearson's query whether the Americans had surrendered, Jones gave the answer that has since become one of the watchwords of the navy, "I have not yet begun to fight!"

Although the *Richard* was hopelessly inferior in her batteries, the force aloft, armed with muskets and grenades, finally turned the tide of victory. The British had been driven out of their own tops, and the Americans dexterously climbed along the interlaced rigging of the two ships, and thus kept the deck of the *Serapis* clear of defenders. Says Pearson in his report, "From the great quantity and variety of combustible material they threw upon our decks, chains, and in short into every part of the ship, we were on fire no less than ten or twelve times in different parts of the ship, and it was with the greatest difficulty and exertion at times that we were able to get it extinguished."[3]

---

[3] Dodsley's *Annual Register,* xxii, 310.

The Bonhomme Richard and the Serapis 37

A very important part in this fight was played by a marine in the maintop of Jones's flagship who succeeded in dropping a hand-grenade into the open hatch of the *Serapis*. A terrific explosion followed, "the flames of which," says Pearson, "running from cartridge to cartridge all the way aft, blew up the whole of the people and officers that were quartered abaft the mainmast; from which unfortunate circumstance all those guns were rendered useless for the remainder of the action, and I fear the greatest part of the people will lose their lives." Pearson was a brave fighter, but this catastrophe on his own ship must have had much to do with the final disorganizing of his men.

At this crisis the *Alliance* made her appearance. She had once before early in the action sailed around the combatants and fired her broadsides so recklessly at the entangled vessels that she did as much damage to the *Richard* as to the enemy. Of her second attack, Jones says: "Landais discharged a broadside full into the stern of the *Richard*. We called to him for God's sake to forbear firing into the *Bonhomme Richard;* yet he passed along the off side of the ship and continued firing. There was no possibility of his mistaking the enemy's ship for the *Richard*, there being the most essential difference in their appearance and construction; besides, it was then full moonlight, and the sides of the *Richard* were all black, while the sides of the prizes were yellow. Yet, for the greater security, I showed the signal of our reconnoissance, by putting out three lanterns, one at the head, another at the stern, and the third in the middle, in a horizontal line. Every tongue cried that he was firing into the wrong ship, but nothing availed; he passed round, firing into the *Richard's* head, stern, and broadside, and by one of his volleys killed several of my best men, and mortally wounded a good officer on the forecastle. My situation was really deplorable. The *Richard* received various shot under water from the *Alliance;* the leak gained on the pump, and the fire increased much on board both ships."

However, Captain Pearson was even more discouraged by the reappearance of the *Alliance* than Jones. In fact, he ascribes his final defeat to Landais. But probably owing to his ignorance of the eccentricities of the Frenchman's character, he did not realize the damage the latter was doing to Jones's ship. Mahan thinks that it was the superiority above decks of the *Bonhomme Richard* which finally turned the scales.[4] At the moment of surrender, the mainmast of the *Serapis*, at which Jones had for some time been discharging one of his 9-pounders, went by the board. The loss in killed and wounded was exceptionally heavy on both sides; that of the *Richard* being 116 men, and of the *Serapis* 129.[5]

The *Countess of Scarborough,* the second of the two vessels under Captain Pearson, was captured after an hour's hard fighting by the *Pallas.* The latter seems to have been the only one of Jones's ships that rendered assistance. The *Vengeance* took no part in the action. The Baltic fleet was allowed to escape because, as Jones says, "I myself was in no condition to pursue, and none of the rest showed any inclination to do so." Unquestionably, Landais was jealous of the American commodore, as was evident from numerous acts of his on the cruise.

The honors in this battle were decidedly in favor of Jones, who, in an old vessel, transformed into a one-decker by the necessary abandonment early in the action of her useless 18-pounders, had fought to a finish a new frigate, which, though classed as a "forty-four," carried in reality

---

[4] Mahan, *Scribner's Magazine*, xxiv, 210.
[5] Paullin, *Navy of the American Revolution,* p. 297.

fifty guns. The *Pallas* had her match in the *Countess of Scarborough;* the *Alliance* did as much harm as good; and the remaining vessel under Jones took no part in the battle. Thus Pearson, instead of sacrificing his two vessels to save the Baltic fleet against a vastly superior force, had in reality matched his two better vessels against two of Jones's squadron, and the escape of the Baltic fleet was an accident so far as Pearson was concerned. There is not the slightest doubt that Pearson was a brave officer and fought as long as there was any hope of success, but he was matched against a man of indomitable courage. As Captain A. S. Mackenzie says, "The *Richard* was beaten more than once; but the spirit of Jones could not be overcome."[6]

After the battle, Captain Jones tried hard to keep the *Richard* afloat. She was on fire in various parts, and at the same time the water was gaining in her hold in spite of three pumps that were kept constantly at work. The fire was extinguished, but on account of the increasing volume of water, she had to be abandoned, and on the morning of the 25th, with her flag still flying, the victorious old hulk sank beneath the waves.

In the *Serapis* Jones now sailed for the Texel, where he arrived on October 3. British men-of-war were lying in wait to capture him; but he bided his time and then, seizing a favorable opportunity, sailed boldly through the English Channel, in plain view of large British fleets at anchor, and reached Groix in February, 1780.

For his brilliant victory, Jones was knighted by France, and presented a sword by the King. On his return to America in 1781, Congress gave him a vote of thanks, and appointed him to command the 74-gun ship *America*, then building at Portsmouth, N. H. As the

---

[6] Mackenzie, *Life of Paul Jones,* i, 205.

war was practically over, Jones's services as a naval officer were no longer needed. In 1783 he was sent to Paris to conduct negotiations regarding prizes of the *Bonhomme Richard*. Jones later accepted a commission in the Russian Navy as vice-admiral, but his experience in Russia was not a happy one. He returned to Paris, where he spent most of the remaining years of his life, honored by the French, the intimate friend of such men as Morris and Lafayette. In this city Jones died July 18, 1792. Of our greatest naval officer during the Revolution, Napoleon is said to have remarked to Berthier in 1805, after the battle of Trafalgar, "Had Jones lived to this day, France might have had an admiral."

Conclusion of the War

While the navy was winning honors in Europe, important events were happening in home waters. Captain Nicholson, in the U. S. S. *Trumbull*, saw some hard fighting, but in 1781 this ship was forced to surrender to the *Iris* and the *General Monk*. It is a strange irony of fate that the *Iris*, formerly the *Hancock*, and the first of the thirteen frigates of Congress to be captured, should thus have received the surrender of the *Trumbull*, the last of the unlucky thirteen. Captain Barry, in the *Alliance*, made a successful cruise and captured a number of prizes. In an encounter with an unknown vessel, probably the *Sibylle*, on March 10, 1783, he fought the last sea fight of the Revolution, in which he was unsuccessful, since the *Alliance* had to relinquish her prey on the appearance of two British frigates.

There yet remain two classes of ships that deserve brief mention, privateers and State navies. From the beginning of the war there were swarms of American privateers that did great damage to British commerce, though it must

Conclusion of the War 41

be admitted, also, that English privateers preyed extensively on American merchantmen. The effect upon the outcome of the war was negligible. The losses suffered were apparently equal, and from the American standpoint, the ill effects probably outweighed the good. Appealing as privateering did to the enterprising and daring type of sailor, it diverted the very men who were most needed in the regular service. State navies were maintained by all the States but two for the protection of their coasts. Their vessels were chiefly small, and of shallow draft, designed for river and harbor defense. One of them, the *Hyder Ali* of the Pennsylvania Navy, mounting eighteen guns, and commanded by Lieutenant Barney, made in April, 1782, a brilliant capture of the English brig *General Monk,* mounting twenty guns.

Meanwhile a strong French fleet under De Grasse had rendered aid of the greatest importance to the land forces, co-operating with Washington. When in 1781 the British power in America was confined to two centres, one at New York and the other in the Chesapeake, with the intervening country in the hands of the Americans, communications between the British forces depended wholly on the sea.[7]

Using one of his frigates as a dispatch boat, De Grasse arranged with Washington for a concerted attack on Yorktown. Early in September, 1781, the French fleet under De Grasse fought the British fleet under Graves, and, although the battle itself was indecisive, De Grasse succeeded in preventing Graves from entering Chesapeake Bay and effecting a junction with Cornwallis. Meanwhile, "a sudden march of Washington brought him to the front of the English troops . . . and the army of Cornwallis was driven by famine to a surrender as humiliating as that of Saratoga."[8]

---

[7] Mahan, *Influence of Sea Power,* p. 385.

[8] Green, *Short History of the English People,* p. 785.

III

THE BEGINNINGS OF A NEW NAVY AND THE WAR WITH FRANCE

The Beginnings of a New Navy

In the chaos that followed the Revolutionary War, all that remained of the Continental Navy disappeared. The ship-of-the-line *America,* which had been completed shortly after the conclusion of peace, was presented by the United States to the King of France, in token of gratitude for the timely aid of France during the war. The three ships that survived the Revolution, the *Deane,* the *Washington,* and the *Alliance,* were sold; and after the disposal of the last of these in 1785, the United States had not a single armed vessel.

With an empty treasury and an overwhelming public debt, the new-born nation was in no condition to maintain a navy; but stronger than the reason of economy was the prevailing notion that an army and a navy were dangerous to the liberties of a republic. Years after the country had settled into its quiet and ordered career under the Constitution, when it was evident that a navy cost less than the annual tribute to pirates or extra insurance on ships and cargoes, the same cry of monarchism continued to be heard.

Yet very soon after the close of the Revolutionary War the necessity of a navy began to be felt. A treaty of peace, in 1785, between Spain and Algiers, opened the Atlantic to the Algerian pirates, and in July of the same year led to the capture of the American schooner *Maria.* Five days later, the ship *Dauphin* of Philadelphia was seized, and the crews of both vessels were

A 32-Pounder Carronade
(Taken from H. M. S. *Cyane*, 1815)

A 24-Pounder Long Gun
(Taken from H. M. S. *Confiance*, 1814. This and the carronade shown above are now at the U. S. Naval Academy)

taken into Algiers as slaves. At this time our consul-general at Paris, Thomas Barclay, was conducting a successful negotiation of a treaty of peace with the Emperor of Morocco. The costs of this treaty amounted to less than $10,000 in presents, with no annual tribute for the future; and it was hoped that some equally good treaty might be made with Algiers.

The capture of the *Maria* and the *Dauphin*, however, complicated the situation because, in addition to the cost of a treaty, the prisoners would have to be ransomed on whatever terms the Dey of Algiers chose. It was soon evident that he was in no hurry to conclude a treaty with America, for the prospect of preying on the shipping of a weak nation was highly attractive. The United States made three distinct efforts to treat with the Dey of Algiers and all were failures, the last being entrusted to John Paul Jones, who died before the orders reached him. By the time a fourth envoy was dispatched, the Dey refused to give him audience, and at the same time a treaty of peace between Portugal and Algiers made still freer for the corsairs the highway into the Atlantic. This treaty, in 1793, was negotiated by the English consul-general, apparently with no authority from Portugal. At this time the British Government was frankly subsidizing the Barbary states to prey on the shipping of rival nations, especially America—a policy which was maintained until the United States made her own terms in the Mediterranean by force of arms.

Taking instant advantage of the treaty with Portugal, Algerian corsairs swarmed into the Atlantic and, in the course of one month, captured eleven American vessels. By this time Algiers held thirteen American prizes, and their crews to the number of 119, seven of whom died in captivity.

This disgraceful situation at last prompted Congress

to measures of force. On March 27, 1794, the President signed an act providing for six frigates, four of forty-four guns, and two of thirty-six, for the purpose of protection against Algiers. The act, however, was careful to make clear that there was no intention of inaugurating a permanent navy, saying that "if a peace should take place between the United States and the regency of Algiers, no farther proceeding shall be had under this act." The fact remains, nevertheless, that this law marks the beginning of the permanent American Navy.

Work on the frigates was promptly begun; and, fortunately, the design of the new vessels was left to the finest ship-builder in the country, Joshua Humphreys. It is a significant compliment to his skill that toward the close of the War of 1812, England built frigates "exactly upon the plan of the large American frigates,"[1] which had been constructed according to his designs. His idea was, "that the vessels should combine such qualities of strength, durability, swiftness of sailing, and force, as to render them superior to any frigate belonging to the European Powers."[2] His chief innovations were provisions for heavier batteries than had hitherto been attempted for frigates, much thicker scantlings, finer lines, and spars longer and stouter than those of any British frigate. The *President*, for example, had a thicker side by one inch than the British 74-gun ship-of-the-line *Hero*, and a mainmast a foot longer than that of a British 64-gun ship.

Types of Ships and Guns

It is worth noting what the term "frigate" meant at the close of the 18th century. The victories of Rodney and of Nelson were won with fleets of "ships-of-the-line."

---

[1] London *Times*, March 17, 1814.
[2] Report of Gen. Knox, Secretary of War, December 27, 1794.

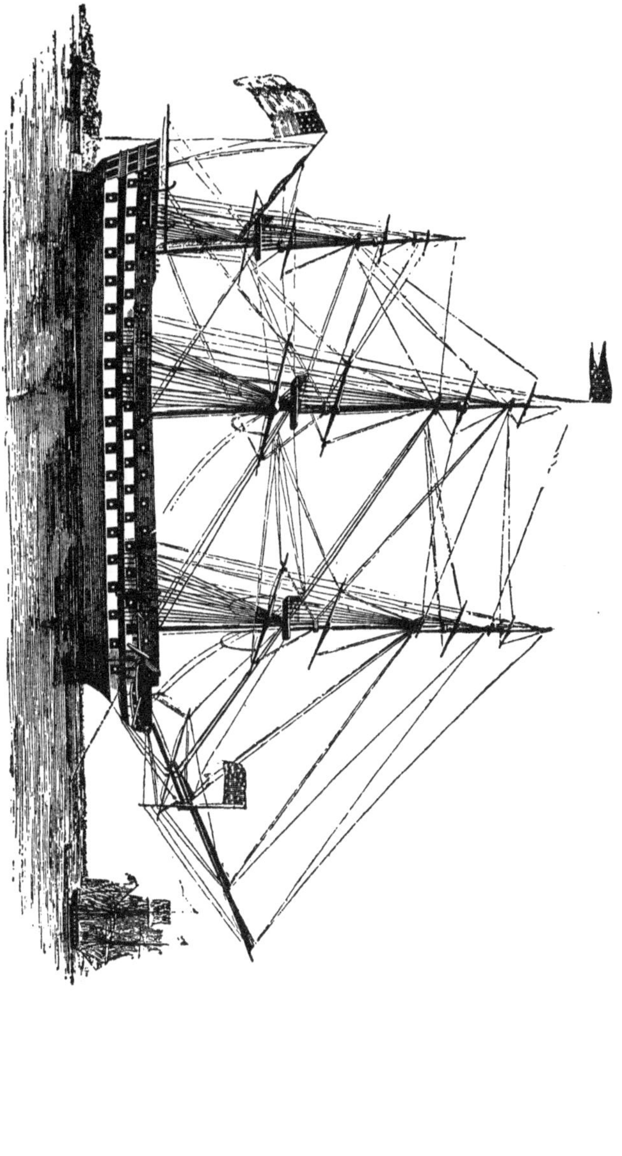

From Brady's *Kedge-Anchor*

UNITED STATES SHIP-OF-THE-LINE COLUMBUS AT ANCHOR

These were heavy vessels of two or three gun decks, carrying from seventy-five to 125 guns. The "frigate" was, like the "ship-of-the-line," ship-rigged, but distinguished by having only *one* gun deck below the spar deck. Being speedier than the heavy ship-of-the-line, the frigate was generally used for scout duty; she was the "cruiser" of this period.

A third class was the "sloop of war." This, the smallest type, was distinguished by the fact that all her armament was mounted on the spar deck. These "sloops" were sometimes ship-rigged, sometimes brigs or schooners, and they varied widely in tonnage. The ship-rigged sloops were frequently spoken of as "corvettes." Between the ship-of-the-line and the frigate there was an intermediary class, the "razee," which was simply a ship-of-the-line that had been cut down one deck, but was still of greater size and heavier metal than the frigate. As a type it is unimportant; but the other three classes, "ship-of-the-line," "frigate," and "sloop," were standard types till the days of steam and steel.

The naval guns of the period may be divided into two classes, long guns and short guns, or "carronades." Both were cast iron tubes, thicker at the breech than at the muzzle, and of smooth bore. The long gun was cast heavy and long, to bear a heavy charge and to strike a distant target; while the carronade was short and wide-muzzled, designed to throw a heavy shot, with a small charge of powder, at close quarters. The carronade (named from the village of Carron in Scotland where the type of gun was first cast) was high in favor in Nelson's day because of its tremendous smashing qualities in a yard-arm fight. The usual practice was to mount the carronades and lighter long guns on the spar deck of a frigate, and to equip the gun deck with the heavier long guns. These carronades and long guns were graded

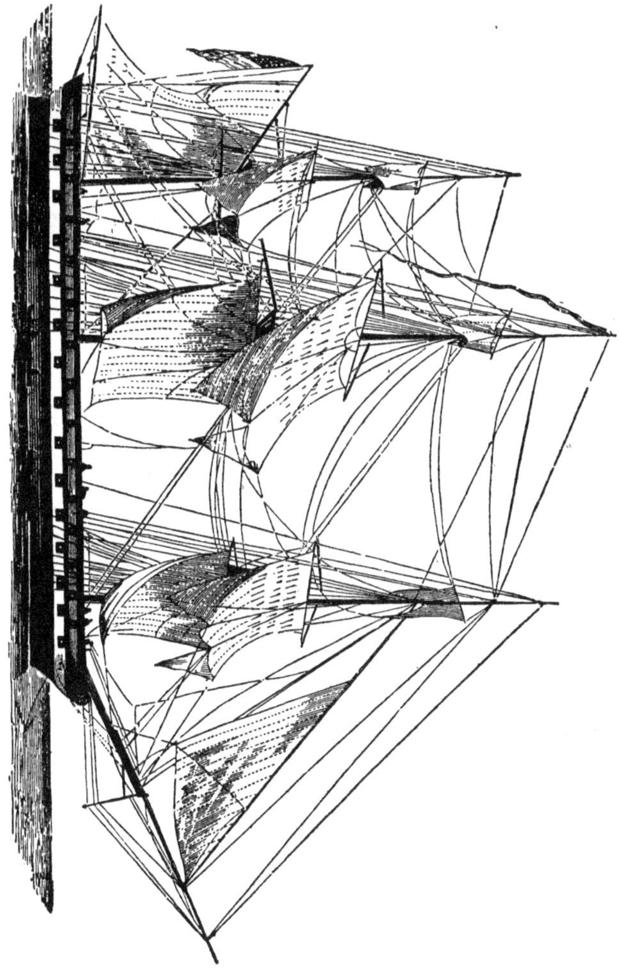

From Brady's *Kedge-Anchor*

FRIGATE WITH HER SAILS LOOSED TO DRY

according to the weight of shot they threw. At the end of the 18th century the long 42-pounder represented the most formidable naval ordnance of the day, but the long guns on a frigate usually varied from twelves to twenty-fours and the short ones from twenty-fours to forty-twos. All these guns were mounted on wooden carriages; the recoil threw the gun inboard as far as the breeching would allow, and when it was reloaded it was run out again by hand tackles. Indeed, all the labor connected with the loading, aiming and firing of a gun was done by hand. Elevating was done by means of a handspike under the breech where a wooden wedge, called a "quoin," was inserted when the desired angle was reached. As a rule, there were no sights; when the matter of sights was called to the attention of Nelson in 1801, he objected to them on the ground that ships should always be at such close quarters that missing would become impossible. This contempt of accurate aim sheds some light on the low state of British gunnery during our War of 1812.

Firing was done on some ships by flint locks, but these missed so often that the priming quill was more popular. This was a split quill, full of powder, inserted in the touch-hole of the gun. The cartridge had already been punctured by a sharp wire thrust through the touch-hole, so that when a slow match in the hands of the captain of the gun touched off the powder in the quill, the discharge followed almost instantaneously. All the men were assigned to the guns of one broadside, a large crew to each gun, every man of whom had a definite duty to perform. In case a ship had to fight both broadsides at once, half the crew of each gun ran to the corresponding gun on the opposite side.

The number of guns a ship carried gave her her rating within her own class. The ships-of-the-line ranged from "74's" to "120's," frigates from "28's" to "44's," but

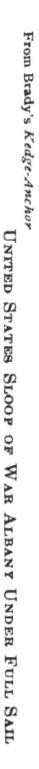

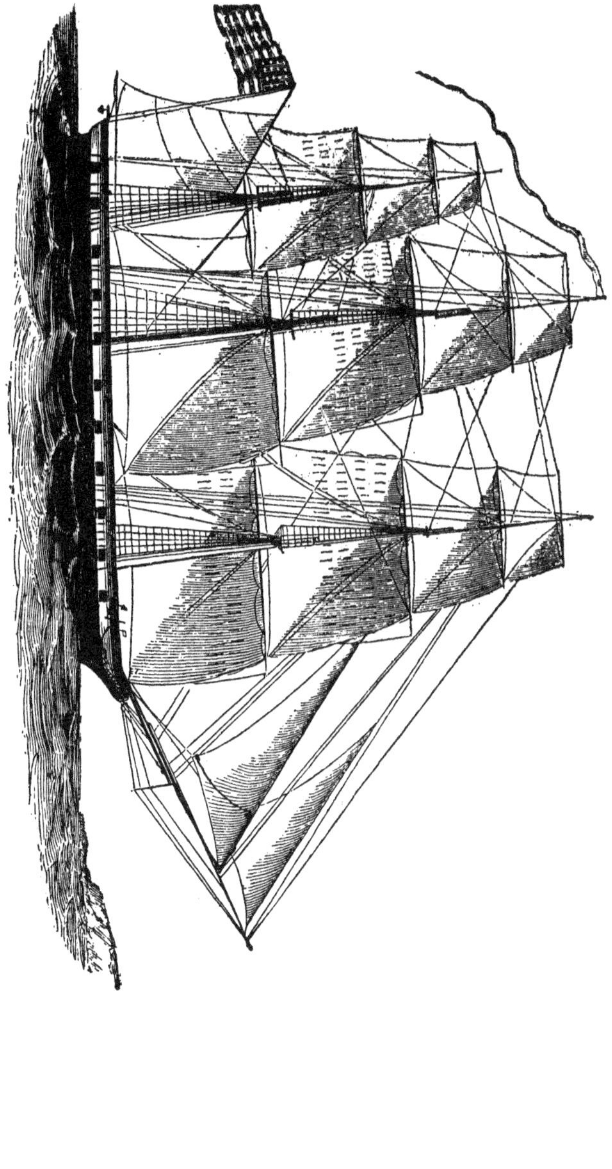

From Brady's *Kedge-Anchor*

UNITED STATES SLOOP OF WAR ALBANY UNDER FULL SAIL

the technical rating was always below the actual number of guns carried. The "44-gun" frigate *Constitution,* for example, carried fifty-four guns in her battle with the *Java.*

In accordance with the act of March 27, 1794, six frigates were laid down as follows:

Constitution, 44 guns, 1576 tons, costing $302,719, at Boston.

President, 44 guns, 1576 tons, $220,910, at New York.

United States, 44 guns, 1576 tons, $299,336, at Philadelphia.

Chesapeake, 36 guns, 1244 tons, $220,678, at Norfolk.[3]

Congress, 36 guns, 1268 tons, $197,246, at Portsmouth.

Constellation, 36 guns, 1265 tons, $314,212, at Baltimore.

It is interesting to compare figures like these with those of one of our latest battleships, the *North Dakota:* ten 12-inch guns, 20,000 tons, costing approximately $8,000,000.

On the fifth of June of the same year, six captains were selected in the following order: John Barry, Samuel Nicholson, Silas Talbot, Joshua Barney, Richard Dale, and Thomas Truxtun. All of these men had distinguished themselves in the struggle for independence. Captain Barney, however, feeling that he was unjustly rated with reference to the men above him, declined to serve, and James Sever was appointed sixth captain, ranking after Truxtun. The lieutenants were to be selected by the captains, the first lieutenant of Barry ranking the first lieutenant of Nicholson, etc.

Meanwhile, efforts were continued to arrange a treaty with Algiers; and finally, toward the close of the year 1795, a humiliating treaty was ratified by the Senate, requiring the United States to pay Algiers maritime stores

---

[3] The *Chesapeake* was intended originally to be a forty-four.

to the value of $21,600 annually. The cost of obtaining this treaty, including ransom of captives, amounted to nearly a million dollars.

The law provided that nothing more was to be done on the frigates if peace was arranged, but three were so far constructed that Congress authorized their completion. The perishable material of the other three was ordered sold, and the rest kept in storage for future use. In 1797 the three frigates completed were launched in the following order: the *United States,* July 10, at Philadelphia; the *Constellation,* September 7, at Baltimore; and the *Constitution,* September 20, at Boston. Captain Barry commanded the *United States,* Captain Nicholson, the *Constitution,* and, as it happened, Truxtun, the fifth on the list, who had been appointed to command the 36-gun *Constellation,* got to sea with his command, while his seniors, Captains Talbot and Dale, were forced into other occupations, because their frigates were not completed. This point, later, gave rise to a question of seniority between these two and Captain Truxtun, because at the time it was not clear whether Talbot and Dale had been retired or merely put on furlough.

According to the terms of the above treaty, as we have seen, the difficulties with Algiers were settled by the payment of a large annual tribute and a cash payment at the time of nearly a million dollars. The last item alone would have been sufficient to build and equip three 44-gun frigates, which could have gone far toward protecting our shipping, and might even have blockaded Algiers and forced a peace on terms of honor.

WAR WITH FRANCE

Long before the first three frigates were launched, other enemies than Algiers had appeared. In the tremendous conflict between Napoleon and England, French and

English cruisers and privateers alike plundered American merchantmen. A treaty of " amity, commerce, and navigation," in 1795, between Great Britain and the United States, temporarily relieved the burden of British oppression, but only increased the hostility of the French. In 1797, the Secretary of State reported that documents concerning the capture of thirty-two ships, brigs, and schooners lay in the department, while the newspapers had reported some 308 others, all by French cruisers. In many cases, these captures were attended with great inhumanity toward the unlucky crews. Finally, to bring their insolence to a climax, early in 1798, French privateers began to make captures in American harbors.

This was too much even for the Congress of that day, and in April of the same year an act was passed authorizing the building, purchase, or hire of "a number of vessels not exceeding twelve . . . to be armed, fitted, and manned." On April 30, 1798, the office of the Secretary of the Navy was established, to which Benjamin Stoddert of Georgetown, D. C., was appointed. Several other acts followed in quick succession, authorizing the further extension of the navy; more especially the building of the three frigates suspended in 1796, and the establishing of a marine corps. Further, all treaties with France were declared void, and rules were made governing the capture of prizes. The entire naval force authorized by these acts consisted of twelve ships of not less than 32 guns, twelve ships of not less than 20 nor exceeding 24 guns, and six not exceeding 18 guns, besides galleys and revenue cutters.

Of this force, Captain Richard Dale, in the *Ganges*, 24 guns, was the first to get to sea, followed in a few days by Captain Truxtun in the frigate *Constellation*, 36 guns, and Captain Stephen Decatur (senior), in the corvette *Delaware*, of 20 guns. These vessels were under orders to capture only such French ships as they found guilty of hostile acts, but it was only a matter of a few

The Baltimore Affair 53

days before the *Delaware* took the *Croyable*, a French privateer of 14 guns, caught red-handed off the American coast. This vessel was taken into the service, under the name *Retaliation,* and put under the command of Lieutenant William Bainbridge.

By the time the other ships were ready for sea, the administration had decided to carry on a vigorous offensive campaign in the West Indies instead of merely patrolling the Atlantic coast. Accordingly, during the winter of 1798-9, the fleet was divided into three squadrons, with definite cruising grounds assigned to each. The frigates *President, Chesapeake,* and *Congress* were as yet unfinished, and the greater number of the vessels in the squadrons were merchantmen hastily transformed into men-of-war. Nevertheless upon the mere sailing of these squadrons for the West Indies, the rates of insurance fell off, in some cases as much as fifty per cent; for one of the important duties of these men-of-war was the safe conduct of fleets of American merchantmen.

While thus convoying a fleet from Charleston to Havana, Captain Phillips, of the 20-gun sloop *Baltimore,* underwent an experience that cost him his epaulets and aroused in the nation a feeling of bitterness against Great Britain that did not subside till after the War of 1812. Shortly before reaching Havana, November 16, 1798, Captain Phillips ran into a British squadron. Signaling his convoy to scatter and make every effort to reach port, he himself bore up to meet the flagship, hoping to divert attention from the merchantmen. On being invited aboard the flagship, he was coolly informed that the British commodore, Loring, would impress all of the *Baltimore's* crew who did not have American "protection papers." Phillips protested, but he was in a difficult situation. He had been provided with no commission to prove that the *Baltimore* was a public vessel, he had been strictly ordered to avoid all hostile acts toward

British men-of-war, "even if they were in the act of capturing American vessels," and, finally, he lay under the guns of an overwhelming force. At last he submitted. Fifty-five of the *Baltimore's* crew were taken off, but of these fifty were returned. As Loring refused to accept the surrender of the American corvette, Phillips continued to Havana. On his return to the United States, he made a detailed report of the affair to the Department, with the result that he was promptly dismissed from the service by Secretary Stoddert.

Immediately after this incident, the Secretary issued orders to each of the commanders of the squadrons in the West Indies in the following vein: "Sir—It is the positive command of the President that on no pretense whatever you permit the public vessels of war under your command to be detained or searched, nor any of the officers belonging to her to be taken from her by the ships or vessels of any foreign nation, so long as you are in a capacity to repel such outrage on the honor of the American flag. If force should be exerted to compel your submission you are to resist that force to the utmost of your power, and when overpowered by superior force, you are to strike your flag and thus yield your vessel as well as your men, but never your men without your vessel."

Four days after the *Baltimore* outrage, the *Retaliation*, Lieutenant William Bainbridge, was overhauled off Guadeloupe, by two French frigates, *Insurgente* and *Volontier*, and compelled to strike. It was due to Bainbridge's quick wit, shortly after his surrender, that the other two American sloops, the *Montezuma* and the *Norfolk*, which happened to be in the neighborhood, were not taken also. The *Insurgente* was rapidly overhauling them, when the captain of the *Volontier*, turning to Bainbridge, asked him the force of the American vessels.

"The ship carries twenty-eight 12-pounders, and the brig twenty 9-pounders," he replied.

The Constellation and the Insurgente 55

Surprised at such force, the Frenchman instantly recalled the *Insurgente* and did not realize the deception till her captain came aboard and reported the facts. In the meantime, the two sloops made good their escape.

On the 9th of February, 1799, the *Constellation* sighted a large sail in the neighborhood of the island of Nevis. The stranger hoisted American colors as Captain Truxtun bore down on her, but was unable to answer the

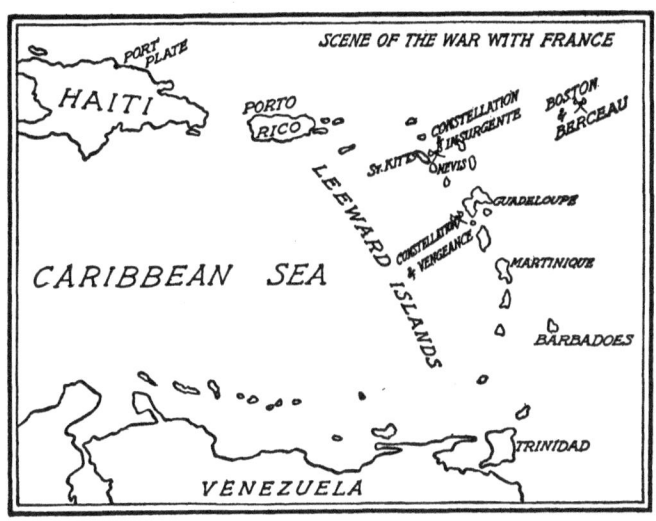

SCENE OF THE WAR WITH FRANCE

private signals which he displayed. She soon declared herself an enemy by raising the tricolor and firing a gun to windward. The following account is from Captain Truxtun's report to the Secretary of the Navy, dated on the 10th of February, the day after the battle:

"I continued bearing down on her, and at a quarter past three P.M. she hailed me several times; and as soon as I got in a position for every shot to do execution, I answered by commencing a close and successful engagement, which lasted until about half-past four P.M., when she struck her colors to the U. S. Ship *Constellation,* and I immediately took possession of her. She proved to be the celebrated French national frigate *Insurgente,* of 40 guns and 409 men, lately out from France, commanded by Monsieur Barreaut, and is esteemed one of the fastest-sailing ships in the French Navy. I have been much shattered in my rigging and sails, and my foretopmast rendered, from wounds, useless—you may depend the enemy is not less so. The high state of our discipline, with the gallant conduct of my officers and men, would have enabled me to have made a more formidable enemy yield, had the fortune of war thrown him in my way. As it is, I hope the President and my country will, for the present, be content with a very fine frigate being added to our navy. I must not omit in this hasty detail to do justice to M. Barreaut; for he defended his ship manfully, and from my raking him several times fore and aft, and being athwart his stern, ready with every gun to fire, when he struck his colors, we may impute the conflict not being more bloody on our side; for had not these advantages been taken, the engagement would not have ended so soon; for the *Insurgente* was completely officered and manned.''

The total loss of the *Constellation* amounted to two badly wounded and one slightly wounded. Early in the action one man was shot by the third lieutenant for deserting his quarters. The loss of the *Insurgente* amounted to twenty-nine killed and forty-one wounded. Both frigates were rated at 36, but the American broadside was fully one-third heavier than the French.

During the action with the *Insurgente,* Midshipman David Porter, who was stationed in the foretop of the *Constellation,* saved the wounded foretopmast from falling over by going aloft, under fire, cutting away the slings of the yards and letting them down. Porter had another and more trying proof of his coolness and

The Constellation and the Vengeance 57

gallantry after the action, when he and Lieutenant John Rodgers were sent with a prize crew of eleven men to take possession of the captured frigate. A gale which arose after the battle separated the two vessels before all the prisoners could be transferred to the *Constellation*, and the two young officers found themselves forced to navigate a ship whose decks were still strewn with dead and wounded, and whose spars, sails, and rigging were cut to pieces, some of which encumbered the decks—a situation made critical by the storm. But the worst danger lay in the fact that, before the surrender, the hatches had been thrown overboard, and the prize crew of two officers and eleven men had the task of guarding 173 prisoners, as well as navigating a crippled ship in a gale. A heavily-armed sentinel was placed at each hatchway, with orders to fire at the first prisoner that attempted to come on deck; and during the three nights and two days that passed before the ship reported to Truxtun at St. Kitts, neither Rodgers nor Porter could take a single minute of sleep or even rest. These two officers rose subsequently to distinction in positions of command, but they never afterward had to go through a more trying test of their courage and efficiency.

During the year 1799, American operations in the West Indies were hampered by the fact that enlistments had been, by law, for only one year. Every ship, therefore, had to leave her station during this year and go to the United States for fresh crews; and the French privateers that made Guadeloupe their base were quick to take advantage of these enforced absences. On the whole, however, the French gained little beyond a brief respite.

The second frigate action of the war also fell to Truxtun and the *Constellation*. On the morning of February 1, 1800, while about fifteen miles west of Basse Terre, the *Constellation* sighted a ship which soon proved to be a French frigate, the *Vengeance*. Captain Truxtun immediately gave chase; but, owing to the light wind, it was not till eight o'clock on the evening of the 2d that he was able to close. The Frenchman, without waiting to hear the hail of the American, opened fire with his stern and quarter guns, which he directed at the *Constellation's* rigging.

Captain Truxtun then gave orders, "not to throw away a single charge of powder and shot. but to take good aim and fire directly into the hull of the enemy." A few minutes later, he gained a good position on the weather quarter of the *Vengeance* which enabled the American batteries to reply. A sharp action followed, lasting till about 1 A.M., when the *Vengeance* stopped firing and sheered off as if to escape. Just as Captain Truxtun was trimming his shattered rigging to come alongside and take possession, his mainmast fell over the side. As the *Constellation* was now unable to pursue the *Vengeance*, the latter made good her escape.

In his report of this action, Captain Truxtun gave the American loss as fourteen killed and twenty-five wounded. The only officer killed was Midshipman Jarvis, who was stationed in the maintop and who, though warned of the dangerous condition of the mast, refused to leave his quarters without orders. The casualties of the *Vengeance* are put at fifty killed and 110 wounded. She was a beaten ship, and was saved from capture only by the fall of the *Constellation's* mainmast. Her first lieutenant stated some years afterward that the tricolor was struck two or three times; but, owing to the darkness and smoke, this fact evidently was not perceived by the officers of the *Constellation*. While it is impossible to state the precise armament of the French frigate during this action, owing to the disparity of the reports,[4] all the authorities are

---

[4] According to the lowest estimate, that of an American prisoner on the *Vengeance*, she carried fifty-four guns, firing 516 lbs. at a broadside. The *Constellation* fired a broadside of only 372 lbs.

Conclusion of the War

agreed in a considerable superiority in weight of metal over that of the *Constellation*.

The third encounter with a French man-of-war took place, October 12, 1800, between the frigate *Boston* of 28 guns and the sloop *Berceau* of 24. The French ship was taken only after a long and stubborn running fight, in which the honors belong to the French captain, Senez.

But the real work of the war lay in the capture of the privateers that swarmed out of the French ports of the West Indies, and there were many spirited combats between our smaller vessels and these privateers. One particularly gallant exploit was performed by Lieutenant Isaac Hull, who ran into Port Plate in broad daylight, spiked the guns of the fort, and surprised and carried away one of the best equipped and most successful of the French privateers. Mention also must be made of the famous cruise of the schooner *Enterprise*, under Lieutenant John Shaw, who, in eight months, captured six privateers and recaptured eleven American merchantmen. This is only the beginning of the fame of this little vessel; for she came to be regarded, next to the *Constitution*, as the "lucky" vessel of the navy.

The foregoing naval operations against France covered in all about two years and a half; at the end of that time, February 1, 1801, they were terminated by a treaty of peace, which had been under way for several months. By the terms of this treaty each side was to return to the other all government vessels that had been captured. This provision was greatly to the advantage of France, because none of our men-of-war had been taken save the *Retaliation*, which, as we have seen, had originally been a French privateer. On the other hand, the *Insurgente*, the *Berceau*, and a small cruiser, the *Vengeance*, had been taken by American ships. The *Insurgente*, dispatched to the West Indies early in the fall of 1800, was never heard from again. The other two were turned over to France. Of the eighty-four vessels remaining in the hands of the United States at the close of hostilities, thirteen were released, and one was sunk, leaving seventy lawful prizes for the American Navy.

The war, while never formally declared, and existing only in the West Indies, was of great benefit to the young American Navy. The large increase in exports due to the protection afforded by our cruisers, and their brilliant successes in battle, gave the navy a standing and popularity that it needed in the days when the maintenance of a man-of-war seemed, to many, a threat of monarchy. To the personnel of the navy, also, it gave a practical training in warfare and self-confidence. The heroes of the war with Tripoli and the second war with Great Britain received their schooling as midshipmen or lieutenants in the West Indian campaigns.

A point, also, which cannot be overlooked is the fact that during these campaigns, while American men-of-war were co-operating with the British in fighting the French, an "Act for the Better Government of the Navy of the United States" was passed by Congress, embodying a set of regulations taken almost word for word from the rules that governed the navy of Great Britain. In short, the discipline and traditions of the British service were then adopted as the standards of our own. Had the United States been allied with France against England at this time, and had the practice of the French Navy been accepted as our own, the results would have been unfortunate, since the discipline of the French men-of-war was at that time demoralized by the levelling ideas of the French Revolution. The point is aptly expressed in the remark of the Duke of Wellington, "I believe in free speech, but not on board a man-of-war."

IV

THE WAR WITH TRIPOLI

An Insult by Algiers

The treaties of peace bought from Morocco in 1786, Algiers in 1795, Tripoli in 1796, and Tunis in 1797, by no means settled the difficulties between American ships and Barbary corsairs. Indeed, the following incident, for which the Dey of Algiers was responsible, was characteristic of the attitude of all the Barbary rulers at that time.

In 1800, when only twenty-six years old, William Bainbridge was promoted to the rank of captain, having served but two years in the navy. In these two years, however, he had come into public notice, especially on account of his experience in the dungeons of Guadeloupe during the war with France. He was assigned the *George Washington*, of 24 guns, one of the ships purchased for the navy at the outbreak of hostilities with France, with orders to carry the annual tribute to Algiers. Captain Bainbridge thus had the distinction of commanding the first American man-of-war to enter the Mediterranean, but the honor was over-shadowed by the humiliating nature of his mission. Bad as this was, the sequel was so much worse that it may fairly be described as the most mortifying incident in the record of the navy.

When the *Washington* arrived in September, 1800, the Dey of Algiers was having difficulties with the Sultan of Turkey—the over-lord of the Barbary rulers—because the Algerians had made peace with Napoleon at a time when Turkey was fighting him. In order to conciliate his master, the Dey of Algiers wished to send presents to Constantinople, and for this purpose requested the loan of the American man-of-war. Naturally, the American consul and Captain Bainbridge protested; but the *George Washington* was anchored under the batteries of Algiers, in a position where she could not escape, and the Dey threatened to declare war instantly if the request was refused. As there were at this time in the Mediterranean a large number of American merchantmen which would probably have been captured if the Dey had made good his threat of war, Bainbridge felt himself forced to yield and play errand boy for the Dey of Algiers. The latter aggravated the humiliation by compelling the American captain to hoist the Algerian flag at the main, an act that virtually put the *George Washington* out of commission and transferred her to the Algerian Navy. As soon as Bainbridge cleared the harbor, however, he hauled down the Algerian colors and hoisted his own.

At Constantinople he had the satisfaction of being received with honor as the representative of a new nation, while the Algerian ambassador was given scant courtesy. During the visit, also, the Turkish admiral gave Captain Bainbridge a "firman," or passport, which insured him respectful treatment in all Turkish ports. On returning to Algiers, the American was careful to anchor out of range of the batteries and promptly refused the demand of the Dey that he make a second trip to Constantinople During an audience with the Dey, Bainbridge countered a fierce threat of instant war by displaying the Turkish "firman." This frightened the pirate into such respect that thereafter Captain Bainbridge and his ship were inviolate. When the Dey declared war with France, under the Sultan's orders, Bainbridge, by using the authority of his "firman," compelled him to allow the French subjects in his city forty-eight hours to leave the country. As it appeared that the unfortunate exiles had no other way of leaving Algiers and escaping slavery, Bainbridge took

The Errand of the George Washington

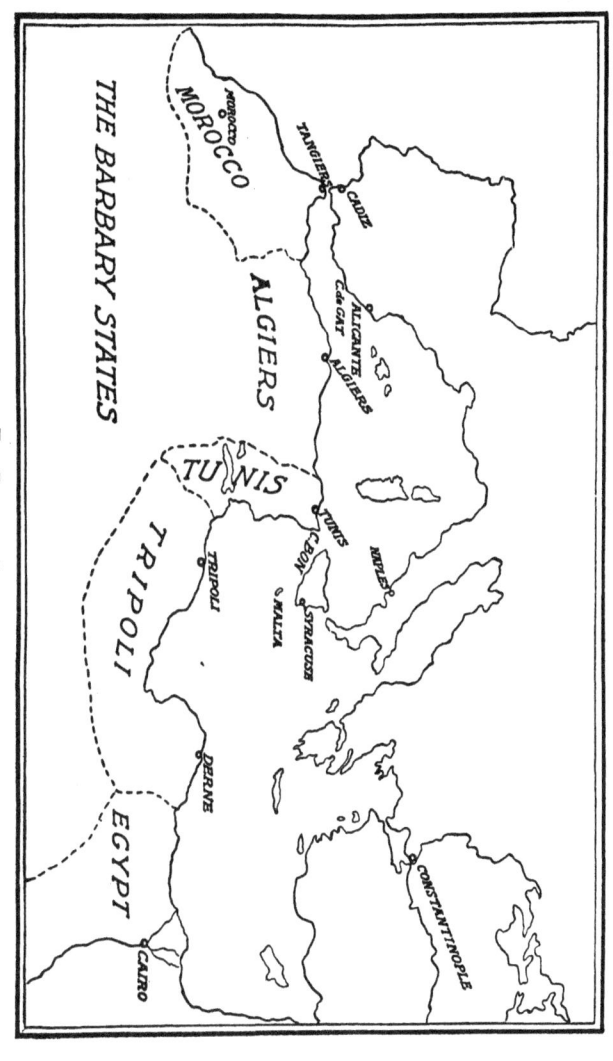

THE BARBARY STATES

them on board the *George Washington,* and conveyed them to Alicante, whence they made their way home. For this service he received the thanks of Napoleon.

THE FIRST YEAR OF THE WAR WITH TRIPOLI

Meanwhile, the Bey of Tripoli also was making trouble. Although he had concluded a treaty with the United States in 1796, realizing in two or three years that he had not made so good a bargain as his neighbors, Algiers and Tunis, he felt obliged to demand more than the treaty called for. Efforts to settle the matter on a reasonable basis failed, and the Bey became more and more insolent. At last, in February, 1801, he repudiated the former treaty, and, the following May, declared war. The negotiations had been dragging on for so long, however, that American merchantmen had had a fair warning, and the Tripolitan cruisers captured little or nothing.

As soon as it became evident that diplomacy would fail, a squadron of "observation" was assembled at Hampton Roads, toward the end of May, with orders to visit the Barbary ports and open hostilities with any or all of the states that had declared war; or, at least, to help diplomatic relations by a show of armed force. This squadron consisted of the frigates *President,* 44 guns, flagship, Captain James Barron; *Philadelphia,* 36 guns, Captain Samuel Barron (brother of James Barron); *Essex,* 32 guns, Captain William Bainbridge; and the schooner *Enterprise,* 12 guns, Lieutenant Andrew Sterett. These vessels were placed under the command of Commodore Richard Dale, famous as Paul Jones's first lieutenant in the battle between the *Bonhomme Richard* and the *Serapis.*

The news of the declaration of war on the part of Tripoli did not reach the United States until after the

The Declaration of War

squadron had sailed, but the ships fortunately arrived at Gibraltar just in time to intercept the passage of two Tripolitan corsairs that were in port, clearly bound for a raid in the Atlantic. Leaving the *Philadelphia* to blockade them in Gibraltar, Commodore Dale dispatched the *Essex* to collect the American ships in neutral ports and convoy them to the Atlantic, while with the remainder of his squadron he cruised along the Barbary coast. The Bey [1] of Tripoli was somewhat disturbed by the appearance of the American ships and offered to treat for peace, but, though Dale remained eighteen days off the harbor, nothing was accomplished. At the end of that time, he was forced to put in for fresh water at Malta, where he arrived in the middle of August.

Meanwhile, on the first of that month, a spirited action had taken place between the schooner *Enterprise* and the *Tripoli*. As the former carried twelve guns and ninety-four men, and the latter, fourteen guns and eighty men, the two vessels were very evenly matched. That the result was so one-sided, is chiefly due to the skill with which Lieutenant Sterett handled his vessel, never allowing himself to be boarded, and time and again raking his antagonist at close range. The following is his report to Commodore Dale:

"I have the honor to inform you that on the first of August, I fell in with a Tripolitan ship-of-war, called the *Tripoli*, mounting fourteen guns, commanded by Reis Mahomet Sous. An action commenced immediately at pistol shot, which continued three hours with incessant firing. She then struck her colors. The carnage on board was dreadful, she having twenty men killed and thirty wounded; among the latter was the captain and the first lieutenant. Her mizzenmast went over the side. Agree-

---
[1] The title of this ruler is variously given as " Bey," " Bashaw," or " Pasha."

able to your orders I dismantled her of everything but an old sail and spar. With heartfelt pleasure I add, that the officers and men throughout the vessel behaved in the most spirited and determined manner, obeying every command with promptitude and alertness. We had not a man wounded, and sustained no material damage in our hull or rigging.''

For this brilliant exploit, Sterett received the thanks of Congress and a sword, while an extra month's pay was awarded to his officers and men. The reason that the *Tripoli* was sent back to Tripoli dismantled instead of being destroyed, was that the commodore's orders from the President did not allow him to take prizes. Jefferson held that, under the Constitution, war had to be declared by Congress, that all he could direct the squadron to do, therefore, was to act on the defensive. This strict interpretation of the Constitution undoubtedly tied Dale's hands somewhat up to the time (February, 1802) when Congress passed an act that gave the President full war powers. Still one would expect from Paul Jones's favorite lieutenant more than the barren results of the first year of the Tripolitan War. The blockade, which at first had been very annoying to the Bey of Tripoli, was gradually relaxed, and, after the departure of Commodore Dale for the United States in March, 1802, apparently amounted to nothing. This blockade duty fell chiefly on the *Philadelphia*, Captain Samuel Barron, which, though in winter quarters at Syracuse, was under orders from Dale to make occasional excursions to Tripoli and Tunis during the spring. According to the report of William Eaton, our consul at Tunis, she appeared but once off Tripoli during the winter and spring, and that only for six hours. Captain Barron made the excuse that the northerly winds were ''very common and excessively heavy,'' and prevented his looking into Tripoli.

The Second Year of the War

Consul Eaton, who criticised Barron's inefficiency, is an interesting figure in the story of our war with Tripoli. A veteran of the Revolution and a captain in the army at the time he was appointed our representative in Tunis (1797), he threw himself into the war with characteristic energy, and spoke his opinions without tact or reserve. His bitter criticism of Bainbridge for submitting the flag to the insult it received from the Dey of Algiers, and his equally scathing remarks about Captain Samuel Barron, awoke against him the hostility, not only of Bainbridge and the Barrons, but of all the naval officers on the station, for they felt that his strictures had involved the honor of the service. Perhaps it was on account of this hostility that, when he suggested attacking Tripoli in the rear by raising a force to the support of Hamet, the deposed brother of the reigning Bey, Yusuf, his plan was disapproved by all the officers in the squadron. His idea was to collect an army of adventurers under the banner of the rightful ruler, Hamet, with which to attack Tripoli in the rear; and, by a joint assault on land and sea, drive Yusuf out of the city or, at least, bring him to terms.

THE SECOND YEAR OF THE WAR

The custom of enlisting men for one year embarrassed the navy in the first year of the war with Tripoli as it had done in the war with France, for all of Dale's ships had to be sent home on account of the expiration of the terms of enlistment. The next enlistments, therefore, were made for two years instead of one. The command of the second squadron was given to Commodore Truxtun, the hero of the French War. Unfortunately, as there seems to have been a scarcity of captains at the time, no one was appointed to command his flagship, the *Constellation*. To act as captain for his own flagship, Truxtun felt to be a descent in grade, and, therefore, declined the post. Since this amounted to a resignation, it cost the nation an officer of the type most needed to prosecute the war against Tripoli. The idea that departmental obstinacy was behind the action in Truxtun's case is suggested by the fact that Richard V. Morris, his successor, was given an acting captain for the flagship, without anything more being said about it.

In the spring of 1802, the ships under Morris set sail for the Mediterranean, one after another, as soon as they were ready for sea. The squadron in the order of their sailing, consisted of the following: the *Chesapeake*, flagship, 36; the *Adams*, 28; the *New York*, 36; the *John Adams*, 28; the *Constellation*, 36; and the *Enterprise*, 12. There were still on the station, the *Philadelphia*, *Boston*, *Essex*, and *George Washington;* but the first and last of these soon left for the United States.

The story of the operations that followed is a mass of confusing detail. Great things were looked for from this naval force, and the Bey of Tripoli was expected to submit at once. As a matter of fact, during this second year of the war the United States lost ground. The blockade was ineffectual except to irritate Tunis and Morocco. In May, 1803, the Americans made feeble overtures to buy peace; but, meanwhile, an American vessel, the *Franklin*, had been seized, and her crew put in irons. These had to be ransomed through Algiers for $35,000. Consul Eaton, also, who was unable to get further in his plan on account of a quarrel with Commodore Morris, left for the United States. During the summer of 1803, however, two Tripolitan cruisers were destroyed by the squadron, and there were also some vigorous skirmishes against the enemy's gunboats, in which the younger officers won distinction. But the results were nothing.

In September, Commodore Morris received a letter

Arrival of Commodore Preble

from the Secretary of the Navy, announcing that he was suspended from duty and ordered home. The following spring, a court of inquiry, composed unfortunately of officers junior to Morris, found him "censurable for his inactive and dilatory conduct of the squadron under his command."[2] Though for some reason no court-martial followed, Morris was summarily dismissed from the service by President Jefferson.

COMMODORE PREBLE

While the court of inquiry was sitting on the case of Captain Morris, a new squadron was being prepared, under the command of Captain Edward Preble. The task of fitting out the ships, especially the flagship *Constitution*, consumed so much of the summer of 1803, that it was August before the new commodore could set sail for the Mediterranean. He had the following vessels in his squadron, named in the order of sailing: *Nautilus*, 12, Lieutenant Richard Somers; *Philadelphia*, 36, Captain William Bainbridge; *Vixen*, 12, Lieutenant John Smith; *Constitution*, flagship, 44, Lieutenant Robinson, acting captain; *Siren*, 16, Lieutenant Charles Stewart; *Argus*, 16, Lieutenant Stephen Decatur, Jr. The *Enterprise*, 12, Lieutenant Isaac Hull, already on the station, was to be included; but Hull, being senior to Decatur, was to exchange commands with him, because the *Argus* was rated above the *Enterprise*. The small schooners and brigs of this squadron were built and fitted to cruise in the shoal waters about Tripoli, where the heavier frigates could not follow.

The new commodore, like his predecessors, was a

---

[2] Captain Samuel Barron, who had himself been criticised by Eaton for "inactive and dilatory conduct" in his blockade of Tripoli, was president of this court.

veteran of the Revolutionary War. He came from New England, and was personally little known to the service, especially as all the other officers, with the exception of Hull, came from the Southern or Middle States. His naturally violent temper was not improved by ill health, and he had iron ideas about discipline. He reciprocated the distrust which the younger officers felt toward their hot-tempered, "taut" commander, for he complained that they were only "school-boys." In fact, all the commanders of his flotilla were under thirty and their lieutenants even younger. A year later, however, the mutual regard between Preble and his young officers amounted to warm affection.

The situation that confronted Commodore Preble was not reassuring. During the two years and a half since war had been declared, the American Navy had gained no decided advantage; on the contrary, the other Barbary powers, especially Morocco, were growing more and more restless and insolent, as is shown by the following incident: Shortly after Bainbridge arrived at Gibraltar in the *Philadelphia*, he learned that two Tripolitan cruisers were off Cape de Gat. While in search of them he fell in with a vessel belonging to the Emperor of Morocco, which upon investigation, proved to be the American brig *Celia*, with the captain and seven of the crew confined below decks. When Bainbridge threatened to hang the Moorish commander for piracy, the latter produced an order from the Governor of Tangiers, authorizing him to capture American vessels. Bainbridge then returned to Gibraltar with his prize, and, upon the arrival of the *Constitution*, reported to Preble the case of the *Celia*.

The commodore, realizing that Morocco must be dealt with promptly, dispatched the *Vixen* and the *Philadelphia* to blockade Tripoli while he, with the remainder of the squadron, joined with Commodore Rodgers and the home-

Edward Preble

bound frigates, *New York, Boston,* and *John Adams,* to make a demonstration at Tangiers. The display of this naval force had instant effect. The Emperor hastily shifted the responsibility for the capture of the *Celia* on the Governor of Tangiers—whom he publicly disgraced— and tried to placate the American officers by gifts. The negotiations concluded with a ratification of the old treaty of 1786, without any payment whatever on the part of the United States.

Meanwhile the *Vixen* and the *Philadelphia* had taken up their station, blockading the port of Tripoli on October 17. About a fortnight later Bainbridge received information of two Tripolitan war vessels cruising in the Mediterranean. Judging that they were probably going westward toward the Straits, he dispatched the *Vixen* to look for them off Cape Bon, a station also which he thought much safer for the little schooner than the coast of Tripoli, at a time when the autumn gales had begun.

Towards the end of October (1803) the *Philadelphia* was driven away by one of these storms. As she was returning to her station on the morning of the 31st, she sighted a Tripolitan vessel making for the harbor. The following account, adapted from Captain Bainbridge's report to the Secretary of the Navy, describes the disaster that resulted:

"Misfortune necessitates my making the most distressing communication of my life, and it is with deep regret that I inform you of the loss of the United States frigate *Philadelphia,* under my command, by being wrecked on rocks between four and five leagues to the eastward of the town of Tripoli. The circumstances relating to this unfortunate event are as follows:

"At nine A.M., being about five leagues to the eastward of Tripoli, I saw a ship inshore of us, standing before the wind to the westward. I immediately gave chase, whereupon she hoisted Tripolitan colors and continued her course very near the shore. About eleven o'clock I had approached the shore to seven fathoms of water, and commenced firing at her, continuing our fire and running before the wind until half-past eleven. Being then in seven fathoms of water and finding our fire ineffectual to prevent her getting into Tripoli, I gave up the pursuit, and was bearing off the land, when we ran on the rocks, in twelve feet of water forward, and seventeen feet abaft. Immediately we lowered a boat from the stern, sounded, and found the greatest depth of water astern. Accordingly, I laid all sails aback; loosed topgallant sails, and set a heavy press of sail canvas on the ship, with the wind blowing fresh, to back her off. I also cast three anchors away from the bows, started the water in the hold, hove overboard the guns, excepting some abaft to defend the ship against the gunboats which were then firing on us. But I found all this ineffectual. Then I made the last resort of lightening her forward by cutting away the foremast, which carried the main topgallant mast with it.''

In testifying before the court of inquiry held in June, 1805, Lieutenant David Porter added a few more details to Captain Bainbridge's account at this point. After the resort of cutting away the foremast had failed to release the *Philadelphia's* bows, ''orders were then given to the ship's carpenter to go forward and bore holes through the ship's bottom, and the gunner to drown the magazine by turning the cock and securing the key. Orders were then given to destroy everything that could be rendered of any use to the enemy.''

''Striking on the rocks,'' continues Captain Bainbridge, ''was an accident not possible for me to guard against by any intimation of charts as no such shoals were laid down on any on board. Every careful precaution (by keeping three leads heaving) was made use of, on

The Loss of the Philadelphia

approaching the shore to effect the capture of the Tripolitan cruiser; and, after the ship struck the rocks, all possible measures were taken to get her off. I determined not to give her up as long as a hope remained, although all the while we were annoyed by gunboats, which took their position in such a manner that we could not bring our guns to bear on them, not even after cutting away a part of the stern to effect it.

"We stood the fire of the gunboats for four hours. By the end of that time, as my officers and I had no hope of getting the frigate off the rocks, and we could see a reinforcement coming out from Tripoli—which there was not the smallest chance of our injuring by resistance—we decided, in order to save the lives of brave men, that there was no alternative but the distressing one of hauling our colors down and submitting to the enemy, whom chance had befriended. . . .

"The gunboats, in attacking, fired principally at our masts. Had they directed their shot at the hull, they undoubtedly would have killed many. . . . The ship was taken possession of a little after sunset, and in the course of the evening I, and all the officers, with part of the crew were brought ashore and carried before the Pasha. . . . We had lost everything but what was on our backs, and even part of that was taken off."

The attempts to scuttle the ship proved to be failures; for, two days later, she was floated off the reef at high tide, her guns were raised and remounted by her captors, and she was towed into Tripoli practically as good as ever.

The Kaliusa reef, on which the *Philadelphia* struck, was, as Bainbridge says, not located on the charts; and yet it is so extensive as to make the omission noteworthy, for it stretches several miles parallel to the coast, here and there broken by channels. It only intensifies the misfortune of Bainbridge to know that if he had kept on a little farther before bearing up, he would have passed through one of these channels safely. If, also, he had held his course toward Tripoli, in the wake of the ketch, he would have escaped grounding.

The imprisonment of the *Philadelphia's* people turned out to be a long one; but, for the officers, at least, not especially severe. They were allowed free intercourse, and, through the kind efforts of the Danish consul, Nissen, were able to buy back their books. By means of these books, Captain Bainbridge with his first lieutenant, David Porter, conducted for the midshipmen the first naval school in the history of the American service. Through Mr. Nissen, also, Captain Bainbridge was enabled to carry on a secret correspondence with Commodore Preble. Throughout their long captivity the officers wore away the heavy hours in laying futile plans for escape. The men, however, received none of the consideration shown to the officers. They were ill-fed, worse lodged, and worked and beaten like slaves; but they seem to have stood their captivity surprisingly well. There were but six deaths and very little sickness during the whole nineteen months of captivity.

Captain Bainbridge's officers, realizing his distress of mind, were hardly in their prison quarters before they drew up a memorial to assure him of their sympathy and respect. "Wishing to express our full approbation of your conduct, concerning the unfortunate affair of yesterday," it ran, "we do conceive . . . that every exertion was made and every expedient tried to get her off and to defend her, which either courage or abilities could have dictated." Commodore Preble, also, as soon as he heard the unwelcome news, wrote Bainbridge a comforting letter, without even a hint of criticism.

But the latter had every reason to feel depressed. His career in the navy, though brief, had been singularly un-

The Loss of the Philadelphia

fortunate. During the French War he had been captured and imprisoned; he was still smarting under the criticism of Eaton and others for the mortifying incident of the *George Washington;* and this final disaster strengthened the hands of the Bey of Tripoli to an extent hitherto not conceivable.

If Commodore Preble had realized the seriousness of his task on taking command of the third squadron, he now felt the difficulties of his situation increased tenfold by the loss of the *Philadelphia*. The Tripolitans now possessed in the *Philadelphia* a larger fighting ship than they had ever owned before, and at the same time the loss to the American squadron amounted to a large proportion of its force, for it left but a single frigate, the *Constitution*, besides the small brigs and schooners. In this way, Preble's operations were crippled at the very outset; and the mere holding for ransom of 300 American prisoners gave the Bey of Tripoli a further tremendous advantage, for he knew that the officers, especially, had influential friends who would bring pressure upon the Government to accept almost any terms of peace that he might dictate.

V

THE WAR WITH TRIPOLI (CONTINUED)

The Destruction of the Philadelphia

THE news of the capture of the *Philadelphia* immediately suggested the idea of cutting her out or destroying her. Bainbridge outlined a plan in one of his secret letters to Preble, and, even before this was received, Preble and Decatur had been discussing a similar course of action. As soon as the subject was mentioned by the commodore, Decatur eagerly volunteered to cut out the *Philadelphia* with his ship, the *Enterprise;* so when Lieutenant Stewart arrived in the *Siren* and offered to perform the same service, Preble informed him that Decatur was already promised the honor. The commodore, believing that it was impossible to save the frigate, decided not to try to cut her out but to destroy her at her moorings. The scheme was greatly helped by the capture of a Tripolitan ketch, the *Mastico,* whose Mediterranean rig would enable her to slip into the harbor without raising the suspicion that the *Enterprise* would have been sure to create.

When Decatur assembled the officers and men of the *Enterprise,* told them of the intended expedition, and called for volunteers, every officer, man, and boy stepped forward. From this number, five officers—Lieutenants James Lawrence, Joseph Bainbridge, and Jonathan Thorn, Surgeon Lewis Hermann, Midshipman Thomas Macdonough—and sixty-two men were chosen. To these were added five officers from the *Constitution*—Midshipmen Ralph Izard, John Rowe, Charles Morris, Alexander Laws, and John Davis—and a Sicilian pilot, Salvatore

The Burning of the Philadelphia 77

Catalano,[1] who was familiar with the harbor of Tripoli. On February 15, the day before the destruction of the frigate, Lieutenant Stewart sent a boat to the *Intrepid* with Midshipman Thomas O. Anderson and six men. The boat party remained on board the *Intrepid,* and shared in the attack on the *Philadelphia.* The following story of the expedition has been taken from the *Autobiography of Charles Morris,*[2] one of the midshipmen detailed from the *Constitution*:

"The brig *Siren,* Lieutenant Stewart, was to accompany us, to assist with her boats, and to receive the crew of the ketch (which had been named the *Intrepid*) in case of her destruction, which was considered probable. The officers were told to take only a single change of linen, and no time was allowed to prepare stores, as we embarked within an hour after receiving notice and sailed immediately, on the evening of the 3d of February, 1804. Combustibles had been previously prepared and placed in the vessel, with ship's provisions for two or three weeks' supply. A Maltese had also been obtained to accompany us as pilot into the harbor, with which he was well acquainted. We arrived in sight of Tripoli about the 10th, but the wind was fresh from the westward, with strong indications of an approaching gale." . . . [Because of the heavy sea the entrance was decided to be unsafe.] "The attempt was abandoned for the time, and the vessels weighed again to get beyond the view of the town before daylight. This was not done without some difficulty, as the gale increased rapidly. It continued for four or five days with great violence, and drove us considerably to

---

[1] A native of Palermo, he apparently joined the squadron at Malta and is referred to by Preble, also, as a "Maltese." He was for many years afterwards a sailing master in our navy.

[2] Edited by Professor James S. Soley, U. S. N., and published for the first time in the *Naval Institute Proceedings,* vol. vi, (1880). Reprinted by permission.

the eastward, and at one time nearer the coast than was agreeable.

"Our situation on board was far from comfortable. The commander, three lieutenants, and the surgeon occupied the very small cabin. Six midshipmen and the pilot had a platform laid on the water-casks, whose surface they covered when they lay down for sleep, and at so small a distance below the deck that their heads could reach it when seated on the platform. The marines had corresponding accommodations on the opposite side, and the sailors had only the surface of the casks in the hold. To these inconveniences were added the want of any room on the deck for exercise, and the attacks of innumerable vermin, which our predecessors, the slaves, had left behind them. The provisions proved to be decayed and offensive. . . .

"On the morning of the 16th, we again obtained sight of Tripoli, with light winds, pleasant weather, and a smooth sea, and stood in for the town. By arrangement, the *Siren* kept far without us during the day, and her appearance had been so changed as to lull all suspicion of her being a vessel of war. The lightness of the wind allowed us to keep up all appearance of an anxious desire to reach the harbor before night, without bringing us too near to require any other change than the use of drags, which could not be seen from the city. All the crew were also kept below, excepting six or eight persons at a time, that suspicion might not be awakened by unusual numbers; and such as were visible were dressed as Maltese.

"As the evening advanced, our drags were taken in, so that we were within two miles of the eastern entrance at dark, the *Siren* being some three miles without us. The concerted arrangements were for the ketch to wait for the boats of the *Siren* to join us after dark, that they might accompany us to the attack; but as the sun descended, the

The Burning of the Philadelphia

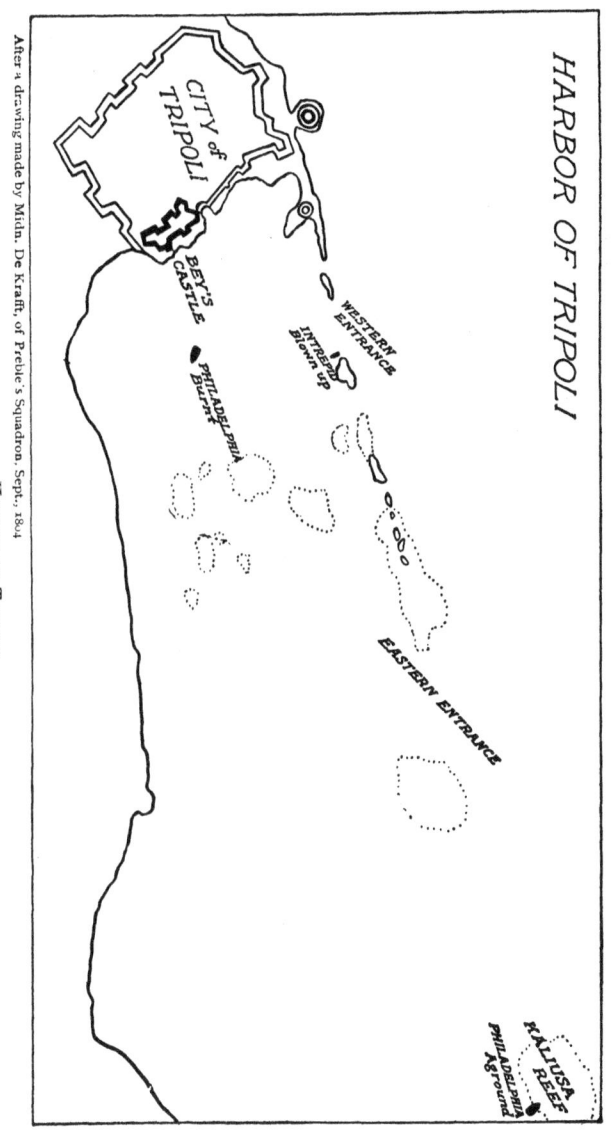

HARBOR OF TRIPOLI

After a drawing made by Midn. De Krafft, of Preble's Squadron, Sept., 1804

wind grew fainter, and there was good reason to apprehend that any delay in waiting for the boats might render it very difficult for the ketch to reach the ship. Decatur, therefore, determined to proceed without waiting, and accompanied his decision with the remark, 'the fewer the number, the greater the honor.' One boat from the *Siren*, with six men, had joined us a few days before, and was still with us.

"The final arrangements were now made, and the respective duties of the several officers, which had been previously allotted, were again specified and explained. The presumed number of our enemy was stated, and the necessity for our utmost exertions enjoined upon us. The watchword '*Philadelphia*' was issued to be used as a means of recognition; and as we advanced into the harbor, strict silence was enjoined and observed. The injunction, however, appeared to be unnecessary. No one appeared to be disposed to enter into conversation, but [each] to be absorbed by his own reflections. My own thoughts were busy, now reverting to friends at home, now to the perils we were about to meet. Should I be able to justify the expectations of the former by meeting properly the dangers of the latter? . . . The officers and crew were directed to conceal themselves as much as possible, excepting some six or eight. Most of the officers could be distinguished by their dress, and they required concealment more than the sailors. Fortunately, owing to the loss of some articles, which had been replaced by loan from the crew, my own dress corresponded to theirs, which enabled me to keep near Decatur, who I supposed would naturally be among the first to leave the ketch. The wind wafted us slowly into the harbor, the water was smooth, and the young moon gave light enough to distinguish prominent objects. One battery was passed, and the *Philadelphia* was in view near several smaller vessels, and

The Burning of the Philadelphia

the white walls of the city and its batteries were before us. We steered directly for the frigate, and at last the anxious silence was broken by a hail from her, demanding our character and object. Then might be seen the eager movement of the heads of the officers and crew who were stretched on the deck, ready to leap forward at the word of their commander, but still resting in silence. The conversation was kept up between the frigate and the ketch through our pilot, acting under the dictation of Decatur. We alleged the loss of our anchors during the last gale, which was true, as a reason for wishing to make fast to the frigate till morning, and permission was obtained; but just as the ketch was about coming in contact with the frigate, the wind shifted, blowing lightly directly from the frigate, and it left us at rest abeam and about twenty yards from her. This was a moment of great anxiety. We were directly under her guns, motionless and powerless, except by exertion which might betray our character. The *Siren's* boat was, however, in tow, and was leisurely manned and took a rope to make fast to the ship. She was met by a boat with another rope, when both were united, and each boat returned to its vessel. This rope was passed along the deck and hauled upon by the crew as they lay stretched upon it, and the vessels brought gradually nearer each other. When nearly in contact, the suspicions of the enemy appeared to be aroused, and the cry of 'Americanos!' resounded through the ship. In a moment, we were near enough, and the order 'Board!' was given; and with this cry our men were soon on the decks of the frigate. The surprise had been complete; there was no time for any preparation, and the enemy made scarcely a show of resistance. A few were killed, one was made prisoner, and the remainder leaped overboard and probably reached their cruisers which were anchored near the ship. . . .

"The plan of attack, prescribed by our commander, was for united action to obtain possession of the ship, with the exception of a boat to intercept communication with the shore, and for the surgeon and a few men to secure the ketch to the ship. When possession was secured, each lieutenant, with a midshipman and specified men, was to receive a portion of the prepared combustibles, and distribute them in designated parts of the berth deck, and in the forward store rooms, and a smaller party under a midshipman to do the same in the cockpit, and there await orders to set fire, that all might be done at the same time, and give all a chance for safe retreat. The party for the cockpit was assigned to my charge. My object in keeping near Lieutenant Decatur when we were approaching the ship was that, by watching his actions, I could be governed by these rather than by his orders when the boarding should take place. It was well that this course was taken, for Decatur had leaped to the main chain plates of the frigate, before the order to board was given. I had leaped with him, and, probably, more favored by circumstances, was able to reach the deck by the time he had gained the rail. The enemy were already leaping over the opposite side, and made no resistance; but Decatur, under the supposition that he was the first on board, was about to strike me, when I accidentally turned and stayed his uplifted arm by the watchword and mutual recognition. On my way to my station, after examining the cabin, and when passing forward, we met again under similar circumstances. Passing through the wardroom, which I found deserted, I awaited in the cockpit the men who had gone for the combustibles. These were so delayed that we had none when the order was given to set fire; but as they came a moment after, they were distributed, and fire communicated before we left our station. In the meantime, the fire on the deck above

The Burning of the Philadelphia 83

us had communicated so rapidly that it was with no small difficulty and danger that our party reached the spar deck by the forward hatchways. All the others had already joined the ketch, except Decatur, who remained on the rail till all others were on board; and the bow of the ketch had already swung off from the ship when he joined us by leaping into the rigging of the ketch. . . . In less than twenty minutes the ship had been carried, the combustibles distributed and set on fire, and all our party were again on board the ketch. By great exertions the two vessels were separated before the fire, which was pouring from the ports of the ship, enveloped the ketch also.

"Up to this time, the ships and batteries of the enemy had remained silent, but they were now prepared to act; and when the crew of the ketch gave three cheers, in exultation of their success, they received the return of a general discharge from the enemy. The confusion of the moment probably prevented much care in their direction, and though under the fire of nearly a hundred pieces for half an hour, the only shot which struck the ketch was one through the topgallant sail. We were in greater danger from the ship, whose broadside commanded the passage by which we were retreating, and whose guns were loaded and were discharged as they became heated. We escaped these also, and while urging the ketch onward with sweeps, the crew were commenting upon the beauty of the spray thrown up by the shot between us and the brilliant light of the ship, rather than calculating any danger that might be apprehended from the contact. The appearance of the ship was indeed magnificent. . . . Favored by a light breeze our exertions soon carried us beyond the range of their shot, and at the entrance of the harbor we met the boats of the *Siren*, which had been intended to co-operate with us, whose crews rejoiced at our success, while they grieved at not having been able to participate in it. . . . The success of this enterprise added much to the reputation of the navy both at home and abroad."

In confirmation of this final remark of Morris, it may be added that Nelson, who was then blockading Toulon, generously described the exploit as "the most bold and daring act of the age."

THE BOMBARDMENT OF TRIPOLI

During the winter and spring of 1804, Commodore Preble maintained as strict a blockade on Tripoli as the weather would allow, and kept two or three of his vessels cruising the Mediterranean in search of any Tripolitan that might have taken advantage of a gale to escape. Meanwhile, he arranged with the King of Sicily for the use of six small, flat-bottomed gunboats and two bomb vessels, together with some extra guns and ninety-six Neapolitan seamen. As soon as these vessels were ready, he proceeded to bombard Tripoli with his entire force. Aside from the gunboats, which carried one long 24-pounder apiece, and the bomb-ketches, each of which mounted a 13-inch mortar, the American attacking force consisted of the frigate *Constitution*, the brigs *Siren*, *Argus*, and *Scourge*, and the schooners *Vixen*, *Nautilus*, and *Enterprise*. The schooners and brigs, however, mounted nothing but carronades, and the only guns fit for the purpose of bombardment were the long guns of the *Constitution* and of the unwieldy gunboats. Against this force was a walled city, strongly fortified, having 115 guns, most of them heavy. Besides these, the Tripolitans had a navy of a brig, two schooners, two large galleys, and nineteen gunboats. The complement of men

The Bombardment of Tripoli

on these vessels alone amounted to more than all under Preble's command.

It was not till August 3 that the weather permitted an attack. Under cover of the bombs and the fire from the heavier vessels, the six gunboats, in two divisions, advanced to attack the two divisions of Tripolitan gunboats which had advanced beyond the line of rocks that sheltered the harbor. The rest of the enemy's shipping and the batteries opened at once in reply. Of the two divisions of American gunboats, Lieutenant Richard Somers commanded the first division, Nos. 1–3; and Lieutenant Stephen Decatur the second, Nos. 4–6.

The following from Preble's report to the Department describes the attack:

"In an instant the enemy's shipping and batteries opened a tremendous fire, which was promptly returned by the whole squadron at grape shot distance; at the same time, the second division of three boats, led by the gallant Captain [3] Decatur, was advancing with sails and oars to board the eastern division of the enemy, consisting of nine gunboats. Our boats gave the enemy showers of grape and musket balls as they advanced; the Tripolitans, however, soon closed, and the pistol, sabre, pike, and tomahawk were made use of by our brave tars.

"Captain [3] Somers, being in a dull sailer, made the best use of his sweeps, but was not able to fetch far enough to windward to engage the same division of the enemy's boats which Captain Decatur fell in with; he, however, gallantly bore down with his single boat on five of the enemy's western division, and engaged within pistol shot, defeated and drove them within the rocks in a shattered condition and with the loss of a great number of men.

---

[3] "Captain" by courtesy, as he was in command of a division.

"Lieutenant [James] Decatur, in No. 2, was closely engaged with one of the enemy's largest boats of the eastern division, which struck to him, after having lost a large proportion of men; and at the same instant that that brave officer was boarding her to take possession, he was treacherously shot through the head by the captain of the boat that had surrendered; which base conduct enabled the poltroon (with the assistance received from other boats) to escape. . . . Captain Decatur, in No. 4, after having with distinguished bravery boarded and carried one of the enemy of superior force, took his prize in tow and gallantly bore down to engage a second,[4] which, after a severe and bloody conflict, he also took possession of. . . . Lieutenant Trippe, of the *Vixen*, in No. 6, ran alongside one of the enemy's large boats, which he boarded with only Midshipman Henley and nine men—his boat falling off before any more could get on board; thus was he left to conquer or to perish, with the odds of thirty-six to eleven. The Turks, however, could not withstand the ardor of this brave officer and his assistants—in a few minutes the decks were cleared and her colors hauled down. . . . Lieutenant Trippe received eleven sabre wounds, some of which were very severe; he speaks in the highest terms of Mr. Henley, and those who followed him. . . .

"Lieutenant Decatur was the only officer killed, but

---

[4] Decatur believed that this second vessel was the one that had struck to his brother a few moments before, and that in killing her commander he had avenged his brother's death. Morris, however, agreeing with Preble, says in his memoirs that the treacherous pirate escaped. At all events, Stephen Decatur very nearly lost his own life in his hand to hand grapple with the Tripolitan commander. One of his seamen, Daniel Frazier, already wounded, interposed his own head to catch the blow of the scimitar, aimed for Decatur.

The Bombardment of Tripoli

in him the service has lost a valuable officer. . . . The enemy must have suffered very much in killed and wounded, both among their shipping and on shore. Three of their gunboats were sunk in the harbor, several of them had their decks nearly cleared of men by our shot, and a number of shells burst in the town and batteries, which must have done great execution.''

On the 7th of August, four days later, the squadron again bombarded Tripoli, but on this occasion none of the enemy's vessels advanced to attack at close quarters. During this attack, gunboat No. 9[5] blew up, killing and wounding eighteen of her crew. Among the killed were Lieutenant Caldwell and Midshipman Dorsey.

The same day brought the frigate *John Adams* with the new commissions of the officers connected with the destruction of the *Philadelphia,* and with the unwelcome news that Preble would be superseded in command by Captain Samuel Barron. This was apparently unavoidable, as the Secretary of the Navy was careful to point out to Commodore Preble, because Barron was senior to him; but the fact hurt Preble, and aroused the indignation of every officer under him. The outcome more than justified their feeling.

Meanwhile, Preble pushed his operations with all vigor. Under a hundred difficulties such as lack of water, lack of men, insufficient or worthless stores, and scurvy, Preble maintained his blockade, and three times again bombarded the city with all his guns. This policy so greatly disturbed the Bey, that he began to moderate very decidedly his terms of ransom and peace.

---

[5] The three Tripolitan gunboats that had been captured (see page 86) were rerigged and taken into service as Nos. 7, 8, 9.

The Intrepid Disaster

The summer campaign of 1804, however, closed with a melancholy episode. "Desirous of annoying the enemy by all the means in my power," wrote Commodore Preble to the Department in his report, "I directed to be put in execution a long contemplated plan of sending a fire ship, or infernal, into the harbor of Tripoli in the night for the purpose of endeavoring to destroy the enemy's shipping and shatter the Pasha's castle and town. Captain Somers, of the *Nautilus*, having volunteered his services, had, for several days before this period, been directing the preparation of the ketch *Intrepid*, assisted by Lieutenants Wadsworth and Israel. About 100 barrels of powder and 150 fixed shells were apparently judiciously disposed on board her. The fuses, leading to the magazine where all the powder was deposited, were calculated to burn a quarter of an hour.

"September 4, the *Intrepid* being prepared for the intended service, Captain Somers and Lieutenant Wadsworth made choice of two of the fastest rowing boats in the squadron for bringing them out after reaching their destination and firing the combustible materials which were to communicate with the fuses. Captain Somers' boat was manned with four seamen from the *Nautilus*, and Lieutenant Wadsworth's with six from the *Constitution*. Lieutenant Israel accompanied them. At eight in the evening, the *Intrepid* was under sail and standing for the port with a leading breeze from the eastward. The *Argus*, *Vixen*, and *Nautilus* convoyed her as far as the rock. On her entering the harbor, several shots were fired at her from the batteries. In a few minutes, when she had apparently nearly gained the intended place of destination, she suddenly exploded, without her people's having previously fired the room filled with splinters and other combustibles. These were intended to create a

The Intrepid Disaster

blaze in order to deter the enemy from boarding while the fire was communicating to the fuses which led to the magazine. The effect of the explosion stunned their batteries into profound silence—not a gun was afterward fired for the night. The shrieks of the inhabitants informed us that the town was thrown into the greatest terror and consternation by the explosion of the magazine and the bursting and falling of shells in all directions. The whole squadron awaited with the utmost anxiety to learn the fate of the adventurers from a signal previously agreed on in case of success—but waited in vain; no signs of their safety were to be observed. The *Argus*, *Vixen*, and *Nautilus* hovered around the entrance of the port till sunrise, when they had a fair view of the whole harbor—not a vestige of the ketch or boats was to be seen. One of the enemy's largest gunboats was missing and three others were seen very much shattered and damaged, which the enemy were hauling on shore.

"From these circumstances, I am led to believe that those boats were detached from the enemy's flotilla to intercept the ketch without suspecting her to be a fire ship. The boat afterwards missing suddenly boarded her The gallant Somers and the heroes of his party, observing the other three boats surrounding them, and no prospect of escape from them, . . . put a match to the train leading directly to the magazine, which at once blew the whole into the air, and terminated their existence. My conjectures respecting this affair are founded on a resolution which Captain Somers and Lieutenants Wadsworth and Israel had formed, neither to be taken by the enemy nor suffer him to get possession of the powder on board the *Intrepid*. They expected to enter the harbor without discovery, but had declared that if they should be disappointed and the enemy should board them before they reached the point of destination in such force as to leave them no hopes of safe retreat, that they would put a match to the magazine and blow themselves and the enemy up together—determined as there was no exchanging of prisoners, that their country should never pay ransom for them, nor the enemy receive a supply of powder through their means.''

Captain Bainbridge was permitted to see the bodies when they came ashore the next day, but all were so mangled as to make recognition out of the question. According to him, no damage whatever was done the Tripolitans; so Preble was probably mistaken in his idea regarding the injury sustained by the enemy's gunboats.

The loss of the *Intrepid's* crew was felt deeply throughout the squadron. Somers, especially, seemed to have a brilliant future in store for him, having many fine qualities in common with Decatur, whose dearest friend he had been from boyhood. After the war, the officers of the squadron subscribed to the erection of the monument, now in the United States Naval Academy grounds, honoring the memory of the six comrades who fell before Tripoli: Somers, Caldwell, James Decatur, Wadsworth, Israel, and Dorsey.

THE FINAL YEAR OF THE WAR

Shortly after the *Intrepid* disaster, Commodore Barron arrived with the frigates *President* and *Constellation*, bringing as passenger Tobias Lear, former consul-general to Algiers, who had full powers to negotiate with the Bey of Tripoli; and in December Commodore Preble sailed for New York on the *John Adams*. The new commodore had under his flag about twice the force that Preble had commanded, but the glory of the war ended with Preble's departure from the Mediterranean. Commodore Barron was, at the time, in wretched health and soon became incapable of command. When, finally, he was compelled to give up his duties, in the spring of 1805, he was succeeded by Commodore Rodgers. The latter then

Eaton's Expedition

had under his pennant five frigates and seven schooners and brigs, the largest of all the American squadrons assembled before Tripoli.

Meanwhile, the energetic Eaton had managed to interest the authorities of Washington in his scheme of backing the deposed Hamet in an effort to regain his throne by means of a land attack against Tripoli. Eaton was authorized to go to Egypt and do what he could, relying on such assistance as the fleet could afford. Starting at Cairo, he collected a motley array of Arabs and freebooters, including Hamet and some of Hamet's officials. This horde he drove by sheer force of will through the desert to the frontiers of the province of Tripoli, and captured the city of Derne.[6] The attack on the city was led in person by Eaton, who was shot through the wrist in the final charge. The fall of Derne thoroughly frightened the Bey, and Eaton was looking forward to a triumphant march on Tripoli when he was met by the humiliating news that he must abandon Derne, because peace had already been concluded on the 10th of June, 1805. Consul Lear, who disliked Eaton and had opposed his plans, had during Eaton's operation hastily agreed to a treaty of peace with the Bey of Tripoli, involving the payment of a ransom of $60,000 for the captives from the *Philadelphia*. Apparently, neither Rodgers nor Bainbridge made any objection to the terms; but that any money should have been paid when a large fleet lay off the batteries of Tripoli and Eaton with an army threatened a revolution in the province itself, seems inexcusable.[7]

---

[6] In this attack Eaton was supported by the fire of the sloop *Hornet*, the brig *Argus*, and the schooner *Nautilus*.

[7] Commodore Preble wrote to Eaton that he was sure "the Senate feel that just sense of indignation which they ought at the sacrifice of national honor which has been made by an ignominious negotiation." Preble Papers, quoted by Allen, *Our Navy and the Barbary Corsairs*, p. 254.

The treaty was satisfactory, however, in that it did away with all annual tribute for the future. Hamet, who was left in the lurch at Derne, became thereafter a pensioner of the United States. Eaton was honored by the State of Massachusetts with a grant of 10,000 acres of land; but he was embittered by the outcome of his efforts to secure an honorable peace, and up to his death in 1811, he was engaged in disputes over that brilliant but luckless expedition.

The war with Tripoli was the beginning of the movement of the civilized world to shake off the yoke of the Barbary pirates. The operations of our little fleet, under Preble, brought honor to the nation and to the service in the eyes of Europe, and at the same time they gave a practical schooling in warfare to the officers of all grades, but especially to the younger men, who later won fame in the War of 1812.

In the popular mind, the hero of the Tripolitan War was Stephen Decatur, and there is no question as to his distinction in the brilliant personal qualities of courage and dash. But the officer who deserved first honors was Commodore Preble. Where others failed with large squadrons, he succeeded with the smallest. He introduced iron discipline into the service at a time when it was most needed, and yet became the idol of his officers and men, because he was as jealous of their success and reputation as of his own. The difficulties that had proved insurmountable to others he overcame. And he inspired his subordinates with ideals of obedience, courage, and efficiency that have ever since been the standards of the American Navy.

VI

THE WAR OF 1812—CAUSES AND EARLY EVENTS

IMPRESSMENT

THE causes of the War of 1812 were mainly the impressment of American seamen, the restrictions upon our commerce by the British Orders in Council and the Napoleonic Decrees, and the Indian troubles in the Northwest—the responsibility for all of which was charged, at least by many, against England.

Great Britain at the close of the eighteenth century entered upon a struggle with Napoleon that was so desperate as to require well-nigh all her resources, both of men and of food and war materials. For her gigantic navy she was constantly experiencing difficulty in finding a sufficient number of seamen. The duty required of them was hard and irksome. Further, many who might otherwise be available were drifting into the rapidly growing American merchant marine. The Yankee ships offered more comfort and very much higher wages. Some seamen of British birth sailing in our ships had become naturalized American citizens; others were deserters from the Royal Navy. It made little difference. England claimed the right of seizing them wherever found and impressing them into her navy. For at this time and for many years to follow she held to the principle, "Once a subject, always a subject." Thus her warships frequently stopped an American merchantman on the high seas and took off deserters. This was bad enough, but when mistakes were made and American-born seamen were removed, there was sharp resentment. The case in which the United States frigate *Chesapeake* was thus treated by His Majesty's ship *Leopard* caused a sense of national humiliation and an indignation that lasted for years.

THE CHESAPEAKE-LEOPARD INCIDENT

The British had been blockading some of our ports to enforce their orders, and several of the vessels on this duty had been very bold in impressing sailors even within a league of our shores. One of these blockaders in Chesapeake Bay had even chased an American revenue cutter with the Vice-President of the United States on board. On the other hand, from the *Melampus,* a British blockader in the Chesapeake, five of the crew deserted, one night in February, 1807, and three of them later enlisted on the United States frigate *Chesapeake.* A demand was made for their return by the British minister at Washington, and while the correspondence was going on, five more men deserted from the *Halifax,* and also took service on the *Chesapeake.* The authorities at Washington made an investigation, but having been convinced that the deserters were Americans, refused to give them up. This refusal was reported to Vice-Admiral Berkeley at Halifax, who at once sent an order to the commanders of all British vessels on the North Atlantic station, requiring them to watch for the *Chesapeake* at sea, and search her for deserters.

On June 22, 1807, as the *Chesapeake* set sail from Hampton Roads to relieve the *Constitution* in the Mediterranean, His Majesty's ship *Leopard,* which had been lying at Lynnhaven, followed her, and when well outside of the jurisdiction of the United States, the British vessel spoke the American. Captain James Barron of the *Chesapeake,* supposing the message to be of a peaceful character, hove to, and received an officer from the *Leopard* who came aboard with Admiral Berkeley's order. Barron refused to give up the men, whereupon the British frigate at once opened fire. The American vessel had just undergone repairs; her powder horns were empty, rammers could not be found, matches had been mislaid, and but few of her guns were mounted. After a number of broadsides had been fired at close range by the *Leopard,* First Lieutenant Allen managed to discharge one gun in return by means of a live coal from the galley. Meanwhile, twenty-one shot had struck the *Chesapeake's* hull, her foremast and mainmast had been carried away, the rigging had been badly cut, and three men had been killed and eighteen wounded. Barron thereupon hauled down his flag. The British boarding party found only one man of the *Halifax's* crew, for the rest had deserted before the *Chesapeake* sailed, but they took off three other men, all Americans. Barron attempted to throw his ship on the British captain as a prize, but the latter, refusing to accept it, left the American vessel to find her way back to port as best she might.[1]

The *Chesapeake* affair angered the nation as had nothing of its kind since the battle of Lexington. But Jefferson sought to avert war. In the negotiations which followed, England was ready to make reparation, but the President thought he could secure with it an abandonment of impressments and demanded also the latter. Since this was refused, many months of uncertainty passed, and it was not until 1811 that Great Britain made a formal disavowal of the wrong by restoring to the United States three of the four men who had been seized—the fourth had been hanged at the yardarm as a deserter.

---

[1] Captain Barron was court-martialed and found guilty of neglecting, on the probability of an engagement, to clear his ship for action. He was suspended for five years without pay.

RESTRICTIONS UPON COMMERCE

The French Revolution, beginning in 1789 and followed soon by wars in which most of Europe including Great Britain was involved, so engrossed the people of the several countries that more and more of the commerce and carrying trade fell to America. For two decades profits were enormous and shipping grew by leaps and bounds. Thus in 1790 the total exports of the country amounted to $19,000,000; five years later $26,000,000 worth of merchandise was brought from French, Spanish, and Dutch possessions to the United States, and thence re-exported. In 1806 the value of the re-exports had grown to $60,000,000. The magnitude of the foreign trade can be seen further by a comparison with later times. In 1810 when the population was about one-tenth that of 1900, and the total national wealth was one-fortieth or one-fiftieth that of the later year, American ships in foreign trade were carrying actually a greater volume of trade.[2]

The conditions that obtained during this period are closely parallel to those of a century and some odd years later in the first years of the World War, when again America was the neutral power and profited from the great demands for ships and cargoes.

It is not strange that England became alarmed over the future of her maritime supremacy, and being goaded on also by the economic phase of her war with Napoleon, passed many restrictive measures.

The British courts having felt the pressure of public opinion handed down a decision on the *"Essex* case." By a previous act, the "Rule of 1756," neutral ships could not in time of war engage in a trade forbidden them in

---

[2] For a fuller discussion of the growth of the American merchant marine see Krafft and Norris, *Sea Power in American History*, chap. iv.

time of peace; e.g., trade between a country and its colonies. American merchants, however, had got around this by bringing the goods from a French or a Spanish colony first to an American port, and, after landing them and paying the duty, reshipping them to France or Spain (or vice versa); the drawback of the duty which was granted made this highly profitable. In the *Essex* case a cargo was thus taken from Barcelona to Havana via Salem. But the highest legal authority in England ruled that since the cargo was never intended for the American market, the broken voyage did not make the trade lawful. As a result of this decision, "about 120 vessels were seized, several condemned, all taken from their course, detained, or otherwise subjected to heavy losses and damages." [3]

Great Britain, as the next step, now ordered a general blockade against France from the Elbe to Brest, and a close blockade from the Seine to Ostend (Order in Council of May 16, 1806). Napoleon retaliated with his famous Berlin Decree (November 21, 1806), proclaiming "that the British Islands were thenceforward in a state of blockade; that all correspondence and commerce with them was prohibited; that trade in English merchandise was prohibited; and that all merchandise belonging to England or (even if neutral property) proceeding from its manufactories or colonies, is lawful prize." [4]

England now countered with a second Order in Council, more drastic than the first, and Napoleon answered with a Decree that was scarcely less than confiscation. American commerce was in consequence ground between the "upper and nether millstones." President Jefferson's remedy for all these wrongs was "peaceable coercion." In 1807 he declared an embargo on all foreign shipping,

---

[3] Monroe to Fox, *American State Papers*, Foreign Relations, III, 114.

[4] Mahan, *War of 1812*, I, 142.

which lasted fifteen months. This cost the New England merchants alone $8,000,000; it was extremely unpopular at home and injured America much more than it did Europe.

Orders in Council and Decrees now followed fast, one after another, in this economic warfare, in which America also took part as she issued her Embargo and Non-Intercourse Acts. Napoleon was by far the worst offender, but he played his game so skilfully that popular feeling in America turned chiefly against England.

Several British statesmen tried hard to avert war with the United States. The lack of bread in England, the distress of her manufacturing towns, and her already great burden in the European War made them hesitate before entering upon further hostilities. The Prince Regent also did his utmost. Thus the Orders in Council restricting American trade were revoked about the middle of 1812, but the action came too late.

INDIAN TROUBLES

While the negotiations between Washington and London and Paris had been proceeding, settlers had been pushing on in the Northwest. Already there was the desire for more space, and land speculators were pressing the Indians for further cessions. Against them Tecumseh attempted to organize the Indians that they might unite in refusing to cede more lands and oppose the settlers' progress.

The Indians had obtained their guns and ammunition from British traders in Canada. Making much of this, the land speculators argued through their spokesmen in Congress that the only way to bring peace to the Northwest was to remove the British from Canada. The West, largely represented by young men in Congress, had as their leader Henry Clay from Kentucky, and they were becoming a strong faction. Clay in a speech declared: "The conquest of Canada is in your power. . . . Is it nothing to extinguish the torch that lights up savage warfare? Is it nothing to acquire the entire fur-trade connected with that country?" Clay, who had been elected Speaker of the House, was with his followers so insistent on aggressive measures that they were dubbed the "War Hawks." Their opponents charged that they had as their real motive territorial conquest.

THE PRESIDENT AND THE LITTLE BELT

Meanwhile another unpleasant affair occurred at sea. On May 1, 1811, the British frigate *Guerrière,* off New York harbor, had boarded the American brig *Spitfire* and impressed a passenger, a native of the United States. Immediately, Captain John Rodgers in the *President* was ordered to seek the *Guerrière.* Rodgers had already been put in command of a squadron of frigates and sloops, with orders to defend on the open sea all vessels of the United States from molestation by foreign armed ships.

While searching for the *Guerrière,* on May 16, 1811, fifty miles off Cape Henry, he sighted a strange vessel. At eight o'clock that evening, though within hailing distance, he could not make out in the darkness the stranger's identity. The latter, after two hails from the *President,* replied with a shot, which struck the American vessel's mainmast. Captain Rodgers at once returned the compliment. After a battle that lasted fifteen minutes, the foreign corvette, which turned out to be the sloop of war *Little Belt,* gave up the unequal contest. She had been badly cut up, and had lost nine killed and twenty-three wounded. Captain Rodgers stood by during the night, and next day offered assistance; but the English captain refused the proffered aid, and continued his voyage. This incident embittered the feeling between the two countries still more.

The Declaration of War

President Madison had called the Congress together on November 4, 1811, and this body had at once voted an army of 35,000 regulars and 50,000 volunteers. To the navy, the President had devoted in his message only three lines. Congress appointed a committee to consider the feasibility of building war vessels, and this committee suggested that twelve ships-of-the-line and twenty frigates should be built to protect our coasts. But Congress, still dominated by a Jeffersonian opposition to naval armaments as expensive and subversive of political freedom, rejected the report by a vote of sixty-two to fifty-nine. Politicians could not see that privateers and the loss of trade were far more expensive than ships-of-war, nor did they yet realize that a well-managed navy would promote patriotism and bring back national self-respect. Congress contented itself in making an appropriation of $600,000 for timber for future warships and while in secret session it passed another embargo, April, 1812, intended to prevent the sapping of our seamen and supplies to aid England in her Peninsular War. Like the other embargoes, the Non-Intercourse Act, and similar legislation, this law also failed in its object. On June 1, 1812, the President sent a message to Congress urging that war be declared against Great Britain, for the reasons that the latter country had ruined America's trade by her Orders in Council, had practically blockaded American ports, and had impressed American seamen into the service of her navy. Congress passed the necessary act, and on June 19, 1812, war was declared.

We thus see that the causes which led to war were: (1) impressment of American seamen, and (2) restrictions upon American commerce resulting from the British Orders in Council, the Decrees of Napoleon, and the

Comparison of Naval Strength 101

retaliatory Embargo and Non-Intercourse Acts. With these there was a third cause, Indian trouble in the Northwest (justifying, as some maintained the taking of Canada). The last, though not proclaimed by the President, had undoubted weight with the section of the country that clamored for war.

THE NAVIES OF THE UNITED STATES AND GREAT BRITAIN

At the outbreak of the war there were sixteen serviceable war vessels in our navy; among them there was not a single ship-of-the-line, but they included the three splendid 44-gun frigates, *United States, Constitution,* and *President,* which were superior to any frigate in the British Navy. The personnel of the navy also was at a high pitch of efficiency, for nearly all the officers and many of the seamen had seen active service in the French War and in the war with Tripoli.

Besides these sixteen men-of-war, there were 257 gunboats which had been built in the years immediately preceding the war; for Jefferson, who strongly opposed a navy, placed great faith in these gunboats, which were intended for coast defence. These, however, proved to be utterly worthless, and need not be considered as any part of our naval force.

On the other hand, Britain's navy in 1812 "stood at a height never reached before or since by that of any other nation."[5] According to the London *Times* of that year, England "had from Halifax to the West Indies seven times the armament of the whole American Navy." Two years later, by the abdication of Napoleon, she had her entire navy free to use against the United States, a huge fleet of 219 ships-of-the-line and 296 frigates, besides a larger number of corvettes.

---

[5] Roosevelt, *Naval War of 1812*, p. 22.

The Chase of the Belvidera

Shortly after the declaration of war, Commodore Rodgers, with his squadron (the only vessels ready for immediate service) consisting of his flagship, the *President*, 44; the *United States*, 44, Captain Decatur; the *Congress*, 36, Captain Smith; the *Hornet*, 18, Master-Commandant Lawrence; and the *Argus*, 16, Lieutenant Sinclair, left New York on June 21, with the intention of capturing the homeward-bound plate fleet from Jamaica. On June 23, Rodgers' squadron sighted the British frigate *Belvidera*, 36, Captain Byron. The *President* was overhauling the enemy, and when she came within gunshot, the American vessel, by means of her bow guns, killed and wounded nine men. At this juncture a main-deck gun on the *President* burst, and in the ensuing confusion, Captain Byron escaped. The *President* had lost much ground by yawing and firing harmless broadsides. By this chase, Commodore Rodgers was taken far out of the course of the plate fleet. He now proceeded to Newfoundland and thence across the Atlantic and back to Boston, where he arrived on August 31, with seven prizes, all merchantmen.

Hull's Escape from Broke's Squadron

The *Belvidera*, after her escape, carried the news of war to Halifax, and acting on this information Vice-Admiral Sawyer, on July 5, 1812, sent a squadron under Captain Philip Bowes Vere Broke to cruise against the United States. This squadron consisted of the flagship *Shannon*, 38; the *Belvidera*, 36, Captain Byron; the *Africa*, 64, Captain Bastard; the *Aeolus*, 32, Captain Townsend; and the *Guerrière*, 38, Captain Dacres. On the 16th, the British vessels captured the United States brig *Nautilus*, of 14 guns. On the same afternoon, off

Chase of the Constitution

Barnegat, they made out a strange sail standing to the northeast. This was the *Constitution*, Captain Hull. When on the following morning they discovered that she was an American frigate, they began a chase, remarkable for its duration, and for the skill with which the *Constitution* was handled.

Commodore Charles Morris, at this time first lieutenant on the *Constitution*, gives in his autobiography an interesting account of this chase:

"The ship [the *Constitution*] had been ordered to New York to meet and join other vessels under the command of Commodore Rodgers, and our course was directed accordingly. We had proceeded beyond the Delaware, but out of sight of land, when, on the afternoon of the 16th [July, 1812], we discovered four vessels at a great distance to the northwest, and a single ship to the northeast, from which quarter a light wind was then blowing. The wind changed to the southward about sunset which brought us to windward, and we stood for the ship, the wind being very light. The chase was evidently a frigate, and the first impression was that she might be a part of Commodore Rodgers' squadron. By eleven P.M. we were within signal distance, and it was soon apparent that she was not an American man-of-war. There being no apprehension that a British frigate would make any attempt to avoid an engagement, Captain Hull felt justified in delaying any nearer approach till daylight of the 17th, when our newly-collected and imperfectly disciplined men would be less likely to be thrown into confusion. The ship was accordingly brought to the wind with her head to the southward and westward, under easy sail, with a light wind from the northwest. The other ship did the same at about two miles' distance. The watch not on duty were allowed to sleep at their quarters, and the officers slept in the same manner.

"As the following morning opened upon us, it disclosed our companion of the night to be a large frigate, just within gunshot, on the lee quarter, and a ship-of-the-line and three other frigates, a brig, and a schooner, about two miles nearly astern, with all sails set, standing for us, with English colors flying. All our sails were soon set, and the nearest frigate, fortunately for us, but without any apparent reason, tacked and immediately wore round again in chase, a maneuver that occupied some ten minutes, and allowed us to gain a distance, which, though short, proved of utmost importance to our safety. By sunrise our ship was entirely becalmed and unmanageable, while the ships astern retained a light breeze till it brought three of the frigates so near, that their shot passed beyond us. The distance, however, was too great for accuracy, and their shot did not strike our ship.

"Our boats were soon hoisted out, and the ship's head kept from the enemy, and exertions were made to increase our distance from them by towing. This, and occasional catspaws, or slight puffs of wind, enabled us to prevent their closing, but as their means were equal to ours, we could gain nothing. A few guns were fired from our sternports, but so much rake [6] had been given to the stern, that the guns could not be used with safety and their further use was relinquished. All means were adopted that seemed to promise any increase of speed. The hammocks were removed from the nettings, and the cloths rolled up to prevent their unfavorable action; several thousand gallons of water were started and pumped overboard, and all the sails kept thoroughly wet to close the texture of the canvas.

"While making all these exertions, our chances for escape were considered hopeless. For many years the ship had proved a very dull sailer, especially during the

---

[6] Slant or inclination.

late cruise, and it was supposed that the first steady breeze would bring up such a force as would render resistance of no avail, and our situation seemed hopeless. At about eight A.M., one of the frigates called all the boats of the squadron to her, and, having arranged them for towing, furled all sails. This brought her toward us steadily, and seemed to decide our fate. Fortunately for us, a light breeze filled our sails and sent us forward a few hundred yards, before her sails could be set to profit by it.

"With our minds excited to the utmost to devise means for escape, I happened to recollect that, when obliged by the timidity of my old commander, Cox, to warp the *President* in and out of harbors where others depended on sails, our practice had enabled us to give her a speed of nearly three miles an hour. We had been on soundings the day before, and, on trying, we found twenty-six fathoms. This depth was unfavorably great, but it gave me confidence to suggest to Captain Hull the expediency of attempting to warp the ship ahead. He acceded at once, and in a short time (about seven A.M.) the launch and the first cutter were sent ahead with the kedge and all the hawsers and rigging, from five inches and upward, that could be found, making nearly a mile of length. When the kedge was thrown, the men hauled on the connecting hawser, slowly and carefully at first, till the ship was in motion, and gradually increasing until a sufficient velocity was given to continue till the anchor could be taken ahead again, when the same process was repeated. In this way the ship was soon placed out of the range of the enemy's guns and by continued exertions when the wind failed, and giving every possible advantage to the sails when we had air enough to fill them, we prevented them from again closing very near us.

"The ship which we had first chased gained a position abeam of us about nine A.M., and fired several broadsides, but the shot fell just short of us, and only served to enliven our men and excite their jocular comments. The exertions of neither party were relaxed during this day or the following night. There was frequent alternation of calms and very light winds from the southeast, which we received with our head to the southwestward. When the wind would give us more speed than with warping and towing, the boats were run up to their places, or suspended to the spars in the chains by temporary tackles, with their crews in them, ready to act again at a moment's notice.

"At daylight of the second day, on the 18th, it was found that one frigate had gained a position on our lee bow, two nearly abeam, one on the lee quarter about two miles from us, and the ship-of-the-line, brig, and schooner, three miles from us in the same direction. The wind had now become tolerably steady, though still light. The frigate on the lee bow tacked about four A.M., and would evidently reach within gunshot if we continued our course. This we were anxious to avoid, as a single shot might cripple some spar, and impede our progress. If we tacked, we might be exposed to the fire of the other frigate on the lee quarter; but as she was a smaller vessel, the risk appeared to be less, and we also tacked soon.

"In passing the lee frigate at five, we expected a broadside or more, as we should evidently pass within gunshot; but, from some unexplained cause, Lord James Townsend, in the *Aeolus*, of 32 guns, suffered us to pass quietly, and tacked in our wake, while the others soon took the same direction. We had now all our pursuers astern and on the lee quarter, and as the wind was gradually increasing, our escape must depend on our superiority of sailing, which we had no reason to hope or expect. Exertions, however, were not relaxed. The launch and first cutter, which we dared not lose, were hoisted on board at six A.M., under the directions of Captain Hull, with so little loss of time or change of sails, that our watching enemies could not conceive what disposition was made of them. This we afterward learned from Lieutenant Crane, who was a prisoner in their squadron. The sails were kept saturated with water, a set of skysails was made and set, and all other sails set and trimmed to the greatest advantage, close by the wind. The ship directly astern gained slowly, but gradually, till noon; though, as the wind increased, our good ship was going at that time at the unexpected rate of ten knots an hour. At noon we had the wind abeam, and as it gradually freshened, we began to leave our fleet pursuer. Our ship had reached a speed of twelve and a half knots by two P.M. Our hopes began to overcome apprehension, and cheerfulness was more apparent among us.

"Though encouraged, we were by no means assured, as all the ships were still near and ready to avail themselves of any advantage that might offer. About six P.M., a squall of wind and rain passed over us, which induced us to take in our light sails before the rain covered us from the view of the enemy; but most of them were soon replaced as the wind moderated.[7] When the rain had passed, we had evidently gained a mile or more during its

---

[7] This was a skilful ruse on the part of Hull to deceive the enemy. " He immediately let everything go by the run, apparently in the utmost confusion, as if unable to show a yard of canvas—his sails were hauled up by the brails and clewlines. The enemy, perceiving this, hastened to get everything snug, before the gust should reach them; but no sooner had they got their sails furled, than Captain Hull had his courses and topsails set, and the *Constitution* darted forward with great rapidity. So coolly, however, did he proceed, that he, . . . though pressed by a pursuing enemy, attended personally to hoisting his launch and other boats, while the ship was going at ten knots through the water. . . . The British squadron cut adrift all their boats, and, after they abandoned the chase, spent two or three whole days in cruising to pick them up." *Naval Monument*, pp. 8–9.

continuance. Still the pursuit was continued, and our own ship pressed forward to her utmost speed. The officers and men again passed the night at quarters. At daylight, on the morning of the 19th, our enemies had been left so far astern that danger from them was considered at an end, and at eight A.M. they at last relinquished the chase and hauled their wind.[8] Our officers and crew could now indulge in some rest, of which the former had taken little for more than sixty hours.

"Captain Hull deservedly gained much reputation for this difficult retreat from a greatly superior force, when superior numbers and other circumstances gave the enemy great advantages. . . . If they had concentrated their efforts at an earlier period to bringing up some one of their ships within fair range, or had adopted our plan of warping at any time during the early part of the chase, they could hardly have failed to inflict such damage as would have prevented our escape, after our dependence was reduced to our sails. The result may be remembered as an evidence of the advantages to be expected from perseverance under the most discouraging circumstances, so long as *any* chance of success may remain."[9]

Captain Isaac Hull, by reason of his coolness, great perseverance, good seamanship, and readiness to take suggestions of his subordinates, had completely outmaneuvered five British captains. This feat in eluding Broke's squadron, and his fight shortly afterwards with the *Guerrière*, according to Roosevelt, "place him above any single-ship captain of the war."

---

[8] That is, came up into the wind.
[9] *The Autobiography of Commodore Morris*, pp. 51–55.

VII

THE CAPTURES OF THE GUERRIÈRE AND THE MACEDONIAN

THE CONSTITUTION AND THE GUERRIÈRE

THE *Constitution,* having been prevented by Broke's squadron from entering New York, proceeded to Boston, where she arrived July 27, 1812. Captain Hull at once dispatched letters to New York and Washington, renewed supplies, and prepared for active service. When he had delayed just long enough to learn that there were no orders from Commodore Rodgers awaiting him in New York, Hull put to sea on August 2. His haste, Morris says, was due to his "apprehension of being blockaded by the enemy's squadron"; but probably he was also influenced by his eagerness to try issues with the British, and by the likelihood that his ship would soon be given to a captain higher on the list. As it turned out, he had a narrow escape in getting to sea; for, on the day following his departure, orders came from Washington which would have held him in port for weeks and perhaps months. It was well for Hull, thus sailing without orders, that he could give a good account of himself upon his return.

After an uneventful cruise to Halifax, he took his station off Cape Race, where he might intercept ships bound to or from Quebec or Halifax. Here he seized two British brigs, saved an American prize from being recaptured, and retook an American brig that had been seized by the British. At this point he heard that Broke's squadron was on the western edge of the Grand Banks. He therefore took a course southward, intending to pass near the Bermudas. On the evening of August 18, he saw a sail, and giving chase overhauled it in two hours. It proved to be an American privateer, the *Decatur*, which, in attempting to escape its supposed foe, had thrown twelve of its fourteen guns overboard. From the *Decatur* Hull learned that a British ship of war had been seen the day previous standing to the southward. He immediately resolved to give chase.

At one P.M., August 19, when the *Constitution* was in latitude 41° 42′ N., longitude 55° 48′ W.[1] (about 750 miles east of Boston), the lookout at the masthead made out a sail somewhat south of east. Two hours later the sail could be seen to be a large ship on the starboard tack under easy canvas, close hauled to the wind, which was blowing fresh from the northwest. Hull was eager to engage a British frigate, and, being to windward, he came rapidly down until he was within three miles, when he ordered the light sails taken in, the courses hauled up, and the ship cleared for action. The stranger, which proved to be the *Guerrière*, had, in the meantime, shown her willingness to engage by backing her main topsail and waiting for her enemy to approach. The American responded smartly, intending to come to close quarters at once.

If the *Constitution* held to her course, Captain Dacres of the *Guerrière* saw that his enemy might pass under his stern and rake. To prevent this, Dacres fired a broadside when his antagonist was barely within range and then wore, firing the other broadside as he came about. The *Constitution,* which had displayed an ensign and a jack at each masthead, also fired occasionally, and yawed to prevent being raked. Thus the frigates maneuvered for three-quarters of an hour, each giving the other no advan-

---

[1] Letter of Captain Hull, August 30, 1812, to the Secretary of the Navy.

tage, but inflicting no injury. The *Guerrière* then gave
the *Constitution* an opportunity to come into close action

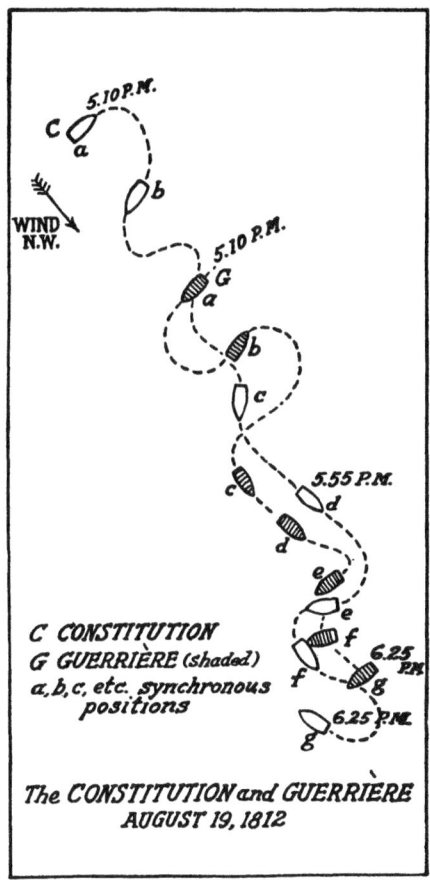

PLAN OF THE BATTLE BETWEEN THE CONSTITUTION AND THE GUERRIERE
AUGUST 19, 1812

by bearing up and sailing slowly under topsails and jib
with the wind on her quarter. Hull, seeing Dacres' willingness, ordered the man at the wheel to steer directly

for the British ship, and had the main topgallant sail set that he might close at once; further, he instructed his gunners to cease firing.

As the *Constitution* approached, the *Guerrière* opened vigorously with her stern chasers, to which the *Constitution* could give no effective reply without yawing, a maneuver which would prevent the American from coming at once into close action. In obedience to Hull's orders, his gunners endured this fire in silence, but made every preparation to strike a telling blow when the word should be given, and double-shotted their guns with round and grape.

It was at 5.55, according to Captain Hull's report, that he came alongside the *Guerrière* within half pistol shot. At the signal a heavy fire burst from his starboard battery as each gun bore on the *Guerrière*. Hull had struck his first blow, and the enemy fairly staggered from the shock. Just before the battle, as the American ensign was unfurled, the crew of the *Constitution* had given three cheers, "requesting to be laid close alongside the enemy." And now when their desire was promptly granted, they responded nobly to the supreme test and maintained a cool and well-directed fire in the face of a furious cannonade from the *Guerrière*. It was only six to eight weeks since Hull had shipped his crew, many of whom were raw hands. But the weeks had been filled with constant practice, and early in this battle the practice began to tell. The main yard of the *Guerrière* was shot away in the slings, and fifteen minutes after she had been engaged at close quarters her mizzenmast was struck by a 24-pound shot, and went by the board, knocking a hole in her starboard counter. On seeing this, Hull is said to have exclaimed, "Huzza, my boys! We have made a brig of her!"

The mast, falling on the starboard side, acted

The Constitution and the Guerrière 113

as a drag, and, though the helm was put hard over, brought the ship's head up. As the *Constitution* then drew ahead, Hull luffed short round the *Guerrière's* bows. The loss of braces, with spanker and mizzen topsails disabled, prevented his coming to as quickly as he desired,[2] but he poured in two raking broadsides, swept her decks with grape, and put several holes in her hull between wind and water. He then attempted to wear that he might retain the advantage of position and perhaps rake again, but as he brought the ship before the wind the bowsprit of the *Guerrière* fouled the port mizzen rigging of the *Constitution*.

Each side now thought of boarding. With the British it was indeed a last desperate chance to retrieve the day. But as they were assembling on the forecastle of the *Guerrière*, the American sailors were being drawn up on the quarter-deck of the *Constitution*. Captain Dacres, seeing what preparation had been made to receive his men, and considering how slow and difficult it would be to cross over because of the rough sea, gave up the attempt.

So near were the two forces to each other, that an American sailor who had discharged his boarding pistol, enraged that he had missed his man, threw the pistol and struck him in the chest. Marksmen in the tops, meanwhile, inflicted severe losses on each side; in fact, nearly all the losses that the *Constitution* suffered during the engagement occurred at this time. Lieutenant Bush of the American marines, who in organizing the boarding-party had exposed himself on the *Constitution's* quarter-deck, was killed; Lieutenant Morris, while attempting to pass some turns of the mainbrace over the *Guerrière's* bowsprit to hold the two ships together, was severely

---

[2] *Autobiography of Commodore Morris*, p. 56.

wounded; Mr. Alwyn, the master, also sustained a slight injury; and Captain Hull escaped only because a devoted sailor who saw him mounting an arm-chest forcibly drew him back and begged he would not get up there unless he took off "those swabs," pointing to his epaulets. Nor did the British suffer less; among the wounded were Captain Dacres (shot through the back), Mr. Scott, the master, and Mr. Kent, the master's mate.

The ships soon drew apart, but the bowsprit of the *Guerrière*, striking the taffrail of the *Constitution*, slacked the British ship's forestay; and as the foreshrouds on the port side had been mostly shot away, the foremast fell over on the starboard side, crossing the mainstay. The jerk suddenly given to the mainmast—not very sound— caused that to fall; and thirty minutes after fighting at close quarters had begun, according to Hull's statement, the *Guerrière* was left without a spar except the bowsprit. The *Constitution* sailed ahead of the *Guerrière* and again took a position to rake, but the British, seeing the uselessness of further fighting, fired a gun to leeward as signal of submission.

The *Constitution* then set fore and mainsails, and hauled a short distance to the east to repair damages. All her braces and much of her standing and running rigging had been injured, and some spars had been shot away. A slight fire, caught in the cabin from the wadding of the enemy's guns, had to be extinguished. A half hour sufficed for reeving new braces and making temporary repairs, whereupon the *Constitution* wore and returned to the *Guerrière*.

The British had during the interim employed all hands in clearing away the wreckage. They had rigged up a spritsail, but when the *Constitution* again bore down, the spritsail yard carried away, and the ship fell into the trough of the sea, with her main-deck guns rolling under.

The Constitution and the Guerrière 115

It was hard for the British to acknowledge defeat on their own element, the sea, but there was no alternative. The small boat sent by the *Constitution* returned with Captain Dacres, and the formal surrender took place.

A few more broadsides would have sent the *Guerrière* to the bottom. As it was, the lieutenant placed in charge of the prize hailed next morning at daylight to say that there was four feet of water in the hold. The possibility of taking her into port was so slight that Hull decided on her destruction; and having removed the prisoners, he set fire to her and blew her up on the afternoon of the 20th. As he had completed the repairs of the *Constitution* about the same time, he set sail for Boston.

The New England States had been opposed to the war at the outset, and more than once during the dreary conflict their discontented citizens threatened secession. However, on Hull's arrival there was no lack of enthusiasm. A splendid entertainment was given by the citizens of all parties in Boston to the victorious captain and his officers; other cities and the officers' respective States honored them with similar spirit, and Congress, besides giving a vote of thanks, appropriated $50,000 as prize money. The encouragement gained from capturing a British frigate was certainly needed after the disgraceful surrender of Detroit, which occurred within the same week.

The victory also had an important influence on the naval policy of the nation. In the years following the war with Tripoli many prominent statesmen were strongly in favor of doing entirely away with the navy as had been done after the Revolution. And on the outbreak of the second war with England, the administration, having no confidence in its ships when opposed to the overwhelming forces of England, was inclining to the course of preventing their capture by holding them locked in the fortified harbors. The victory of the *Constitution* made permanent the establishment of the navy, and induced the Government to give the ships their share in the fighting.

Exultation in America and depression in England were both marked with extravagance. Strangely enough, when the British officers had seen the *Constitution* in the West Indies and the Mediterranean, they had spoken slightingly of her, as of the other "Yankee" frigates.[3] The low estimation put on their power is indicated by Dacres' entry on the register of the American brig *John Adams*, as he fell in with her two or three days before meeting the *Constitution:* "Captain Dacres, commander of His Britannic Majesty's frigate *Guerrière*, of 44 guns, presents his compliments to Commodore Rodgers, of the United States frigate *President*, and will be very happy to meet him, or any other American frigate of equal force to the *President*, off Sandy Hook, for the purpose of having a few minutes' *tête-à-tête*." Thus, in meeting a sister ship of the *President*, Dacres got precisely what he sought.

The opinions of the British on the inferior qualities of the American frigates were now quickly reversed. Captain Dacres, before the court-martial which tried him for the loss of his ship, testified to the American's "superior sailing" which "enabled him to choose his distance." And an officer of the *Guerrière* wrote home shortly after the fight: "No one that has not seen the *Constitution* would believe there could be such a ship for a frigate;

---

[3] The English people as a whole underrated the power of their enemy. *The Morning Post*, the organ of the Government, had observed shortly before the loss of the *Guerrière:* " A war of a very few months, without creating to England the expense of a single additional ship, would be sufficient to convince America of her folly by a necessary chastisement of her insolence and audacity." Quoted by Coutts, *Famous Duels of the Fleet*, p. 244.

The United States and the Macedonian

the nearest ship in the British Navy, as to her dimensions and tonnage, is the *Orion*, of 74 guns.''

A comparison of the two forces will show at a glance that, courage and skill being at all equal, there really could be no excuse for the Americans' not winning:

	Guns	Broadside-weight	Crew	Killed	Wounded	Total
Constitution	55	736[4]	468	7	7	14
Guerrière	49	570	263	15	63	78

Yet the British had fought with the French and Spanish against odds fully as great, and had won. They had come to think British courage and discipline much more than an offset for a few additional guns. Now, as they suddenly apprehended, they were dealing with quite a different foe. They had also to face the fact that the disparity in force, which, according to Roosevelt's estimate, was about as three to two, was very much less than the disparity in losses, so that the advantage was very decidedly with this new foe.

THE UNITED STATES AND THE MACEDONIAN

In the first frigate action of the war there is some weight to be given to the explanation that the *Guerrière* was not an English-built ship (she had been captured from the French six years before), and that at the end of a long cruise she was very much in need of overhauling. In the second action this was not at all the situation. The British frigate, the *Macedonian*, 38 guns, just out of drydock, and built only two years before, was supposed

---

[4] American shot regularly was lighter than British of the same size. To bring the two to a like standard, subtract from the figures given for American guns one-eighteenth, following the suggestion of James (*Naval Occurrences*, p. 10); Roosevelt would make a reduction slightly larger than James, or seven per cent.

to be one of the finest ships of her class in the Royal Navy. Her captain, John Surman Carden, gave the closest attention to the personnel as well as to the discipline of his crew. To such men as he found below the standard he gave opportunity to desert; those whom he found efficient he held under strictest rule; and with his able lieutenant, David Hope, drilled them daily in seamanship and gunnery.

The ship that was to engage in duel with the *Macedonian* was the *United States,* 44 guns, commanded by Captain Stephen Decatur. She had left Boston, October 8, 1812, in Commodore Rodgers' squadron. The other ships of the squadron, the *President, Congress,* and *Argus,* returned after a three months' cruise, having accomplished little. Decatur had parted company after three days out, and it was on October 25, 1812, off the Canary Islands (lat. 29° N., long. 29° 30′ W.) that he encountered the *Macedonian.*[5]

Carden, who was less than a month out from Portsmouth, had heard at Madeira that the American frigate *Essex* was in the vicinity, and as the lookout at the masthead early on the morning of the 25th reported a sail twelve miles distant on the lee beam, Carden made haste and stood over in its direction. Instead of the *Essex,* inferior to his ship in power, he was about to meet the *United States,* which was decidedly superior. Yet had he known who the stranger was, it is probable he would have been scarcely less eager for an engagement. The utmost confidence prevailed on board the *Macedonian,* and neither Carden nor his lieutenant, Hope, was the kind of Englishman that is careful in considering the odds against him. Carden had not yet learned of the fate of the *Guerrière.*

---

[5] Letter of Captain Decatur, October 30, 1812, to the Secretary of the Navy.

STEPHEN DECATUR, JR.

The United States and the Macedonian 119

In the crew of the *Macedonian* were seven Americans impressed into the British Navy. They had heard only rumors of the existence of war between the two countries; but when they saw the preparations for battle and an American frigate approaching, one of their number, Jack Cand, known among his shipmates for his bravery, addressed the captain, requesting that they might be regarded as prisoners of war and be excused from fighting against their own flag. Captain Dacres, although short of men, had in precisely the same situation allowed the Americans to go below. Captain Carden, never too gentle with his crew, roughly ordered the man to his quarters, threatening to shoot him if he made the request again. It was a hard fate for Cand, whichever course he took, and he was killed during the battle by a 24-pound shot.

The *Macedonian*, on first sighting the *United States*, was sailing northwest by west, and in closing had the advantage of the weather-gage.[6] The wind was blowing fresh from the south-southeast.

Decatur, wishing to secure a better position, just before coming into range wore round on the port tack and hauled short up. The *Macedonian*, by continuing on the course she was then sailing, would have crossed the *United States'* bow at short range and would have entered at once into close action.[7] This was what Lieutenant Hope advised. But in so doing the *Macedonian* must have relinquished the weather-gage. Rather than do this Carden hauled close to the wind, still keeping his distance. Had he been fighting the *Essex*, as he still supposed,

---

[6] Weather-gage: the term applied to the position of a ship to windward of another; in the days of sailing vessels this was regarded as a decided advantage, for it gave the ship possessing it in battle, everything else being equal, the greater speed and facility in maneuvering.

[7] Court-martial of Captain Carden.

120   *The United States Navy*

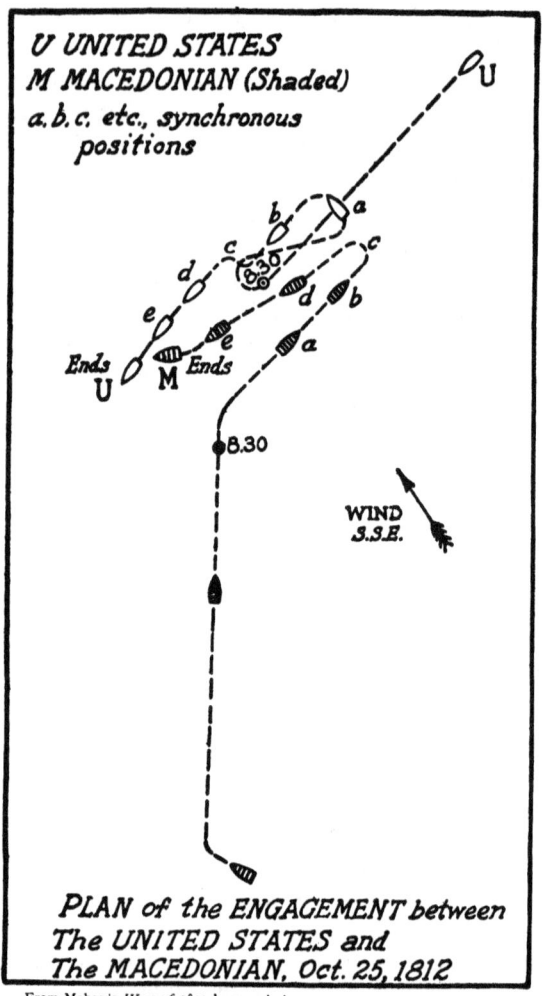

PLAN OF THE ENGAGEMENT BETWEEN THE UNITED STATES AND THE MACEDONIAN, OCT. 25, 1812

The United States and the Macedonian 121

Carden's decision would have been wise, for that ship, though well equipped with carronades, was weak in long guns. As it was, he gave his enemy a decided advantage, for the *United States* excelled in long guns of unusual weight.

When the ships passed on opposite tacks, the *United States* fired, but the distance was too great to inflict injury. The *Macedonian*, which had already shown herself much the faster sailer, then wore in pursuit and caught up with her enemy, reaching a position, at long range, off the American's port quarter. An exchange of broadsides cost the *United States* her mizzen topgallant mast, and the *Macedonian* her gaff-halyards and mizzen topmast, the latter falling into her maintop. This loss deprived the *Macedonian* of her superiority in sailing. As long as the two ships sailed on parallel courses or yawed to fire a full broadside, the advantage was not of position but of long guns, and the latter was decidedly with the *United States*. To overcome this superiority, and to bring his ship near enough to use her carronades, Carden changed from a parallel to a converging course. Decatur yawed and fired a broadside; and then, running ahead a little to prevent the *Macedonian* from closing, he repeated the maneuver. On came the *Macedonian*, exposing her starboard bow to the *United States;* whereupon the latter, by a severe diagonal fire, dismounted all the carronades on the starboard side of the *Macedonian's* quarter-deck and forecastle and at the same time damaged her hull and disabled many of the crew.

If in time of peace there had been considerable sullenness among the crew of the *Macedonian* because of the stern rigidity of the discipline and the cruel use of the lash, as is reported, the men certainly showed admirable spirit in fighting. "Our men kept cheering with all their might," wrote Samuel Leech,[*] a boy serving one of the guns. "I cheered with them, though I confess I scarcely knew for what. Certainly there was nothing very inspiriting in the aspect of things where I was stationed. So terrible had been the work of destruction round us, it was termed the slaughter-house." After many gruesome details he continues, "Our men fought like tigers. Some of them pulled off their jackets, others, their jackets and vests; while some, still more determined, had taken off their shirts, and, with nothing but a handkerchief tied around the waistband of their trousers, fought like heroes." Mr. Hope, the first lieutenant, was wounded by an iron ring torn from a hammock by a shot. "He went below, shouting to the men to fight on. Having had his wound dressed, he came up again, shouting to us at the top of his voice, and bidding us fight with all our might." This lieutenant had been brutal in enforcing discipline and in administering extreme penalties for slight offenses; and the gunner's boy pauses in his narrative to observe that there was not a man in the ship who would not have rejoiced if something much larger had struck the petty tyrant.

At 10.15, when the *United States* had been pouring in an effective fire for half or three-quarters of an hour, Decatur laid his maintopsail to the mast and allowed the *Macedonian* to come into close action. But it was too late to be of any benefit to the Englishman, who had only his main-deck guns remaining, and the maneuver but increased the disparity of forces. A few minutes after eleven the *Macedonian* had her mizzenmast shot away; her fore and maintopmasts were also shot away at the caps, her lower masts were wounded, and she had received more than 100 shot in her hull. No longer steadied by her sail, she was rolling her main-deck guns under, while

---

[*] In his *Thirty Years from Home,* p. 132, ff.

the *United States,* having no sail she could not set but her mizzen topgallant, was perfectly steady.

There was just one wild, desperate chance remaining for the British, and putting their helm hard aport they prepared to board the American frigate. Lieutenant Hope wrote afterwards, "At that moment every man was on deck, several who had lost an arm, and the universal cheer was, 'Let us conquer or die.' " Just then, however, the forebrace was shot away, and the yard, swinging round, threw the ship up into the wind. The *United States,* seeing her opponent's helpless state, then withdrew a short distance for repairs; at which the irrepressible "Macedonians," deluded into thinking that their enemy had spied an English man-of-war coming to the rescue, gave a final cheer.

Returning at noon, the *United States* took a position off her opponent's stern. There had already been a council of war on the quarter-deck of the *Macedonian.* Lieutenant Hope, though wounded again, this time somewhat seriously in the head, had still much fight in him, and advised "not to strike but to sink alongside." The counsel of those who put a higher valuation on life, however, prevailed.

It must have been a surprise for Carden when he learned on surrender, that he was to meet his old acquaintance, Decatur. As he offered his sword, Decatur generously declined it, saying, "Sir, I cannot receive the sword of a man who has so bravely defended his ship." With a like chivalry and kindness Decatur gave orders that all the personal effects of the English officers should be respected as still theirs, even including a large stock of wine which they had laid in at Madeira, giving them as equivalent $800. Further, everything was done by the Americans to give their late enemies, while on the *United States,* the comforts and cheer due to honored guests.

Decatur's good fortune did not end with the capture. Having determined to take his prize in, he spent two weeks after the fight in making repairs. With the many squadrons that the English had scattered about the Atlantic and along the American coast, the long voyage home involved great risk of recapture. However, without having so much as sighted a British sail, the two ships arrived at New London and then proceeded to New York. The *Macedonian* was repaired and fitted out anew, and had a long and honorable career in the American Navy.

The following shows the comparative force of the two ships:

	Guns	Broadside	Crew	Killed	Wounded	Total
United States	55	786	478	5	7	12
Macedonian	49	547	292	36	68	104

In speed the *Macedonian* had the decided advantage (the nickname of the *United States*, "Old Wagoner," suggests her lumbering gait, which seems later to have been somewhat remedied). In every other particular the advantage was with the American frigate. She was the larger ship, had thicker scantlings, was higher out of the water (of importance in the rough sea), had heavier guns and more of them, and finally was superior in her crew. Further, Decatur showed better seamanship than Carden. An instructive comparison is to be gained by considering the coming into close action by Captain Carden on the *Macedonian* and by Captain Hull on the *Constitution*. Each at the beginning of the engagement had the advantage of the weather-gage; Hull yawed when his opponent wore, giving him no opportunity to rake; Hull pursued a zig-zag course, and coming up in the British ship's wake, was within pistol shot before the enemy could do any harm. Carden obstinately held to the weather-gage; and when he closed he did so without maneuvering, and **exposed his ship to such a disastrous diagonal fire that** he was virtually defeated before he had reached close quarters.

Strangely enough, the comparative effectiveness of 24- and 18-pounders, as well as the superiority of their respective ships, had been the subject of a friendly argument between Carden and Decatur a few months previous to the war, when, as the two ships were together in Chesapeake Bay, the commanders were discussing the merits of each.

The inequality in force was approximately the same as that between the *Constitution* and the *Guerrière*, three to two, but the disparity in losses was almost nine to one. Yet David Hope wrote some years later to his old commander, "In no ship in the British service could there have been more attention paid to the practical part of gunnery than was done by you to the crew of the *Macedonian.*" If this is true, the results of the action are evidence of the very superior quality of the crew under Decatur. Perhaps, also, they illustrate the principle uttered by Farragut at Port Hudson, "The best protection against the enemy's fire is a well-directed fire from our own guns." It is plain, on reading the extravagant speeches and newspaper articles that dealt with the capture, that our country was young and unaccustomed to victory. Yet without magnifying the size and armament of the *Macedonian* or reducing that of the *United States*, this victory, like that of the *Constitution*, was a notable achievement in the history of the navy and of the nation. The leading naval power of the world had lost a frigate of which an officer of the *United States*, while admitting the *Macedonian's* inferiority in force, goes on to observe, "But she is just such a ship as the English have achieved all their single-ship victories in; . . . she is, in tonnage, men, and guns, such a ship as the English prefer to all others, and have, till the *Guerrière's* los always thought a match for any single-decked ship afloat."

VIII

A VICTORY AND A DEFEAT

THE CONSTITUTION AND THE JAVA

THE third squadron sent to cruise against British commerce during the War of 1812 was placed under the command of Captain William Bainbridge, and consisted of three ships, the *Constitution*, 44 guns, flagship; the *Essex*, 32 guns, Captain David Porter; and the sloop *Hornet*, 18 guns, Master-Commandant James Lawrence. The *Hornet* and the *Constitution* left Boston together on October 26, 1812, but the *Essex*, which was fitting in the Delaware, was unable to get to sea till the 28th.

The orders for this little squadron were, to sail first for the Cape Verde Islands, where fresh water could be procured; thence, by November 27, to Fernando Noronha, an island about 200 miles off the coast of Brazil; and thence along the coast to Rio de Janeiro. From this port the course was to be laid directly across the South Atlantic for the neighborhood of St. Helena, where the home-coming English East Indiamen frequently touched. These plans were never carried out.

In the first place, the *Essex*, which Porter characterized as the "worst frigate in the service," was unable to catch up with the other two; and when Porter arrived at Fernando he found that the *Constitution* and the *Hornet* had already gone to Bahia, but that Bainbridge had left orders for him to proceed to Rio. There, finding no sign of his commodore, Porter struck out on his own authority and began his famous roving cruise in the Pacific. Meanwhile the actions between the *Constitution* and the *Java*, and between the *Hornet* and the *Peacock*, compelled the *Constitution* and the *Hornet* to give up the intended cruise, and repair to the United States.

On the 13th of December, the *Constitution* and the *Hornet* arrived at Bahia, where they found a British sloop, the *Bonne Citoyenne*, with a large amount of specie aboard. The American vessels kept her blockaded for some time, during which Lawrence challenged the British commander to come out to single combat, Bainbridge pledging his honor not to interfere. The Englishman, however, declined, excusing himself on the ground that he did not believe the American commodore would keep his hands off. Finally on the 26th of the month, Bainbridge made sail for open sea, hoping thereby to tempt the *Bonne Citoyenne* to come out and meet the *Hornet*.

At nine o'clock, on the morning of the 29th, Bainbridge discovered two sails to the northeast, which proved to be a British frigate, the *Java*,[1] and an American prize. On sighting the American frigate, the Englishman directed his prize to make for Bahia, while he himself made all sail to come up with the *Constitution*. Captain Bainbridge responded by tacking and heading southeast, in order to draw the other to a safe distance beyond neutral waters. The *Java* came on at a ten-knot gait, and rapidly overhauled the *Constitution* till about 1.30, when Bainbridge put his ship about, shortened sail, and headed for the enemy. The *Java* now held off, trying for an opportunity to rake, which the *Constitution* prevented by wearing and resuming her course to the southeast. A half hour later, with the *Java* in a windward position and a half mile distant, Bainbridge fired ahead of the enemy to make her display her colors. The response was

---

[1] Like the *Guerrière*, the *Java* was a French prize, originally named the *Renommée*, and captured only the year before.

an instant hoisting of the ensign to the gaff, followed by a broadside, and the contest was on.

The earlier part of the battle consisted of maneuvering on the part of the *Java* to get a raking position, and the simultaneous wearing of the *Constitution* to avoid it,

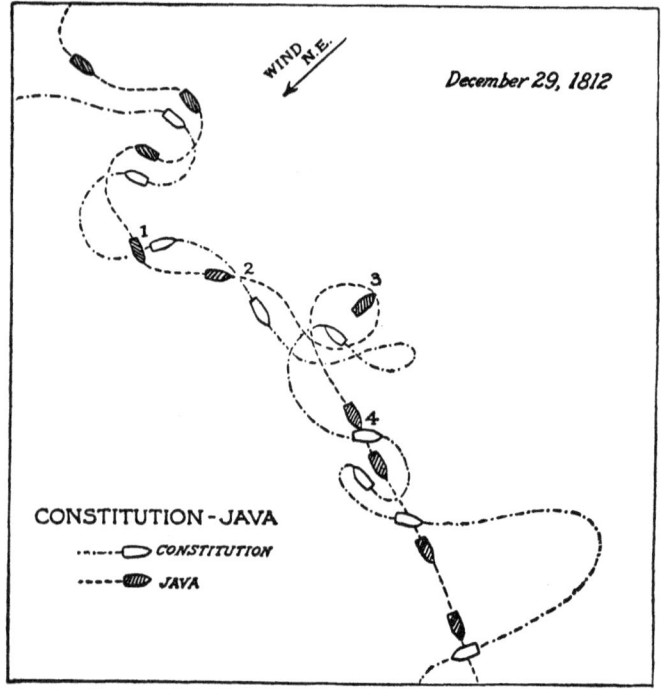

PLAN OF ENGAGEMENT BETWEEN CONSTITUTION AND JAVA

accompanied by heavy firing on both sides. The *Java* was a better sailer than the *Constitution*, and Bainbridge had his hands full to match her movements, particularly as at 2.30 a round shot from the *Java* smashed the *Constitution's* wheel, and the ship had to be steered thereafter by relieving tackles, handled two decks below. Earlier in the action, Commodore Bainbridge had received a musket ball in his hip, and the shot that smashed the wheel also drove a copper bolt deep into his thigh. In spite of these painful wounds, he kept the deck throughout the battle.

Shortly after the disaster to his wheel, he determined to close with his adversary even at the risk of being raked, and luffed up. For some reason, however, the *Java* missed the opportunity to rake as she passed under the *Constitution's* stern (see diagram, 1), for she fired only one 9-pounder. She then luffed up and crossed the wake of the *Constitution* again, delivering a semi-raking fire which was not effective on account of the distance (2). Bainbridge then set the courses and luffed up again in order to close with his nimble adversary. At this point the *Java* had the end of her bowsprit with the jib and jib-boom shot away, and with this sudden loss of her head sails she pointed up into the wind, where she lay for a few moments helpless (3). The *Constitution* instantly wore and, passing under the *Java's* stern, raked with great effect. The American wore again, and the English ship attempted to save the day by laying alongside and boarding; but she lost her foremast at the outset of the maneuver and succeeded only in running the stump of her bowsprit into the mizzen shrouds of the *Constitution* (4).

From this moment on, though the *Java* maintained a heroic defense, she was a beaten ship. The *Constitution* sailed round her, pouring in an accurate fire at close quarters that shot away every spar but the mainmast, and that went by the board a few minutes before the surrender.

Meanwhile, the American gunners had been also sweeping the *Java's* decks with a diagonal fire, seconded by a deadly sharp-shooting of the marines in the tops. It was a musket bullet from the maintop that gave Captain Lambert his mortal wound, shortly after the two vessels came in contact. The command then devolved upon his first lieutenant, Chads, who continued the hopeless fight with great spirit.

At five minutes after four,[2] the fire from the *Java* had been completely silenced, and she rolled on the seas a dismasted hulk, her decks lumbered with the fallen spars, sails, and rigging. As she displayed no colors, Captain Bainbridge took it for granted that she had struck; and, hauling down his courses, he shot ahead to repair his badly cut rigging. On his return, at about 5.30, he found that the enemy had his colors flying again; but, as the *Constitution* drew across the *Java's* bow, ready to rake, they were instantly struck.

The *Constitution* had about the same superiority in metal over the *Java* as she had had over the *Guerrière;* but, as in the action with the latter frigate, the relative damage inflicted was wholly disproportionate to the respective armaments. It must be remembered also that the *Java* had one considerable advantage in her superior speed. The British frigate[3] was so thoroughly shot to pieces that Bainbridge had no alternative but to blow her up, while the *Constitution* was in condition to make a long voyage back to the United States without refitting. The American loss in this engagement amounted to nine killed and twenty-five wounded, three mortally. Chads's official report of the British casualties gave twenty-two killed and 102 wounded.[4]

In 1804 Captain Lambert distinguished himself, in a

---

[2] According to the British account, 4.35. There is such a wide discrepancy in the matter of time between the two reports that an English writer suggests that "perhaps someone's watch or clock was adrift." (*Famous Duels of the Fleet*, p. 261.)

[3] A relic of the *Java* that for a long time remained on the *Constitution's* quarter-deck was her wheel, which replaced the one shot away early in the action.

[4] Captain Bainbridge, inclosing as evidence a letter written by one of the British officers and accidentally left on board the *Constitution*, gives the figures of that officer, which are sixty killed and 170 wounded.

The Constitution and the Java

heavy action at close quarters, by beating off a French ship with a broadside of 240 pounds opposed to his own total of 99 pounds. But the crew he then commanded had just been under a captain known as a "crank" in gunnery, and Lambert got the benefit of his predecessor's work. During the six weeks he was in command of the *Java*, he had held gun drill only once, and then with blank cartridges. In seamanship he was probably unsurpassed, for the *Java* was expertly handled; but, like so many of his brother-officers, he had small interest in gunnery. The *Java's* firing grew wilder as the battle progressed, while that of the *Constitution* steadily improved.

Among the American wounded was Lieutenant Alwyn, who had been shot through the shoulder in the engagement with the *Guerrière*. When the *Java's* bowsprit fouled the mizzen rigging of the *Constitution,* and boarders were called away, he leaped upon the hammock nettings to lead the party, and was shot through the very shoulder that had been wounded before. Despite the painful character of the wound, he kept at his station till the enemy had struck, but died on the voyage home.

While at Bahia, where the *Constitution* put in after the battle, Commodore Bainbridge, himself suffering severely, was brought before the dying Lambert; and, with the stately courtesy of the time, returned to him his sword with the expression of an earnest hope for his recovery. There are also letters from General Hyslop, a passenger on the *Java*, to Commodore Bainbridge, which bear grateful testimony to the chivalrous bearing of the victorious commander. Later, General Hyslop presented Bainbridge with a gold-mounted sword in token of appreciation.

Of the engagement with the *Java*, Admiral Mahan says: "This battle was not merely an artillery duel, like those of the *Constitution* and the *Guerriere*, the *Wasp* and the *Frolic*, nor yet one in which a principal maneuver, by its decisive effect upon the use of artillery, played the determining part, as was the case with the *United States* and the *Macedonian*. Here it was a combination of the two factors, a succession of evolutions resembling the changes of position, the retreats and advances, of a fencing or a boxing match, in which the opponents work round the ring; accompanied by a continual play of the guns, answering to the thrusts and blows of individual encounter.''

This victory can hardly be passed without some mention of its personal significance to Commodore Bainbridge. Up to this time, though he was admittedly an excellent officer, his professional career had been marked by the most trying misfortunes that can befall a commander. In the French War he had been taken by a superior force and imprisoned, with the mortifying knowledge that his was the only American man-of-war to strike to the tricolor. Scarcely was he again on the quarter-deck, when he was forced by the Dey of Algiers to submit to the worst humiliation ever suffered by an American naval officer. During the war with Tripoli, the greatest disaster to the American cause was the loss of his ship, the *Philadelphia*, and, while his brother officers were winning distinction and applause, he was compelled to remain a prisoner. He had been sharply criticised on more than one occasion, and, even his own crew, the men who under Hull had worked the ship free from Broke's squadron and recently beaten the *Guerrière*, apparently felt little confidence in their new commander, as is shown by the long list of punishments for infractions of discipline. To all this criticism and distrust, Bainbridge's conduct in the battle with the *Java* was a sufficient answer.

THE CHESAPEAKE AND THE SHANNON

In spite of the fact that Commodore Bainbridge left the *Hornet* alone to blockade the *Bonne Citoyenne,* Captain Greene of the British sloop still refused Lawrence's challenge. This was taken by Lawrence as cowardice, and he did not avoid saying what he thought. His criticism of Greene on this occasion put him on his mettle, when, six months later, the situation was exactly reversed and Captain Broke, with the *Shannon,* blockaded alone the young American commander in the ill-fated *Chesapeake.*

Lawrence's relations with the *Bonne Citoyenne* were suddenly cut short by the arrival of a ship-of-the-line that chased him into port. By immediately standing out to sea, under cover of the night, he escaped the new enemy, and headed north. During this cruise he made his famous capture of the sloop *Peacock.* On the 24th of March, 1813, he reached New York and discharged his prisoners, after a cruise of 145 days, during which he had captured one ship, two brigs, one schooner, and one man-of-war, a record that none of his brother officers could equal.

Lawrence, already the most popular officer in the service, became at once the toast of the nation. By this time, his rank [5] would not permit his retaining command of the sloop *Hornet,* though he requested to be allowed to do so; and the Department appointed him to command a frigate, the *Chesapeake,* then refitting at the Boston Navy Yard. Lawrence would have preferred the *Constitution,* but, as his orders were not changed, he took command of the *Chesapeake* on May 20, 1813.

Lawrence was under orders to put to sea at the earliest

---

[5] Lawrence had been promoted in March from Master-Commandant to Captain.

opportunity, and to head north to strike at the British fisheries on the Banks. On this cruise he was to meet, at Cape Breton, Master-Commandant Biddle, commanding the *Hornet*, and the two vessels were to act together in a commerce-destroying cruise. Although in the early months of the war the Admiralty had left the coast of New England alone, in order to encourage the hostile attitude of that section toward the war, by the spring of 1813 it had abandoned this policy and instituted a blockade from New York to Nova Scotia. Early in April the *Shannon* and the *Tenedos* appeared off Boston Light and maintained as close a blockade as the weather conditions would permit. Shortly before Lawrence arrived, the frigates *President* and *Congress* ran the blockade in a fog, leaving the *Constitution*, which was undergoing repairs, and the *Chesapeake*, which was nearly ready for sea.

On taking command, Lawrence notified the Department that he found the *Chesapeake* "ready for sea," lacking only a small number of men and a few supplies. On May 30, ten days later, he cast loose from Long Wharf and dropped down to the Roads, "with the intention of lying there a few days and shaking down before going to sea."[6] The following afternoon, while dining with a friend in Boston, he received news that only one English frigate was in sight off the port, and he immediately returned to his ship to prepare for action. Between eight and nine o'clock the next morning, June 1, 1813, the British frigate was again sighted, and Lawrence made instant preparations for going out to meet her. The

---

[6] Gleaves, *Life of James Lawrence*, p. 172.

[7] Although the *Chesapeake* was rated as a "36," she carried two more carronades than the "38-gun" *Shannon*, and fifty more men in her crew.

stranger was the 38-gun [7] frigate *Shannon;* and it happened that while Lawrence was making ready to slip his moorings, her commander, Captain Philip B. V. Broke, was writing a lengthy but courteous challenge to Lawrence, inviting him to single-ship combat, ''wherever it is most convenient to you.'' This challenge was sent ashore by a discharged prisoner, but by the time it reached Boston, the beaten *Chesapeake* was already on her way to Halifax.

The American commander was under orders to strike a blow at a definite area of the enemy's commerce, but, with the memory of the *Bonne Citoyenne* fresh in his mind, Lawrence was not the man to hesitate an hour in the face of an opportunity for single-ship combat. That one ship should attempt to maintain the blockade was enough to call him out as soon as he could trip his anchor and swing his yards. The *Chesapeake* was not, however, in the best condition to meet a seasoned enemy. Her first lieutenant, Octavius Page, was lying ill with pneumonia in the hospital ashore, where he died a few days after the battle. Two other officers were on leave, so that Lieutenant Ludlow, then only twenty-one, became first lieutenant, and two midshipmen, Cox and Ballard, were promoted to the position of acting lieutenants. These officers were new to their duties and to the men, and the crew, for their part, were as yet unorganized and undisciplined.

On the other hand, their antagonist, the *Shannon,* was manned by a veteran crew, some of them men who had fought under Rodney and Nelson, and who had been drilled together aboard the same ship, and under the same captain, for about seven years. Her commander, though only five years older than Lawrence, had seen active service since his midshipman days. He had been a lieutenant in the great victory off St. Vincent, and had become post captain [8] at the age of twenty-five.

In 1806 he was given the *Shannon*, and it was not long before he made her famous as a "crack" ship. At a time when most of the British officers echoed Nelson's contemptuous remark on gun-sights, Broke fitted out at his own expense dispart sights and quadrants for every gun on his ship. Behind each gun he cut out arcs of circles on the deck, with degrees notched in, and filled with putty, so that all the fire of a broadside could be concentrated accurately upon a target. Nor were the devices idle. Twice a day, except Saturdays and Sundays, the watch below were exercised at the guns, not merely in practice with the side-tackles, but in actual firing at a barrel floating three or four hundred yards away.

When hostilities broke out, Broke was the senior British officer on the American station. Early in the war, he had endured the chagrin of seeing the *Constitution* slip away from his squadron when he was so sure of her that he had told off a prize crew from his *Shannon* to bring her into Halifax. Then followed the mortifying captures of the *Guerrière*, the *Macedonian*, the *Frolic*, the *Java*, and the *Peacock*, without a single British naval success to offset them. Confident of his own ship and her crew, he dismissed the *Tenedos* from the blockade of Boston in order that he might meet the *Chesapeake* alone, and restore the prestige of the British Navy by a victory.

His opponent, James Lawrence, was now in his thirty-

---

[8] Post captain: "A designation formerly applied . . . to a naval officer holding a commission as captain, to distinguish him from an officer of inferior rank, to whom the courtesy title of captain was often given, either as being an acting captain, or as being master and commander of a vessel not rated to be commanded by a full-grade captain, and so not said to 'give post.'" *New English Dictionary.*

second year. Like most of the naval heroes of the War of 1812, he had entered the navy as a midshipman in 1798, at the outbreak of the war with France, and he had received his early training under Captain Tingey on the *Ganges*. He had won distinction in the war with Tripoli, notably as Decatur's lieutenant in the burning of the *Philadelphia*, and had reached the height of his fame by his recent brilliant capture of the *Peacock*. Handsome, impetuous, and winning, he was perhaps, next to Decatur, the most romantic figure in the navy.

Before unmooring ship to meet the *Shannon*, Lawrence mustered his crew aft, and made the customary patriotic speech before an action. At the end two members stepped forward, requesting the prize money which had long been due them. Lawrence sent them below to the purser to get checks for the amount due, and then retired to his cabin to write last letters to his wife and the Secretary of the Navy.

By noon, the *Chesapeake* was heading for the *Shannon*, and Broke, seeing that Lawrence intended to fight, led the way some distance to sea, and then hove to, awaiting his approach. The Englishman made no effort to maneuver, allowing Lawrence to choose his own method of attack. For his part, the American commander refused the opportunity of securing a raking position under the *Shannon's* quarter, but rounded-to to run alongside and fight "yard-arm to yard-arm."

At 5.50, as the *Chesapeake's* bows doubled on the *Shannon's* starboard quarter, the British gunners struck the first blow. As soon as each gun of the *Shannon* bore on the *Chesapeake*, it was fired, rapidly reloaded, and fired again. The effect was terrible at such close quarters, but the American gunners responded smartly, and for five or six minutes the two frigates sailed on parallel courses, pounding each other at a range of about fifty yards.

Lawrence, however, had made the mistake of coming up with too much headway, and he saw that his ship would soon forge too far ahead. Accordingly, he tried to luff her, but as her sails blanketed those of her enemy, her headway carried her still farther till she lay on the *Shannon's* weather bow. At this critical point the two upon whom the safety of the vessel most depended

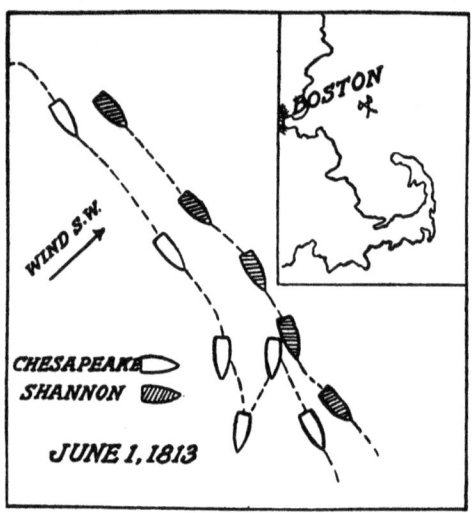

THE CHESAPEAKE AND THE SHANNON

were disabled, Lawrence was wounded, and his sailing-master killed. Disasters then crowded each other in rapid succession. The cutting of the fore-topsail tye by the enemy's fire let fall the yard, so that the foresail became useless; at the same time the wheel was disabled and the brails of the spanker and the jib-sheet were shot away. The combined result was that, as the ship had no head sails left, and her wheel was useless, she pointed up into the wind, and lay helpless in the most desperate position imaginable; that is, with her quarters exposed to her

The Chesapeake and the Shannon 139

enemy's broadside only about seventy yards distant. The *Shannon* took instant advantage of the opportunity by a terrible diagonal fire that swept the *Chesapeake*. To add to the confusion, about this time a grenade tossed from the *Shannon's* mainyard exploded an arms chest on her enemy's deck.

Seeing that the *Chesapeake* was now gaining sternboard, and would soon foul the *Shannon*, Lawrence called the boarders away. But the negro bugler, whose duty it was to sound the call, had hidden himself in terror, and the word was passed with difficulty by word of mouth. Just before the two ships touched, Lawrence received his second and mortal wound, and was carried below. Like Lambert of the *Java*, he had been picked off by one of his enemy's marines.

As the *Chesapeake's* stern fouled the main chains of the *Shannon*, the two ships were lashed together by the British, who made instant preparation to carry the American frigate by boarding. Meanwhile, at Lawrence's call for boarders, the *Chesapeake's* men had responded promptly, but they found no leaders. Lawrence was being carried below; and, of the officers on the spar deck, first lieutenant, sailing-master, captain of marines, and boatswain had already received their death wounds, leaving none but a few midshipmen.

The second lieutenant was at the forward end of the gun deck with no idea of what was happening on the quarter-deck; the fourth lieutenant had been mortally wounded at the first fire; and the third lieutenant, on hearing the call for boarders, led his men on deck, but stopped to help his beloved commander down to the steerage ladder; and when he attempted to get back again, found the hatch battened down by the enemy's boarders.

Left wholly without officers, the crew, already demoralized by a raking fire at close quarters, made an ineffectual attempt to resist the British boarding party, and then a large number actually broke and ran below into the hold. The marines, however, under their sergeant, made a gallant defense; out of a total of forty-four they lost twelve killed and twenty wounded.

Shortly after Captain Broke and his men boarded the quarter-deck of the *Chesapeake,* the American frigate fell off sufficiently to catch the wind. The lashings parted and the *Chesapeake* broke away with the enemy's boarders on her deck. Here was a chance for the Americans to save the day, but there were no officers to rally the panic-stricken crew. Second Lieutenant Budd, who had gained the forecastle and begun a desperate resistance, was twice severely wounded, and thrown to the deck below. In a few minutes the last effort at defense was abandoned.

In this hand-to-hand struggle on the forecastle, Captain Broke himself received a sabre cut on the head that very nearly proved mortal, and incapacitated him for the rest of his life. Meanwhile, his first lieutenant, Watts, lost his life by a blunder; soon after boarding the *Chesapeake* he had lowered the colors, and bent on an English ensign, but in his excitement he stopped the English colors under, instead of over, the American. At this, the "Shannons," thinking that the Americans must have regained the quarter-deck, fired one of the main deck guns, killing Watts and four or five of his men.

It was only fifteen minutes from the first shot of the battle to the final rout of the American crew, just the time it took Lawrence to destroy the *Peacock* a few months before. Unfortunately, the brutality of the young English lieutenants and their men on taking possession bears no such parallel with the magnanimity of Lawrence on a similar occasion, and it is the most discreditable feature of the *Shannon's* victory. No blame, however, can be attached to the gallant Broke, whose wound had already rendered him unconscious.

The Chesapeake and the Shannon 141

For four days, Lawrence lingered in great agony, repeating in his delirium, the words that have since become the motto of the navy, "Don't give up the ship!" His kindness to the men of the *Peacock* had won him friendly regard among all Englishmen, and no honor was spared him in the subsequent funeral ceremonies at Halifax.

Naturally, the victory of the *Shannon* caused the greatest exultation in England, and corresponding gloom in the United States. The fact that the *Shannon* had captured the *Chesapeake* in fifteen minutes with an unprecedented slaughter of officers and men was mortifying, and it was not long before a "patriotic" legend twined around the ugly fact. This legend reports, in brief, that the *Chesapeake's* crew was made up of landlubbers and foreigners, and those were either dead drunk during the battle, or mutinous and cowardly. The muster roll, however, proves that there was not one "landsman" on board, and gives only fifteen foreign names out of a total of 340. Just two men were reported drunk, and the idea of a mutinous spirit is based wholly on the request for prize money made just before going out. This request was reasonable enough. The money was long overdue, and the men wanted it to their credit on the eve of battle. The purser expressly testified before the court of inquiry, that there was nothing disorderly or mutinous in the conduct of the crew as they came to him for the prize checks. Lawrence, in writing to the Secretary of the Navy after this incident, says, "My crew appear to be *in fine spirits*, and I trust will do their duty."

While it is true that many of the crew became panic-stricken at the end when they had no leaders, yet of their own accord they gave three hearty cheers when the *Chesapeake* swung alongside the enemy; and they stood splendidly by their guns in that terrible first broadside from the *Shannon*. In fact, during those six minutes, when the two vessels were running on parallel courses, the slaughter on board the *Shannon* was apparently as bad as that on board the *Chesapeake*. During those minutes, the *Chesapeake* killed and wounded more on the *Shannon* than the *Constitution*—a much heavier frigate—did in thirty minutes' pounding of the *Guerrière*. It was when the *Chesapeake* hung in irons, unable to reply to a diagonal fire, that the American loss grew to such a terrible disproportion.

In his official report of the action, Lieutenant Budd gave a loss of forty-eight killed and ninety-seven wounded, and of the latter fourteen died after the battle. The British loss was given at forty-three killed (including those who died shortly after the engagement) and twenty-nine wounded.[9] In this brief action the victor suffered more than the vanquished *Guerrière* or *Macedonian*. "The total loss of both ships [*Chesapeake* and *Shannon*] was only forty-five less than the combined losses of the French and English fleets at Cape St. Vincent where forty-two ships were engaged."[10]

The defeat was partly due to the fact that "the *Chesapeake* was a ship much inferior to the *Shannon*, as a regiment newly enlisted is to one that has seen service, and the moment things went wrong seriously, she could not retrieve herself."[11] But, equally it can be attributed to what may be called "the fortune of war," in the unprecedented slaughter of the *Chesapeake's* officers at the outset of the battle, with a simultaneous destruction of her wheel and head sails. The fact may be accepted, however, that it was a fair fight and fairly won.

It was fortunate for Lawrence that he died a hero, for the defeat was a severe blow to our national pride.

---

[9] Figures from Gleaves's *Life of James Lawrence*, p. 209.
[10] *Ibid.*, p. 210.
[11] Mahan, *War of 1812*, ii, 145.

The Chesapeake and the Shannon 143

As it was, Midshipman Cox—acting third lieutenant—who made the mistake of assisting his commander to the deck below, was expelled from the service with the burden of the defeat laid on his shoulders; and this, despite the fact that it was he who trained and discharged the last gun fired in defense of the flag.

Much has been written concerning Captain Lawrence's judgment in going out to fight the *Shannon,* and the opinion is widely accepted that he acted rashly and impulsively; with great gallantry, but with inexcusable lack of judgment. And yet, it is hard to see how a brave officer could have done otherwise. For months the harbor had been blockaded by two frigates; and, as far as Lawrence knew, at any moment the blockade of two or even three frigates, would be renewed. The fact that the *Shannon* alone stood on blockade meant an opportunity to get to sea, and win honor besides. It is clear, from his letter to the Secretary of the Navy, that he regarded his ship as ready for sea, and he knew that if he delayed a week, or even a day or two, simply to get his ship's organization into better shape, he ran the risk of never having another chance to leave port. As it turned out, the *Constitution,* which was then undergoing repairs after her battle with the *Java,* was blockaded until late in 1814, when the war was practically over. Had the *Chesapeake* also remained, she would have shared the same fate. It must be added to Lawrence's credit, that when he did offer battle, he chose the style of fighting that was best adapted to an unpracticed crew, namely, close quarters. At all events, he did not strike his colors; and the harshest critic must be gentle in the face of his heroic death.

IX

THE SLOOP ACTIONS OF THE WAR

IN the single-ship engagements between frigates in this war, the United States was three times victorious and once defeated. All these actions occurred during the first twelve months of the war, for after the several reverses the British Admiralty had grown wary and had instructed their captains to refuse battle when English 18-pounders were opposed to American 24's, and to obtain added security for their frigates by cruising in couples. The activity of American frigates was further checked, as the British, on increasing their naval force on our shores, extended the blockade so as to include New England. Whenever it was known that an American frigate was in a harbor, an English squadron would hover about, making it impossible for a large ship to get to sea. Thus the *Congress* was shut up in Portsmouth on her return in 1813; the *Constellation,* which was undergoing repairs in the Chesapeake at the outbreak of hostilities, was prevented from sailing till their close; and the *United States,* after defeating the *Macedonian,* was permitted to sail with her former prize only from New York to New London, where both frigates were closely held till the end of the war.

The sloops of war, drawing less water and being much more nimble than the frigates, easily eluded the blockade, and their activity continued unabated throughout the war. Besides inflicting great damage on the enemy's commerce, they engaged in battle British craft of their own kind, fighting in all eight single-ship actions; in just one, the third encounter, the British were successful; in the other seven, our sloops were victorious.

The Frigate and the Sloop Actions 145

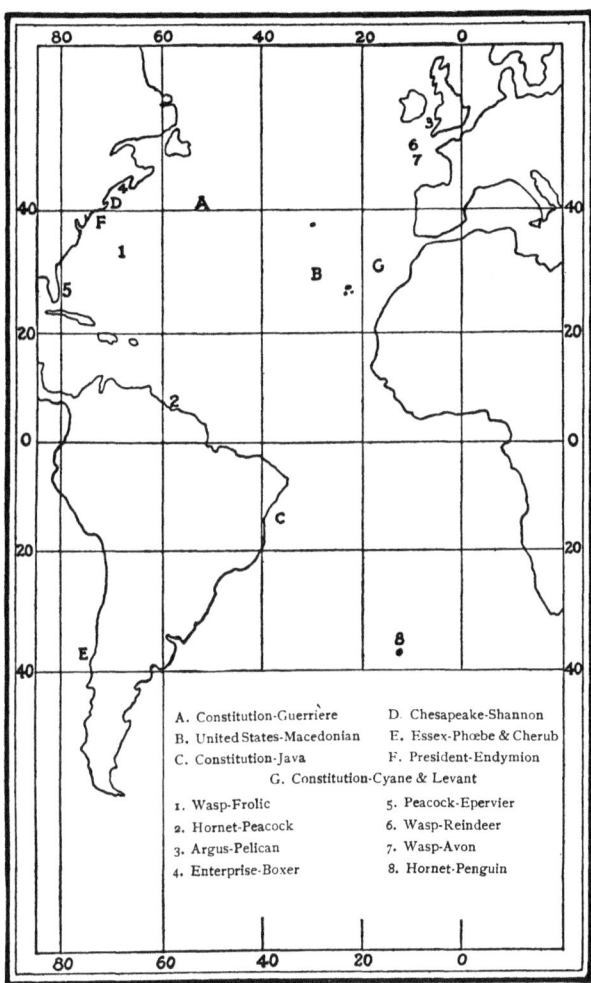

THE FRIGATE AND THE SLOOP ACTIONS OF THE WAR OF 1812

THE WASP AND THE FROLIC

On the 18th of October, 1812, the American sloop of war *Wasp*, 18 guns, Master-Commandant Jacob Jones, engaged the British brig *Frolic*, 22 guns, Captain Thomas Whinyates. The *Wasp* had sailed from the Delaware on October 13; two days later she had encountered a violent storm that carried away her jib-boom with two men. On the 17th, a half hour before midnight, when about 500 miles east of Chesapeake Bay (lat. 37° N., long. 65° W.) Jones made out a convoy; but, as there appeared to be at least two large ships, he cautiously stood off till daylight should disclose their force. The convoy consisted of six vessels returning from Honduras in the charge of the *Frolic*. The gale which had so severely handled the *Wasp* had been no kinder to the English brig, for the *Frolic* had lost her main yard as well as her topsails and had sprung her maintopmast.

When, as day broke, Jones had determined the character of the enemy, he bore down to attack.[1] Whinyates, seeing his intention, ordered the convoy to run before the wind, while he dropped astern and hoisted Spanish colors, hoping by this ruse to deceive and delay his enemy.

The action did not begin until the two were within fifty yards of each other, and as they sailed along parallel courses, there was little maneuvering. In very few naval battles has the equality of force been so marked. For though the *Wasp* had an advantage in the number of men, 135 to her opponent's 110, the *Frolic*, to offset this, had a heavier broadside, 274 pounds to the American's 250; both alike had suffered from the gale.

There was a heavy sea running, which frequently threw spray over the decks or even rolled the muzzles of

---

[1] Jones's official report may be found in *Niles's Register*, iii, 217; Whinyates', in the *Naval Chronicle*, xxix, 76.

The Wasp and the Frolic 147

the guns under, yet the gunnery was unusually good. The *Wasp* suffered many wounds in her spars and rigging; within four or five minutes her maintopmast was shot away, and, falling with the maintopsail yard across the port fore and foretopsail braces rendered the head yards unmanageable; four minutes later, the gaff and mizzen topgallant mast fell; and after twenty minutes of fighting every brace and most of the rigging had been shot away. Meanwhile, the distance between the two ships had gradually lessened and the *Wasp*, drawing ahead of her opponent, secured an advantageous position off the *Frolic's* bow. Captain Whinyates in his official report of the battle wrote:

"The superior fire of our guns gave every reason to expect its speedy termination in our favor; but the gaff head-braces being shot away, and there being no sail on the mainmast, the brig became unmanageable, and the enemy succeeded in taking a position to rake her, while she was unable to bring a gun to bear."

The *Frolic* now fouled the *Wasp*, running her bowsprit between the main and mizzen rigging of the *Wasp*. This was not disadvantageous for Jones; for, with his rigging so badly cut up, he was apprehensive that his masts might fall, and he had already decided to take the enemy by boarding. First, however, he seized the opportunity to rake, and was intending further to hammer away, when the eagerness of his crew for still closer action could scarcely be restrained. Jack Lang, once impressed into the British service, leaped on his gun, cutlass in hand, and thence to the *Frolic*. Lieutenant Biddle was for calling him back, but, seeing the enthusiasm of the crew, quickly changed his mind, and led them on. His feet, however, got tangled in the rigging, and, as a midshipman caught hold of his coat to help himself up, the lieutenant fell back upon the deck of the *Wasp*. Quickly jumping up again, Biddle passed Lang and a seaman who had gained the bowsprit of the *Frolic,* and was the first to go aft. There to his astonishment, he found only four men on deck alive, Captain Whinyates with two other officers and a seaman who held to his station at the wheel. On Biddle's approach the officers, all wounded, threw down their swords in token of submission, and as there was no one to haul down the colors Biddle himself climbed the rigging and did so.

A few minutes after the *Wasp* had freed herself from the *Frolic,* both masts of the latter fell, the mainmast close to the deck, the foremast twelve or fifteen feet above the deck. The action had lasted forty-three minutes. The most surprising feature of the engagement is that with the unusual equality of force there should have been such a great difference in losses. On the American side there were five killed and five wounded, a total of ten; on the British, not twenty men escaped injury, and the total loss was about ninety. In explanation of this it was reported that, in the heavy sea running, the *Frolic* fired when rising on the crest of the waves, so that nearly all her shot which struck injured the spars and rigging of her enemy; and that the *Wasp* fired while going down so that her shot swept the decks or pierced the hull of her opponent. When Whinyates spoke of the "superior fire" of the British guns, he probably meant the more rapid fire (three to two, according to Cooper) for, as Vice-Admiral Jurien de la Gravière of the French Navy observes, the accuracy of the American fire, in spite of the unfavorable conditions prevailing, was indeed astonishing.

The determined and obstinate resistance of the *Frolic* illustrates the value of holding out to the last, even when things are going wrong. Whinyates subjected his ship and crew to awful losses, yet not without result; for soon after the *Frolic* had surrendered, another sail appeared on the horizon. Jones supposed it to be one of the convoy of the *Frolic,* several of which were heavily armed, and he loaded his guns and cleared for action. But the stranger proved to be the British 74-gun ship-of-the-line *Poictiers,* Captain Beresford; and as the *Wasp* could not flee, Beresford took the *Wasp* and recaptured the *Frolic,* and sailed with them to Bermuda.

THE HORNET AND THE PEACOCK

It has been told in the previous chapter how James Lawrence, when captain of the *Hornet,* vainly sought an engagement on equal terms with the *Bonne Citoyenne* off the coast of Brazil. At length, compelled by the British ship-of-the-line *Montague,* 74 guns, to choose a new station, he followed the coast to British Guiana, a favorite cruising ground of American privateers, and on his way captured the British brig *Resolution,* 10 guns, with $23,000 in specie on board.

On February 24, 1813, when off the mouth of the Demerara River, British Guiana, Lawrence discovered on his weather quarter, a brig which showed a willingness to engage. It was the *Peacock,* a sister ship of the *Frolic,* and thus of about the same size as the *Hornet,* but with only two-thirds as heavy a broadside; for her 32-pound carronades, because of her light scantling, had all been replaced by 24's.

As the ships neared each other, Lawrence kept close to the wind, and secured the weather-gage. At 5.25 the ships, passing on opposite tacks, exchanged broadsides at half pistol-shot range. Then Lawrence, seeing that the *Peacock* was about to wear, bore up and, receiving her starboard broadside, ran close on her starboard quarter, where, by a heavy and well-directed fire, he cut the brig to pieces. By this fire the British commander, Captain William Peake, was killed, and soon the *Peacock* was in a desperate condition. Less than fifteen minutes after the action had begun, the *Peacock* surrendered, hoisting an ensign, union down, as a signal of distress. The ship was sinking fast, already having six feet of water in her hold.

Lieutenant Conner, who, with a small force of American seamen, had been sent aboard, made every effort to keep the *Peacock* afloat until the prisoners could be removed; they threw guns overboard, plugged some of the holes, and resorted to pumping and baling. But she continued to settle, and went to the bottom so suddenly as to carry down nine of her crew and three Americans.

The loss on the *Peacock* was five killed, including her commander, and thirty-three wounded; on the *Hornet*, one killed and four wounded (two by the bursting of a cartridge)[2]; the rigging of the *Hornet* was cut, but the hull had received no damage. While it must be admitted that the advantage favored the Americans in number of crew and weight of gun metal, still this does not explain the astonishing difference in the effects of the fire of the two ships. As some writer has observed, "Had the guns of the *Peacock* been of the largest size they could not have changed the result, as the weight of shot that do not hit is of no great moment."

Another British brig, the *Espiegle*, of approximately the same strength as the *Peacock*, lay at anchor six miles distant throughout the engagement. At its termination, Lawrence quickly patched his rigging and prepared for a second fight which he supposed would be soon forced upon him. But as the *Espiegle* remained unconcernedly at her anchorage in the harbor, he sailed away.

---

[2] Official report of Captain Lawrence, March 19, 1813.

The Argus and the Pelican

THE ARGUS AND THE PELICAN

On June 18, 1813, the American brig-of-war *Argus*, Master-Commandant William H. Allen, sailed for L'Orient, with Mr. Crawford, the newly appointed minister to France. On the voyage over of twenty-three days, Allen made just one prize, but, later, in thirty-one days of cruising in the chops of the English Channel, he captured and destroyed nineteen British merchantmen. The explanation of the difference is that on the regular thoroughfares ships were not allowed to sail except in convoy, while nearer home, in the vicinity of England and Ireland, ships followed a hundred courses, as in time of peace, and there were no ships-of-war stationed near to protect them. The career of the *Argus* was soon to be cut short, but she had shown the advantage of preying on unprotected parts of the enemy's coast.

Early in the morning, August 14, 1813, the *Argus*, after capturing a prize between Wales and southern Ireland and setting fire to her, fell in with the British brig-of-war *Pelican*, Captain Maples, which had been sent out from Cork, expressly to meet her. The wind was from the south and the *Pelican* had the weather-gage. Allen attempted to pass to windward, but finding he could not, he shortened sail and allowed the *Pelican* to close. The action began at six A.M., when the *Argus* wore round and fired her port broadside within grape distance, the *Pelican* promptly responding with her starboard battery. Although early in the action, Allen was severely wounded in the leg by a round shot, he held to his post, until he fainted from loss of blood—bravery that cost him his life. A few minutes later, the first lieutenant, W. H. Watson, was struck in the head and stunned by a grape shot, whereupon the command devolved on the second lieutenant, W. H. Allen, Jr.

A large part of the rigging of the *Argus* had now been disabled, yet as the enemy edged off to pass under her stern, Second Lieutenant Allen skilfully prevented this by luffing with the maintopsail aback, at the same time firing a raking broadside. The wheel ropes of the *Argus*, as well as the running rigging, were soon shot away and she became unmanageable. Her enemy, only slightly damaged, could then choose his position at will.

When, at 6.30, Lieutenant Watson, on recovering consciousness, again came up on deck, he found the enemy raking from under the stern of the *Argus*. The Americans were plainly beaten, unless they could bring their ship up and board; and this maneuver, since all their braces were cut, proved impossible. The action continued a few minutes longer, the *Argus* exposed to a cross or raking fire to which she was able to respond with little more than musketry. Finally, at 6.47, when the action had been in progress about three-quarters of an hour, the *Argus* surrendered.

The American loss was six killed and seventeen wounded, five so severely that they died within a few days. The British had two killed and five wounded. The British brig was twenty per cent larger, and her broadside seventeen per cent heavier. Yet this does not explain why the American fire at short range caused so little injury. Even when the *Argus* had a raking position she could not use it to advantage. Her gunnery was decidedly poor. Lieutenant Watson observes in his official report that the crew had been under a long strain because of the "very rapid succession of captures."

The Enterprise and the Boxer

On September 5, 1813, the American brig *Enterprise*, of 14 guns, commanded by Lieutenant William Burrows, while near Monhegan Island, Maine, fell in with the

The Peacock and the Epervier

British brig *Boxer*, of 14 guns, Captain Samuel Blyth, and decisively defeated her in an action lasting forty minutes.

Both vessels were dull sailers. The *Enterprise* had a slight superiority in guns, and also a larger complement; but while the *Enterprise* had just got to sea, the *Boxer* had been cruising for six months, certainly an enviable opportunity for drilling.

The loss of the Americans was fourteen killed and wounded; that of the British was not reported, but was evidently larger. The *Enterprise* had inflicted considerable damage in the hull of her enemy, while receiving little in return; both had suffered in spars and rigging. The *Enterprise* seems to have been more skilfully maneuvered, and, to quote the findings of the British court-martial, she had "a greater degree of skill in the direction of her fire." Almost at the first broadside, Captain Blyth of the *Boxer* was killed, and, at about the same time, Lieutenant Burrows of the *Enterprise* was struck down by a musket ball. Lieutenant Edward R. McCall, who then assumed command of the *Enterprise*, and carried the fight to a successful conclusion, had never so much as seen a battle before.

THE PEACOCK AND THE EPERVIER

The Government, though so slow in building new frigates that none took part in the war, had in the latter part of 1813 three new sloops approaching completion, the *Peacock*, the *Frolic*, and the *Wasp*, names given in honor of Lawrence's and Jones's splendid victories. On April 29, 1814, the *Peacock*, 18 guns, Master-Commandant Lewis Warrington, while off the southeast coast of Florida, engaged the British brig *Epervier*, 18 guns, Captain Wales. The American ship, nominally equal in strength to her antagonist, was slightly superior in every particular. Still when the *Epervier* surrendered, after an action lasting forty-five minutes, the difference in losses showed, even more decidedly than in previous engagements, that it was something more than heavier guns which brought victory.

The *Peacock* had not a man killed, and but two slightly wounded; the *Epervier*, eight killed and fifteen wounded. Not a round shot had touched the hull of the *Peacock*, and her masts and spars were as sound as ever, while her enemy had masts badly cut up and forty-five shots in the hull which had admitted five feet of water in the hold.

After making some repairs, Warrington decided to take his prize into Savannah. The sloops were chased by two British frigates, but escaped by clever maneuvering, and succeeded in reaching port in safety.

THE WASP AND THE REINDEER

An important share in the credit for the *Enterprise's* splendid victory over the *Boxer* was due to Master-Commandant Johnston Blakely. It was he who had fitted out the brig and drilled the raw crew, and thus made it possible for the young and inexperienced Lieutenants Burrows and McCall, immediately on getting to sea, to give such good account of the *Enterprise*. He himself did not sail, for he had just received a better command, the new sloop of war *Wasp*, now nearly ready for sea. The story of this, the second *Wasp*, is that of a swift and daring cruiser which met with signal success.

Leaving Portsmouth, New Hampshire, on May 1, 1814, Blakely slipped through the blockading line, and, according to his instructions, took up a station in the approaches to the English Channel, almost exactly where Allen, in the *Argus*, had, a year before, captured so many merchantmen. Blakely had a sloop that probably was not surpassed in all European waters; his crew of 173 was made up almost entirely of New Englanders, and, though they averaged only twenty-three years in age, many without previous sea training, they were spirited and ambitious, the kind that an efficient commander like Blakely could quickly mould into the best of crews.

Not until he had been thirty-two days at sea did he make a capture; he was then probably near his station in the Channel, for, in the next thirty-five days he took seven more prizes. Not every sail he saw was legitimate prey; as he observes in a letter of July 8, 1814, "After arriving on soundings, the number of neutrals which were passing kept us almost constantly in pursuit." It was a daring game he was playing, for he adds, "I found it impossible to maintain anything like a station, and was led in chase farther up the Channel than was intended."

Early on the morning of June 28, 1814, Blakely, having discovered two sails on his lee beam, started in chase; but as soon afterwards he made out a single sail on his weather beam, he altered his course, and stood for this. The stranger, which was the brig *Reindeer*, Captain William Manners, might easily have escaped, and as the superior character of American sloops was now pretty well known, Manners must have been aware that he was about to engage a stronger antagonist; but William Manners had a crew said to be the pride of Plymouth, and was himself a commander that, for courage and ability, had scarcely a superior. Instead of avoiding battle, Manners came about with the wind nearly aft, and stood for his opponent.

The breezes were so light that the ships moved on almost an even keel; and it was quarter after one before Blakely had the drummer call the men to their quarters. Two hours more elapsed before the fight began, Blakely having tacked and attempted to pass to windward of his enemy; Manners, much too clever to surrender any advantage needlessly, had tacked at the same time, and standing from the American, had foiled him. Blakely, seeing that his enemy would weather him, changed to the other tack, and, furling most of his sail, allowed the *Reindeer* to approach.

The English brig came up on the weather quarter of the *Wasp*, about sixty yards distant, and opened with a 12-pound carronade loaded with round and grape shot, a fire that must have severely tested the discipline of the crew of the *Wasp*, for, as the *Reindeer* did not draw abeam, the guns of the *Wasp* would not bear. Blakely got out of this awkward position, however, by suddenly putting his helm alee; and beginning with the after carronade he fired, in succession, all the guns of his broadside as they bore.

The *Reindeer*, somewhat disabled by this fire, now ran aboard of the *Wasp*, her port bow against the *Wasp's* quarter, in which position the *Wasp* raked with telling effect. Meanwhile the American marines and riflemen, with the skill for which they were famed, picked off many of the exposed officers and crew of the brig. Captain Manners, though wounded, kept the deck and urged on the fight. A second wound caused by a shot that went through both thighs, brought him to his knees; but he was up again quickly, and would give no heed to his wounds, which were bleeding profusely. Finally, perceiving the execution of the musketry from the tops of the *Wasp*, he called out, "Follow me, my boys, we must board." With the words, he climbed the rigging to lead them on, but two balls from the *Wasp's* maintop, passing through his skull, killed him instantly.

The Americans, in turn, now prepared to board. The English, badly crippled by the death or disability of nearly all their officers, as well as of half their men, could make but little resistance, and soon surrendered.

The action occupied nineteen minutes.[3] The *Wasp* received six round shot in her hull, and a 24-pound shot that passed through the centre of her foremast, and had her sails and rigging injured. The *Reindeer,* wrote Blakely, "was literally cut to pieces in a line with her ports." The *Wasp* had five killed and twenty-one wounded, the *Reindeer,* twenty-five killed and forty-two wounded. Almost equal honor was due the two forces for the brave fight. When, as in this case, it is a picked American crew against a picked English crew, both splendidly disciplined, and directed by the finest of captains, victory depends on something else than determination and courage; and here it is fair to conclude that it was due to superiority in power. The *Wasp* had twenty 32-pounder carronades and two long guns against the *Reindeer's* sixteen 24-pounders and two long guns, and as the complement of the *Wasp* was in a like degree larger, she surpassed the English brig in at least the ratio of three to two.

THE WASP AND THE AVON

That he might secure the best care for his wounded and as well make needed repairs on the *Wasp,* Blakely sailed for L'Orient, where he remained till the 27th of August. Then putting to sea, in less than a month, he made six more valuable captures. How free and fearless were his movements may be seen from the capture of the British brig *Mary,* loaded with cannon and other military stores, and convoyed with nine other ships by a bombship, and the ship-of-the-line *Armada,* 74 guns. The *Wasp* not only succeeded in cutting out the *Mary,* but having burned it within sight of the convoy attempted to make another capture; she was prevented, however, by the *Armada,* which chased her away.

---

[3] For Blakely's report, see *Niles's Register,* vii, 114.

On the evening of the same day, September 1, 1814, the lookout sighted four sails, two on the starboard and two on the port bow. Blakely immediately set sail in chase of the ship on the starboard bow farthest to windward. The chase was the brig *Avon*, Captain James Arbuthnot. After an engagement of three-quarters of an hour she surrendered, with a loss of nine killed and thirty-three wounded. The *Wasp* had two killed and one wounded, about an eighth or ninth of her loss in the fight with the *Reindeer;* since the *Avon* was superior to the *Reindeer* by having 32-pounders where the *Reindeer* had 24's, this shows something of the quality of Manners and his crew.

When Blakely was about to take possession of the prize, he discovered a second brig, the *Castilian*, of 18 guns, standing towards him and he received a broadside from her as she ran up under his stern. Since two other sails were also approaching, Blakely left his prize and standing off to reeve new braces, attempted to decoy the second brig from her supports. But the *Avon* was firing guns of distress, and the *Castilian* went to her rescue; scarcely had the last man been removed from the *Avon* before she went down.

Sailing now to the south, Blakely captured off the Madeiras the brig *Atlanta*, which, being of exceptional value, he sent with official despatches to Savannah. Three weeks later, the *Wasp* was spoken 900 miles farther south and this is the last ever heard of the brilliant captain and his gallant crew. Their end is entirely shrouded in mystery.

The Hornet and the Penguin

On January 20, 1815, the *Hornet*, Master-Commandant James Biddle, slipped through the British blockading squadron off New York and set sail for the South Atlantic,

The Hornet and the Penguin

where, with several other ships that were to rendezvous at the lonely island of Tristan da Cunha, 1500 miles west of the Cape of Good Hope, it was planned she should cruise against British commerce.

On her arrival, March 23, 1815, as she was about to anchor, the lookout sighted a sail to the southeast, passing behind the island. The *Hornet* immediately got under way, and after a little maneuvering, at 1.40 that afternoon, entered into an artillery duel with the British sloop of war *Penguin*, Captain Dickinson. The two were running on parallel courses, the *Hornet* to leeward. In armament, the *Penguin* had sixteen 32-pounder carronades, two long 12's, and one 12-pounder carronade; opposed to this, the *Hornet* had eighteen 32-pounder carronades and two long 12's. Thus it will be seen that the *Hornet* had only very little superiority in gun metal.

The story of the fight is like that of many other actions. The *Penguin* kept drifting nearer, and as she was being decidedly worsted in the artillery duel, Dickinson suddenly put his helm hard up and fouled the *Hornet* with the intention of boarding. But the American crew was ready and kept the British off while the small-arms men poured in a murderous fire. The *Penguin* wrenched loose with the loss of her bowsprit and foremast, and then surrendered. The action lasted twenty-two minutes. The British guns were active, yet the fact that the *Hornet* did not receive a single round shot in her hull or any material injury in her spars shows the inaccuracy of their fire. Her loss was one killed and eleven wounded, to be contrasted with fourteen killed on the *Penguin,* including the captain, and twenty-eight wounded. This was the last naval action of the war; in fact, it occurred several weeks after the terms of peace had been approved by the President and ratified by the Senate.

THE IMPORTANCE OF THE SLOOP ACTIONS

Although the loss of seven sloops from such a navy as Great Britain's could have little direct effect upon the war, yet the service of our small cruisers was far-reaching in its influence. The daring enterprise of our sloops, their ability to move almost at will in the face of a heavy blockade, the skill with which they were handled, in short, their almost uninterrupted success in coping with the first navy of the world, fostered in our country the much needed spirit of self-respect, earlier stimulated by the frigate actions, and awoke in Europe a general feeling of admiration.

Of no trifling importance, further, was the service of our sloops in their attack upon England's commerce. The *Argus, Peacock* (2d), and *Wasp* (2d) were extremely daring, and the number of prizes they took can be compared favorably with the work of even the most celebrated of the privateers. The sloops had found a vulnerable spot in the great sea power. Their attack was similar in strategy, though not in magnitude, with that of the German U-boats a century later. Such communications as the following, sent to the British Admiralty by the Royal Exchange and London Assurance Corporations in August, 1814, were weighty arguments for concluding hostilities:

"Should the depredations on our commerce continue, the merchants and traders will not be able to get any insurance effected, except at enormous premiums on vessels trading between Ireland and England, either by the chartered companies or individual underwriters; and as a proof of this assertion, for the risks which are usually written fifteen shillings nine pence per cent the sum of five guineas is now demanded."[4]

---

[4] *Niles's Register*, vii, 174.

X

THE BATTLE OF LAKE ERIE

STRATEGIC IMPORTANCE OF THE GREAT LAKES

ALTHOUGH the United States did not rouse itself to maintain a navy on the Great Lakes until after hostilities had begun, long before the beginning of the war Great Britain had appreciated their strategic importance. Indeed the British had, ever since the days of the French occupation in Canada, realized the advantage of these inland oceans on the borderland as rapid means of conveying troops, supplies, and communications. The nation in power on these waterways had also the lucrative fur trade, and with it the Indian interests in that section. The woods on both Canadian and American sides were all but impassable. Since Britain's salt water navy could reach with its mighty arm as far as Montreal, control of the lakes would easily give her the upper hand in all the territory bordering on these waterways as far as Mackinac. Kingston, Detroit, and Mackinac were the important links in the chain of communication from the Atlantic to the Northwest. Besides, the fact that two of these places, Detroit and Mackinac, were on narrow bodies of water, furnished an additional element of defense.

It should have been the policy of our Government to take the offensive on the northern border, while it sought to maintain a defensive attitude on the seaboard. Preparations for a control of the lakes should have been made ten years previous to the war, but a parsimonious government, naturally opposed to navies, did not foresee the need of warships at sea, much less on the lakes. It was a similar shortsighted policy that prompted Hull and

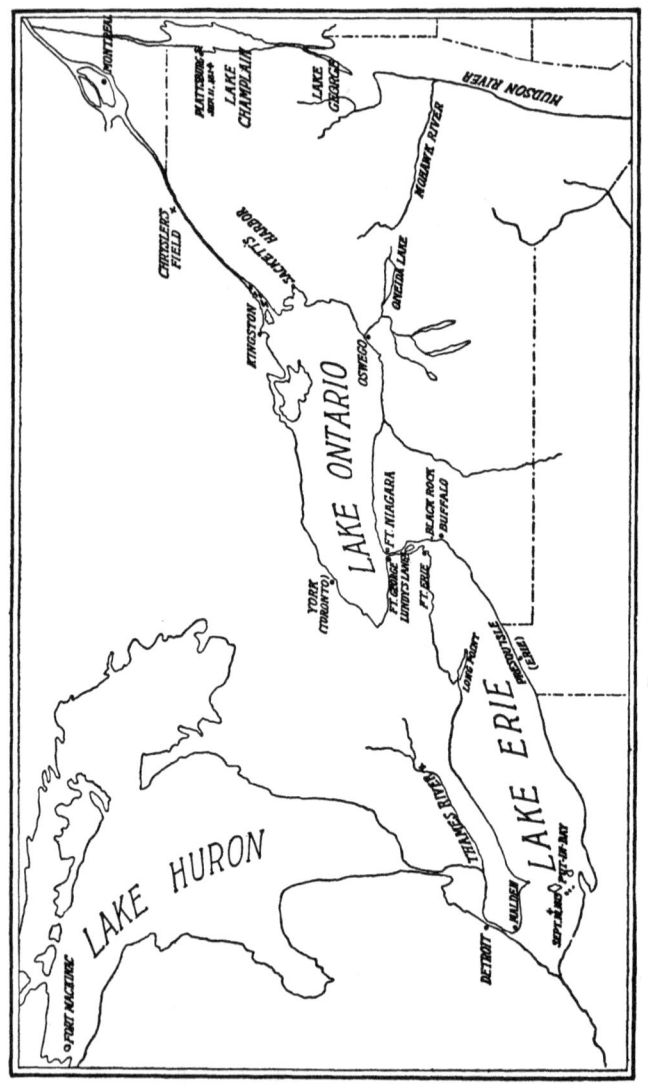

The Lake Campaigns, 1812–1814

Dearborn to concentrate their efforts in the Northwest, rather than at Lake Champlain and against Montreal, the true objective in an offensive war for control of the Northwest. Hull's disastrous campaign in Michigan, and the fall of Detroit and Mackinac in the summer of 1812, spurred our people to efforts which culminated in a partial control of Lake Ontario, and in Perry's victory on Lake Erie. Detroit and Mackinac would never have fallen if we had had control of the Great Lakes. Indeed, shortly after Perry's capture of the British flotilla on Lake Erie, Detroit and the territory of Michigan came back into our possession.

CHAUNCEY AND ELLIOTT SENT TO THE LAKES

On September 3, 1812, Captain Isaac Chauncey was ordered by the Navy Department to take command of Lakes Erie and Ontario with the purpose of building fleets on these waters and wresting the naval supremacy on them from the British. Chauncey took charge of the work on Ontario himself, and on September 7 he dispatched Lieutenant Jesse D. Elliott to Lake Erie to establish a naval base. The latter arrived at Buffalo on September 14, and was busily engaged in equipping at Black Rock, his temporary navy yard, some schooners which he had recently bought, when, on October 8, he was informed that two British armed brigs had come to anchor off Fort Erie. These were the *Detroit,* formerly the U. S. S. *Adams,* and the *Caledonia.*

With the aid of ninety seamen, who had arrived that very day from New York, and with about fifty soldiers, Elliott determined to cut out these brigs. He succeeded in bringing the *Caledonia* to Black Rock, but the *Detroit* ran aground off Squaw Island, and, under the fire of both the British and American forts, had to be burned. The

Caledonia had a cargo of furs valued at $200,000, and the *Detroit* had a quantity of ordnance; four of the latter's 12-pounders and a quantity of shot were later recovered at night by a party of American seamen.

Lieutenant Elliott had quickly seen his opportunity and grasped it; he had realized that with these two vessels added to his squadron he might wrest the control of the Upper Lakes (*i.e.*, the lakes west of Lake Erie) from Great Britain. But as the *Detroit* had to be destroyed, the British still possessed a naval force too great for Elliott to encounter. General Brock, commanding the British forces, however, felt the loss of these brigs very much. In a letter to the Governor-General of Canada, he wrote: "This event is particularly unfortunate and may reduce us to incalculable distress. The enemy is making every exertion to gain a naval superiority on both lakes; which if they accomplish, I do not see how we can retain the country. More vessels are fitting for war on the other side of Squaw Island, which I should have attempted to destroy but for your Excellency's repeated instructions to forbear. Now such a force is collected for their protection as will render every operation against them very hazardous."[1] Elliott kept hard at work until the winter closed the lake to navigation, and his labors laid the foundations for Perry's success the following year.

Perry in Command on Lake Erie

On March 27, 1813, Master-Commandant Oliver Hazard Perry took charge of the work on Lake Erie, and removed the flotilla from Black Rock to Presqu'isle (Erie), where he established his base. A race in shipbuilding now took place between Perry on the American

---

[1] Quoted in Mahan's *War of 1812*, i, 356.

Oliver H. Perry

Perry and Barclay on Lake Erie 165

side and the British naval commander, Barclay, on the Canadian side. Both were young and full of energy. Both had to work under great difficulties. The Canadians gave Barclay little help; the severer winter and less developed country on the north shores made his task harder. Although the salt water navy of Great Britain could reach as far as Montreal to bring men and arms, still the Government was in great straits for sailors for the European war. Captain Sir James Lucas Yeo, the able young British officer on Lake Ontario, could spare his subordinate on Erie but few men, as he needed them too much himself in his struggle for supremacy against Chauncey. On the other hand, Perry had in New York a better developed country to operate in. But he likewise found it difficult to persuade his superior, Chauncey, to spare him men and supplies; and he had to bring his mechanics and seamen for the most part from New York City, a distance of 500 miles. The American commander had to depend largely on militia and negroes to defend his shipbuilding operations, as his British rival depended on Canadians and Indians. As many of the Canadians had originally come from New England and New York, they had been from the beginning as much opposed to the war as the people in our northern States, and were not to be relied upon. Roosevelt is of the opinion that the Canadians, being naturally lake sailors, fought better at the battle of Lake Erie than British tars did a year later at the battle of Lake Champlain. Barclay, however, lamented greatly his lack of British officers and seamen.

Taking advantage of a temporary naval control on Lake Ontario, Chauncey, in conjunction with General Dearborn, captured York, now Toronto, in April, 1813 A month later Chauncey assisted in the capture of Fort George, on the Niagara River, an event which compelled the British to abandon their hold on this river. This made it possible for Perry to tow up the river to Presqu'-isle the brig *Caledonia,* the purchased schooners *Somers, Tigress,* and *Ohio,* and the sloop *Trippe.* The warping of these vessels up against the powerful current was an arduous task. The rest of Perry's squadron, the two 20-gun brigs *Lawrence* and *Niagara,* and three more schooners, the *Ariel, Scorpion,* and *Porcupine,* were being hastily constructed at the navy yard at Presqu'isle.

Barclay, too, was very busy in building and equipping his flotilla, which consisted of the ships *Detroit* (a new vessel named after the former *Detroit*) and *Queen Charlotte,* the brig *Hunter,* the schooners *Lady Prevost* and *Chippewa,* and the sloop *Little Belt.* As soon as most of his vessels were ready, Barclay put to sea and at once blockaded Perry at Presqu'isle. The American commander was now in difficult straits, because he could not get his brigs, with their guns mounted, across the bar at the mouth of Erie harbor; and to try to get them over with guns unmounted, while Barclay's flotilla was hovering about, would be foolhardy. The British commander maintained a close blockade until August 2, when, for no apparent reason, he disappeared to the westward. Perry now hurried matters, and on the 4th he towed the *Lawrence* to the deepest part of the bar, hastily took out her guns, and that night got the brig across the bar. The method used by Perry in getting the *Lawrence* over is thus described by Cooper: "Two large scows, prepared for the purpose, were hauled alongside, and the work of lifting the brig proceeded as fast as possible. Pieces of massive timber had been run through the forward and after ports, and when the scows were sunk to the water's edge, the ends of the timbers were blocked up, supported by these floating foundations. The plugs were now put in the scows, and the water was pumped out of them. By this process the brig was lifted quite two feet, though when she was got on the bar it was found that she still drew too much water. It became necessary, in consequence, to cover up everything, sink the scows anew, and block up the timbers afresh. This duty occupied the whole night."[2]

At eight o'clock on the morning of the 5th, just as the *Lawrence* had been safely got across, Barclay reappeared. But he was too late, and after the exchange of a few shots with the American schooners, Barclay went back to his base at Malden (Amherstburg) to await the completion of his most powerful ship, the *Detroit*. Shortly after, Perry brought the *Niagara* across the bar without trouble. After sailing westward towards Malden, Perry returned to Erie to lay in provisions, and on August 10 took on 102 seamen whom Lieutenant Elliott had just brought as a much-needed reinforcement. Elliott, as second in command, took charge of the *Niagara*. Perry could now range the lake at will. He made his headquarters at Put-in-Bay, a good harbor thirty miles southwest of Malden, where he could watch the movements of Barclay and prevent him from getting to the British source of supplies at Long Point. As the roads were impassable, and as blockade-running was impracticable, Captain Barclay was soon forced to come out for supplies. In his report to Sir James Yeo after the battle, he wrote: "So perfectly destitute of provisions was the port [Malden], that there was not a day's flour in store, and the crews of the squadron under my command were on half allowance of many things, and when that was done there was no more." The Indians had been wantonly killing cattle in this region, and these warriors and their families, in all 14,000, whom the British had to provide for, were becoming restive because of the lack of food.

---

[2] J. Fenimore Cooper, *The History of the Navy of the United States of America*, ii, 389.

The Battle of Lake Erie

At sunrise on September 10, 1813, the lookout at the masthead of the *Lawrence* saw the British flotilla coming out from Malden. The wind was at first southwest, which gave Barclay the weather-gage. But after Perry had got under way, the wind shifted to the southeast and thus was in his favor. Barclay, in his report of the battle, says: "The weather-gage gave the enemy a prodigious advantage, as it enabled them not only to choose their position, but their distance also, which they did in such a manner, as to prevent the carronades of the *Queen Charlotte* and *Lady Prevost* from having much effect; while their long guns did great execution, particularly against the *Queen Charlotte*."

Both commanders formed their vessels in columns, with the most powerful ships in the centre—a formation which gave the whole line a strong cohesive force. Perry had intended to have each of his stronger vessels keep its position parallel to a correspondingly powerful opponent. This is proved by the fact that after he noticed the formation of Barclay's centre to be constituted in the following order: *Detroit, Hunter,* and *Queen Charlotte,* he rearranged his own centre thus: *Lawrence, Caledonia,* and *Niagara.* His first plan had been to have the *Niagara* ahead of the *Lawrence,* thinking that the British centre would be led by the *Queen Charlotte.* This change in formation should be noted carefully, as it has an important bearing on the Perry-Elliott controversy which arose after the battle, and which caused our people to take sides with the two American commanders.

The battle began at 11.45 and continued until three o'clock. Shortly after the British opened fire, Perry determined to abandon his first formation parallel to the enemy's column. He found that the *Lawrence* with her carronades was not within effective range. Accordingly, with the schooners *Ariel* and *Scorpion,* and the flagship *Lawrence* in the van, he tried to reform his flotilla in column ahead obliquely, that is, in echelon, or bow and quarter line. At the same time he sent word to the rear ships, which by reason of the lightness of the wind were straggling behind, to close up. For some reason Elliott did not follow his commander's lead; instead, he kept his position behind the slow-sailing *Caledonia,* and as four-

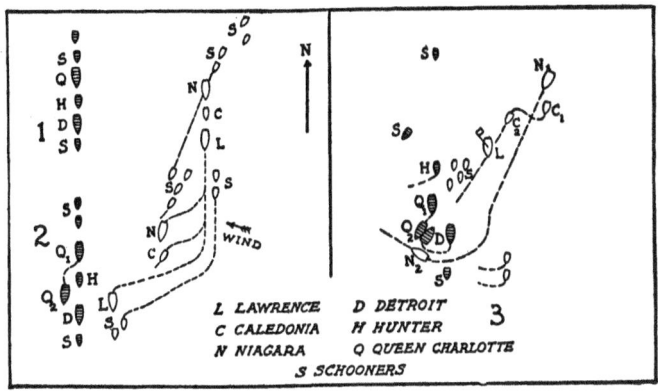

From Mahan's *War of 1812*, by permission
THE BATTLE OF LAKE ERIE

fifths of the *Niagara's* guns were carronades, Elliott's vessel fell behind, out of range. Meanwhile, her intended antagonist, the *Queen Charlotte,* finding that the long guns of the *Caledonia* were doing great damage, sailed ahead to take part in the terrific fire that was already being concentrated on the *Lawrence.* By reason of Elliott's misunderstanding of orders, or his poor judgment, there was now a considerable gap between the *Caledonia* and the vessels in the van.

The *Lawrence* was thus compelled to bear the brunt of the battle from twelve o'clock until half-past two. Both the British and the American larger ships in the van were suffering terribly. At the end of the first stage of the battle, at two-thirty, the *Lawrence* was a wreck. Four-fifths of her crew were either dead or wounded. Finally, Perry had to call on the surgeons and even on the wounded to lend a hand, and he himself, assisted by the purser and chaplain, fired the last effective gun. But the *Detroit* was also "a perfect wreck," according to Barclay's report. The *Queen Charlotte* had lost her able captain, Finnis, early in the action, and was now being badly handled by an inexperienced Canadian officer.

It was at this crucial moment, that Perry, while his ship was drifting helplessly astern out of action, made his famous passage in a boat from the flagship to the *Niagara,* which was still perfectly fresh. He at once sent Elliott to hurry up the American vessels astern, and he himself in the *Niagara* stood down for the badly shattered British flagship. On passing, Perry fired his port guns into the smaller vessels of the enemy, and his starboard into the *Detroit,* the *Queen Charlotte,* and the *Hunter.* The *Detroit* and the *Queen Charlotte* were at this moment trying to wear, to bring fresh broadsides into action; but as every brace and almost every bowline on both had been shot away, the two vessels fouled each other, and thus gave the *Niagara* an excellent opportunity to rake within half pistol-shot. The terrific fire of the *Niagara,* supported by the *Caledonia* and the schooners now coming up, quickly brought the battle to a close.

Perry then transferred his broad pennant back to the *Lawrence,* so that he might receive the surrender of the British commanders on the deck of his old flagship. In the smoke and confusion, the *Chippewa* and the *Little Belt* had crowded on all sail to escape, but they were soon overhauled by the *Trippe* and the *Scorpion,* and were forced to send their officers to the *Lawrence* to give up their swords. Immediately after the formalities of surrender, Perry sent to General William Henry Harrison, who had succeeded Hull in the command of the American Army in the Northwest, his famous message, "We have met the enemy and they are ours—two ships, two brigs, one schooner, and one sloop."

The forces opposed in the battle were very unequal. The Americans had nine vessels[3] with a total broadside of 896 pounds against Barclay's six vessels and total broadside of 459 pounds. Perry's superiority in long gun metal was as three is to two, and in carronade metal as two is to one. Barclay's gunnery was excellent in spite of the fact that, having no locks, he had to fire his guns by flashing pistols at the touch-holes. The total American crew numbered 532, of whom only 416 were fit for duty; the British crew amounted to 440. In all this comparison, however, it must be borne in mind that the Americans were not able to take advantage of their superiority in ships and equipment until nearly the end of the action, when Elliott finally brought up the *Niagara*.

Elliott's conduct in the battle is difficult to explain. He seems to have misunderstood his commanding officer's orders. Perry had sent back word by trumpet early in the engagement to close up the line. Whether Elliott ever received this order we cannot now determine, as the charges and counter-charges were never carefully sifted. Lieutenant Elliott had rendered excellent service in his earlier work on Lake Erie, but in this battle he seems to have displayed bad judgment and lack of initiative in not following Perry's lead in getting into close action, and in not engaging the *Queen Charlotte* according to the original plan. Elliott's pleas were that he understood he

---

[3] The *Ohio* was not present at the battle; she had some time previously been sent down the lake.

was to maintain his position in the line behind the *Caledonia*, and that the wind was too light to keep up with the faster sailing *Queen Charlotte*.

Hitherto American naval officers had had little or no practice in fleet operations, for the sea fights of the early days had been all single-ship actions. The traditions of the middle of the 18th century required that the line must be maintained at all hazards, with the opposing fleets sailing in parallel courses. In the famous Battle of the Saints, fought with De Grasse in the West Indies, April 12, 1782, Rodney, at the suggestion of his fleet captain Douglas, introduced a new maneuver, that of breaking the enemy's line. By this means he concentrated the fire of many of his ships upon an inferior number of the enemy, and determinedly clung to them until after a desperate resistance they were worn out and compelled to surrender. These also were Nelson's tactics at Trafalgar, and the remarkable results still more positively demonstrated the soundness of this style of fighting. The principle of concentration, although carried out in a different way, holds as good now as in the time of Rodney and Nelson.

Perry's method of attack seems at first to have followed the older tradition of ships sailing in column abreast the enemy, and Elliott's reluctance to leave his station astern of the *Caledonia* indicates that this was the style of battle which he, at least, expected. This unwillingness of his to leave his position in column, and the maneuver of the *Queen Charlotte* in sailing ahead to join in the attack on the *Lawrence*, the *Ariel*, and the *Scorpion*, very nearly enabled Barclay to accomplish the feat of destroying in detail a superior enemy. From the moment Perry boarded the *Niagara*, however, he abandoned all line formation, and, by breaking through his enemy's flotilla, turned defeat into victory.

Captain Barclay, who was thirty-two years of age, had

The Battle of Lake Erie 173

an excellent record, and had been in the battle of Trafalgar under Nelson. In the action on Lake Erie he was twice wounded. He refused to leave the deck the first time he was hurt, but the second time he was wounded so terribly that his condition later brought tears to the eyes of the officers who sat on his court-martial. Barclay behaved with splendid courage during the battle; his great mistake was in giving up the blockade of Presqu'isle and thus letting Perry get to sea. In his report, the British commander states the number of killed as forty-one, and wounded ninety-four; Perry gives his losses as twenty-seven killed and ninety-six wounded.

Although the forces were unequal, this very inequality redounds to the glory of Perry, whose energy created so quickly a superior flotilla. Roosevelt remarks that Perry by reason of his victory over an inferior force does not deserve the high place above such men as Hull and Macdonough that is generally accorded him in American histories. But he goes on to say: "It was greatly to our credit that we had been enterprising enough to fit out such an effective little flotilla on Lake Erie, and for this Perry deserves the highest praise." [4] Further, when we contrast the determined work on Lake Erie with the lack of results on Lake Ontario, we must admit that Perry accomplished wonders. His intense energy got together a fleet which within a few months gave the United States control of Lake Erie, the Upper Lakes, and the adjacent territory. On the other hand, on Lake Ontario, the shipbuilding race between Yeo and Chauncey kept on without result, and ended only with the war. The extravagant praise of Perry in American histories, criticised by Roosevelt, is due to the melodramatic features of the battle, which appealed to the popular imagination:

---

[4] Roosevelt, *Naval War of 1812*, p. 278.

the heroic resistance of the *Lawrence,* the passage of Perry in an open boat to the *Niagara,* and the sudden turning of the tide of victory. His fame should rest, rather, upon the hopeless days when the timbers of his future ships were still growing in the forest. In a word, Perry's work on Lake Erie attests the fact that what counts in an officer's career is not the spectacular event which appeals to the public, but the quiet, yet tireless energy, the sound judgment, and the farsightedness that always precede, and sometimes follow, a successful battle.

RESULTS

The results of the battle of Lake Erie were far-reaching. Detroit and Michigan fell back into our possession. Then followed the victory of the Thames, in which Tecumseh, the great Indian leader, was slain. Thereupon the Indians, leaving the British, ceased to be a terror to the American settlements in the Northwest. The scheme which the British had fostered of creating in this section an independent Indian state, carved out of United States territory—a state which should be under the protection of Great Britain, constituting a buffer against the United States—was ended once and for all.

XI

THE CRUISE OF THE ESSEX

IN Chapter VIII it was said that the 32-gun frigate *Essex*, after missing the *Constitution* and the *Hornet*, set sail on a roving cruise in southern waters. There were several reasons for this independent action on the part of Captain Porter. In the first place, after waiting in vain two weeks off Cape Frio (near Rio de Janeiro) to meet Bainbridge, Porter found his ship running short of supplies. He, therefore, hurried on to the next rendezvous agreed upon, the Island of St. Catharine's, which was also on the Brazilian coast. There he failed to find either the *Constitution* or the *Hornet*, but heard of the capture of the *Java*, with rumors to the effect that the *Hornet* had been taken by the ship-of-the-line *Montague*, and learned that several heavy British ships were soon expected in those waters. Fearing that he should be blockaded, or attacked in port by an overwhelming force, Captain Porter immediately put to sea.

"It was then necessary,"[1] he wrote in his journal, "to decide promptly on my proceedings, as our provisions were getting short. I called on the purser for a report and found that we had about three months' bread at half allowance. There was no port on this coast where we could procure a supply, without a certainty of capture, or blockade (which I considered as bad); to attempt to return to the United States at a season of the year when our coast would be swarming with the enemy's cruisers, would be running too much risk, and would be going

---

[1] *Porter's Journal*, i, 56, ff.

diametrically opposite to my instructions. I was perfectly at loss now where to find the commodore, as, in remaining before Bahia, he had departed from his original intentions, and had already disappointed me at three rendezvous. The state of my provisions would not admit of going off St. Helena's to intercept the returning Indiamen, nor would my force justify the proceeding. . . . I, therefore, determined to pursue that course which seemed to be best calculated to injure the enemy and would enable me to prolong my cruise. This could only be done by going into a friendly port, where I could increase my supplies without the danger of blockade, and the first place that presented itself to my mind was the port of Concepcion on the coast of Chile. The season was, to be sure, far advanced for doubling Cape Horn; our stock of provisions was short, and the ship in other respects not well supplied with stores for so long a cruise; but there appeared no other choice left to me except capture, starvation or blockade.''

Accordingly he put all hands on half rations and steered for the Cape. After a rough three weeks spent in beating against the storms for which Cape Horn is famous, the *Essex* turned northward again, the first American man-of-war to weather the Horn or to enter the Pacific. It happened by an odd coincidence that this little vessel had been also the first American man-of-war to round the Cape of Good Hope. [2]

On March 13, 1813, Captain Porter dropped his anchor in the harbor of Valparaiso,[3] and proceeded at once to replenish his exhausted stores. The Chilean Government treated him with courtesy, for, being at that time already

---

[2] In 1800, under Captain Edward Preble.

[3] Porter was prevented from carrying out his original intention of entering Concepcion by a gale that drove him so far north of that port that he made for Valparaiso instead.

David Porter

The Cruise of the Essex

in revolt against Spain, it did not profess an alliance with England, as did the still loyal colonies of Spain and Portugal. Peru, for example, was so zealous in England's cause that she had already commissioned several privateers to prey on the returning American whalers.

While lying at Valparaiso, Captain Porter learned from an American whaler that there were likely to be many English whalers in the vicinity of Galapagos Islands, a noted whaling rendezvous about five hundred miles west of Ecuador, and that the presence of the *Essex* in that neighborhood would serve also to give warning and protection to home-bound American vessels, whose masters were still ignorant of the fact that war had broken out. Acting on this information, as soon as he had finished storing ship (March 20), Captain Porter left Valparaiso for the Galapagos, skirting, *en route*, the coast line of Chile and Peru, looking for a Peruvian privateer which he heard had captured two American whalers. In a few days he succeeded in finding and capturing the privateer, whose captain, on demand, furnished a list and description of all the British whalers he knew in those waters. Two days later, he recaptured the *Barclay*, one of the two American ships taken by the privateer. After this, he sailed direct for the Galapagos Islands, arriving there on the 17th of April.

While cruising in this neighborhood, the *Essex* captured six ships, carrying in all eighty guns and 340 men. Finding himself burdened with prisoners and prizes, which were too far from any American port to send home, Porter took his squadron to the coast to land his prisoners and dispose of some of his prizes. He touched first at Tumbez, a town at the mouth of the Tumbez River, in the Gulf of Guayaquil, Ecuador. There he put the largest of the prizes, the *Atlantic*, mounting twenty light guns, under the command of the first lieutenant, Master-Commandant

Downes, and renamed her the *Essex Junior.* To another prize, the *Greenwich,* he transferred all the supplies he had taken from his captures and made her thereafter the store ship of his squadron.

Having completed these arrangements, Porter returned to the Galapagos in the *Essex,* accompanied by the *Greenwich,* and a prize ship of 16 guns, the *Georgiana.* The remaining prizes he sent to Valparaiso under the escort of the *Essex Junior.* By this time he had captured so many vessels that he was compelled to draw on the midshipmen for prize masters, and in the trip from Tumbez to Valparaiso, he put the ship *Barclay,* with her ex-captain retained on board to help navigate her, under the command of Midshipman Farragut, then not quite twelve years old. At the very outset, the lad was compelled to settle the question of command with the big whaler, who swore that he would take the *Barclay* to New Zealand instead of Valparaiso, and went below to get his pistols. The other vessels of the squadron were by this time too far away to communicate with, but Farragut, after telling his right-hand man of the prize crew what the situation was, shouted down the cabin ladder that if the whaler came up with his pistols he did so at the risk of going overboard. Finding that the crew were ready to stand by their young commander, the ex-captain had to give in. From that moment Farragut was master of the situation, and navigated the *Barclay* without mishap to Valparaiso.

Captain Porter continued to make valuable captures in the neighborhood of the Galapagos, and by the end of September, when he was rejoined by the *Essex Junior,* he had captured nearly every English ship on the southern coast. Master-Commandant Downes, on his arrival, brought the news from Valparaiso that the 36-gun frigate *Phœbe* and the sloops *Cherub* and *Raccoon* were on their

The Cruise of the Essex

way round the Horn. Porter looked forward to an opportunity of trying the *Essex* against the *Phœbe*, but his ship was in great need of overhauling. Accordingly, he set sail with his squadron for the Marquesas Islands, where he could dismantle his ship without fear of being disturbed by a British man-of-war.

While the squadron lay at Nukahiva, one of the Marquesas Islands, the work of refitting was interrupted by a lively campaign on shore in defense of the coast tribe, which had received them with hospitality, against hostile tribes of the interior. On the 12th of December, 1813, the overhauling of the *Essex* was completed. Captain Porter left Lieutenant Gamble [4] of the marines with three midshipmen and twenty-six men in charge of a small battery, under which the four prizes were moored; and made sail for Valparaiso, accompanied by the *Essex Junior*. He hoped now to meet an English man-of-war of equal force, and conclude his commerce-destroying cruise with the capture of a frigate.

The results of this famous cruise, Captain Porter summarized in his report to the Secretary of the Navy, as follows: [5]

"I had completely broken up the British navigation in the Pacific; the vessels which had not been captured by me were laid up and dared not venture out. I had afforded the most ample protection to our own vessels, which were, on my arrival, very numerous and unprotected. The valuable whale fishery there [of the British] is entirely destroyed, and the actual injury we have done

---

[4] A mutiny broke out shortly afterwards. Lieutenant Gamble escaped with his life and eventually made his way to one of the Sandwich Islands, and was captured afterwards by the *Cherub*. The mutineers were British deserters in the crew of the *Essex* aided by six prisoners.

[5] *Porter's Journal*, ii, 161.

them may be estimated at two and a half million dollars, independent of the expenses of vessels sent in search of me. They have supplied me amply with sails, cordage, cables, anchors, provisions, medicines, and stores of every description—and the slops on board them have furnished clothing for the seamen. We have, in fact, lived on the enemy since I have been in that sea; every prize having proved a well-found store ship for me. I have not yet been under the necessity of drawing bills on the Department for any object, and have been enabled to make considerable advances to my officers and crew on account of pay. For the unexampled time we have kept at sea, my crew have continued remarkably healthy.''

On the way to the mainland, Captain Porter kept his men exercised daily at gun and sword drills in anticipation of meeting the *Phœbe*. On February 3, 1814, the *Essex* and the *Essex Junior* reached Valparaiso. Five days later, the *Phœbe* and the *Cherub* came in together. The *Raccoon* had previously parted company from her consorts and headed north. What happened between the two forces is graphically told by Farragut in his journal.[6]

"In January, 1814, we arrived off the coast of Chile. After looking into Concepcion, we ran down to Valparaiso, where we lay until the arrival of the British frigate *Phœbe* and sloop of war *Cherub*. This occurred early in February. The frigate mounted thirty long 18-pounders, sixteen 32-pounder carronades, one howitzer, and six 3-pounders in the tops, with a crew of 320 men. The *Cherub* had eighteen 32-pounder carronades, eight 24-pounders, two long nines, and a crew of 180 men.

" When they made their appearance off the port, our whole watch, being a third of our crew, were on shore on liberty. The mate of an English merchantman, which

---

[6] Loyall Farragut, *Life of David Glasgow Farragut*, p. 32, ff.

The Arrival of the British Ships

was lying in port at the time, went immediately on board the *Phœbe*, and stated to Captain Hillyar that one-half of our men were on shore and that the *Essex* would fall an easy prey. The two ships then hauled into the harbor on a wind. The *Phœbe* made our larboard quarter, but the *Cherub* fell to leeward about half a mile. On gaining

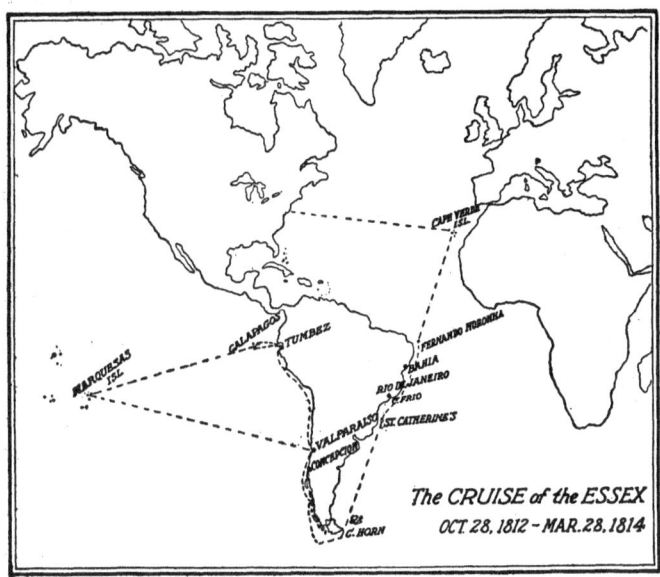

The Cruise of the Essex, Oct. 28, 1812—Mar. 28, 1814

our quarter, the *Phœbe* put her helm down, and luffed up on our starboard bow, coming within ten or fifteen feet of the *Essex*.

"I should say here, that as soon as the enemy hove in sight, we fired a gun and hoisted a cornet for all boats and men to return, and in fifteen minutes every man was at his quarters, and but one was under the influence of liquor, he a mere boy. When the *Phœbe*, as before mentioned, was close alongside, and all hands were at quarters, the powder-boys stationed with slow matches ready to discharge the guns, the boarders, cutlass in hand, standing by to board in the smoke, as was our custom at close quarters, the intoxicated youth saw, or imagined that he saw, through the port, some one on the *Phœbe* grinning at him. 'My fine fellow, I'll stop your making faces,' he exclaimed, and was just about to fire his gun, when Lieutenant McKnight saw the movement and with a blow sprawled him on the deck. Had that gun been fired, I am convinced that the *Phœbe* would have been ours. But it was destined to be otherwise. We were all at quarters and cleared for action, waiting with breathless anxiety for the command from Captain Porter to board, when the English captain (Hillyar) appeared, standing on the after gun in a pea-jacket, and in plain hearing said:

" 'Captain Hillyar's compliments to Captain Porter, and hopes he is well.'

"Porter replied, 'Very well, I thank you; but I hope you will not come too near, for fear some accident might take place which would be disagreeable to you,' and with a wave of his trumpet the kedge anchors went up to our yard-arms, ready to grapple the enemy.

"Captain Hillyar braced back his yards and remarked to Porter that if he did fall aboard him, he begged to assure the captain that it would be entirely accidental.

" 'Well,' said Porter, 'you have no business where you are. *If you touch a rope-yarn of this ship, I shall board instantly.*' He then hailed the *Essex Junior,* and told Captain Downes to be prepared to repel the enemy.

"But our desire for a fight was not yet to be gratified. The *Phœbe* backed down, her yards passed over ours, not touching a rope, and she anchored about half a mile astern. We thus lost an opportunity of taking her, though we had observed the strict neutrality of the port under very aggravating circumstances.

The Arrival of the British Ships 183

"We remained together in the harbor for some days, when the British vessels, having completed their provisioning and watering, went to sea and commenced a regular blockade of our ships. One night we manned all our boats for the purpose of boarding the enemy outside. The captain in his boat, with muffled oars, pulled so close up to the *Phœbe* that he could hear the conversation of the men on her forecastle, and thereby learned that they were lying at their quarters prepared for us; so the attempt was given up, and we returned on board.

"It was understood in our ship, one day, that Captain Porter had sent word to Captain Hillyar that, if he would send the *Cherub* to the leeward point of the harbor, he would go out and fight him. We all believed the terms would be accepted, and everything was kept in readiness to get under way. Soon after, the *Phœbe* was seen standing in with her motto flag flying, on which was *God and our Country! British Sailors' Best Rights!* This was in answer to Porter's flag, *Free Trade and Sailors' Rights!* She fired a gun to windward, and the *Cherub* was seen running to leeward. In five minutes our anchor was up, and under topsails and jib we cleared for action—in fact, we were always ready for that. When within two miles of our position, the *Phœbe* bore up and set her studding-sails. This I considered a second breach of faith on the part of Hillyar; for, by his maneuvers in both instances, it was evident that he was either wanting in courage or lacked the good faith of a high-toned chivalrous spirit to carry out his original intention. However, as Captain Hillyar subsequently proved himself a brave man, in more than one instance, I shall not deny him that common characteristic of a naval officer, and have attributed his action on these two occasions to a want of good faith. He was dealing with a far inferior force and it was ignoble in the extreme, on his part, not to meet his foe, when he had the ghost of an excuse for doing so, ship to ship.

"On the 28th of March, 1814, it came on to blow from the south, and we parted our larboard cable, dragging the starboard anchor leeward; we immediately got under way and made sail on the ship. The enemy's vessels were close in with the weathermost point of the bay; but Captain Porter thought we could weather them, so we hauled up for that purpose, and took in our topgallant sails, which had been set over close reefed topsails. But scarcely had the topgallant sails been clewed down, when a squall struck the ship and, though the topsail halyards were let go, the yards jammed, and would not come down. When the ship was nearly gunwale under, the maintopmast went by the board, carrying the men who were on the maintopgallant yard into the sea, and they were drowned. We immediately wore ship and attempted to regain the harbor; but, owing to the disaster, were unable to do so; therefore we anchored in a small bay, about a quarter of a mile off shore and three-quarters of a mile from the small battery.

"But it was evident, from the preparations being made by the enemy, that he intended to attack us; so we made arrangements to receive him as well as we possibly could. Springs [7] were got on our cables, and the ship was perfectly prepared for action.

"I well remember the feelings of awe produced in me by the approach of the hostile ships; even to my young mind it was perceptible in the faces of those around me,

---

[7] A spring is a rope taken from the stern of a ship to an anchor off the bow. By hauling on it the crew can turn or "wind" the ship in the desired direction without having to depend on sail power. In this action the springs were bent to the anchor cable instead of to the ring of the anchor itself, an unfortunate arrangement which exposed them to the enemy's fire.

The Action with the Phœbe and Cherub

as clearly as possible, that our case was hopeless. It was equally apparent that all were ready to die at their guns rather than surrender; and such I believe to have been the determination of the crew almost to a man. There had been so much bantering of each other among the men of the ships, through the medium of letters and songs, with an invariable fight between the boats' crews when they met on shore, that a very hostile sentiment was engendered. Our flags were flying from every mast, and the enemy's vessels displayed their ensigns, jacks, and motto flags, as they bore down grandly to the attack.

"At 3.54 P.M. they commenced firing; the *Phœbe* under our stern, and the *Cherub* on our starboard bow. But the latter, finding out pretty soon that we had too many guns bearing on her, likewise ran under our stern. We succeeded in getting three long guns out of the stern ports, and kept up as well directed a fire as possible in such an unequal contest.

"In half an hour they were both compelled to haul off to repair damages. During this period of the fight, we had succeeded three times in getting springs on our cables, but in each instance they were shot away as soon as they were hauled taut. Notwithstanding the incessant firing from both of the enemy's ships, we had, so far, suffered less than might have been expected, considering that we could bring but three guns to oppose two broadsides. We had many men killed in the first five or ten minutes of their fire, before we could bring our stern guns to bear.

"The enemy soon repaired damages, and renewed the attack, both ships taking position on our larboard quarter, out of reach of our carronades, and where the stern guns could not be brought to bear. They then kept up a most galling fire, which we were powerless to return. At this juncture the captain ordered the cable to be cut, and, after ineffectual attempts, we succeeded in getting sail on the ship, having found that the flying jib-halyards were in a condition to hoist that sail. It was the only serviceable rope that had not been shot away. By this means we were able to close with the enemy, and the firing now became fearful on both sides. The *Cherub* was compelled to haul out, and never came into close action again, though she lay off and used her long guns greatly to our discomfort, making a perfect target of us. The *Phœbe* also, was enabled, by the better condition of her sails, to choose her own distance, suitable for her long guns, and kept up a most destructive fire on our helpless ship.

" 'Finding,' as Captain Porter says, 'the impossibility of closing with the *Phœbe*,' he determined to run his ship ashore and destroy her. We accordingly stood for the land, but when we were within half a mile of the bluffs the wind suddenly shifted, took us flat aback, and paid our head off shore. We were thus again exposed to a galling fire from the *Phœbe*. At this moment Captain Downes of the *Essex Junior* came on board to receive his orders, being under the impression that our ship would soon be captured, as the enemy at that time were raking us, while we could not bring a gun to bear, and his vessel was in no condition to be of service to us.

"Captain Porter now ordered a hawser to be bent on to the sheet anchor and let go. This brought our ship's head around, and we were in hopes that the *Phœbe* would drift out of gun shot, as the sea was nearly calm; but the hawser broke, and we were again at the mercy of the enemy. The ship was now reported to be on fire, and the men came rushing up from below, many with their clothes burning, which were torn from them as quickly as possible, and those from whom this could not be done were told to jump overboard and quench the flames. Many of

The Action with the Phœbe and Cherub

the crew, and even some of the officers, hearing the order to jump overboard, took it for granted that the fire had reached the magazine, and that the ship was about to blow up; so they leaped into the water and attempted to reach the shore, about three-quarters of a mile distant, in which effort a number were drowned.

"The captain sent for the commissioned officers, to consult with them the propriety of further resistance; but first went below to ascertain the quantity of powder in the magazine. On his return to the deck, he met Lieutenant McKnight,[8] the only commissioned officer left on duty, all the others having been killed or wounded. As it was pretty evident that the ship was in a sinking condition, it was determined to surrender, in order to save the wounded, and at 6.30 P.M. the painful order was given to haul down the colors."

In this action, the *Essex* lost fifty-eight killed, sixty-six wounded, and thirty-one missing. Most of the last were probably drowned in the attempt to swim ashore. If the number of the missing is included, this is the heaviest loss sustained by any American vessel during the war. The British reported four killed and seven wounded on the *Phœbe;* and one killed and three wounded on the *Cherub*. Among the killed on the *Phœbe* was Captain Hillyar's first lieutenant, Ingram, who, it is said, begged his captain to close with the *Essex*, saying that it was

---

[8] The loss of the *Essex* is linked with the tragedy of the *Wasp*. After the battle in Valparaiso, Lieutenant Stephen Decatur McKnight and Midshipman James Lyman were exchanged against a number of Englishmen in one of the *Essex's* prizes that remained in port, and these officers consented to go in the *Phœbe* to Rio to testify before the prize court in behalf of the *Phœbe's* prize claims. Afterwards they embarked in a Swedish brig sailing for England. On October 9, 1814, the brig fell in with the *Wasp*, in mid ocean. The two officers were transferred to her, and she was never heard from again.

deliberate murder to lie off at long range and fire into the Americans like a target, when they were unable to return the fire. Hillyar, however, naturally preferred to make the capture at least cost to himself.

The result was conclusive as to the folly of arming a frigate's main deck with carronades. Porter himself had protested, on taking command, and begged to be allowed to substitute long guns, but the Department refused. It may fairly be said that the country owes the loss of the *Essex* to this refusal.[9]

Though the British captain showed Captain Porter and the survivors of the American crew every consideration, as Porter freely admits, the latter could not but feel a bitter resentment over Hillyar's attacking him in neutral waters. This was particularly hard to endure after Porter's forbearance when the *Phœbe* came into the harbor with the evident intention of taking the *Essex* by surprise. Captain Hillyar's conduct, however, was in keeping with the policy of those days, common to Napoleon and to the British Government alike, which recognized neutral rights only when it was convenient.

Like another famous commerce-destroyer, the Confederate cruiser *Alabama*, the *Essex* was not taken till after she had struck her blow. By destroying British commerce in the Pacific she did far more to hurt the enemy than she could have done by the capture of a frigate; for in 1814 England had frigates to spare, but her merchantmen were her very means of existence.

---

[9] The armament of the *Essex* in her action with the British ships consisted of forty 32-lb. carronades and six long 12's.

XII

BATTLE OF LAKE CHAMPLAIN AND THE CONCLUSION OF THE WAR

Operations on Lake Ontario

On Lake Ontario the shipbuilding contest between Sir James Lucas Yeo and Captain Isaac Chauncey, referred to in a previous chapter, continued. At the beginning of the summer of 1814, each had four ships and four brigs. This contest in building went on with the nicety of a mathematical problem. When one commander had a slight superiority, the second hid in port until he could build enough to outstrip the other. Then the second sallied forth, and the first took his turn in port. Both were overcautious.

During the previous spring, Yeo had managed to get to sea some time before Chauncey, and at once made a successful attack (May 5) on Oswego, destroying the barracks and sailing away with the *Growler*, together with heavy ordnance and supplies. The British, however, did not pursue their advantage, but, instead, now blockaded the American commodore at Sackett's Harbor, where he was doing his best in hurrying forward the heavy guns for his new ships. On June 5, Yeo raised the blockade; and Chauncey, on July 31, took the lake, only to find that the British commander had shut himself up at Kingston to await the completion of a ship-of-the-line then building.

When Major-General Brown asked the co-operation of Chauncey in the offensive campaign against Canada, the latter, who had rendered valuable assistance the year before in the attacks on Forts George and York, objected on the plea that he had his hands full in attempting the "capture and destruction of the enemy's fleet." This was, of course, his immediate duty; and if he had accomplished it, General Brown's mission on the Niagara peninsula would have received the kind of co-operation it most needed. But Chauncey's cautious and dilatory tactics gained nothing for himself, or for the American cause anywhere. It was the opinion of Winfield Scott that if the British had not had free access to the lake, Lundy's Lane, instead of being a drawn battle, might have been a victory so decisive as to have turned the scales of war. The Americans soon found themselves, instead of taking the offensive against Canada, forced to prepare for a threatened invasion through Lake Champlain.[1]

BATTLE OF LAKE CHAMPLAIN

Although the condition of affairs on the Great Lakes remained unchanged during the year 1814, events of the greatest importance were taking place on Lake Champlain. This lake had not hitherto played a part in the war at all commensurate with its important position. With Lake George and the Hudson River it formed a series of water connections from the source of American supplies at New York to what should have been the true objective of an offensive war on the Canadian border, Montreal. The British, naturally on the defensive in Canada, had paid no heed to this waterway during the early years of the war, and the Americans, in their efforts, under Hull and Dearborn, to concentrate their attention on the Northwest, had neglected their opportunity. Hence we find little or no mention of Lake Champlain until June, 1813. As three of the armed sloops here were American, against one

---

[1] Mahan, *War of 1812*, ii, 306–311.

Thomas Macdonough

Rivalry for Control 191

British, the former could sail where they pleased, while the British remained at their base in the lower narrows, at Isle aux Noix. On June 2, 1813, two of the American sloops, the *Eagle* and the *Growler,* while approaching too near the British garrison at the narrows, were raked from the shore and captured. The British now followed up their advantage. Captain Everard, of the British sloop *Wasp,* lying at Quebec, volunteered with some of his men to make a raid on the lake. He destroyed the public building at Plattsburg and the barracks at Saranac, and captured some small vessels, while Macdonough, the American commander on the lake, taken utterly by surprise, and helpless because of the loss of his two vessels, had to sit by and look on. Everard hurried back, and with Captain Pring stirred up the authorities to building ships at once on Lake Champlain.

Now began a contest in shipbuilding like the rivalry on the Great Lakes, and it continued until the fall of 1814. Macdonough had already established his base at Plattsburg, and had all his vessels, except the *Eagle,* ready by the latter part of May. He could then range the lake at will and bring stores from Burlington, while the British were awaiting the completion of their most powerful ship, the *Confiance,* which was not launched until August 25. Captain Downie took command of the British flotilla on September 2, and in response to the goading of the Governor-General of Canada, hurried the equipment of his vessels to the utmost in order to co-operate with Prevost's invading army. By this time, the American flotilla consisted of the ship *Saratoga,* 26; the brig *Eagle,* 20; the schooner *Ticonderoga,* 17; the sloop *Preble,* 7; and about ten row-galleys or gunboats: in all fourteen vessels, with 882 men, eighty-six guns, and total broadside of 1194 pounds, 714 from short and 480 from long guns.

On the other hand, the British had the *Confiance* (rated after her capture in our navy as a frigate), mounting twenty-seven long 24-pounders, of which one was a pivot gun and thus available for both broadsides, and ten carronades; they had, besides, the brig *Linnet*, 16; the *Chub*, 11; the *Finch*, 11; and about twelve gunboats: in all, sixteen vessels, with 937 men, ninety-two guns, and total broadside of 1192 pounds, 532 from short and 660 from long guns. Thus the superiority was on the British side. The *Confiance* had an approximate tonnage of 1200, as against the *Saratoga's* 734 tons. "The two largest British vessels, *Confiance* and *Linnet*, were slightly inferior to the American *Saratoga* and *Eagle* in aggregate weight of broadside; but, like the *General Pike* on Ontario in 1813, the superiority of the *Confiance* in long guns, and under one captain, would on the open lake have made her practically equal to cope with the whole American squadron, and still more with the *Saratoga* alone, assuming that the *Linnet* gave the *Eagle* some occupation." [2]

A British army of 11,000 men, part of four brigades recently sent from Wellington's Peninsular veterans to Canada, was slowly marching, under the command of Sir George Prevost, Governor-General of Canada, up the western side of Lake Champlain. The American general, Izard, had been ordered to proceed with most of the troops at Plattsburg to Sackett's Harbor, leaving General Macomb with scarcely 2000 men to meet the invaders. Prevost kept urging Downie to set sail, so as to co-operate with him in the attack on Plattsburg. The Governor-General drove Macomb across the Saranac, which divides Plattsburg, and then he sat down and waited for Downie. The latter thus had to offer battle prematurely to Macdonough; but although the British flotilla was somewhat

---

[2] Mahan, *War of 1812*, ii, 371.

Rivalry for Control

handicapped by this haste, the American vessels were likewise not yet fully prepared. The crews of both flotillas had had little time for that training necessary to organized effort. The locks of some of the guns of the *Confiance* were useless, and similar difficulties presented themselves on the American vessels. But in these disadvantages, the opposing fleets were equally handicapped.

Macdonough, though only thirty years old, had made preparations for battle worthy of a much older head. The mouth of Plattsburg Bay, where the engagement took place, extends from Cumberland Head southwestward to the shoals of Crab Island. When Downie's fleet, early on the morning of September 11, was known to have set sail under a northeast wind, Macdonough anchored his ships in a line across the entrance of Plattsburg Bay, the larger vessels off Cumberland Head, in the following order: *Eagle, Saratoga, Ticonderoga,* and *Preble;* the gunboats he drew up in a line forty yards behind. Thus the heavier vessels at Cumberland Head, and the shoals at Crab Island, would check any attempt at turning Macdonough's flanks. The enemy, in a channel too narrow to beat, would have to approach bows on, close to the wind, while the Americans had the weather-gage for easy maneuvering. Besides, in case of failure of wind, or for presenting a new broadside quickly at the same berth, Macdonough had provided his vessels with springs.

The British naval commander, who could plainly see across the narrow Cumberland Head Macdonough's formation, planned his own line accordingly. The *Confiance* was to round the point, fire a broadside at the *Eagle* at the upper end of the line, and then come to anchor across the bows of the *Saratoga*. The *Chub* and the *Linnet* were then to anchor off the *Eagle's* bow and stern, and the *Finch*, assisted by the British gunboats, was to oppose the *Ticonderoga* and the *Preble*.

As Downie rounded Cumberland Head, he was surprised to find no co-operation from Prevost, but he nevertheless bravely adhered to his part of the attack. The *Confiance* laboriously made for the upper end of the

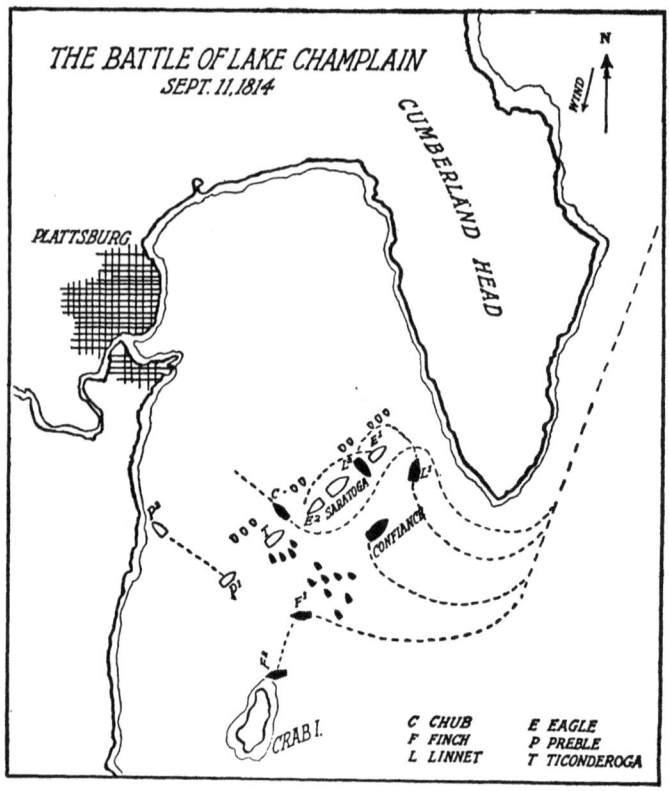

THE BATTLE OF LAKE CHAMPLAIN, SEPT. 11, 1814

American line, but under the concentrated fire from Macdonough's vessels and the shifting winds, she was compelled to abandon her first plan of going to the head of the line, and she came to anchor some 500 yards to the east of the *Saratoga*. Both port bow-anchors of the

Battle of Lake Champlain 195

British flagship had meanwhile been shot away, and a ball from one of the *Saratoga's* long 24-pounders, fired by Macdonough himself, struck the *Confiance* near the hawse-hole, killing and wounding several men in its course along the length of the deck. Downie, who coolly made fast his ship before he fired a gun, now, at about nine o'clock, fired a deadly broadside which is said to have killed or wounded one-fifth of the *Saratoga's* crew.

Meanwhile the *Linnet* and the *Chub* had engaged the *Eagle*. The *Chub*, before she could anchor, received considerable damage to her sails and rigging; and, with her commander wounded, she drifted helplessly through Macdonough's line, where an American midshipman took charge of her. The *Linnet*, having anchored to windward of the *Eagle*, kept pouring a diagonal fire into the American vessel. After standing the broadsides of the *Linnet* and part of the fire of the *Confiance*, the *Eagle* at 10.30 cut her cables and slipped down to a position between the *Saratoga* and the *Ticonderoga*. In this way she brought her fresh broadside into play against the *Confiance* without exposure to shots from either the *Confiance* or the *Linnet*. The *Eagle's* change of berth gave the *Linnet* an opportunity, after some slight skirmishing with the American gunboats, to shift her anchorage to a raking position off the *Saratoga's* bows.

At the southern end of the American line, the *Finch* and some of the British gunboats were attacking the *Ticonderoga* and the *Preble*. As the *Finch* did not keep near enough to the wind, she failed to reach the position assigned to her abreast the *Ticonderoga*, nor could she gain it later when the wind died down. Silenced by a few broadsides from the American schooner, she drifted on the shoals at Crab Island, where a 6-pounder mounted on shore forced her finally to surrender. Although some of the British gunboats kept at a safe distance from their enemy's long guns and later ingloriously fled, four pressed forward to attack with desperate courage. The little *Preble* was obliged to cut her cable and take refuge under the American shore batteries at Plattsburg. As the American gunboats were too light to be of much assistance, the *Ticonderoga* was left practically unsupported, but her commander, Lieutenant Cassin, handled his schooner with marked ability. Heedless of the great danger from musketry and grape, he directed the fight from the taffrail, and gave the close-approaching gunboats loads of canister that finally drove them off, though not till some of them had got within a boat's length of their foe.

At the head of the line, where the main fighting took place, the contest dwindled down to one between the *Saratoga* and *Eagle* on the American side, and the *Confiance* and *Linnet* on the British. The vessels were firing at stationary targets, at point-blank range, and in smooth water, and under such conditions even inexperienced crews could inflict terrible damage. Downie was killed early in the action, and his death was a great loss to the British side. Gradually, owing to the inexperience and lack of longer training of the crews, confusion became apparent in both flotillas. The American sailors, when their officers were killed or wounded, overloaded the carronades, and thus destroyed the effectiveness of these guns. On the *Confiance* the quoins were gradually loosened by the heavy firing, and as this error was not rectified, her guns kept shooting higher and higher. Such confusion reigned at times on the British flagship, that the gunners rammed home shot without any powder, or cartridges without any shot. The first broadside of the *Confiance*, before Captain Downie was killed, had been directed with deadly precision, but the later confusion

Battle of Lake Champlain 197

showed the need of that organization and co-operation which are necessary to make crew and officers a unit in action.

The damage aboard the *Saratoga* was also great, nearly her whole starboard battery having been rendered useless; but it was at this crisis that Macdonough's foresight and preparation were able to bring into play the unused guns of his vessel. By means of the springs previously prepared for just such a contingency, he now winded his ship, and thus brought to bear her fresh broadside. The British tried to do the same, and as the *Confiance's* stern anchor had been shot away, Lieutenant Robertson tried to wind her by a spring from the bow. The attempt was not successful, and the flagship hung with her bow to the wind, affording the *Saratoga* an excellent opportunity to rake. With the British vessel's hold partly full of water, and a crew that refused to work the guns any longer, Robertson, in his exposed position, was compelled to strike his colors. This was at about eleven o'clock. Macdonough at once, by means of his springs, again turned his ship so that her broadside would bear on the *Linnet*, and after fifteen minutes forced Captain Pring also to strike. At just this time the *Ticonderoga* was ending her fight with the gunboats.

The battle had been fought with the greatest obstinacy on both sides. The *Saratoga* had been hulled by round shot fifty-five times, and the *Confiance* 105 times. The *Eagle* and the *Linnet* also were badly shattered. The number of killed and wounded on the American side was approximately 200; that of the British, 300. The greatest praise is due to Macdonough for this signal victory; in the careful choice of his position and in the thorough preparations for battle, he had shown unusual skill and judgment. In addition to these qualities, Macdonough possessed indomitable courage. "Down to the time of the Civil War he is the greatest figure in our naval history."[3]

The results of the battle of Lake Champlain were of the highest importance. Prevost's army at once fled in confusion back to Canada, thus abandoning the policy of the British Government for an offensive war. It had also a decisive effect on the pending peace negotiations in forcing England to relinquish her claim to American territory.

Concluding Events of the War

The battle of Lake Champlain practically ended the war. The Treaty of Ghent was signed on December 24, 1814, but, owing to the slowness of means of communication in those days, it was not ratified by our Government until February 17, 1815. Since it had been expressly stipulated that hostilities were not to cease until ratification, and since it was difficult to get news of peace to vessels cruising in distant waters, several important battles took place after the signing and even after the ratification of the treaty. These included one land battle, New Orleans; and several naval engagements, the capture of the *President* by the British blockading squadron off New York, the battle between the *Constitution* and the *Cyane* and *Levant*, and the sloop action between the *Hornet* and the *Penguin*.

The part of the navy in the battle of New Orleans was small; yet the aid of the *Carolina* in attacking the invaders on December 23, 1814, and the assistance rendered by the crew of the *Louisiana*, with its naval battery mounted ashore so as to enfilade the troops of the enemy, on January 1, 1815, showed of what excellent use even a trifling naval force can be.

---

[3] Roosevelt, *Naval War of 1812*, p. 399.

Loss of the President

The frigate *President,* lying in New York harbor, had, in May, 1814, been transferred to Captain Stephen Decatur, who had brought with him the crew from his former command, the *United States,* then hopelessly blockaded at New London. As a formidable force under Admiral Cochrane and General Ross was now threatening our coast, the citizens of New York and Philadelphia were anxious that Decatur should remain in the vicinity.

This, and the fact that a vigilant blockading fleet was outside, kept the *President* shut up in New York until the night of January 14, 1815, when, in a bad northwester, she slipped out of the harbor, but unfortunately went aground in the channel. After considerable effort, the *President* cleared the bar, damaged so badly that her former speediness was gone. To add to her misfortune, she ran at five o'clock next morning into the blockading fleet, under Captain Hayes, consisting of the razee *Majestic,* 56, and the 38-gun frigates *Endymion, Pomone,* and *Tenedos.* In the fierce gale, the British vessels were scattered, and Captain Hayes had not yet succeeded in getting his ships together.

While Captain Hayes was directing his attention to a suspicious sail to the south, which turned out to be his own frigate, the *Tenedos,* the *Endymion* started a chase of the *President* which lasted until nearly midnight of the fifteenth. Decatur steered his course eastward, parallel to the shore of Long Island. The *Endymion,* by constantly yawing, was able to bring her broadsides to bear without losing distance. Decatur endured this fire for a half hour, and then suddenly putting his helm to port headed south, with intent to cross the *Endymion's* bows. But the latter imitated the maneuver, and the two ships, on parallel courses, exchanged broadsides until Decatur had accomplished his purpose, which was to strip his pursuer's sails from the spars and thus prevent further pursuit. The *President* now, with even studding-sails set, continued her course, but although the *Endymion* was badly crippled, Decatur's maneuver had given the *Pomone* and the *Tenedos* a chance to overtake him. At eleven P.M., the American commander surrendered without firing another broadside.

CAPTURE OF THE CYANE AND LEVANT

The *Constitution*, Captain Stewart, after a long blockade in Boston harbor, managed, in December, 1814, to get to sea. Some 200 miles northeast of Madeira, on February 20, 1815, she sighted two vessels, which later were found to be the frigate *Cyane*, 32, and the sloop of war *Levant*, of 20 guns. When first seen, the British ships were ten miles apart, but in spite of the light easterly wind, they gradually joined each other, and were only 100 yards apart when they attacked the *Constitution*. At 6.05 P.M. the American vessel, being to windward, at 300 yards' distance, opened with her guns. The wind was so light that in the enveloping smoke the antagonists had to cease firing at times to see where they were. Stewart, with remarkable nimbleness, not only avoided being raked himself, but managed to wear the *Constitution* so adroitly that he raked both British vessels several times. The *Cyane* struck at 6.50. Stewart now set out in pursuit of the *Levant*, which had withdrawn while a prize crew was taking possession of the *Cyane;* but at 8.50 P.M. the plucky little *Levant* wore, and on opposite tacks the vessels exchanged broadsides. Stewart, by another quick turn, raked the *Levant* from the stern. The British vessel now sought safety in flight, but at ten P.M. the *Constitution* overtook and captured her. The divided force of the enemy in this engagement was in the *Constitution's* favor, but it was especially the quick and skilful maneuvering of Captain Stewart that won the battle. The *Constitution* and the *Cyane* later escaped from a British squadron and safely reached the United States, but the *Levant* was recaptured.

PRIVATEERING

At least a passing consideration should be given to the very important service of the American privateers, although, strictly speaking, they had no place in our navy. Privateering, especially towards the end of the war, was a favorite way of harrying British trade. By diverting large numbers of seamen, it weakened the regular navy; and as the results were far less than might have been secured by men-of-war, it seems from our point of view to have been of doubtful advantage. Yet our country, when it awoke to the fact that it had entered upon hostilities wretchedly prepared, welcomed assistance from private enterprise. Privateering was profitable business to those who succeeded, and it must be admitted commercial instinct quite as often as patriotism was the impelling motive. There were about 500 of these vessels, and they captured or destroyed 1350 British ships.

RESULTS OF THE WAR

The treaty signed at Ghent on December 24, 1814, was silent regarding the two great issues of the war, impressment and illegal seizures under the Orders in Council. The orders had been repealed before war was declared by the United States, and though Great Britain stoutly maintained her prescriptive right to impressment, she did not later continue her practice in this regard. On the other hand, the British made concessions in the treaty that were hard for them to yield. On the strength of their possession, in 1814, of Forts Mackinac and Niagara, and of the country east of the Penobscot, England had at first laid claim to the surrender of some of our territory. The British also had sought to make military barriers of the Great Lakes, which thenceforth should be controlled by Great Britain and used by Americans only for commercial purposes. Further, they had laid claim to some of our territory in the Northwest for an independent Indian state. In the face of a possible European war, however, and more particularly by reason of Prevost's precipitous retreat to Canada, the British gave up these territorial demands, and the American position, no grant of territory whatever, was incorporated in the treaty. Moreover, to avoid future complications, the treaty provided for the adjustment of the boundary as far as the Lake of the Woods in Minnesota. Both parties also pledged themselves to use every effort to stamp out the slave trade.

The war had an excellent effect in firing anew the spirit of patriotism in the young nation, and in promoting respect abroad. The narrow selfishness of many of the merchant classes and the hostile attitude of New England to the war, had given way to a stronger national unity and a broader patriotism. The navy had contributed in no small degree to bringing about this result. While battles were being lost on land, the brilliant feats of the navy kept up the courage of our people. Although Great Britain with her thousand vessels might little miss the loss of a few frigates, still the ship-duels of this war brought the navy, and consequently the country, a world-wide respect.

XIII

MINOR OPERATIONS

THE WAR WITH ALGIERS

THE war with Tripoli had put an end to all paying of tribute by the United States to that principality, but ever since the treaty of 1795 we had been sending annual tribute to the Dey of Algiers. The return of the *Hornet* to the United States, in 1807, left the Mediterranean without a single American man-of-war; and after the *Leopard* incident in 1807 the American Navy was confined so closely to home waters, on account of impending war with Great Britain, that one year succeeded another without the appearance of an American cruiser before Algiers. Encouraged by this situation, the Dey seized three American merchantmen, late in 1807, on the excuse that his tribute of naval stores was overdue. The crew of one of these ships, the *Mary Ann*, managed to kill their Algerian prize crew and retake their vessel, but the other two were brought into port. Scarcely had the matter been settled by cash payment for arrears, when the Dey demanded $18,000 for the nine Algerians who had been the prize crew of the *Mary Ann*. Consul Lear had to pay this, also, in order to avoid instant declaration of war.

In 1808, this Dey was assassinated, as was his successor the year following. Early in 1812, the reigning Dey received a special envoy from the British Government, presenting a friendly letter from the Prince Regent himself. Feeling now that he had the support of Great Britain, the Dey decided that he could safely assume a hostile attitude towards the United States. When the *Alleghany* arrived in July with the tribute of naval stores, he instantly found fault with them. There was some tribute money—less than $16,000—still in arrears, but he demanded $27,000, on the ground that, by the Mahommedan way of reckoning (354 days to a year) seventeen years and a half had elapsed since the treaty of 1795, instead of seventeen. He gave Consul Lear five days in which to make the payment, with the alternative of going into slavery, together with all other American residents and the crew of the *Alleghany*. The consul finally borrowed the money at twenty-five per cent interest from a Jew in Algiers, and, with three other American residents, left the country on the *Alleghany*.

Fortunately the expectation of war with England had kept American merchantmen out of the Mediterranean, so that when the Dey sent out his cruisers they took only one brig, the *Edwin*. Her crew of ten were sold into slavery. During the war with England, efforts were made to ransom them, but without success.

The conclusion of peace with Great Britain left the United States free to deal with Algiers, and Congress acted promptly. On March 2, 1815, war was declared against Algiers and two squadrons were ordered to the Mediterranean. One, which was to assemble at Boston, was placed under the command of Commodore Bainbridge, and the other, at New York, under Commodore Decatur. The latter squadron got to sea first, on May 20. It consisted of the frigates *Guerrière*,[1] 44, flagship; *Constellation*, 36; *Macedonian*, 38; the sloops *Epervier*, 18, and *Ontario*, 16; and the brigs *Firefly*, *Spark*, and *Flambeau*, each 14 guns. Of these the *Firefly* was so badly damaged by a gale that she had to put back to New York.

Before entering the Mediterranean, Decatur made inquiries of the American consuls at Cadiz and Tangiers

---

[1] A new frigate named after the one destroyed by the *Constitution*.

Operations under Decatur

as to the whereabouts of Algerian cruisers, and learned that a squadron had just entered the straits under the command of the Algerian admiral, Rais Hammida. Decatur touched at Gibraltar only long enough to communicate with the American consul, and then set off in pursuit, hoping to take the Algerians by surprise.

On June 17, the *Constellation* sighted a large frigate off Cape de Gat and signaled an enemy. Decatur immediately ordered English colors hoisted to deceive the Algerian, but the mistake of a quartermaster on the *Constellation* in sending up American colors gave the corsair warning and she made all sail to escape. The *Constellation* then opened fire, and the Algerian, apparently giving up the idea of making the port of Algiers, suddenly wore ship to reach the neutral waters of Spain. This maneuver brought her close to the *Guerrière*, and Decatur, laying aboard, delivered two broadsides. This fire did such execution that it drove below decks all the survivors of the crew but the musketeers in the tops, and killed Rais Hammida himself. Seeing that the Algerian frigate was making no resistance, Decatur ceased firing and drew a short distance away. The little *Epervier*, however, under Captain John Downes, came up on the starboard quarter of the enemy, who was trying to escape, and, by skilful maneuvering, held this position, delivering nine broadsides. This forced the frigate to come up into the wind and surrender. She proved to be the *Mashuda*, 44 guns, the flagship of the Algerian fleet.

Two days later the squadron drove an Algerian brig ashore, and on the 28th arrived at Algiers. Decatur immediately sent to the Dey the terms of a treaty which he insisted should be ratified at once, threatening, in case of delay, to capture every Algerian ship that tried to enter the port. The loss of the *Mashuda*, together with the death of Hammida, had its effect on the Dey. On the appearance of an Algerian cruiser, whose capture by Decatur was only a matter of minutes, he sent out a boat in great haste to give word of his assent.

Thus, by Decatur's dashing methods, peace was concluded with Algiers in less than six weeks from the time the squadron left New York. The treaty provided for no tribute in the future, the instant release of American captives, the restoration of American property seized by the Dey, the payment of $10,000 for the brig *Edwin*, the emancipation of every Christian slave who should escape to an American man-of-war, and the treatment of captives, in case of a future war, not as slaves, but as prisoners of war, exempt from labor.

After settling with Algiers in this masterful style, Decatur proceeded to Tunis and Tripoli, having learned meanwhile that these states had permitted British men-of-war to recapture American prizes in their waters. From Tunis he exacted $46,000—the estimated value of the prizes taken there—and from Tripoli $25,000 with the added condition that ten Christian slaves should be liberated. Two of these were Danes, selected by Decatur out of gratitude to the Danish consul, Nissen, who had shown so much kindness to the captives from the *Philadelphia*.

Meanwhile, Commodore Bainbridge had sailed with his squadron from Boston, July 3. With characteristic bad luck, he arrived at Gibraltar only in time to discover that his junior, Decatur, had done all that needed to be done, and had carried off all the glory. Nevertheless, he took his squadron to the Barbary ports to reinforce the impressions left by Decatur. As it was no longer of any advantage to Great Britain to subsidize Algiers, she dispatched, the following year, a large fleet under Lord Exmouth to bombard the city. That blow ended the pretensions of the Barbary states to special privileges in piracy and Christian slavery.

Suppression of Piracy in the West Indies

We have already seen the extent to which French privateers, in the closing years of the 18th century, preyed on American ships in the West Indies and even in our own waters, eventually bringing on our war with France. These privateers were, to all purposes, pirate craft, which used the French colony of Guadeloupe as their base of operations. During the West Indian campaigns against France, the pirates were checked by British and American men-of-war, but by no means exterminated. The capture of Guadeloupe by the British in 1810 drove them from their refuge; but they found other rendezvous in the Gulf coast, where some resorted to smuggling and others continued their piracy.

The bayous of Louisiana were especially adapted to their profession, and here the celebrated brothers Lafitte made their headquarters for preying on the commerce of the coast. The war with Great Britain saved them from interruption by American authorities till September, 1814, when Master-Commandant Patterson, with six gunboats and a schooner towing several barges of troops, attacked and destroyed ten of the pirate vessels. The Lafittes, with some of their followers, escaped to New Orleans, where, oddly enough, they offered their services to General Jackson and fought under him in the famous defense of that city in January, 1815. One of the brothers went afterwards to Texas, where he resumed his profession. As late as 1822, his name was the terror of every skipper on the Gulf.

The Lafittes were not the only pirates in this region in the decade after the war. There were French and Spanish privateersmen, and—it must be admitted—some American as well, to whom the business of robbing merchantmen was too agreeable to give over on conclusion of peace. Nearly all of these obtained letters of marque from some Spanish colony in revolt, as Venezuela, for example, and used them for protection against capture by a man-of-war. This abuse grew to such proportions that scarcely a ship passed through the Gulf or the Caribbean without at least one desperate adventure with these so-called privateers.

In 1819, the United States took action by sending a squadron to the Gulf under the command of Commodore Oliver H. Perry, the hero of Lake Erie. He went directly to Angostura, Venezuela, to open negotiations concerning the matter of Venezuelan letters of marque. But there he was suddenly taken ill with yellow fever, and died on the way to Trinidad. His death ended the expedition without result.

Further efforts in the year 1821–22, by a squadron under Commodore James Biddle, made a good beginning. One small gunboat, the *Shark*, distinguished herself by capturing five pirate craft and aiding in the capture of a sixth. Her commander was Matthew C. Perry, a younger brother of Oliver Hazard Perry, and famous later for his mission to Japan. To continue the work, the Government dispatched another squadron the following year, February, 1823, commanded by Commodore David Porter. He was accompanied, as in the *Essex* days, by his adopted son, David G. Farragut.

This service in the West Indies was beset with difficulties. In order to destroy the pirates it was necessary to make land attacks upon their strongholds. Frequently the ground was almost impassable, and the Americans advanced in constant danger of ambush. Further, the yellow fever, which had recently been brought to the West Indies by the slaves, proved a far more dangerous enemy than the pirates themselves. In the midst of his campaign, Commodore Porter was forced for a time to

The Fajardo Affair 209

withdraw his entire squadron to Key West on account of the epidemic. It cost him one of his best officers, Lieutenant Watson; indeed, he himself lay for some days at the point of death. Perhaps the greatest obstacle, however, was the fact that many, if not most, of the Spanish officials were secretly hand in glove with the pirates, as they were then and later with the slavers.

An instance of this duplicity was the famous "Fajardo case." In October, 1824, Lieutenant Platt, commanding the schooner *Beagle*, was informed that $5000 worth of goods had been stolen from the American consul at St. Thomas. As the robbers were reported to have taken a boat for Fajardo, Porto Rico, Lieutenant Platt sailed for that place. On going ashore to explain his errand, he was insulted by the officials of Fajardo and thrown into prison.[2] After a long deliberation, enabling the stolen goods to be put safely out of the way, the "alcalde" allowed Lieutenant Platt to return to his ship. As soon as the commodore heard of the affair, he proceeded to Fajardo with a large force. The Spaniards, who had prepared a defense, deserted their guns and ran at the approach of the American seamen and marines. Porter spiked the battery that had been thrown across the road, and proceeded to the outskirts of the town. Under a flag of truce, he sent a demand for the officials of the town to appear and make instant and public apology to Lieutenant Platt. This they hastened to do, with the humblest promise of good behavior in the future toward all American officers. Thereupon Porter retired to his ship, having settled the whole affair in less than three hours.

Although Spain had made no protest whatever, this

---

[2] They pretended to believe that Platt was not an American officer because he had come ashore in civilian clothes, and when he showed his commission they declared that it was a forgery.

impulsive conduct offended the Secretary of the Navy, as being an offense against neutral rights, and Captain Porter was ordered home in December, 1824, to explain his action. By this time, however, he had so thoroughly done the difficult work intrusted to him that the year 1824 may be said to be the last in which the black flag was seen in the West Indies.

On reaching the United States, Porter found that he had to face a court-martial on account of his conduct at Fajardo. Unfortunately, there were some members of the court who were reputed to be personally hostile to the commodore, notably the president, James Barron. At least, Porter believed that the latter bore a grudge against him because he had been a member of the court that suspended Barron for the affair of the *Chesapeake* and the *Leopard*. At all events, the court found Commodore Porter guilty of "disobedience of orders and conduct unbecoming an officer," and suspended him from the service for six months. The court added, however, that the "censurable conduct" of the accused was due to an "anxious disposition on his part to advance the interest of the nation and the service."

Strictly speaking, there is no question but that the landing of an armed force on Spanish soil, except in pursuit of actual pirates, was an act of hostility and unauthorized by the United States Government; but to many who were acquainted with the ways of West Indian officials the circumstances were an ample justification. Porter naturally felt that the sentence was unjust, and resigned. Shortly after, he accepted the command of the naval forces of Mexico, but after three years of this service he left in disgust and returned to the United States. President Jackson then appointed him consul-general to Algiers and later minister-resident to Turkey, in which office he died in 1843.

Commodore Porter's name is associated chiefly with his celebrated cruise in the *Essex*, but it should be remembered that by abolishing in one year the long-established piracy of the Gulf and Caribbean, he performed a task far more difficult and hazardous.

THE SLAVE TRADE

Although the Constitution forbade the prohibition of the slave trade to the United States prior to the year 1808, Congress, as early as 1794, passed an act prohibiting the export trade and providing for the humane treatment, during their passage, of slaves imported into the United States. In 1800 it was made a crime, punishable by two years' imprisonment and a fine of $2000, for any American citizen to engage in the slave trade. In 1808, the trade was prohibited entirely, and in 1820 it was declared piracy and punishable by death. Our men-of-war were ordered to take slavers wherever found. A bounty of twenty-five dollars a head was offered to the captor for every slave on board.

In spite of these severe measures, the slave trade increased enormously for two principal reasons; first, the great profits in the business, and second, the carelessness of United States authorities. As an example of the first, in 1835 the Baltimore schooner *Napoleon*, of ninety tons, delivered in one voyage 350 slaves. These cost $16 a head on the African coast and sold at $360 each in Cuba. As for the second, although the slave trade was declared piracy, scarcely a week passed in the decade before the Civil War when a slaver did not leave New York harbor; and the first American slave trader hanged as a pirate went to his death in November, 1861, after the Civil War had begun.

The efforts of our navy to suppress the traffic were

weakened by several conditions. For a number of years the courts in England and America would convict a slaver only when the negroes were actually on board. The result of this ruling is exemplified in the case of the slaver *Brilliante*. On one of her trips, in 1831, her captain found himself becalmed and surrounded by four British cruisers. Anticipating being boarded if the wind did not rise, he stretched on deck his entire chain cable, suspended it clear of everything, and shackled it to his anchor, which hung on the bow ready to drop. To this chain he lashed his 600 slaves. He waited for a breeze till he heard the oars of the British boats close at hand, when he cut away the anchor. As it fell, it dragged overboard the entire cable with its human freight; and, though the British heard the screams of the victims and found their manacles still lying on the deck, because there were no slaves left on board the officers had to leave the vessel amid the jeers of her captain and crew.[1]

It was not long after this incident when the preposterous ruling was set aside in favor of common sense. A more serious obstacle to the suppression of the trade arose from the unwillingness of the United States to co-operate heartily with Great Britain. In 1824 the English Parliament declared the slave trade piracy, though the foundations of Liverpool's commercial greatness had been only recently laid by the profits of her slavers. England soon went still further by asking and gaining the co-operation of several of the European powers in suppressing the slave traffic to their colonies. But when she made an appeal for a mutual right of search to be exercised by United States and British cruisers upon the merchantmen of England and America in the "Middle Passage" she met with an indignant refusal. Those who were financially

---

[1] Spears, *The American Slave Trade*, p. 145.

The Slave Trade 213

interested in the trade raised the cry of "sailors' rights," and appealed to the principles of the War of 1812.

This patriotic clap-trap succeeded; and as the American ships were the only ones safe from British search, almost the entire slave trade passed under the protection of the American flag. Although in 1842 the United States, in a treaty with England, agreed to maintain a squadron of not less than eighty guns off the African coast, the Secretary of the Navy in his instructions to the commodore laid more emphasis on the necessity of preventing any attempted search of American ships by English cruisers than on capturing slavers. Accordingly, the commander of this squadron, Commodore Matthew C. Perry, cruised about without finding a single slaver. Meanwhile, every English officer who boarded a slaver was obliged to leave with an apology if the captain could show American papers, real or forged.

Early in the fifties Lieutenant-Commander Andrew H. Foote captured two slavers off the coast of Africa. On his return he wrote a book, *Africa and the American Flag;* and this book, by describing the hideous conditions of the traffic and the protection it received from the American ensign, did more to stop the abuse than all the American squadrons put together. It opened the eyes of the Americans to the fact that their flag had become the symbol of the slave trade.

During President Buchanan's administration the Government was secretly anxious to bring about the annexation of Cuba. In order to create a sentiment of some sort on which to base an appeal to the nation, especially to the anti-slavery sections, the Secretary of the Navy ordered American naval vessels to cruise in Cuban waters and capture slavers there. In spite of Spain's formal renouncement of the slave trade, made under pressure from England, it was common knowledge that Cuba was the most profitable slave market in the world, for the black-mailing charges of the Cuban officials were so low as not to interfere seriously with the great profits of the business. In the year 1860 alone, twelve Cuban slavers were captured by our men-of-war, although that was insignificant compared with the actual number of slavers that were landing negroes at various points along the coast. One great difficulty was the fact that the slavers, usually American-built "clipper" ships, or sometimes converted yachts, could easily outsail a man-of-war. At all events the trade was never so flourishing as in the five years preceding the Civil War.

During that time the pro-slavery men were making active efforts to repeal all existing legislation against the slave trade, most of which was admittedly dead-letter. But the change of administration and the outbreak of war altered the situation. The limited right of search asked by England was readily granted in 1862, enlarged in 1863, and in 1870 extended still further. From the moment the United States showed a sincere desire to allow her navy to co-operate with the British, the slave trade was doomed.

The Mutiny on the Somers

In the fall of 1842, the brig *Somers*, 10 guns, was ordered to the African coast with dispatches for Commodore Perry's squadron. On her return trip to New York, November 26, the purser's steward got word to the captain, Commander Alexander Slidell MacKenzie, that Acting-Midshipman Philip Spencer had tried to induce him to join a conspiracy to seize the ship, murder all the officers, together with such of the crew as would not be wanted, and turn pirate.

At first, Commander MacKenzie laughed at the story

as a boy's joke, but since the bearing of the crew had been insubordinate from the time they left Madeira, the other officers were inclined to regard the matter as serious. Accordingly, Spencer was put in irons and his effects were searched, with the result that a paper with Greek characters was discovered. It happened that there was one person on board besides Spencer who understood the Greek alphabet—Midshipman Rogers. He interpreted the words as a list of the crew, marked "certain," or "doubtful," with a few observations as to the policy to be pursued with the rest of the crew.

From the time of Spencer's arrest the conduct of the crew became more and more sullen and insubordinate. That afternoon there was a sudden and mysterious falling of the maintopmast and unnecessary confusion in clearing it away. The men gathered in whispering groups, and Spencer was observed making signals to them from the quarter-deck where he sat in irons.

From the evidence of the purser's steward, a boatswain's mate named Cromwell, and a seaman named Small also were arrested as ring-leaders and put in irons. As it was evident from the temper of the crew that the situation was extremely grave, Commander MacKenzie convened all his officers in a court of inquiry, while he, with a midshipman, took charge of the vessel. After deliberating about a day and a half, the officers returned a report that the prisoners were guilty of a "determined intention to commit a mutiny on board this vessel of a most atrocious nature," and in view of the "uncertainty as to what extent they are leagued with others still at large, the impossibility of guarding against the contingencies which a day or an hour may bring forth, we are convinced that it would be impossible to carry them to the United States, and that the safety of the public property, the lives of ourselves, and of those committed to our charge, require that . . . they should be put to death."[2]

Commander MacKenzie concurred in this opinion, and on December 1, he caused the three conspirators to be hanged from the yard-arm. Upon receiving sentence, Spencer and Small admitted their guilt; Cromwell protested his innocence to the end. The execution had a salutary effect on the crew, who immediately returned to their duties with an alacrity that was in striking contrast with their previous conduct.

On the arrival of the *Somers* at New York, the report of this execution aroused the greatest excitement, particularly as Spencer was the son of the Secretary of War. MacKenzie immediately called for a court of inquiry; but before its findings were reported, he was hurried to a court-martial. Though both courts rendered an honorable acquittal, for a long time thereafter the father of Spencer made unsuccessful efforts to have MacKenzie indicted in the civil courts for murder. The newspapers naturally made a great deal of the matter, to the disparagement of the navy as well as of MacKenzie, and even so distinguished a writer as Fenimore Cooper published a pamphlet reviewing the evidence of the court-martial with a severe criticism of Commander MacKenzie's conduct. Indeed, the feeling was so strong that it became a point of etiquette among naval officers never to discuss the mutiny on the *Somers*.

Theoretically, the death sentence, then as now, could not be inflicted without the approval of the President. But a commander's first duty is to save his ship, and the lives of the officers and men under him. To appreciate the circumstances, one must realize that the *Somers*

---

[2] *Proceedings of the Naval Court-Martial in the Case of Alexander Slidell MacKenzie,* p. 35.

was about the size of a pleasure yacht of to-day. There were only small scuttles leading from the officers' quarters to the deck, and it would have been a simple matter for the mutineers to seize the deck and kill the officers one by one as they came up. In fact, if there had been a leader ready, after the three were put in irons, a single concerted rush by the crew would have overpowered the officers instantly. Further, on account of the cramped quarters, the prisoners had to be kept in irons on the quarter-deck where they were in sight of the crew and offering a constant temptation to rescue, if the men were so disposed. As the *Somers* was at this time more than 500 miles from St. Thomas, there was no knowing when she would be able to reach New York; and the mutiny might have broken out at any moment. Finally the dying confession of Spencer showed that a plot for a mutiny of the most diabolical type was actually afoot, so that the apprehensions of Commander MacKenzie and his officers were not due to sudden panic. At the time this affair occurred, Commander MacKenzie had as fine a professional reputation as any other officer in the service, and though he had a difficult decision to make, it is safe to concur with the opinion of his brother officers that he followed the only proper course.

This incident had a wider significance than was realized at the time. It suddenly focused the attention of the naval officers and the public upon the evils of a practice that had become prevalent, that of throwing upon the navy such young scapegraces as proved on shore hard to keep out of jail. Philip Spencer was probably the worst example of this type, and his case, like most of the others, was aggravated by the fact that he was backed by strong political influence. He came to the receiving ship *North Carolina* with a bad college record, and made mischief at once. When the first lieutenant, Craney, tried to have him punished, the father set in motion all his political influence to persecute the unfortunate officer, who finally escaped only by resigning his commission. After Spencer had made a brief cruise on the Brazilian station in the *John Adams*, he was forced to resign on account of his "disgraceful and scandalous conduct"; but, apparently he was reappointed to the *Somers*, through his father's influence. In fact, Spencer admitted to Commander MacKenzie just before the execution that he had cherished the plan of mutiny and piracy ever since he entered the navy.

THE FOUNDING OF THE NAVAL ACADEMY

Hitherto the idea of a naval school corresponding to the Military Academy had often been urged, but without success. Congress did not wish to spend any more money on the navy, and the officers, especially the older men, laughed at the idea of "teaching sailors on shore." The Spencer incident, however, showed clearly enough the demoralizing influence of taking undisciplined young rascals into the service without any training or qualifications whatever. Furthermore, the use of steam for men-of-war had by this time passed the experimental stage and become recognized as necessary. It began to be evident that steam engineering could not be picked up, like seamanship, simply by going to sea. Accordingly, when the historian, George Bancroft, accepted the post of Secretary of the Navy, in March, 1845, he did so with the determination of founding a Naval Academy. Knowing the obstacles he had to overcome, he went about the work with consummate tact. He managed it so that the suggestion for a school appeared to come directly from the officers themselves. He first asked an examining board, consisting of older officers, to make a report on the best

GEORGE BANCROFT

The Founding of the Naval Academy 219

location for the school, and by submitting the same question to another board, composed of the younger element, won their approval as well. The recommendation of the first board that Fort Severn, Annapolis, was a suitable place was formally seconded by the second board, and thus the entire navy was committed to the idea.

Bancroft then overcame the unwillingness of Congress to make an appropriation; first, by getting a transfer of Fort Severn from the War to the Navy Department; and secondly, by putting all but a selected few of the navy "schoolmasters" on the waiting list, using the money appropriated to their salaries for the necessary expenses of the new academy.

By these means, he managed in a few months from the time he accepted his post, to have the Naval Academy in actual operation. From the point of view of its effect on the personnel of the navy, the founding of this school may be regarded as the most important event between the War of 1812 and the Civil War.

The Naval Academy was formally opened October 10, 1845, with fifty midshipmen and seven instructors. Commander Franklin Buchanan, U. S. Navy, was the first superintendent. For fifteen years the institution struggled along, handicapped by inadequate equipment and insufficient funds. In the Civil War period it first justified its existence. Practically all midshipmen, with the exception of the fourth class, were at once transferred to the fleet, where the need of officers was acute. The notable work of these young officers in a time of national emergency awakened new interest in the Naval Academy, and at the end of the war it was Vice-Admiral Porter, next to the ranking officer in the navy, who was detailed as its superintendent. The Spanish-American War was the first to be conducted by its graduates, and firmly established the Academy as a national institution.

XIV

THE MEXICAN WAR
PERRY'S EXPEDITION TO JAPAN

The Mexican War

WHILE President Polk, early in his administration (1845-1849), was framing a treaty with Great Britain that should establish our claim to Oregon—the name applied to the vast territory in the extreme northwest—he was also attempting to secure the Pacific slope to the south; for he had already recognized the immense future value of California with its harbor of San Francisco. This territory, owned by Mexico and as yet undeveloped, President Polk wished to purchase at a fair price; but Mexico, ill disposed because of the annexation of Texas to the United States and torn by civil dissension, would not consent. Her refusal, however, did not discourage the determined President.

On the 13th of May, 1846, when troubles relating to Texas had become acute, Congress by a joint resolution recognized a state of war as existing between Mexico and the United States. Nearly a year previous, Commodore Sloat in command of the American squadron on the Pacific coast had been given confidential instructions as to his course of action should Mexico show herself "resolutely bent on hostilities."[1] When he heard that war had begun, Commodore Sloat sailed north, and, on July 7, 1846, took possession of Monterey. Two days later, by his orders, Captain Montgomery took possession of San Francisco, and when Commodore Stockton, who had relieved Sloat,

---

[1] *Report of the Secretary of the Navy*, 1846, p. 378.

entered Los Angeles the month following, our flag was flying over every commanding position in California.

A campaign in the extreme west had also been planned by the army. Brigadier-General Kearny had begun a march to the Pacific early in July, stopping long enough before Santa Fé to scatter an army of Mexicans, three times his force, and to occupy the city. When he arrived at the eastern border of California and heard that the navy had largely anticipated him, he sent most of his troops back. But just about this time the Mexicans recaptured Los Angeles. Kearny had now only 110 dragoons and mounted riflemen; but, co-operating with Stockton, who furnished a large force of sailors and marines, he marched from San Diego to Los Angeles and after a two days' battle made permanent the authority of the United States in California.[2] The rest of the war was on the east, or Gulf, side of Mexico.

The general situation at the beginning of the war corresponded in many respects with the situation a half century later, when the United States was fighting, not Mexico, but Mexico's mother country, Spain. Commodores Sloat and Stockton in the far west, like Admiral Dewey in the far east, acted with decision, and, falling upon a detached portion of the enemy that were ill prepared, at once took possession of a vast territory. In consequence, the plans of the Navy Department in both wars were chiefly concerned with the slower and more extensive operations nearer home.

The chief work for the navy was, therefore, to blockade and seize the Mexican ports on the Gulf; these were from north to south, Tampico, Tuxpan, Vera Cruz, Alvarado, and Frontera. Later, the co-operation of the navy was required for the army, when the plan of military

---

[2] Bancroft, H. H., *History of California*, vol. v.

campaign changed a long march from the Rio Grande through the interior by General Taylor, to a short advance from Vera Cruz to the City of Mexico by General Scott. The navy was to assist in the transportation of troops to Vera Cruz and in the attack on that city.

The "Home Squadron," upon which this duty fell, was at the beginning of the war under the command of Commodore David Conner. Its early work was lacking in results because of two reasons: First, it was handicapped by having no gunboats of shallow draft to cross the bars at the mouths of rivers. Second, the commander of the squadron, though possessing many excellent qualities, was ill adapted to the service required. Captain W. H. Parker says of him: "I knew Commodore Conner well; I was his aid for some time. He had served with distinction in the War of 1812, and was in the *Hornet* when she captured the *Penguin*, where he was badly wounded. He was an educated man and a brave officer; but during the war he always seemed to be too much afraid of risking his men; he lacked moral courage, and would not take the responsibility his position imposed upon him. Consequently he failed."[3]

The naval operations before Vera Cruz were naturally of much greater magnitude than at any other point. Here the ships covered the landing of the army, and by a very nice piece of organization disembarked 10,000 in one day. Later, a naval battery with guns and men from the ships did excellent service in the attack upon Vera Cruz.

Among the officers who had a minor part in the operations on the Gulf were Farragut and Porter, who were later to win renown, but were as yet unknown. At the outbreak of hostilities both had applied to the Department for active duty; but although they possessed unusual

---

[3] Parker, *Recollections of a Naval Officer*, p. 53.

qualifications for service about Vera Cruz, they were kept waiting for several months.

Farragut knew Vera Cruz, for he had served five years in the Gulf, and had been present on the U. S. S. *Erie* when, nearly twenty years earlier, the French had taken the Castle of San Juan de Ulloa, the chief defense of the city. And it was because he was confident in his knowledge that he wrote to the Department, urging that the fleet early in the war should bombard the castle or attack by escalade [4] at night. Knowing the character of the Mexicans, he believed either method of attack would be successful, and he wanted to win honors for the navy. In referring to what he had learned from the operations of the French, he later remarked, "I . . . had taken great pains to inform myself as to the local advantages in attacking the place, measured the depth of water all around the fort, and marked the penetration of every shell from the French ships; . . . in so doing I had not at the time looked forward to a war with Mexico, but *I had made it a rule of my life to note these things with a view to the possible future.*" [5] It was just this thoroughness of Farragut that eventually was to enable him to fly the admiral's flag, but in the Mexican War the opportunity for making it tell was denied him. When at length he was given a ship, he was ordered to blockade Tuxpan. There for five months and a half, where nothing ever happened, he remained; and the only enemy he had to deal with was yellow fever, which very nearly proved fatal.

Porter also knew Vera Cruz, for when he was a boy of fourteen his father was commander-in-chief of the Mexican Navy, and with his father he lived for a while

---

[4] Escalade: surmounting the walls or ramparts of a fortification by means of ladders or scaling.

[5] Loyall Farragut, *The Life of David Glasgow Farragut*, p. 157.

in this very Castle of San Juan. It was, however, not until nearly ten months after the beginning of hostilities that his request for active service was granted. He had, in the meantime, submitted to the Department a plan in many respects resembling Farragut's. It provided for the exploding of several cases of gunpowder placed under the bastions of the castle by Captain Taylor, the submarine engineer. Porter had volunteered to rush in through the breach made by the explosion with fifty picked men, and seize the top of the castle.[6] The scheme was novel and suggested many difficulties in its operation, but Porter had nerve and knew how effective were surprise and deeds of daring in fighting Mexicans. Porter's plan, like Farragut's, failed to gain serious consideration.

To Porter's great satisfaction, however, he was sent to Vera Cruz in time to take part in the attack. His duty was that of first lieutenant on the *Spitfire*, Captain Josiah Tattnall, of the "Mosquito Fleet." When the army had been landed, Commodore M. C. Perry, who had relieved Conner, wished to learn the position of the enemy's guns, and directed the Mosquito Fleet to draw their fire. The night previous Porter spent in a row boat, moving daringly about under the enemy's guns in order to take soundings. In the morning he acted as a pilot and guided in the *Spitfire* and the *Vixen*, each with two gunboats in tow. They advanced to a position between the Castles of San Juan and Santiago and opened fire on the fortifications. In reply, the heavy guns of the forts began a furious cannonade, which if it had been well directed would have quickly sunk the little vessels. Shot and shell splashed around them, but, incredible as it may seem, did practically no harm. The army and the navy looked on breathless and amazed. Commodore Perry

---

[6] Soley, *Admiral Porter*, p. 59.

anxiously signalled a retreat; but Tattnall, following the famous example of Nelson at Copenhagen, told his quartermaster not to look at the flagship and continued the bombardment. At length, Perry sent his fleet captain, Mayo, to the *Spitfire* with peremptory orders to retire, and was reluctantly obeyed.

The war ended on February 2, 1848, when according to the treaty the United States came into possession of an immense area which included, not only Texas, but the present States of California, New Mexico, Nevada, Arizona, Utah, and parts of Wyoming and Colorado. In return Mexico was given $15,000,000 and released from the payment of claims, amounting to $3,000,000, held against her by American citizens.[7]

Although our naval officers and seamen for several months continued to exhibit courage, resource, and daring, yet the Mexican War cannot be regarded as of great importance in the history of the navy. As the enemy had no force to meet our ships on their element, the army bore a far more conspicuous part. At the same time the navy, through its spirited co-operation, made possible several victories of the army, the most important of which was Vera Cruz; and for this service gained recognition.

PERRY'S EXPEDITION TO JAPAN

The acquisition of California opened the way for trade with the Orient. American merchants had already made a beginning, and for some years our whalers had been carrying on extensive operations in the Japanese Sea. The United States earnestly desired friendly relations with Japan for three reasons: 1. To protect our shipping; in stress of weather foreign vessels could not take refuge

---

[7] *Cambridge Modern History*, vii, 397.

in Japanese ports, and when wrecked on the Japanese coast the crews were thrown into prison. 2. To facilitate trade with Asia; Japan had rich industries, she lay on the route to China, and she had deposits of coal of the greatest value to steamers making the long voyages. 3. To succeed where England, France, Portugal, and Russia had failed, for they had long been seeking trade relations in vain.

There were several steps that led up to the opening of Japan. The first was the success that Commodore Lawrence Kearny achieved in China. We had had no legitimate commerce with that country, but when in 1842 Commodore Kearny with the *Constellation* and the *Boston* arrived at Macao, he heard of the favorable treaty that England had just obtained from China and decided to act at once. Addressing a direct and friendly communication to Viceroy Ke, minor guardian of the heir apparent and governor of two provinces, he asked that the citizens of the United States should "be placed upon the same footing as the merchants of the nation most favored." This he followed up by fearlessly sailing to Canton for an answer. The reply was favorable, and he strengthened the good feeling that had been created, with the assurance that the United States would not protect her merchants caught smuggling opium. Thus it was Commodore Kearny who was largely responsible for a proclamation issued a few months later giving to the United States and other nations the same commercial privileges that had been granted to Great Britain.

Four years later Commodore Biddle with the *Columbus* and the *Vincennes* entered Yedo Bay. Nine years earlier the *Morrison*, an unarmed ship that attempted to land shipwrecked Japanese sailors, had been fired upon by the forts. Biddle was treated with more respect. The Japanese, with a show of great generosity, brought him supplies, but they would allow no one to land; and to the offer of friendly intercourse, they replied, "Go away and do not come back any more." In 1849 Commander Glynn with the *Preble* visited Nagasaki and compelled the release of some American sailors who had been shipwrecked the year before and imprisoned. During this transaction he discovered that the Japanese knew all about our recent victory over Mexico and had been considerably impressed. Returning home he reported that the time was unusually favorable for the United States to try the moral effect of an armed demonstration. A large expedition was accordingly authorized, and to Commodore Matthew Calbraith Perry, on March 24, 1852, was given the command.

In organizing his squadron Perry encountered many vexatious delays. Had he waited for the twelve ships assured him, he might never have seen Japan. However, the months of waiting were not given entirely to idleness. Charts of Japanese waters were secured from Holland at a cost of $30,000. And, through book collectors in New York and London, Perry gathered all the important literature relating to the Japanese. By these and other means he carefully acquainted himself with Japanese history, customs, and manners.

Commodore Perry sailed from Norfolk, November 24, 1852. On arriving in China, he continued his study and preparation. Finally, when all was ready, he directed his course toward the very heart of Japan. On July 8, 1853, with the steam frigates *Susquehanna* and *Mississippi*, towing the sloops of war *Saratoga* and *Plymouth*, he moved slowly up the bay of Yedo and dropped anchor off Uraga, a city twenty-seven miles from the capital, Yedo (Tokio). This was the first appearance of a steamer in Yedo Bay; and great was the astonishment of the natives to see the huge ships approaching directly against the wind. A cordon of small boats soon surrounded the vessels, and the curious natives caught at the chains and attempted to clamber on board. This and many other liberties had been permitted by foreign ships in the past, but now the Japanese were forcibly given to understand

JAPAN

that they must keep off. Perry, in coming to the exclusive nation, had decided fairly to outdo them in exclusiveness, and had given orders forbidding communication with the natives except from the flagship. Even when the Vice-Governor of Uraga appeared in a small boat and an interpreter declared his rank, he was kept waiting until he had explained why he, and not the Governor, had come.

And when the gangway was lowered and the dignitary came on board, he was by no means permitted to see Commodore Perry. Perry, because of his rank as the great ambassador of the President, would meet no one less than a "counsellor of the Empire" (cabinet minister). However, Lieutenant Contee, acting as Perry's representative, informed the Vice-Governor of the friendly mission on which the Americans had come, and of the letter written by the President to the Emperor, which Commodore Perry would deliver with appropriate formalities. The Vice-Governor's immediate answer was that "Nagasaki was the only place, according to the laws of Japan, for negotiating foreign business, and it would be necessary for the squadron to go there." To this "he was told that the commodore had come purposely to Uraga because it was near to Yedo, and that he *should not go to Nagasaki;* that he expected the letter to be duly and properly received where he then was; that his intentions were perfectly friendly, but that he would allow of no indignity."[8]

Perry had resolved to use force only as a last resort; yet that he might be prepared for emergency he had already cleared the decks and begun drilling the crews as in war. It was indeed a time of uncertainty. Though on the ships all was very quiet that evening, on the shores the blazing of beacon fires from every hill top and the tolling of a great alarm bell gave indication of the tremendous excitement that was rapidly spreading among the people.

At seven o'clock the next morning two large boats that came alongside the *Susquehanna* brought the Governor of Uraga. Again the exclusive commodore would not deign to treat with an official beneath his rank, but dele-

---

[8] This and the following quotations relating to the opening of Japan are from Hawks's *Narrative of the Expedition to Japan.* This is the official account, compiled from Perry's notes under his immediate supervision.

gated Captains Buchanan and Adams to confer with him. The first suggestion from the new conferee was "Nagasaki"; and again this met with an emphatic refusal. The captains said that the commodore "would persist in delivering the letter where he was; and, moreover, that if the Japanese Government did not see fit to appoint a suitable person to receive the documents in his possession addressed to the Emperor, that he, the commodore, whose duty it was to deliver them, would go on shore with a sufficient force and deliver them in person, be the consequences what they might." The Governor now requested an opportunity to send to Yedo for further instructions. This he said would require four days; he was informed the commodore would wait only three. Before departing the Governor asked what the ships' boats, busily engaged since daylight in surveying the bay and harbor, were doing. And when he was told, he strongly protested, urging that it was against the Japanese law to permit such examinations. The quick reply was "that the American laws command them, and that Americans were as much bound to obey the American as he was to obey the Japanese laws."

Perry was well aware "that the more exclusive he should make himself, and the more unyielding he might be in adhering to his declared intentions, the more respect these people of forms and ceremonies would be disposed to award him." And thus it happened that on the day following the Governor's visit, Sunday, Perry, who from his boyhood up had been careful in Sabbath observance, refused to admit on board his ship several mandarins who had come to make an unofficial visit. If the Japanese had been familiar with the language of their visitors they would have been further edified by one of Isaac Watts's hymns sung in the morning service: "Before Jehovah's awful throne, Ye nations bow with solemn joy."

As can be easily imagined, the communications taken

to Yedo by the Governor of Uraga had the effect of an earthquake. For even if the Japanese were not to be shaken out of their prejudice against foreigners by Perry's friendly purpose, they were tremendously disturbed by his individual firmness and power. They were shrewd enough to recognize that if they forcibly resisted him, he might land, and by dwelling in it defile the Holy Country. They especially dreaded this, because the government was already in an unstable condition and the dynasty in power was threatened with rebellion.

Of this internal disorder Perry had no knowledge. But he was rejoiced by the Governor's returning, on the day appointed, with the answer that the President's letter would be received by an official of superior rank with fitting ceremonies. Almost immediately the Governor proceeded to arrange with Captains Buchanan and Adams, the time, place, and even the minutest details for the formal delivery and acceptance of the letter.

Two days later (July 14), shortly before eight o'clock, the *Susquehanna* and the *Mississippi* moved down the bay, and inshore, towards a large and highly decorated reception hall which the Japanese had quickly erected. At a signal from the *Susquehanna*, 300 officers, sailors, and marines filled fifteen launches and cutters, and with stately procession moved toward the shore. When they had gone half way, a salute of thirteen guns from the *Susquehanna* began to boom and re-echo among the hills; this was to announce that the great commodore, the august ambassador of the President, upon whom no Japanese eye had yet been privileged to gaze, was embarking in his barge.

"On the arrival of the commodore, his suite of officers formed a double line along the landing place, and as he passed up between, they fell into order behind him. The procession was then formed and took up its march toward the house of reception, the route to which was pointed out by Kayama Yezaiman [the Governor of Uraga] and his interpreter, who preceded the party. The marines led the way, and the sailors following, the commodore was duly escorted up the beach. The United States flag and the broad pennant were borne by two athletic seamen, who had been selected from the crews of the squadron on account of their stalwart proportions. Two boys, dressed for the ceremony, preceded the commodore, bearing in an envelope of scarlet cloth the boxes which contained his credentials and the President's letter. These documents, of folio size, were beautifully written on vellum, and not folded, but bound in blue silk velvet. Each seal, attached by cord of interwoven gold and silk with pendent gold tassels, was encased in a circular box six inches in diameter and three in depth, wrought of pure gold. Each of the documents, together with its seal, was placed in a box of rosewood about a foot long, with lock, hinges, and mountings all of gold. On either side of the commodore marched a tall, well-formed negro, who, armed to the teeth, acted as his personal guard." These negroes, the pick of the squadron, were giants in stature and attracted great attention from the Japanese, who had never seen blacks before. This pomp and parade, carefully planned for effect, seems to have been highly successful.

As Perry and his suite entered the reception hall, magnificent in its hangings of violet-colored silk and fine cotton, two princes, who were seated on the left, rose, bowed, and then resumed their seats. They had been appointed by their government to receive the documents, and their dignity was appalling; during the entire interview they sat with statuesque formality uttering not a word nor making a gesture.

The complete ceremonies occupied not more than a half hour. For some minutes after the commodore had

From a lithograph by W. Heine, an artist accompanying the expedition

DELIVERY OF THE PRESIDENT'S LETTER

taken his seat there was absolute silence, broken finally by the Japanese interpreter asking the American interpreter if the letters were ready for delivery and stating that the princes were ready to receive them. "The commodore, upon this being communicated to him, beckoned to the boys who stood in the lower hall to advance, when they immediately obeyed his summons and came forward, bearing the handsome boxes which contained the President's letter and other documents. The two stalwart negroes followed immediately in rear of the boys, and marching up to the scarlet receptacle [prepared by the Japanese for the letters], received the boxes from the hands of the bearers, opened them, took out the letters, and, displaying the writings and seals, laid them upon the lid of the Japanese box—all in perfect silence."

The commodore then directed his interpreter to inform the Japanese that he should leave in two or three days, but would return the following spring for an answer. When they inquired if he should return with all four vessels, he gave the prompt assurance, "All of them and probably more, as these are only a portion of the squadron." After a further impressive silence, and a repetition of the formal bowing with which the conference had begun, Perry took his departure.

Before leaving the bay of Yedo the *Susquehanna* had another visit from Yezaiman, Governor of Uraga, who, after being shown over the ship, was urged to remain and see the engine in motion. The interest of the Japanese was keenly aroused and there could be no doubt of the favorable impression produced by this striking example of American inventive genius. Perry advanced farther up the western shore of the bay within ten miles of Yedo, all the while taking soundings, and again he caused the Japanese evident uneasiness. Then he retraced his course and sailed for China.

While the American ships were wintering in Hong Kong, Commodore Perry had his suspicions aroused by the unusual movements of some French and Russian ships in the vicinity, and he feared lest they were secretly planning a visit to the bay of Yedo, with the purpose of snatching the advantages he had gained. He resolved not to be anticipated; and although navigation in those waters was supposed to be extremely dangerous in winter, he sailed for Japan on the 14th of January, 1854. Entering Yedo Bay with three steam frigates and four sloops of war he steamed twelve miles beyond Uraga, and on February 13 came to anchor twenty miles from Yedo.

Shortly after Perry's first visit, the Japanese Emperor had died. The Japanese officials had sent the Americans news of this while the squadron was at Hong Kong, and had requested that they defer their return as it might create confusion. Perry suspected the genuineness of the report; at least he could see no reason why he should not be near to comfort his new friends in their bereavement. On arrival he was well received, but the Japanese dignitaries who conferred with his captains—for Perry was still playing his rôle of exclusiveness—at once requested that the ships put back to Uraga, where they said preparations had been made to treat with the Americans and to give an answer to the President's letter. Perry, feeling that it would be dangerous to yield in a single instance, replied, through his captains, that Uraga was unsafe and inconvenient for the ships, and further that it was the custom of civilized nations to treat at the metropolis. When the dignitaries continued to insist on Uraga and the captains to refuse, and several days had been spent in useless conferences, Perry settled the difficulty in a characteristic way. Without warning, he moved the squadron forward until within sight of Yedo. This induced the Japanese promptly to adopt a conciliatory tone; they then proposed for the treaty ground Yokohama, almost opposite where the ships were anchored, and this was at once accepted.

On the eighth of March, the day that had been set for beginning the negotiations, the commodore with 500 men and three bands of music, went ashore to the "Treaty House," erected for this especial occasion. At an early stage in the negotiations, the Japanese expressed a willingness to enter into friendly intercourse with the United States, but were seemingly determined to grant nothing. Three weeks of conference followed, and as the commodore continued to show the firmness and dignity that had already won prestige for him and as he kept his men strictly under discipline, the Japanese came to regard their persistent visitors with increasing tolerance.

In the middle of the negotiations Perry delivered to the Japanese the presents that the storeship had lately brought from America, designed especially for this people, and he sent ashore officers and workmen to prepare the gifts for exhibition. Among them were agricultural implements, clocks, two telegraph instruments, three Francis life-boats, and a Lilliputian railway. The last had a locomotive, tender, car, and rails, but was so small that it could scarcely carry a child of six. "The Japanese, however, were not to be cheated out of a ride, and, as they were unable to reduce themselves to the capacity of the inside of a carriage, they betook themselves to the roof. It was a spectacle not a little ludicrous to behold a dignified mandarin whirling around the circular road at the rate of twenty miles an hour, with his loose robes flying in the wind, . . . [clinging] with a desperate hold to the edge of the roof, [and] grinning with intense interest." In return the Japanese brought generous presents of lacquered work, pongee, umbrellas, dolls, and various other things, together with the substantial remembrances of 200 sacks of rice and 300 chickens. Then, after this evidence of friendliness, they entertained their guests with wrestling matches between their champions, enormously fat and muscular. Later the Americans received seventy of the Japanese on board the *Powhatan* and the cook fairly outdid himself in setting forth a dinner which, as the Japanese did not pay much attention to order in eating the various dishes of food loading the tables, is described as the most "confused commingling of fish, flesh, and fowl, soups and syrups, fruits and fricassees, roast and boiled, pickles and preserves"; all of which the Japanese consumed in large quantities, and became fairly "uproarious under the influence of overflowing supplies of champagne, Madeira, and punch, which they seemed greatly to relish."

On Friday, March 31, 1854, Commodore Perry and four Japanese commissioners signed a treaty written in the English, Dutch, and Chinese languages. This guaranteed succor and protection to shipwrecked Americans; permission for a ship in distress, or overtaken by storm, to enter any Japanese port; the opening of the ports Simoda and Hakodadi, where Americans could secure water, wood, coal, and provisions, and enjoy, with some restrictions, trade relations.[9]

Larger privileges were later granted by the treaties of 1857 and 1858. England, quick to follow the advantage gained by the United States, six months after Perry

---

[9] An interesting souvenir of Perry's expedition is preserved at the U. S. Naval Academy. It is an ancient bronze bell, said to have been cast in 1168, which was presented to Perry by the Regent of Napha, one of the Lew Chew Islands, a dependency of Japan. Among the many flowery sentences inscribed on the outside, one gave the assurance that if the people would bear in mind to act rightly and truly, and the lords and ministers would do justice in a body, the barbarians would never invade their country.

The Treaty with Korea

(September, 1854), also secured commercial rights, and Russia and Holland were only a few months later. Thus if Perry's expedition had been planned solely for our own commercial profit, there might have been disappointment. But the prestige gained by the American commodore, who had shown himself such an able diplomat, and the honor that came to our nation in having drawn Japan from her isolation, proved an ample recompense.

A similar achievement by an American naval officer, requiring not less skill and patience, was that of Commodore Robert W. Shufeldt in opening up Korea. A previous attempt by Rear-Admiral John Rodgers had resulted in a battle in which 350 Koreans were killed or wounded, but the Korean government would not enter into any negotiations. For four years Shufeldt strove, first through the Japanese, and then through the more friendly Chinese, to reach the Korean King. Finally the high dignitaries in Peking were convinced of the advantages that would result to them if Korea would establish treaty relations with the western powers, and they lent their influence. As a result the long-sought-for treaty was secured and signed with elaborate ceremony (1882). It was more comprehensive than the initial treaty with either China or Japan. Great Britain, Germany, and other nations were watching, and soon they pressed forward to obtain like treaties. In each case they accepted the American draft as their model.

XV

THE CIVIL WAR: THE FIRST YEAR

In the great struggle with Secession certain conditions that had existed in our wars with England were reversed. The odds were as decidedly in favor of the United States Navy as earlier they had been against it. Yet the varied duty that fell to the navy was full of hazard and difficulty, and often involved extreme tests of endurance.

It was not merely that the South showed daring and brilliancy in the few single-ship actions, and, by developing the idea of the ironclad, threatened destruction to whole squadrons of wooden vessels; the National Navy had also to fight against powerful forts guarding the harbors and the rivers; it had to blockade a coast over 3000 miles in length; and with the army it was assigned the task of opening the vast system of waterways comprised in the Mississippi and its tributaries.

The Navy Unprepared

Here were difficulties for any navy, and they were more formidable because of the wretched condition of the National Navy at the outbreak of the war. On March 4, 1861, when President Lincoln took his oath of office, there were in commission, including supply ships and tenders, forty-two vessels, of which there were only twenty-three propelled by steam that might be called efficient. On that day but four of the twelve ships constituting the home squadron were in Northern ports, available for service [1]; the other squadrons were in the Mediterranean,

---

[1] *Report of the Secretary of the Navy*, 1861, p. 10.

The Navy Unprepared

Pacific, and off Brazil, the East Indies, and Africa. With the time necessary for the transmission of orders and for the return voyage, it was several months before these squadrons could be utilized. Threats of war had been heard long before fighting began; why then, when the crisis came, was the navy so utterly unprepared?

First, President Buchanan (1857–1861) was the victim of his environment; three of his Cabinet advisers were, to say the least, lukewarm in their allegiance to the Union; and a fourth, Mr. Toucey, the Secretary of the Navy, although from Connecticut, was so strong in his Southern sympathies, that he had earlier failed of re-election to the Senate. Secondly, Congress had by its indifference and blindness disorganized the navy quite as much as had the administration. Because of the wide-spread financial disaster, beginning in 1857, the national revenue had fallen off, and Congress, in attempting to economize, had severely crippled the navy.

Opposition to building or even repairing ships came from Northern as well as Southern sources. Congressmen from Ohio and Illinois led in the attack on the navy and the naval appropriation bill. Congress as a whole was apathetic. Strange as it may seem now, even a few months before hostilities began, the Northern members had no real apprehension of the titanic struggle at hand. Outside of Congress such a clear-sighted observer as James Russell Lowell, writing on the eve of Lincoln's election, made light of the threats of secession.

When Lincoln was elected and secession had been accomplished, President Buchanan still remained inactive; thus no preparation was made to meet the great emergency. Admiral Chadwick ably remarks on the state of affairs at the time: "The whole Government was in a state of sad flabbiness. There was but a nucleus of an army; the navy was moribund; there was a captain afloat in command nearly seventy years of age; the commandant of the Norfolk Navy Yard was sixty-eight; the commandant at Pensacola, sixty-seven. The general-in-chief of the army was seventy-four. There was no settled belief or opinion. The New York *Tribune,* which held the position of leadership among Republican journals, and which was a power throughout the North, was proclaiming that 'if the Cotton States shall become satisfied that they can do better out of the Union than in it, we insist on letting them go in peace'; and, again, that 'five millions of people, more than half of them of the dominant race, of whom at least half a million are able and willing to shoulder muskets, can never be subdued while fighting around and over their own hearthstones'—expressions which had a powerful effect for ill throughout the South."[2] The opinion that the South could never be subdued was freely uttered in the North, and universally believed in Europe.

THE EARLY PLANS FOR OPERATIONS

With the firing on Fort Sumter, April 12, 1861, war began, and the new and efficient Secretary of the Navy, Gideon Welles, took vigorous hold of affairs. He had an invaluable helper in the Assistant Secretary, Gustavus V. Fox. Mr. Fox had had eighteen years' experience in the navy, resigning to enter business in 1856, the year he was commissioned lieutenant. His training and rare ability made him just the man for the position. The assistant secretaryship was a new office felt to be necessary in order to introduce harmony in the various bureaus of the Department. Fox was the professional adviser, and was given the greatest responsibility in planning operations, choosing leaders, and removing superannuated and

---

[2] *Causes of the Civil War,* p. 164.

Early Plans for Operations 241

inefficient officers. The last was the weakest point of the navy at the beginning of the war. One of Lincoln's Cabinet characterized Fox as "the able man of the administration."

The Department early made plans for an immense naval armament. The annual appropriation made by the previous Congress for the navy of about $13,000,000 was increased to $43,500,000. As Mr. Welles outlined in his report of December, 1861, three lines of operation had been determined on: 1. The naval occupation of the Potomac, and the blockade of all Southern ports. 2. The organization of combined naval and military expeditions against various points on the Southern coast and along the Mississippi. 3. The active pursuit of Confederate cruisers and privateers.

The Northern navy yards, in which work had been almost entirely suspended during the years preceding, became scenes of great animation. Within a few months after the firing on Sumter, the North had 11,000 men engaged in fitting out the old ships that had been dismantled, in overhauling those returned from foreign waters, and in building new ships especially adapted to the service for which they were required. At the same time the Navy Department, drawing from every source, was purchasing and making over ships from the merchant service.

The added ships required crews to man them, and before the year was ended the number of seamen had grown from 7600 to 22,000. Meanwhile, one-fifth of all the officers in the old navy (322, if all grades and corps are included) had joined fortunes with the seceded States.[3] To meet the emergency, the upper classes at the Naval Academy were given active duty; and promotion was so

---

[3] Soley, *The Blockade and the Cruisers*, p. 8.

rapid that many midshipmen became lieutenants before they had reached the age of nineteen. Volunteer officers were also called for, and 7500 of them received appointments during the war.

President Lincoln, by official proclamation on April 19 and 27, declared his intention to blockade all the Southern coast. But according to international law, as formulated in the Declaration of Paris, 1856, "a blockade in order to be binding must be effectual, that is to say, maintained by a force, sufficient in reality to prevent access to the coast of the enemy." For the Union Navy at once to blockade the coast from Alexandria, Virginia, to the Rio Grande, 3549 statute miles, with 189 harbor or river openings, was discovered to be an impossible task. It could not be accomplished in a month nor in several months; but the beginning was made at Hampton Roads shortly after the proclamation, and as ship after ship, purchased or built, was fitted out, it was assigned its place in the long line.

The Potomac Flotilla

Washington, both because of its being the national capital and because of its proximity to the Confederate lines, became an important centre of operations. And when at the outbreak of the war the loyalty of Maryland, the nearest State, seemed to be wavering, it caused the greatest concern. The people of Baltimore attempted to prevent the Northern troops from passing through the city, though it was known that those troops were indispensable to the protection of the national capital. Thus, for various reasons, it was highly important that the Union forces should control the Potomac and maintain Washington's communications by water.

For this service Commander J. H. Ward organized a small flotilla in May, 1861. Already the buoys had been

The Expedition to Hatteras Inlet 243

largely removed from the Potomac by the Confederates, and men and supplies were being constantly ferried across from Maryland into Virginia. Then, too, the Confederates had begun to fortify the heights near Aquia Creek. Ward bombarded them without much result on May 31 and June 1. This was the first naval engagement of the war.

The flotilla was active and efficient, but its duties, as the year advanced, became increasingly difficult. Buoys that had been replaced were again removed; light-house keepers were intimidated into extinguishing their lights; and so many were the convenient points for crossing the river that it was impossible to stop more than a part of the men and supplies entering Virginia. Finally, the Confederates, having come into possession of large guns by the capture of the Norfolk Navy Yard, made fortifications along the river of such strength that they were more than a match for the ill-protected paddle-wheel steamers of the flotilla. On October 15, Commander T. T. Craven had to report that in spite of the utmost efforts of the flotilla the navigation of the river was practically closed. In the following spring, however, the operations of the Army of the Potomac against Richmond compelled the Confederates to contract their lines and abandon the fortifications on the Potomac.

CAPTURE OF BATTERIES AT HATTERAS INLET

Naval stations and harbors convenient for refuge from the heavy storms common to the South Atlantic coast were, as the Department saw, indispensable for carrying on hostilities and maintaining a blockade. Accordingly, a board was appointed, consisting of Captain Samuel F. DuPont and Commander Charles H. Davis of the navy, and Major John G. Barnard of the Coast Survey, to make " a thorough investigation of the coast and harbors, their access and defenses," and recommend a plan of immediate action. As a result, two combined naval and military expeditions were organized in the late summer and fall of 1861.

The first was directed against Hatteras Inlet. This position was important as the key to Pamlico Sound, and here the Confederates had erected two defenses, Forts Clark and Hatteras. On August 26, an expedition of fourteen vessels under Flag-Officer Silas H. Stringham, accompanied by Major-General Benjamin F. Butler with 860 troops, sailed from Hampton Roads. The resistance made by the forts was rather weak, and after a two days' bombardment the Confederates surrendered; the captured numbered 615 officers and men, including Samuel Barron, flag-officer of the Confederate Navy, who for nearly fifty years previous had served in the National Navy. Not a man in the Union Navy was killed during the engagement, an immunity due in part to Stringham's clever maneuvering of his ships when near the forts; he passed and repassed the forts, varying his course so as to prevent their securing the range.

The Capture of Port Royal

For the second point of attack, the Department decided on Port Royal, S. C., and made Captain Samuel F. DuPont, lately appointed flag-officer of the South Atlantic blockading squadron, leader of the expedition. Port Royal was by inland routes thirty miles from Savannah and fifty from Charleston. Though somewhat neglected, it was the finest natural harbor on the Southern coast.

On October 29, the fleet of fifty vessels (including army-transports carrying nearly 13,000 troops under Brigadier-General Thomas W. Sherman) left Hampton Roads. Great pains had been taken to conceal their

The Capture of Port Royal

destination, but without success. The Confederates heard of the plans even earlier than most of the officers of the fleet.[4]

The weather, which had promised well as they started, changed to a gale off Hatteras, and for a while its violence approached that of a hurricane. The fleet was utterly dispersed and on November 2 but one sail was to be seen from the deck of the *Wabash*. Some of the ships that had been purchased or chartered because of the great need were quite unfit to encounter such a wind and sea. Thus two were lost—the men being saved with great difficulty—and a third had to throw her battery overboard to keep from foundering. However, as the severity of the gale abated, prospects brightened and on the morning of the 4th, DuPont, with twenty-five of his vessels, anchored off the bar of Port Royal, while others were appearing on the horizon.

The buoys that marked the channel across the long bar before Port Royal had been removed. But they were replaced by Commander Davis, the fleet-captain, and Mr. Boutelle, of the Coast Survey, so that the gunboats and lighter transports could enter the roadstead that evening. DuPont had grave fears in crossing the bar with his flagship, the *Wabash*, for with her deep draft there would be but a foot or two to spare. But on making the attempt next morning, he succeeded, and was soon followed by the frigate *Susquehanna* and the large transports.

The entrance to Port Royal was guarded by two strongly built fortifications, two and five-eighths miles

---

[4] Although the ships were sailing under sealed orders, the following telegram was sent, on November 1, from Richmond, to Governor Pickens and Generals Drayton and Ripley of South Carolina: "I have just received information, which I consider entirely reliable, that the enemy's expedition is intended for Port Royal. J. P. Benjamin, Acting Secretary of War."

apart, Fort Beauregard, mounting twenty guns on Bay Point, the northern side, and Fort Walker, mounting twenty-three guns on Hilton Head, the southern side. To reduce these forts with wooden ships was what Flag-Officer

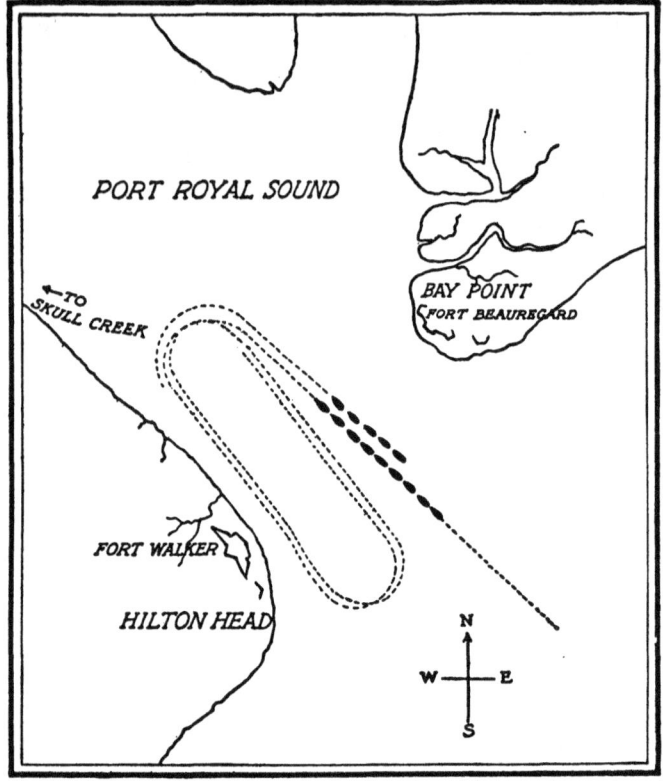

BATTLE OF PORT ROYAL

DuPont had decided on. The 13,000 troops accompanying the expedition had no part in the attack on the forts. This change in plans was due to the fact that the greater part of the means for disembarkation had been lost in the storm, and that the only convenient place for the troops

The Capture of Port Royal 247

to land was five or six miles from the anchorage of the transports. It was therefore decided to reduce the forts by the naval force alone.

Calling his captains on board the *Wabash*, DuPont explained the strength and the weakness of the enemy's position, and then carefully outlined his plan of attack and order of battle. The fleet was to divide, "a main squadron ranged in a line ahead, and a flanking squadron which was to be thrown off on the northern section of the harbor to engage the enemy's flotilla, and prevent their raking the rear ships of the main line when it turned to the southward, or cutting off a disabled vessel."[5] The main squadron, consisting of nine of the heaviest frigates, sloops, and gunboats, was led by DuPont's flagship, the *Wabash;* and the flanking squadron of five gunboats was led by the *Bienville*.

"The plan of attack was to pass up midway between Forts Walker and Beauregard, receiving and returning the fire of both, to a certain distance about two and a half miles north of the latter. At that point the line was to turn to the south, round by the west, and close in with Fort Walker, encountering it on its weakest flank, and at the same time enfilading, in nearly a direct line, its two water faces. . . . When abreast of the fort the engine was to be slowed and the movement reduced to only as much as would be just sufficient to overcome the tide, to preserve the order of battle by passing the batteries in slow succession, and to avoid becoming a fixed mark for the enemy's fire. On reaching the extremity of Hilton Head . . . the line was to turn to the north and east, and, passing to the northward, to engage Fort Walker with the port battery nearer than when first on the same course. These evolutions were to be repeated."

Captain DuPont had worked out an unusually skilful

---

[5] *Naval War Records*, xii, 262.

plan, which was executed with faultless precision. At eight A.M., November 7, the commander made signal to get under way. A half hour later the two columns were headed in for the forts, the flanking squadron to the right; and soon the ships, decreasing the intervals, came into close order. At 9.26 there was a flash and a roar from Fort Walker, and another immediately followed from Fort Beauregard. The challenge was taken up by the *Wabash*, and the other ships followed with their fire as their guns bore. At ten o'clock the head of the main squadron had reached the point two and a half miles above the forts; then as the ships turned, they changed the course so that when abreast of Fort Walker they should be only 800 yards distant; and in this closer formation they steamed with great deliberation southward.

From a reconnoissance DuPont had learned of the weakness of the northern flank of Fort Walker, and on this point each ship opened with her forward pivot as soon as she came in range. The Confederates, unprepared for an attack on this quarter, suffered from the enfilading fire, which dismounted a few of the guns and greatly annoyed the defenders. And their confusion increased when in addition to the enfilading fire, still kept up by the rear of the Union line, full broadsides swept the parapets from the leading ships, now abreast of the fort.

Meanwhile, a small Confederate squadron of four gunboats under Commodore Tattnall came down the river and endeavored to make its presence known. Tattnall was a cool and daring officer who had served long in the old navy, and when the Union columns had first moved against the forts he had advanced as if to give battle to the entire fleet. Taking a raking position he fired several ineffectual broadsides at the *Wabash*. But as that ship came within range, he wisely retreated in haste up Skull Creek; there he was out of the fight, yet still showed his spirit by

The Capture of Port Royal

dipping his blue flag three times, "regretting his inability to return the high-flown compliments of Flag-Officer DuPont in a more satisfactory manner."[6] The flanking squadron, by remaining at the northern end of the loop, prevented Tattnall's emerging from Skull Creek, and also kept up the enfilading fire on Walker.

The main squadron reached its starting place at 11 A.M. and then proceeded to execute another ellipse; but this time the ships as they turned to southward moved still nearer to Fort Walker, taking a course less than 600 yards distant.

The forts were considered strong and well equipped, yet the defense crumbled under the fire of the fleet. The commanding officers gave various explanations in their reports to Richmond: only a part of the guns could be used against the ships, many of the shells would not fit the guns and were useless, ammunition was insufficient, and gun crews became exhausted—all of which indicated lack of preparation and discipline. Yet, had the forts been fully manned and equipped, the slight losses sustained by the fleet give reason for believing that it might still have been successful. More troops and ammunition would not have made up for the defects in the construction of the forts. The batteries were arranged to command the sea-front; but against an attack from inside the sound they had no defense. The guns were nearly all mounted *en barbette,* that is, above a parapet, thus affording the advantage of wide range, but with the disadvantage of little protection to the gunners. Consequently, although it was estimated at this time that one gun on shore was equal to four on ship, the superiority of the land batteries was lost almost the moment the ships took the enfilading position. For though the fire of the fleet did not do great

---

[6] *Savannah Republican,* November 12, 1861, quoted in the *Naval War Records,* xii, 295.

damage to the guns themselves, it drove the gunners to shelter.

Major Huger, C. S. A., one of the defenders of Fort Walker, recognized its weakness, as in his official report he said: "Three of them [the Union ships] took position to enfilade our batteries from our northwest flank, while others which had not yet got into action assumed direction opposite our southeast front, and their largest ship [the *Wabash*] . . . returned down our front, delivering a beautifully accurate fire at short range, supported at rather longer range by the fire of two other large ships of war. So soon as these positions had become established, the fort was fought simply as a point of honor, for, from that moment, we were defeated, except perhaps by providential interference." [7]

When the main squadron had reached the northern end of the ellipse for the third time and was about to begin another bombardment on the southern course, the *Ottawa* signaled that the works at Hilton Head had been abandoned. Commander John Rodgers was sent ashore with a flag of truce, and, finding that the fort was indeed deserted, at 2.20 P.M. raised the flag of the Union. The transports now came up, and before night troops had landed and occupied the works. At sunset it was discovered that Fort Beauregard was no longer flying the Confederate flag, and early next morning that defense also was occupied by Union troops.

The victory was extremely important. It created alarm in South Carolina, and caused troops about to leave for Virginia to be retained for the protection of their own State. It gave the Union an excellent harbor, of the greatest advantage for fitting out expeditions against the strongholds along the coast, and for protecting the blockade. Incidentally, the engagement demonstrated the value of steam power, and showed that ships could be used even

---

[7] *Naval War Records*, xii, 308.

The Trent Affair

in attacking strongly armed forts. Finally, the victory, coming in the latter part of 1861, when a gloom was overhanging the North from the many disasters on land, brought cheer and encouragement. A stronghold had been seized in South Carolina, the State that had been first to secede.

THE TRENT AFFAIR

On the same day the Union flag was raised over Fort Beauregard there occurred elsewhere an event which at first was hailed as a great achievement on the part of the navy, but which soon proved a grave menace, for it involved the United States almost in a European war. It was the "Trent affair."

The Confederacy had early sought recognition from the leading European states, but although their representatives were given a friendly reception in England and elsewhere, they were received merely as private citizens. President Davis then resolved to send commissioners of the highest ability to England and France, hoping that they might succeed where the others had failed; he accordingly selected James M. Mason of Virginia and John Slidell of Louisiana, with J. E. Macfarland and George Eustis as their secretaries; both Mr. Mason and Mr. Slidell were United States senators when their States seceded, and both had earlier held important posts in the diplomatic service. Eluding the blockade, they sailed from Charleston to Nassau and then to Cardenas, Cuba; on November 7 they took passage on the British mail-steamer *Trent*, Havana to St. Thomas, on their way to England. It was the seizing of these commissioners on the *Trent* by an armed United States ship that so violently aroused all Europe and America.

Captain Charles Wilkes, commanding the *San Jacinto* in West Indian waters, who had earlier distinguished himself in Antarctic exploration, resolved to intercept the Confederate commissioners. As they made no effort to maintain secrecy after arriving in Cuba, Captain Wilkes learned of their intended departure on the *Trent*, and took up his station in the Old Bahama Channel. At 11.40 A.M., November 8, the smoke of a steamer was reported, which was rightly guessed to be the *Trent*. What followed Captain Wilkes states in his official report.[8]

"We were all prepared for her, beat to quarters, and orders were given to Lieutenant D. M. Fairfax to have two boats manned and armed to board her and make Messrs. Slidell, Mason, Eustis, and Macfarland prisoners, and send them immediately on board. . . .

"The steamer approached and hoisted English colors. Our ensign was hoisted, and a shot was fired across her bow; she maintained her speed, and showed no disposition to heave to; then a shell was fired across her bow, which brought her to. I hailed that I intended to send a boat on board, and Lieutenant Fairfax, with the second cutter of this ship, was dispatched. He met with some difficulty, and remaining on board the steamer with a part of the boat's crew, sent the boat back for more assistance. The captain of the steamer having declined to show his papers and passenger list, a force became necessary to search her. Lieutenant James A. Greer was at once dispatched in the third cutter, also manned and armed.

"Messrs. Slidell, Mason, Eustis, and Macfarland were recognized and told they were required to go on board this ship; this they objected to, until an overpowering force compelled them. Much persuasion was used and a little force, and at about two o'clock they were brought on board this ship and received by me. Two other boats were then sent to expedite the removal of their baggage

---

[8] *Naval War Records,* i, 130.

and some stores, when the steamer, which proved to be the *Trent,* was suffered to proceed on her route to the eastward, and at 3.30 P.M. we bore away to the northward and westward. The whole time employed was two hours, thirteen minutes.

"It was my determination to take possession of the *Trent* and send her to Key West as a prize, for resisting search and carrying these passengers, whose character and objects were well known to the captain, but the reduced number of my officers and crew, and the large number of passengers on board bound to Europe who would be put to great inconvenience, decided me to allow them to proceed."

The prisoners were taken to Boston and confined in Fort Warren. Captain Wilkes became at once a popular hero. He was given a grand ovation in Boston and New York, lauded by the public press, and thanked by a joint resolution of Congress. Even the Cabinet with one exception, the Postmaster-General, were delighted with the capture. But while the country was being thus swept by an outburst of enthusiasm, President Lincoln, with his rare discernment, perceived the complications that were soon to follow. He remarked: "I fear the traitors will prove to be white elephants. We must stick to American principles concerning the rights of neutrals. We fought Great Britain for insisting, by theory and practice, on the right to do exactly what Captain Wilkes has done. If Great Britain shall now protest against the act, and demand their release, we must give them up, apologize for the act as a violation of our doctrines, and thus forever bind her over to keep the peace in relation to neutrals, and so acknowledge that she has been wrong for sixty years."[9]

Great Britain did protest, and Lord Lyons, the British

---

[9] Lossing, *History of the Civil War,* ii, 156.

minister, was instructed, unless redress including the surrender of the commissioners was forthcoming within seven days, to depart with "the archives of the legation, and . . . repair immediately to London."[10] Meanwhile, the British Government, without waiting for developments, embarked troops for Halifax, conveyed muskets from London Tower for shipment, and made ready all kinds of warlike munitions.

Although the matter primarily concerned only England, the Emperor of France, the King of Prussia, and the Emperor of Austria had within a month of the receipt of the news communicated with the Foreign Office, London, and their own diplomatic representatives in Washington, expressing their approval of England's attitude in the controversy. In short, just as emphatically as the United States had approved of Wilkes's act, Europe disapproved.

War was averted, however, by the United States' disavowing the act and surrendering the prisoners to English custody, January 1, 1862. As the affair involves such an important point in international law much has since been written on it. The best authorities of recent years agree in condemning the act of Captain Wilkes. While he had the right to stop the *Trent* and search her, he could not possess himself of any persons on her without taking the ship into port as a prize. Neither the commissioners nor their dispatches, being of a non-military character, could be regarded as contraband of war, and therefore the ship was not liable to capture except on the ground of resistance to search. Since obstacles in the way of search were interposed by the captain of the *Trent*, Wilkes would have been justified in taking the ship into port, though whether a court would have considered the resistance as sufficient to condemn her is a matter of conjecture.[11]

---

[10] *Naval War Records*, i, 161.
[11] Harris, *The Trent Affair*, p. 264.

XVI

THE BATTLE OF HAMPTON ROADS: THE DESTRUCTION OF THE CUMBERLAND AND THE CONGRESS

NORFOLK NAVY YARD ABANDONED

SOME of the large guns the Confederates used at Hatteras and Port Royal, as well as later about New Orleans, Port Hudson, and Vicksburg, were secured from the Norfolk Navy Yard. The loss of this yard in the latter part of April, 1861, was the greatest disaster sustained by the navy during the war. It was caused, not by an overwhelming force of hostile arms, but by the prevalent policy of inaction, and by panic. The administration, the Navy Department, and several of the senior officers of the army and the navy, all shared in the blame.

The situation in Virginia previous to the firing on Sumter had been extremely delicate; as the State wavered in her choice of sides, friends of the Confederacy who were closely watching the Norfolk Navy Yard found it easy to dissuade the administration from taking any measures to protect the government property there, arguing that this would indicate distrust and thus alienate the State.

General Scott, the head of the army, a Virginian, and conservative by reason of age (he was nearly seventy-five years old), did not favor sending troops to Norfolk. And when Commodore C. S. McCauley, commandant of the yard (sixty-eight years old), was instructed on April 10 that "great vigilance should be exercised in guarding and protecting the public interests and property," he did nothing. He was misled by Southern advisers, and seemed to lack all power of action; so far as is known, he made not even a plan in defense of the yard.

A week before Virginia passed the ordinance of secession (April 17), the Department had become apprehensive and had sent confidential orders for the removal of the *Merrimac* and other ships at the Norfolk Yard. On April 12 Engineer-in-Chief Isherwood was sent from Washington expressly to take out the *Merrimac*. He found her engines in bad condition; but putting a large force of men to work on Monday morning, the day after his arrival, and employing shifts so as to push the work day and night, he reported Wednesday afternoon that everything was in readiness for firing. On Thursday morning he had steam up, and waited only for the commandant's order to cast loose and take the *Merrimac*, with the *Germantown* in tow, to a place of safety. But the commandant hesitated, and hesitation at this critical moment was fatal. Finally, when Isherwood reminded him of the peremptory orders given by the Department for sending the ship out, McCauley said that he had decided to retain her, and directed that the fires be drawn.

The patriotism of Commodore McCauley was never seriously doubted. But he was quite unequal to the emergency. Distressed and anxious, he was led by some of his officers who shortly entered the Confederate service to believe that moving the *Merrimac* would incite to violence the mob collecting outside the yard. Although he had a force which, with the guns of the ships, could have resisted several regiments of militia without artillery, he was persuaded that the security of the yard depended on avoiding a rupture. He was also induced to believe that some obstructions the Confederates had placed in the channel, really insignificant, would prevent the *Merrimac's* passing.

When Engineer-in-Chief Isherwood and Commander

Alden (who was to have been captain of the *Merrimac*) found they could do nothing, they departed for Washington and made their report.[1] Immediately Commodore Hiram Paulding, in the *Pawnee*, and a detachment of 500 men were dispatched to relieve McCauley and save the ships. But it was too late.

The greater part of McCauley's officers had resigned or deserted. Mechanics and watchmen had joined the secessionists outside, who were collecting in scattered groups. The unfortunate commandant, dejected by this, and dismayed by the reports that State troops were arriving from Richmond and Petersburg, decided to destroy all the ships in the yard except the *Cumberland*. Accordingly, on Saturday, April 20, he scuttled the *Merrimac*, *Germantown*, *Plymouth*, and *Dolphin*.

At the very hour when the destruction began, Commodore Paulding, who had progressed as far as Fortress Monroe, was embarking a regiment of Massachusetts volunteers. They were only twelve miles away, and were coming as fast as the *Pawnee* could bring them to save the ships.

On Paulding's arrival Commodore McCauley's courage revived, and he was in favor of remaining and defending the yard. There is little doubt that it might have been held for some weeks even without the reinforcements already on their way. Commodore Paulding had altogether 1000 effective men under his command. Though not much reliance could be placed on the strength of the walls enclosing the yard, the guns of the receiving-ship *Pennsylvania*, the *Cumberland*, and the *Pawnee* commanded the entire yard, and could have set fire to Norfolk and Portsmouth. On the other hand, the Confederates had only a few companies of soldiers and no heavy guns.

---

[1] To be found in the *Naval War Records*, iv, 280.

Whatever Commodore Paulding's possibilities may have been, he was just as plainly a victim of panic as Commodore McCauley had been before him. Within an hour after his arrival, Paulding decided to abandon the yard. On reaching this decision he immediately began making preparations. One hundred men were to render useless the guns in the yard by knocking off the trunnions with sledges; they pounded well, but accomplished nothing. Other men were set to work rolling cannon and shells into the river. Still others were to prepare the ships and buildings for firing. The *Cumberland*, the only ship to be saved, was towed a short distance out by the *Pawnee*, and at four or five in the morning, a rocket from the *Pawnee* gave signal that the fires were to be ignited.

But even the work of destruction suffered from panic, and evidently had been poorly planned. The moment the National forces had withdrawn, the crowds outside the yard rushed in. Extinguishing a slow fuse attached to a mine designed to destroy the drydock, they saved it intact. At the same time others checked the flames in the buildings (only a few of which had been really set on fire), and secured most of the valuable shops uninjured. As but very few of the cannon were destroyed, the Confederates gained nearly 3000 pieces of ordnance of all kinds, 300 of them Dahlgren guns of the latest type.[2]

The events at the Pensacola Navy Yard furnish a companion piece to the story just narrated. On January 12 preceding, Captain James Armstrong, in command, had weakly surrendered to the State militia of Florida.

---

[2] These are the figures given by Commodore Paulding in his report to the Department of April 23, 1861; Commodore McCauley's estimate is about the same; other estimates vary greatly, but all are less; Scharf in his history states, "There were 1198 guns of all kinds captured with the yard, of which fifty-two were 9-inch Dahlgren guns."

Development in Guns

Had it not been for the guns captured at Pensacola and Norfolk, according to the belief expressed later by Admiral Porter, the Confederates could not have armed their fortifications until they had built gun factories of their own, or imported cannon from Europe; that is, not until nearly a year after the beginning of hostilities.

The Union lost at Norfolk the steam frigate *Merrimac*, 40 guns, the sloop of war *Germantown*, 22, the sloop of war *Plymouth*, 22, the brig *Dolphin*, 4, all of which were practically ready for sea; also, the older ships, still possessing some usefulness, *Pennsylvania, United States, Columbus, Delaware, Raritan,* and *Columbia;* and, last an unfinished ship-of-the-line, the *New York*. But "great as was . . . the loss of our ships, it was much less than the loss of our guns."[3]

DEVELOPMENT IN GUNS AND SHIPS

The Civil War marks the end of the old in the ships and guns of our navy, and the beginning of the new. Since the events following the loss of the Norfolk Navy Yard instituted this revolution, it is worth while here to pause and note certain changes that had taken place in the half century preceding.

Smooth-bore guns, firing solid shot, had increased from the earlier 18- and 24-pounders to 32's. The " Columbiads " used in the War of 1812 and in the Civil War were guns of this type, though previous to the later war the model had been changed by lengthening the bore and increasing the weight of metal so as to adapt it for a heavier charge. As it was discovered that the improved guns frequently did not possess the requisite strength, they were degraded to the rank of shell-guns, and fired with diminished charges of powder.

---

[3] Porter, *Naval History of the Civil War*, p. 33.

The "Dahlgren" gun, designed by Admiral Dahlgren in the '50's, was regarded as the most advanced type of smooth-bore at the time of the Civil War. This was of large calibre and made of cast-iron. Its special feature was the "curve of pressures," making it heavy at the breech and light at the muzzle. It meant a great gain in power with a minimum of weight, and thus was especially adapted for naval use.

All smooth-bore ordnance was muzzle-loading. These pieces fired round shot, canister, common shells, and shrapnel shell. The first rifled guns were also muzzle-loaders; and it was not until 1875–80 that breech-loading rifles were generally accepted.

Experiments in rifled cannon began in Russia about 1836. In the Crimean War these guns did not prove very successful, but by the beginning of the Civil War they were regarded no longer as experiments. The moment armor was introduced on ships they became a necessity. Rifled cannon had the advantage of greater penetrating power, greater range, and increased accuracy.

The "Parrott" rifle gun was probably the best of the large ordnance that found extensive use in the war. This was a cast-iron rifled tube, strengthened by a coiled wrought-iron hoop shrunk on the breech. The Parrott guns were 100-, 200-, and 300-pounders.

In the construction of ships there had been but one important innovation since the War of 1812, and that was caused by the introduction of steam as the propelling power. Ships were still built on the general lines of frigates and sloops of war, and were fully rigged, for it was supposed that warships would ordinarily use steam only as auxiliary power. There were some side-wheelers, but ships of the latest approved type built in the United States, such as the *Merrimac* and the *Hartford*, had screw propellers, which evidently would be much less vulnerable in battle. Such vessels were capable of making, under steam alone, from eight to twelve knots. The first steam man-of-war ever launched was the U. S. S. *Fulton*, 1814, and the first screw warship, the U. S. S. *Princeton*, 1843. In thus leading the navies of the world, the United States Navy, insignificant as it was in number of ships, won distinction.

By the introduction of steam as the motive power, ships not only gained in speed, but could be maneuvered regardless of the wind. In consequence, they were much better able to attack or pass forts commanding harbors and rivers. Further, they were adapted for a new mode of attacking other vessels, that is, by ramming. This method of fighting was virtually a return to the tactics of the Greek and Roman galleys, and it proved very effective in the confined space of rivers and narrow bays.

The Confederate Navy Department early recognized that, having no ships, shipbuilders, or seamen, they could not hope to battle successfully with the National Navy except by some new and quite superior kind of fighting machine. They began studying the torpedo and the ironclad, the principles of both of which were well known in navy circles.

The ironclad, of which alone we shall speak in this chapter, had its beginning in the Crimean War, in which it was used by the French. On October 17, 1855, three so-called floating batteries, the *Lave, Tonnante,* and *Dévastation,* their hulls of timber covered with four inches of iron armor, advanced to the attack of Kinburn and delivered a very destructive fire, which, with that of the ships-of-the-line, frigates, and mortar boats, compelled the Russian forts to surrender after three hours' resistance. The significant feature of the engagement was that although the floating batteries took a position only a few hundred yards distant from the forts, and received a terrific bombardment in return, they suffered practically no injury. This set progressive naval constructors to thinking; France shortly planned in her navy various changes which Great Britain viewed with apprehension.

THE REBUILDING OF THE MERRIMAC

On the 23d of June, 1861, Mr. Mallory, the Confederate Secretary of the Navy, met a board consisting of Chief Engineer William P. Williamson, Lieutenant John M. Brooke, and Naval Constructor John L. Porter, to make plans for an ironclad. Since the Confederates had failed in their attempt to purchase one, they were obliged to rely on their own resources. Mr. Porter, who had submitted the plans for an ironclad to the U. S. Navy Department as early as 1846, brought to the conference a model of a boat of shallow draft, its upper works entirely inclosed by a shield with armored sloping sides. But the building of such a vessel would require twelve months, and presented many difficulties, for the South had practically no facilities for making engines, and almost no machinists. Aid was found in the Norfolk Navy Yard.

When Commodore Paulding was leaving the yard, he set fire to the abandoned ships; but as the *Merrimac* had already been scuttled, the flames destroyed only her upper works, and, stopping with the berth deck, left her engines and boilers practically uninjured. To save time, and to take advantage of the machinery of the *Merrimac*, the board, meeting at Richmond, adapted its plan to this vessel, which already had been raised and placed in drydock.

The South showed splendid energy in the reconstruction of the *Merrimac*, as most of the world have continued to call her, rather than the *Virginia*, as she was renamed by the Confederates. Officers and constructors

The Rebuilding of the Merrimac

did their utmost to hasten the work; even the blacksmiths, machinists, and bolt drivers caught the spirit, and signed a voluntary agreement to work until eight o'clock every evening without extra pay.

The *Merrimac* was originally a screw frigate, of 3500 tons burden. Her hull, 263 feet long, was covered amidships with a shield of 178 feet; the sides of which slanted at an angle of 35°, and rose, when she was trimmed for battle, seven feet above the water. The shield was made of rafters of yellow pine, fourteen inches thick; on this was a course of four-inch pine planks running fore and aft, and on this another of four-inch oak planks placed up and down. Superposed on the wood was a layer of rolled iron bars, eight inches wide and two inches thick, running fore and aft, and on these another layer of similar size, up and down. The whole was bolted through and through. Thus the vessel had an armor which, measured perpendicularly to the slanting sides, was four inches of iron supported by twenty-two inches of wood, but which horizontally gave a thickness very much greater. The knuckle, where the armor joined the hull, and the two ends of the vessel beyond the armor, were submerged to a depth of two feet, rendering those parts invulnerable. The rudder and propeller were protected by a heavy solid deck or fan tail.[4] The top of the shield was protected from a plunging fire by an iron grating in which

---

[4] There is considerable variance in the descriptions of the *Merrimac*, even in statements made by officers who served on her; *e.g.*, some give the slant of her shield as 45°, affirming that her decks were merely awash when in battle, instead of submerged, and that her rudder and propeller were unprotected, etc. In this account, the authors have relied chiefly on statements by Naval Constructor J. L. Porter, *Battles and Leaders of the Civil War*, i, 716, and by John W. H. Porter, *A Record of Events in Norfolk County*, pp. 327-366.

the bars were two inches wide and thick, separated by meshes two inches square.

The armament of the *Merrimac* consisted of ten guns; of the eight, comprising her broadsides, six were smoothbore 9-inch Dahlgrens, part of her original battery, and two were 6.4-inch rifle guns; there were also two 7-inch rifle guns on pivot, one at each end. The rifle guns were made at the Tredegar Iron Works, Richmond, where the armor plate was rolled, the work being under the supervision of Lieutenant Brooke. The *Merrimac* was further armed with a cast-iron beak, wedge shaped, weighing 1500 pounds.

The *Virginia,* or, as we shall call her, the *Merrimac,* moved slowly down Elizabeth River, at the same time making ready for battle about midday, March 8, 1862, the very earliest moment she was available. Many of the workmen were still on her and hurried to give the finishing touches as she drew out of the navy yard. The engineer was running cautiously, for the shaft had scarcely been given a turn previous to this day. The officers moved among their men, and sought to give them some acquaintance with their duties. The crew surely needed instruction, for it was made up largely of volunteers from the army. No wonder many of the people of Norfolk, as they cheered the *Merrimac,* supposed that she was going merely on a trial trip.

The Ramming of the Cumberland

It was about twelve o'clock when Lieutenant George U. Morris, of the *Cumberland,* 24 guns, discovered three vessels under steam standing down Elizabeth River towards Sewell's Point. The sense of peace and security then prevailing on the Union side was indicated by the sailors' washing, which decorated the rigging, and hung

The Ramming of the Cumberland

limp in the breathless air. The captain of the *Cumberland*, Commander William Radford, was absent, having been ordered to the *Roanoke* as member of a court of inquiry. The *Congress*, 50 guns, was a quarter of a mile

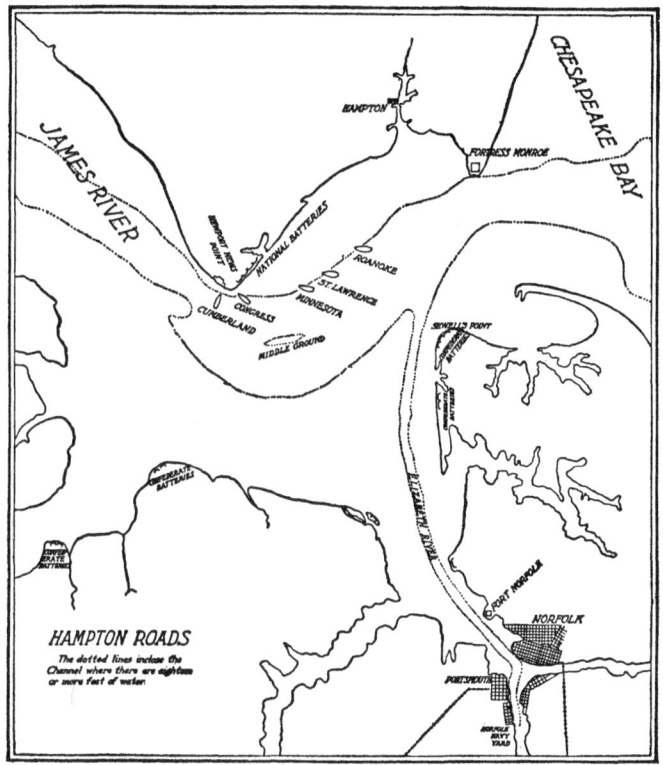

HAMPTON ROADS

distant from the *Cumberland;* both were near Newport News, while the remaining ships of the fleet, the *Roanoke, Minnesota,* and *St. Lawrence,* were anchored off Fortress Monroe, eight miles distant.

The *Cumberland* and the *Congress,* though suddenly

awakened from their repose, had ample time to clear for action and to study the strange foe [5] approaching. The *Merrimac* was deliberate in her movements; her engines, condemned as worn out and useless a year before, when the yard was in the possession of the Government, had since not been improved by fire and water. At their best they could not drive her five knots an hour. The great bulk of the *Merrimac*, and her draft, made her difficult to maneuver. She drew twenty-one feet forward and twenty-two aft, and many times in the battle of this day and the day following her keel dragged in the mud. It took over half an hour to wind her.

The commanding officer of the *Merrimac* was Captain Franklin Buchanan, who had been forty-six years in the United States Navy, and who was in command of the Washington Navy Yard at the outbreak of hostilities. By one of the accidents not infrequent in this war, his favorite brother was purser on the *Congress*, which the Confederate ram was about to engage.

When the *Merrimac* had passed the Confederate batteries at Sewell's Point, where she was heartily cheered by the troops that lined the shores, she was seen to take the South Channel and head for Newport News. The two National ships lying there at anchor opened fire on her when she was three-quarters of a mile distant, the *Cumberland* first with her heavy pivot guns. The shore batteries at Newport News also brought their guns into action.

Many of the shot struck the *Merrimac*, but bounded off without effect. Of this hostile demonstration the strange monster took no notice, but in silence, and with an awful deliberation, continued to advance. Finally, when within close range, Lieutenant Charles Simms carefully aimed

---

[5] Stiles, in his *Military Essays and Recollections*, says the *Merrimac* looked "like a house submerged to the eaves, borne onward by a flood."

The Ramming of the Cumberland 267

her forward pivot, and the shell, going true to its mark, swept away practically the entire crew of the after pivot-gun of the *Cumberland*.[6] Passing near the *Congress*, the *Merrimac* gave the old frigate a destructive broadside with her starboard battery, and received a heavy fire in return though with no effect. Without stopping to repeat the fire, the ironclad then headed direct for the *Cumberland*, and rammed her under the starboard forechannels.

The beak of the *Merrimac* was under water, but when it pierced the side of the *Cumberland* the smashing of timbers could be heard above the roar of cannon. The shock was scarcely felt on the *Merrimac*, but the *Cumberland* had received a fatal wound. The tide began to swing the *Merrimac* around, and as she was disengaging herself and backing clear, the ram broke off short. The hole made in the *Cumberland* was large enough to admit a man.

Just previous to the moment of impact, the forward pivot-gun of the *Merrimac* had again been fired, a second time doing terrible execution. On the other hand, as one of the *Merrimac's* crew in his excitement and enthusiasm imprudently leaped into the porthole to sponge out his gun, he was immediately shot through the head by a musket ball.

Although the *Cumberland* had been rammed, her men, controlled by splendid discipline, did not flinch because of the hopelessness of the contest or the carnage on their decks, and, reforming the gun-crews, continued the fight. Their shot did not penetrate the ironclad, yet they were not altogether wasted. For when the ships, close alongside, chanced to fire at the same moment, the shot shattered the muzzles of two guns of the *Merrimac* and rendered them useless. Fragments of guns and shells killed one man on the *Merrimac*, while "sixteen more were

---

[6] *Battles and Leaders of the Civil War*, i, 698.

scorched with powder or scratched with minor particles of the debris.'' (Surgeon Phillips, of the *Merrimac*.)

The *Merrimac*, on disentangling herself, laboriously proceeded to turn, that she might engage the *Congress*. Meanwhile the crew of the *Cumberland*, under Lieutenant Morris, heroically held to the fight. As she began to settle, the men were driven from the lower decks, but fought with the guns on the spar deck. Nor did they leave them so long as the guns were above water, that is, not until forty-five minutes after the ship had been rammed. As the Union vessel careened and went down, some of the wounded were saved by being placed on racks or mess-chests, but the loss was large. Out of a complement of 376 officers and men, only 255 responded to muster the following day; nearly all of the others had been killed or drowned.

The *Cumberland* partly regained an upright position on sinking in the shallow water; her mastheads were not submerged, and the American flag still flew. Thus Commander Radford, who had come from Fortress Monroe on horseback, and who reached his ship only in time to witness her end, had the consolation of seeing the colors still flying.[7]

THE DESTRUCTION OF THE CONGRESS [8]

Meanwhile Captain Buchanan, who, on leaving the *Cumberland*, had headed up the James, put his helm hard-a-starboard, and as he was coming about, Colonel J. T. Wood, in charge of the after pivot, put three raking shells into the *Congress*. Lieutenant Joseph B. Smith,

---

[7] Radford's and Morris' reports will be found in the *Naval War Records*, vii, 20 ff.

[8] Built at Portsmouth, N. H., in 1841, and connected only in name with the old *Congress*, one of the six frigates forming the first permanent navy of the United States.

The Destruction of the Congress

commanding the *Congress*, attempted to save his ship by setting jib and topsails, and, with the assistance of the tug *Zouave*, running under the protection of the shore batteries. But the *Congress* soon grounded in shoal water, out of reach of the *Merrimac's* prow, but not of her guns. Of the events that followed, Lieutenant Pendergrast, the executive officer, says in his official report:

"At 3.30 the *Merrimac* took a position astern of us, at a distance of about 150 yards, and raked us fore and aft with shells, while one of the smaller steamers kept up a fire on our starboard quarter.

"In the meantime, the *Patrick Henry* and *Thomas Jefferson* [*Jamestown*], rebel steamers, approached us from up the James River, firing with precision and doing us great damage.

"Our two stern guns were now our only means of defense. These were soon disabled, one being dismounted and the other having its muzzle knocked away. The men were swept away from them with great rapidity and slaughter by the terrible fire of the enemy.

"At about 4.30 I learned of the death of Lieutenant Smith, which happened about ten minutes previous. Seeing that our men were being killed without the prospect of any relief from the *Minnesota*, which vessel had run ashore in attempting to get up to us from Hampton Roads, not being able to bring a single gun to bear upon the enemy, and the ship being on fire in several places, . . . we deemed it proper to haul down our colors without any further loss of life on our part.

"We were soon boarded by an officer from the *Merrimac*, who said that he would take charge of the ship. He left shortly afterwards, and a small tug came alongside, whose captain demanded that we should surrender and get out of the ship, as he intended to burn her immediately.

"A sharp fire with muskets and artillery was maintained from our troops ashore upon the tug, having the effect of driving her off. The *Merrimac* again opened on us, although we had a white flag at the peak to show that we were out of action."⁹

The Confederates thought that the fire directed against them came in part from the ship, and were highly indignant. Captain Buchanan, who was naturally excitable, snatched a carbine from one of his men, and, exposing nearly his whole body above the shield of the *Merrimac*, began firing. His anger and recklessness, however, met with a heavy penalty. His thigh bone was broken by a musket ball from the shore, and he was obliged to yield the command to his lieutenant, Catesby ap R. Jones. The Confederate steamers, although driven away from the *Congress* by the rifle guns on shore, set the Union ship on fire by red-hot shot. She burned until past midnight, when the flames reached the magazine and blew her up.

At the beginning of the battle, the *Minnesota,* the *Roanoke,* and the *St. Lawrence,* leaving Fortress Monroe, had attempted to move up the Roads and take part in the action. But by the middle of the afternoon the tide was ebbing, and, as they drew considerable water, all three grounded; the *Minnesota,* which had gone farthest of the three, succeeded in getting within a mile and a half of Newport News, and witnessed the *Cumberland* sink and the *Congress* surrender, without any power on her part to aid. However, if the *Minnesota* could not rush forward and grapple with the *Merrimac,* no more could the *Merrimac* cross the shoal water and engage the *Minnesota,* and to this the *Minnesota* owed her salvation.

The fire of the *Merrimac* was not very accurate, and at the distance of a mile her gunners succeeded in putting only one shell through their enemy's bow. But the *James-*

---

⁹ *Naval War Records,* vii, 23.

The North Alarmed 271

town and the *Patrick Henry*, taking positions on the *Minnesota's* port bow and stern, with their rifle guns did considerable damage until the Union vessel, bringing a heavy gun to bear, forced them to withdraw.

About this time the *St. Lawrence* succeeded in reaching a position near the *Minnesota* before grounding again, where she fired several broadsides at the *Merrimac*. Hostilities ceased about 6.30, when the pilot of the *Merrimac* declared that the tide would leave her aground if she continued longer in her present position. The Confederate vessels then steamed back to Sewell's Point, where they anchored for the night.

The South had won a decided victory. The conflict, according to the Confederate historian Scharf, was "twenty-seven guns [the combined batteries of the *Merrimac* and the small steamers] against an armament of over 300 guns, of which 100 could be brought into action at every moment, and on every point." The *Merrimac* had moved about at will in the destruction of the Union ships, checked only by the shallow water of the Roads and her own awkwardness. The heavy guns of the Union ships and shore batteries had swept her decks, carrying away davits, anchors, and flagstaffs. Her smokestack and steampipe were riddled; her beak was broken off and prow twisted; the muzzles of two guns had been shattered. But as her armor had been scarcely so much as dented, the injuries were insignificant, and the Confederates awaited only daylight to complete the work of destruction.

Reports of the victory of the *Merrimac* were soon spreading in all directions. No wonder that the South became ecstatic and that the North was filled with the gravest apprehension. When the news reached Washington next morning (Sunday), a Cabinet meeting was immediately called. As the members assembled it was evident that they were suffering from the general alarm. In the deliberation that followed, excited fears were expressed that the blockade might now be broken, and the Richmond campaign thwarted; and, who could tell, even New York might soon be laid under contribution, and Washington burned![10]

For where were the helpless ships of the Union to find succor? Without seeking on their part, however, help came in a strange, most unseamanlike craft, the *Monitor*, which arrived in Hampton Roads that evening at nine o'clock.

---

[10] Nicolay and Hay, *Abraham Lincoln*, v, 226.

XVII

THE BATTLE OF HAMPTON ROADS (CONTINUED): THE MONITOR AND THE MERRIMAC

A Race in Shipbuilding

It was seemingly a strange coincidence that within eight hours after the first ironclad of the South had entered so brilliantly on her career, an armored champion of the North, also the first of its kind, should come upon the same scene. But the coincidence admits of explanation.

The South, recognizing her inability to build and man a navy, was virtually forced into trying the ironclad, and, as we have seen in the last chapter, began work on the *Merrimac* two months after the beginning of the war. News of this alarmed the North, and three or four months later the Department signed contracts for three ironclads. The smallest of these, the *Monitor*, was to be completed in the almost unprecedented time of 100 days. As the navy departments of the North and South were kept fairly well informed of the progress made by each other, there ensued a race in shipbuilding of grave importance; in which the North had the advantage of superior shops and mechanics, the South of a long start and intensity of feeling, stimulated by the constant presence of her enemy. This nearness of her foe promised the South another important advantage: her ironclad would have to steam fewer hours than the *Monitor* would days before striking the first decisive blow.

The South won the race by half a day, and thus was able to destroy two staunch old sailing ships. This, compared with the losses suffered by the army, was trivial,

But although the navy did not in general bear the brunt of the fighting, much depended on the ships. If the *Monitor* had been delayed another week in reaching Hampton Roads, the whole character of the war might have been changed.

Early in August, 1861, Congress, convened in extra session, had appropriated $1,500,000 "for the construction or completing of iron- or steel-clad steamships or steam batteries." Commodore Joseph Smith, Commodore Hiram Paulding, and Commander Charles H. Davis were appointed a board to investigate the plans and specifications that were submitted. These old and tried officers, schooled in everything that pertained to the earlier navy, admitted in their report that they approached "the subject with diffidence, having no experience and but scanty knowledge in this branch of naval architecture." Nevertheless, they did not shirk their responsibility, and after careful consideration approved the plans for the *Monitor*, the *Galena*, and the *New Ironsides*, which ships were soon begun. In fact, the *Monitor's* keel-plate was passing through the rolling mill while the clerks of the Navy Department were drawing up the formal contract. The *Monitor* was launched January 30, 1862, and was turned over to the Government on February 19.

The inventor of the *Monitor* was John Ericsson,[1] born in Sweden in 1803. His strange craft showed nothing less than genius in its adaptation to the service required. She was of light draft to navigate the shallow bays and

---

[1] Already Ericsson had given evidence of genius. While living in England he invented the screw propeller (1836); and it was because his invention met with utter indifference from British shipowners and naval officers that on the encouragement of an American consul and naval officer he came to the United States. The U. S. S. *Princeton*, already mentioned as the first warship with a screw propeller, was of his designing.

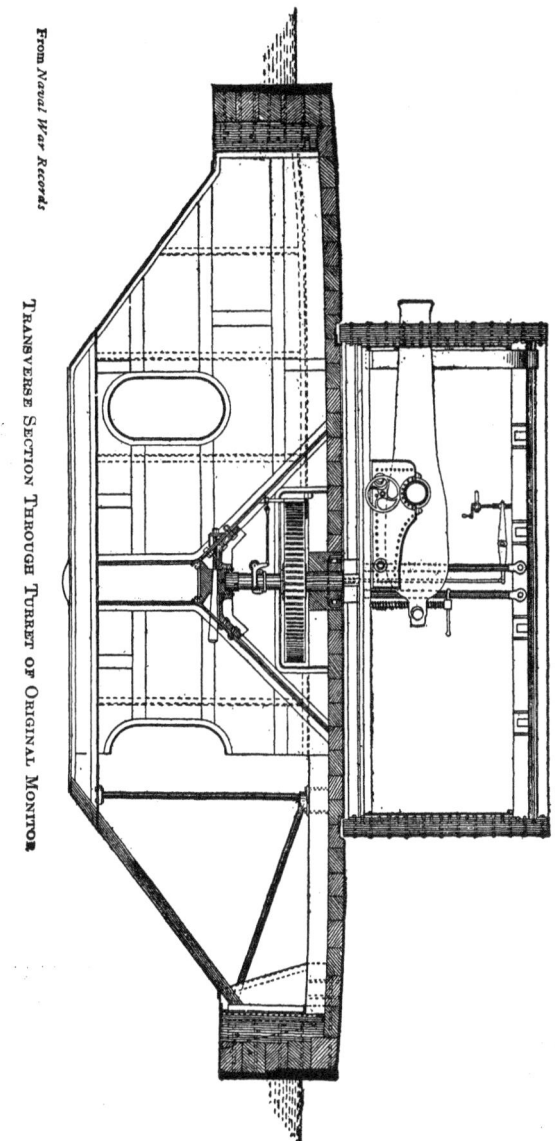

TRANSVERSE SECTION THROUGH TURRET OF ORIGINAL MONITOR.
From *Naval War Records*

rivers of the Southern States. As light draft made impossible high armored sides, her exposed surface was small, but heavily armored, and thus invulnerable to any guns of this period. A revolving turret was introduced that she might use her few guns in narrow streams where maneuvering would be impossible. Engines below the water line, and propeller and rudder protected by a wide overhang, were other elements of strength; the overhang, on sides as well as ends, protected her from ramming and also from shot directed at the water line, besides giving her increased stability in a rough sea.[2]

The original *Monitor* was, in simple terms, a turret on a raft, and the whole was superposed on a flat-bottomed boat. She was of 776 tons burden. Her extreme length was 172 feet; breadth, forty-one and a half feet; draft, ten and a half feet; inside diameter of turret, twenty feet; height of turret, nine feet.[3] The turret was composed of eight thicknesses of wrought-iron plates, each one inch thick, firmly riveted together. The sides of the hull, which rose scarcely two feet above the water, were protected by five inches of armor, and the deck was covered with a plating one inch thick. She had an armament of two 11-inch Dahlgren guns, the muzzles of which were run out through ports placed side by side. When the guns were drawn back, the ports were closed by heavy iron stoppers, acting like pendulums.

Even after the *Monitor* had been launched and had convinced the skeptical—of whom there were many—that she would at least float, duty on her was thought to be so hazardous that a crew was not detailed to man her,

---

[2] Church, *Life of John Ericsson*, i, 263.

[3] Executive Doc., House of Rep., 48th Cong. 1st Sess., Report No. 1725.

The Trip to Hampton Roads

but volunteers were called for. Lieutenant J. L. Worden was given the command, and Lieutenant S. D. Greene was made executive officer.

THE HAZARDOUS TRIP TO HAMPTON ROADS

The *Monitor* was built at Green Point, Long Island. After two short and rather unsatisfactory trial trips, she started for Hampton Roads. She left New York on Thursday, March 6, towed by the tugboat *Seth Low*. Of the experiences on that dangerous voyage, Lieutenant Greene wrote to his mother a week later: "About noon [Friday] the wind freshened and the sea was quite rough. In the afternoon the sea was breaking over our decks at a great rate and coming in our hawse-pipe forward in perfect floods. Our berth-deck hatch leaked in spite of all we could do, and the water came down under the tower like a waterfall. . . . The water came through the narrow eye-holes in the pilot house with such force as to knock the helmsman completely around from the wheel."[4]

The men on the *Monitor* had to meet all kinds of dangers. Water swept over the craft in such a volume that it went down the blowers and the smokestack. Engineers and firemen narrowly escaped asphyxiation, and when the engines stopped, the pumps were rendered useless, and the water in the hold increased rapidly. As the wind was from the west, by signaling the tug to go nearer the shore, the crew found relief in smoother water. At eight P.M. they succeeded in starting the engines, and all went well till midnight, when, passing a shoal, they once more encountered a heavy sea. The wheel ropes then jumped off the steering gear and became jammed. The vessel came very near foundering, but by heroic perseverance, Worden and his men finally succeeded in weathering

---

[4] Published in *United Service*, April, 1885.

the storm. At four P.M. the following afternoon the *Monitor* passed Cape Henry, and shortly after dark reached Fortress Monroe. According to orders already sent by the Department to Captain Marston of the *Roanoke*, the senior officer present, the *Monitor* on arrival was to proceed immediately to Washington; but in view of the desperate state of affairs at Hampton Roads, Captain Marston decided to disregard the orders and detain her for the defense of the fleet.

THE BATTLE OF THE IRONCLADS

Shortly after sunrise on Sunday morning, March 9, 1862, the *Merrimac*, attended by the *Patrick Henry* and the *Jamestown*, got under way and headed for Fortress Monroe; then, striking the channel up which the *Minnesota* had labored the day before, the squadron came slowly about and made for the Union ship. When still a mile distant, the *Merrimac* opened fire and planted a large shell under the counter near the water line. Before any considerable damage had been done, however, the *Monitor* appeared from the shadow of the *Minnesota* and boldly advanced to meet the *Merrimac*. Such a novelty in ship construction mystified the lookouts on the *Merrimac*. Lieutenant Davidson of the Confederate ship is said to have remarked, "The *Minnesota's* crew are leaving her on a raft." Soon the new vessel was recognized as Ericsson's invention, and many were the observations concerning the absurdity of this "immense shingle floating on the water, with a gigantic cheese box rising from its centre."

At a time seemingly so unpropitious, the officers and crew of the *Monitor* showed no ordinary courage in offering battle. All the night before they had been hard at work preparing for action; two days and a night previous to that, they had been struggling for their lives, and twice

The Monitor and the Merrimac 279

had narrowly escaped shipwreck; thus for forty-eight hours they had had almost no sleep or food. Further, it required unusual spirit to disregard the gloomy forebodings that surrounded the Union fleet, and advance in a small, untried craft to meet a foe that had just been proved to be practically invulnerable.

At about 8.30, on the *Monitor's* coming within short range, Lieutenant Worden changed his course so as to pass the *Merrimac* abeam, and gave the order to commence firing. Up went a port, a gun was thrust out, and a heavy shot struck the *Merrimac;* the latter responded with a broadside. Then the vessels, after passing, came about and passed again somewhat nearer. The firing now became regular; the *Monitor* discharged her guns every seven or eight minutes, and used solid shot; the *Merrimac* with her larger number of guns fired more often, and used only shells. Most of the early shot of the *Merrimac* had gone wide of the mark, for her gunners had a far smaller target than that offered the day before by a frigate. And later, as their missiles struck, they made no impression on the *Monitor's* turret, which continued to revolve freely—a fact which brought great relief to the men inside the turret, now being tested for the first time. When, however, as happened in three cases, a man was leaning even slightly against the wall of the turret on its being struck, he was knocked down and stunned. Thus Master Stodder, who had charge of the machinery controlling the turret, was disabled about ten o'clock, and had to be carried below. Fortunately, Chief Engineer Stimers, who was on board as official inspector, was eager to take part in the action; and as he knew more about the machinery of the turret than any one else on the vessel, his service was of great value.

The *Monitor*, because of the anchor-well in her bow, was scarcely adapted for ramming. The well was a device of Ericsson that permitted the anchor to be raised or lowered through the bottom without exposing men or machinery to the fire of the enemy. Nevertheless, Lieutenant Worden, on seeing that his heavy 11-inch shot were glancing off the slanting sides of the *Merrimac,* secured a favorable position and made a dash for the ram, hoping thereby to disable her rudder and propeller. He missed his mark by three feet, and the *Monitor* passed clear of the *Merrimac.*

It had been a part of Worden's plan in engaging the *Merrimac* to protect the *Minnesota* by offering battle at some distance from her. The *Merrimac* was, however, within long range of the *Minnesota,* and when in the middle of the engagement the *Monitor* withdrew for a few minutes, Lieutenant Catesby ap R. Jones, who was commanding the *Merrimac,* gave all his attention to the wooden ship. Captain Van Brunt of the *Minnesota* says, "On her second approach, I opened with all my broadside guns and 10-inch pivot, a broadside which would have blown out of water any timber-built ship in the world. She returned my fire with her rifled bow gun with a shell, which passed through the chief engineer's stateroom, through the engineer's mess room, amidships, and burst in the boatswain's room, tearing four rooms all into one in its passage, exploding two charges of powder, which set the ship on fire, but it was promptly extinguished by a party headed by my first lieutenant; her second went through the boiler of the tugboat *Dragon.*"[5] By the time the *Merrimac* had fired a third shell, the *Monitor* had again taken the offensive, and coming between the *Minnesota* and the *Merrimac,* compelled the latter to change her position, in doing which she grounded. Fifteen minutes later she was free, and then headed down the bay, with

---

[5] *Naval War Records,* vii, 11.

The Monitor and the Merrimac

the *Monitor* in pursuit. This was but a ruse on the part of the *Merrimac*, for, getting into deeper water, after considerable maneuvering she attempted to ram the *Monitor*. But the smaller craft, much the more agile, put her helm over and received only a glancing blow. The heavy beak of the *Merrimac* that had gone down with the *Cumberland* had not yet been replaced, and the light iron shoe now on her stem was cut by the *Monitor's* sharp edge. This opened a leak on the ram, which had been started the day before and had been only temporarily checked. At the moment of contact, Lieutenant Greene, who with his own hands fired all the guns of the *Monitor* until he left the turret near the close of the battle,[6] planted a solid 180-pound shot in the forward casemate of the *Merrimac*. The shot broke some of the iron plate and bent in the timber. Another shot striking in the same place would probably have penetrated. By order of the Department, only fifteen pounds of powder was used to a charge. Had thirty pounds been used, which later was found to be not too heavy for the guns, it is thought that several of the shot might have pierced the shield. A gun crew on the *Merrimac* were so affected by the concussion that they bled from nose and ears, but there was no further injury.

After the *Monitor* had been fighting for two hours, ammunition began to fail in her turret, and as this could be replenished only by bringing a hole in the turret directly over a scuttle, she withdrew into shallow water, where the *Merrimac* could not follow. Fifteen minutes later she was back and ready for the fight.

---

[6] By the strange fortune of war, Lieutenant Butt, an old Naval Academy chum of Greene, also took part in this battle. As Greene wrote to his mother, "My old room-mate was on board the *Merrimac*. Little did we think at the Academy we should ever be firing 150-pound shot at each other, but so goes the world."

The engagement had at this time been fought for three hours without either antagonist's securing the advantage. Each was powerful in defense, and each met with many difficulties on assuming the offensive. The *Merrimac* was cumbrous and unwieldy, and her draft of twenty-two feet was ill adapted to Hampton Roads. Her smokestack had been so riddled by the fight of the previous day, that the fires did not draw well, and steam got so low as scarcely to drive her defective engines. The *Monitor*, much shorter, and with a draft of less than twelve feet, responded quickly to her helm; as she also had twice the speed of her antagonist, she showed a marked superiority in maneuvering. She would dart about, assume a position where for a time the *Merrimac* could not bring a gun to bear, and, when threatened, retreat to shoal water, where her huge enemy could not follow. But the turret of the *Monitor* could be operated only with great difficulty; it was hard to start, and when started it was still harder to stop. Consequently the guns had to be fired "on the fly," and it was anything but a simple matter to secure a good aim when all that a man in the turret could see of the outside world was what he saw through the narrow cracks between the guns and the sides of the ports. By the revolving of the turret, the men at the guns lost their sense of direction; white guide marks painted on the stationary platform below were soon covered with grime, so that when word was brought from the pilot house that the *Merrimac* bore off the starboard or port bow, the gunners had little to guide them. It was a constant source of anxiety to Lieutenant Greene [7] lest in the smoke and confusion the guns of the *Monitor* might be trained on their own pilot house, which, being in almost the extreme

---

[7] Greene's story of the battle will be found in *Battles and Leaders of the Civil War*, i, 719.

The Monitor and the Merrimac 283

bow, was separated from the turret by a third of the length of the ship. Communication between pilot house and turret was by a speaking-tube, and when this was disabled early in the engagement, the paymaster and captain's clerk were employed as messengers; since they were without sea-training, orders were not always rightly understood.

At about half past eleven, the gunners of the *Merrimac*, despairing of doing any injury to the turret of the *Monitor*, directed their fire against the pilot house. This projected four feet above the deck, and was made of wrought-iron beams, nine inches thick and twelve inches deep, dovetailed together at the corners. By crowding, it now held three people, Lieutenant Worden, the quartermaster, and the pilot. While Worden was looking through the long narrow slit interposed between the iron beams, which served as a sight hole, a shell fired by the *Merrimac* only a few yards distant exploded directly outside, and his face and eyes were painfully wounded with powder and fine fragments of iron. The explosion also partially raised the heavy iron cover of the conning tower, which had been laid in a groove, not bolted down. Though suffering extreme pain, and temporarily blinded, Worden retained his presence of mind; conscious of the flood of light streaming in from above, he feared that the pilot house had been demolished, and gave orders to sheer off, a maneuver that brought the vessel into shallow water towards Fortress Monroe.

Lieutenant Greene, who had been summoned to take command, after helping Worden to the cabin, found that the *Monitor*, though drifting aimlessly about beyond the reach of the *Merrimac*, was practically as fit for engagement as ever; the pilot house had suffered little harm, and the steering gear was uninjured. Accordingly, after fifteen or twenty minutes' absence, the *Monitor* was again pointed towards the *Merrimac;* but it was towards a retiring foe. The *Merrimac* was on her way back to Norfolk. The *Monitor* followed her a short distance, fired a few shot to indicate her willingness to continue the engagement, and then returned to the *Minnesota.* This was shortly after twelve o'clock; the battle had been fought nearly four hours without either ironclad's losing a man.

Both sides later expressed surprise that the *Merrimac* should have retired when she did. Captain Van Brunt of the *Minnesota* in his official report said that on seeing the *Monitor* withdraw after Worden's accident, he inferred she was leaving because she had run short of ammunition or had met with serious injury. And he admitted that, since the *Minnesota* was immovably aground, and had expended most of her solid shot, he had decided, when the *Merrimac* returned to the attack, to destroy his ship.

Lieutenant Catesby Jones, who was severely criticised, defended his action as follows:

"We had run into the *Monitor,* causing us to leak, and had received a shot from her which came near disabling the machinery, but continued to fight her until she was driven into shoal water. The *Minnesota* appeared so badly damaged that we did not believe that she could ever move again. The pilots refused to place us any nearer to her (they had once run us aground). About twelve [o'clock] the pilots declared if we did not go up to Norfolk then, that we could not do so until the next day."[8] If this explanation is not wholly satisfactory, further light may be gained from a letter of Lieutenant Davidson, C. S. N.: "Our officers and men were completely broken down by two days' and a night's continuous work with the heaviest rifled ordnance in the world."[9]

---

[8] *Naval War Records,* vii, 59.
[9] *Ibid.,* vii, 61.

During the engagement, the *Monitor* fired forty-one solid cast-iron shot. A proof of the fair marksmanship was found when the *Merrimac* went into drydock; twenty of the 100 indentations in her armor were recognized as caused by the shot of the *Monitor*. While six of the outer plates of the *Merrimac* were cracked, and had to be replaced, none of the inner course were broken. The *Monitor* had been struck twenty-two times. The armor of her turret had been indented in one place two and a quarter inches, but none of the plates had been cracked. As has been narrated, one of the wrought-iron beams of the pilot house, however, had been fractured by a 68-pound shell.

RESULTS

The fight between the *Monitor* and the *Merrimac*, so far as the ironclads were directly concerned, ended at noon, March 9; but on paper, a contest of the same name has been fought over again and again in a fruitless effort to decide who was victor. Whether it was a defeat, a victory, or a drawn battle, it relieved the North of the greatest apprehension. The *Monitor*, by her remarkable defense, had saved the *Minnesota*, the *Roanoke*, and the *St. Lawrence*. She had prevented the blockade from being broken at Hampton Roads, its most important point. She insured the supremacy of the sea to the North. She allayed the discouragement and terror felt through the loyal States on the overwhelming defeat of the previous day, and checked the wild rejoicing of the South.

These results were of such moment that the battle is to be classed with Gettysburg and Vicksburg in its influence on the war. Its fame, for other reasons as well, went far beyond the United States. "Probably no naval conflict in the history of the world ever attracted so much attention as did the battle in Hampton Roads, between the *Monitor* and the *Merrimac*. It revolutionized the navies of the world, and showed that the wooden ships, which had long held control of the ocean, were of no further use for fighting purposes."[10]

The conservative London *Times* observed, on receiving the news of the battle, "Whereas we [the English] had available for immediate purposes 149 first-class warships, we have now two, these two being the *Warrior* and her sister *Ironside*. There is not now a ship in the English Navy, apart from these two, that it would not be madness to trust to an engagement with that little *Monitor*."[11]

As the North immediately proceeded to construct other monitors of an improved type, the danger of armed intervention by England and France in behalf of the seceded States was materially lessened.

The Subsequent Careers of the Monitor and the Merrimac

Each side made elaborate plans for boarding or ramming the ironclad of the other in a later engagement; but each, recognizing how disastrous would be a defeat, refused to fight except on terms promising a decided advantage.

The *Merrimac*, after being repaired, appeared twice in the Roads, but made no further attempt against the Union fleet, and no engagement followed. On the 10th of May, 1862, when the Confederates evacuated Norfolk and Portsmouth, it became a question what should be done with the *Merrimac*. Commodore Tattnall, who had succeeded to the command of the ram, despairing, because of her draft, of taking her up the James for the defense of Richmond, as had been planned, applied the torch and destroyed her on May 11.

---

[10] Knox, *Decisive Battles since Waterloo*, p. 228.
[11] Quoted by Knox.

The Sinking of the Monitor 287

The career of the *Monitor* was also brief, and she survived her great rival by only little more than half a year. She was once more actively engaged; the occasion, May 15, 1862, was a bombardment of Drewry's Bluff, seven miles below Richmond, by the *Monitor, Galena, Aroostook, Naugatuck,* and *Port Royal.* The ironclad *Galena* was perforated eighteen times by plunging shot, and had thirteen men killed and eleven wounded. The *Monitor* was struck three times, but not injured. The end of this, the most famous ship of modern history, came at the very conclusion of the year 1862. On December 29 the *Monitor* left Hampton Roads, towed by the *Rhode Island,* bound for Charleston, S. C. All went well until the evening of the 30th, when, being about fifteen miles south of Cape Hatteras Shoals, she struck a rough sea and yawed badly. The wind was from the south. Had the *Rhode Island,* with her tow, early come about, and run before the gale, the *Monitor* might have been saved; but the *Rhode Island* held determinedly to her course. About eight o'clock in the evening the sea rose rapidly; from that time till midnight Commander J. P. Bankhead, with his men on the *Monitor,* made a heroic fight against the waves, which swept repeatedly over the decks, poured through innumerable crevices, and made the engines work harder and harder. Shortly before midnight two boats of the *Rhode Island* began taking off the shipwrecked crew. This, in the raging sea, with the *Monitor* submerged much of the time, was a most hazardous undertaking; and four officers and twelve men of the *Monitor* were lost. Shortly after Commander Bankhead had reached the *Rhode Island,* the red light in the turret of the *Monitor* disappeared, for the waves had closed over her.[12]

---

[12] Commander Bankhead's report will be found in the *Naval War Records,* viii, 347.

XVIII

OPERATIONS ON THE WESTERN RIVERS

THE organization of combined naval and military operations for gaining control of the Mississippi and its tributaries was one of the three cardinal recommendations of the Secretary of the Navy at the beginning of the war. This appealed with especial directness to the people of the North Central States, who realized that with the Union divided the vast system of waterways, the avenues of commerce, might become useless. They also perceived that the side which held the Mississippi could easily carry war into the territory of the other.

Cairo, Illinois, at the junction of three States as well as two great rivers, occupied a strategic position, and became the naval arsenal and depot of supplies for the Union flotilla. Nearly all the Mississippi south of Cairo, 1097 miles by stream, 480 by direct line, was in 1861 controlled by the Confederates. They had also a strong line of fortifications from Columbus, Kentucky (twenty-one miles down the river from Cairo), extending east to Fort Henry, Fort Donelson, and to the Cumberland Mountains. Attacking this line of Confederate defenses, the Union forces early in 1862 gained several important victories; and the navy, though not always the chief factor, was undeniably essential.

Gunboats, well protected and adapted to service on shallow rivers, were at once demanded, and the Government contracted in August, 1861, with James B. Eads of St. Louis for seven ironclads. In size and form these were practically all the same, 175 feet long, fifty-one and

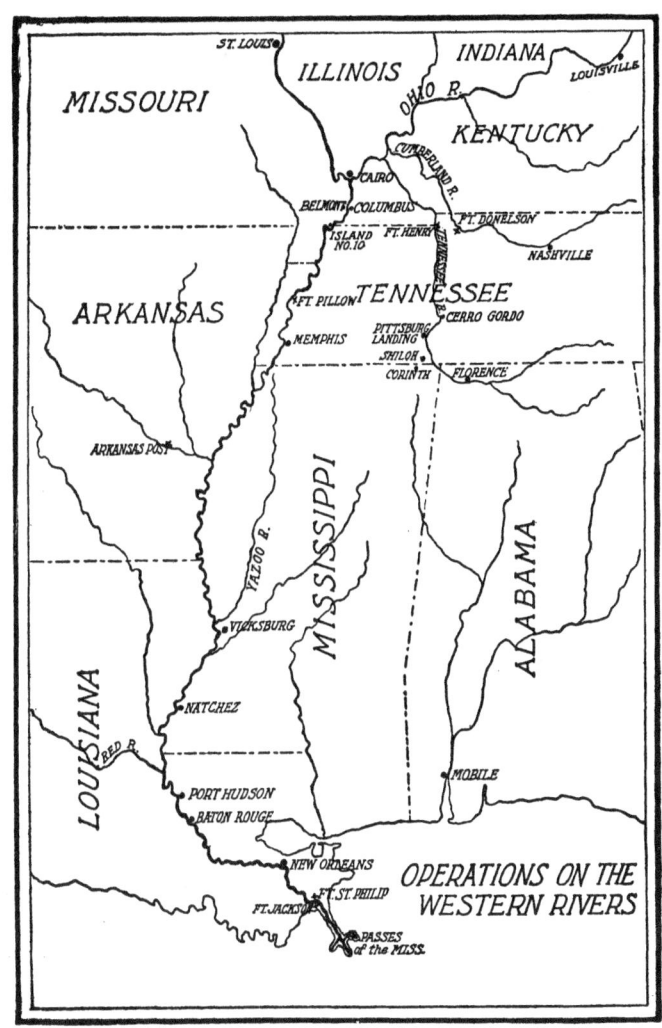

OPERATIONS ON THE WESTERN RIVERS

a half feet beam, and six feet in draft; each carried thirteen heavy guns, and had a casemate, sloped at an angle of 35° and plated at the forward end and abreast the engines with two and a half inches of iron. There was a single, large paddle wheel placed in an opening forward of the stern and thus protected from shot by the casemate and sides. The speed required by contract was nine miles an hour. Thus were built and made ready for active service in January, 1862, the gunboats *St. Louis, Carondelet, Cincinnati, Louisville, Mound City, Cairo,* and *Pittsburg.* These with the *Benton,* a government snagboat that had been made over into an ironclad larger and stronger than any of the rest, formed the backbone of the river fleet throughout the war.[1]

The fleet was built under the general supervision of the War Department. However, the Navy Department co-operated by detailing one of its officers to direct the work. Commander John Rodgers began the construction, and Captain Andrew H. Foote, relieving him on September 6, 1861, carried it on to its completion. Foote, a true sailor, would have much preferred a command on the sea; for the peculiar duty given him included operations on land and swamp as well as river, and he met problems utterly different from any encountered previously in his long service. The fact that he was under the direction of the War Department, receiving orders from generals who little comprehended what a gunboat could and could not do, was not the least of his difficulties. In fitting out the fleet he was frequently embarrassed by lack of materials, money, and credit, but he carried forward the work with magnificent patience and determination. He later gained high praise for the successes he won with this fleet, yet

---

[1] Eads, *Recollections of Foote and the Gunboats,* in *Battles and Leaders,* i, 338 ff.

From Hoppin's *Life of Foote*
ANDREW H. FOOTE

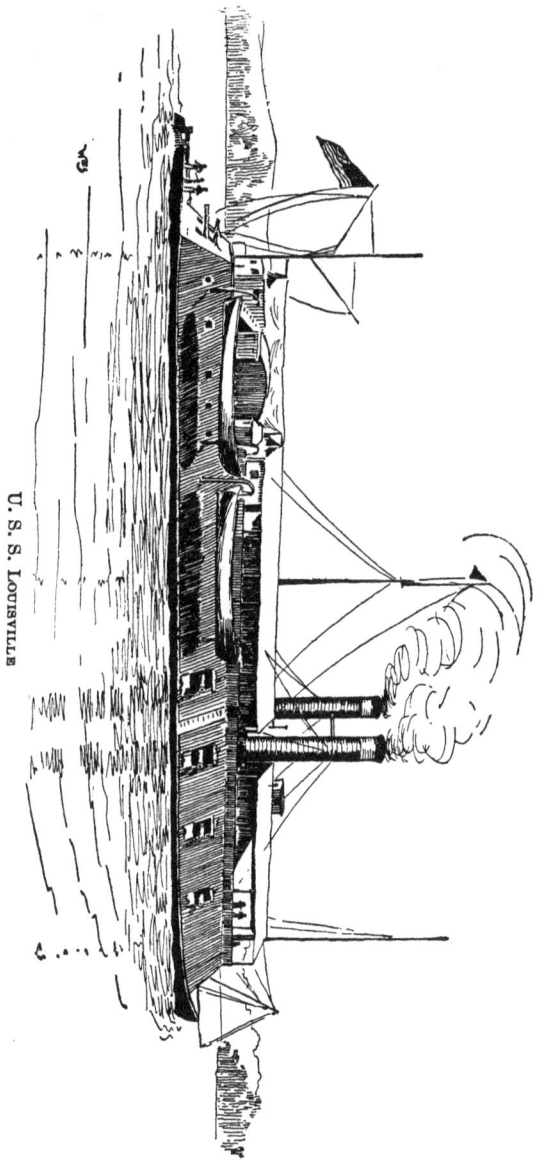

U. S. S. LOUISVILLE

he is said to have looked upon the fighting as secondary, and the creation of this fleet as being the great achievement of his life.

THE ACTION AT BELMONT

The first important service rendered by the river navy was on November 7, 1861, the day Port Royal was taken by DuPont. General Grant, with 3000 troops, surprised a Confederate force of 2500 at Belmont, Missouri, just across the Mississippi from Columbus. The Union army had come down the river in transports, convoyed by the *Tyler*, Commander Walke, and the *Lexington*, Commander Stembel. These were river boats which, with the *Conestoga*, had been purchased and made into wooden gunboats the summer preceding by Commander Rodgers.

The Union army swept all before them, but when a decisive advantage had been gained, were slow in obeying orders to fall back. As a consequence they were in imminent danger of being overwhelmed by the large Confederate reinforcements that had crossed over from Columbus. The gunboats, which had three times engaged the heavy Confederate batteries above Columbus commanding Belmont, now from an advantageous position opened on the Confederate troops advancing to attack the retreating army even at their transports; with grape, canister, and 5-second shell they enfiladed the Confederate lines and drove them back with considerable loss. They had occasion to protect the transports even after they had got under way; moreover, when they had proceeded a few miles up the river, and General McClernand discovered that some of the troops had been left behind, the gunboats went back, picked up the troops with their wounded and forty prisoners, and then returned to Cairo. The incident may seem not very important in the history of the navy, and

The Capture of Fort Henry

yet without the *Tyler* and the *Lexington* the capture of a large part of the Union force could scarcely have been averted. Such a disaster would have caused distrust of Grant, and might have long prevented his being given an opportunity to show his great abilities.

THE CAPTURE OF FORT HENRY

In January, 1862, when Grant had his army fairly well disciplined, and Foote had the seven ironclads ready, they considered attacking the Confederate lines. Columbus, with its admirable situation and heavy batteries, gave promise of being able to withstand a direct attack for a long while. Forts Henry and Donelson were not so strong, and if they should fall the Union forces would have access to Tennessee, Alabama, and Mississippi, and could compel the evacuation of Columbus.

Having gained General Halleck's permission to attack Fort Henry, Foote left Cairo, on February 2, with four ironclads and three wooden gunboats. Progress up the Tennessee was slow because of torpedoes, eight of which the squadron fished out of the channel. At the same time Grant's army came up the river in transports, convoyed by gunboats, and landed within a few miles of the fort. For the plan was that the troops, making a detour, should attack the rear of the fort when the squadron attacked from the river. Fort Henry in the official report of J. F. Gilmer, Chief Engineer, Western Department, C. S. A., is described as "a strong field work of fine bastion front. . . . in good condition for defense," with "seventeen guns mounted on substantial platforms, twelve of which were so placed as to bear well on the river." The twelve guns were, one 10-inch columbiad, one 60-pounder rifle, two 42-pounders, and eight 32-pounders, "all arranged to fire through embrasures formed by raising the parapet between the guns with sand bags carefully laid."[2]

On the morning of February 6, according to agreement, Foote steamed towards the batteries, and at half past twelve, when 1700 yards distant, opened fire. "The three old [wooden] gunboats," writes Foote, "took position astern and inshore of the [four] armored boats doing good execution there in the action, while the armored boats were placed in the first order of steaming, approaching the fort in a parallel line."[3] Foote's plan was to present the bows, the least vulnerable part of his boats, to the enemy, and rely on his bow guns, of which in the armored vessels he had eleven; then, by advancing, to compel the Confederate gunners constantly to alter their aim and make it difficult for them to secure the right elevation for their pieces.

The fire of the gunboats called forth a spirited reply from the fort, and as the squadron slowly approached to within 600 yards, the shooting on both sides increased in rapidity and accuracy. About an hour after the battle had begun, the armored *Essex* had her casemate penetrated by a shot; this killed one man, then plowing its way back, exploded the boiler and wounded by scalding twenty-eight, among them Commander W. D. Porter. The *Essex*, rendered helpless, slowly drifted out of line astern, and was carried by the current from the fort down the river. The other gunboats also were struck several times. The flagship *Cincinnati*, particularly, was a target and had many plates of her casemate broken, while her smoke stacks, after-cabin, and boats were completely riddled. She received only one shot that caused loss of

---

[2] *Army War Records,* vii, 132.
[3] *Ibid.,* vii, 122.

The Capture of Fort Henry

life; this, penetrating the forward casemate on the port side, killed one man and wounded several.

Meanwhile the Confederates were finding it increasingly difficult to defend their works. Their gunners were "under a most terrific fire from the advancing foe, whose approach was steady and constant."[4] Early in the action their rifled cannon burst, killing three of the men at the piece and disabling a number of others. Next, one of the 32-pounders was struck by a heavy shell, which rendered the gun useless and wounded all its crew. Then the 10-inch columbiad became silent; the priming wire had been jammed and broken in the vent, and efforts to remove it were unavailing. At 1.45 P.M., General Tilghman, commanding the fort, saw that further resistance was useless, for he had but two guns now in action. After an engagement that had lasted one hour and fifteen minutes, he lowered his flag and surrenderd to Foote.

An hour later Foote turned over the fort with the prisoners to Grant. The army had been so impeded by well-nigh impassable roads and swollen streams (the result of heavy rains for two days previous to the battle), that it had been able to take no part in the attack. In recognition of the splendid service rendered by the gunboats and their commanding officer, the captured fort was at once renamed "Fort Foote."

On the surrender of Fort Henry, Lieutenant-Commander Phelps, with the three wooden gunboats, proceeded twenty-five miles up the Tennessee, where he destroyed the bridge and rendered useless for through traffic the important Memphis and Charleston Railroad. Having compelled the Confederates, whom he surprised near the bridge, to destroy three boats loaded with military stores to prevent their capture, he continued to Cerro

---

[4] Report of Chief Engineer Gilmer.

Gordo, Tennessee. There he seized a large steamer, the *Eastport,* which was being remade into a gunboat. She was such a valuable prize that the *Tyler* remained to guard her and to put on board the materials that had been gathered for her rebuilding. She was later taken into the navy, and served for two years in the river operations. The *Conestoga* and the *Lexington,* going farther up the river, had seized two more steamers, one freighted with iron to be sent to Richmond. At Florence, Alabama, they discovered three steamers, but these were fired on their approach. They could not go beyond Florence because of the Muscle Shoal. Destroying the military stores along the route which they could not carry back, the gunboats then returned to Cairo, just in time to join the expedition against Fort Donelson.[5]

THE ATTACK ON FORT DONELSON

Because the Union army had been delayed in reaching the position in the rear of Fort Henry, most of the Confederate army had escaped. While a hundred men under General Tilghman had been replying to the attack of the gunboats, the main force had slipped past the Federal army and gone to Fort Donelson, twelve miles distant on the Cumberland River. Here the Confederates, drawing in their lines, concentrated about 18,000 men, the commands of Generals Floyd, Pillow, and Buckner. The fort occupied a bluff on the west bank of the Cumberland, and commanded the navigation of the river. It was much stronger than Fort Henry, and the Confederates realized its great importance to them. It was defended on the water side by two batteries, each about thirty feet above high water and well constructed; the lower, or downstream, battery was armed with nine guns, one 10-inch

---

[5] For Phelps's report see *Army War Records,* vii, 153.

The Attack on Fort Donelson

columbiad and eight 32-pounders; the upper battery with three guns, a 6½-inch rifled gun and two 32-pounder carronades.

After the capture of Fort Henry, General Grant, knowing that the Confederates would make every effort to increase their force at Donelson, recommended that the Union forces move forward at once and make a combined attack. Foote protested that the flotilla needed time for preparation, but as Halleck and Grant both deemed immediate action to be a military necessity, he yielded to their judgment. Since he had a force insufficient to man more than four of his ironclads, he substituted for the two gunboats that had been most injured in the recent battle two others that had been left behind at Cairo, and on February 12 he advanced up the Cumberland.

At three o'clock in the afternoon of the 14th, Foote engaged the water batteries at Fort Donelson. His plan of attack was similar to that employed at Fort Henry. With the armored gunboats *St. Louis, Carondelet, Louisville,* and *Pittsburg* in line abreast, he slowly advanced upon the enemy's works, beginning the action at the distance of a mile, and reaching a position less than 400 yards away. The wooden gunboats *Tyler* and *Conestoga,* forming a second division, were to shell the batteries from a position considerably astern. As a slight protection from the plunging shot of the fort, all the hard materials of the boats, such as chains, coal in bags, and lumber, had been placed along the upper decks.

The contest was sharply fought, and lasted for an hour and a half. The fire of the batteries was terribly accurate, and not only swept the tops of the ironclads, destroying everything that was exposed, but occasionally penetrated the casemates or ports. "The *St. Louis* alone," Foote writes of his flagship, "received fifty-nine shots, four between wind and water, and one in the pilot house, mortally wounding the pilot and others."[6] The shot that entered the pilot house of the *St. Louis* carried away the wheel. About the same time the Confederates' fire injured the tiller-ropes of the *Louisville*. The attempt made to steer by relieving tackles failed in the rapid current, and the two boats, becoming unmanageable, drifted down the river and out of action. On the *Carondelet*, two pilots had already been disabled, and now the third was wounded. The wheel had been injured, and finally her starboard rudder was broken by the *Pittsburg's* fouling her. There was no alternative—the gunboats were unequal to the task and had to withdraw.

Admiral Mahan remarks on the attack, "Notwithstanding its failure, the tenacity and fighting qualities of the fleet were more markedly proved in this action than in the victory at Henry. The vessels were struck more frequently (the flagship fifty-nine times, and none less than twenty), and though the power of the enemy's guns was about the same in each case, the height and character of the soil at Donelson placed the fleet at a great disadvantage. The fire from above, reaching their sloping armor nearly at right angles, searched every weak point. . . . Despite these injuries, and the loss of fifty-four killed and wounded, the fleet was only shaken from its hold by accidents to the steering apparatus, after which their batteries could not be brought to bear."[7]

In his report, Foote expressed confidence that the gunboats would have captured both batteries, had their steering apparatus not been disabled, and had the action continued fifteen minutes longer. But the statements made by the defenders of the fort scarcely support his belief. General A. S. Johnston reported at the close of the engage-

---

[6] Foote's report will be found in the *Army War Records*, vii, 166.

[7] Mahan, *The Gulf and Inland Waters*, p. 27.

ment, "No damage done to our battery and not a man killed," and Chief Engineer Gilmer said the same. The gunboats when near were at a disadvantage because of the elevation of the batteries. Foote perhaps could have fought on more equal terms by bombarding the works from a distance, but later experience at Island No. 10 and at the forts below New Orleans showed that a bombardment from a safe distance might be kept up day after day and cause little damage. Foote was looking for immediate results, and his dashing style of attack would have secured them had not the fort been so ably defended.

A hard fought battle followed the next day between the Union and Confederate armies, in which the Confederates at first had the advantage, but later were driven back to their fortifications. Early on the morning after, February 16, Fort Donelson surrendered. Grant had shown wisdom in beginning operations immediately on the capture of Fort Henry. The gunboats had been necessary for bringing up the troops in safety, and although the river attack had been checked, the navy was essential to the ultimate success.

OPERATIONS AT ISLAND NO. 10

Less than a week after the capture of Fort Donelson, the Confederates had begun to transfer the military supplies at Columbus to a point farther south, but they contrived to make the evacuation so skilfully that Flag-Officer Foote, making a reconnoissance while it was in progress, suspected nothing. The next stand the Confederates made at Island No. 10, so called because of its numerical position in the series of islands south of Cairo. It was fifty-five miles from that city, and lay near the shore opposite Missouri close to the boundary separating Kentucky from Tennessee. The island has since been swept away, and the river has somewhat changed. Here, at that time, the river by an extraordinary twist, like an "S" reversed (∽), gained in its flow of twelve miles just three to the south. The island, two miles long by two-thirds of a mile wide, lay at the bottom of the loop to the right, occupying, with the batteries on the Tennessee shore, a position admirably adapted for defense. For the Con-

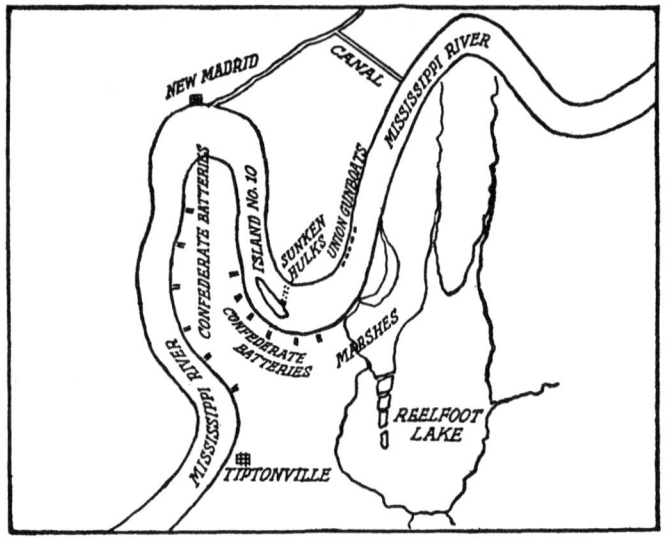

ISLAND No. 10

federates had the river before them, and behind them (to the east) a large, impassable swamp, which made attack by land forces impossible so long as the defenders could control the river. But their position was one of great isolation. Supplies could reach them only by the river from the south, and when their communications from that quarter were cut off, they were helpless, and retreat was practically impossible.

On March 15, 1862, Flag-Officer Foote, with a squadron consisting of six ironclads and ten mortar boats, supported by Colonel Buford with 1200 troops, moved down the river to attack the island. General Pope, who had begun operations previous to their arrival, had occupied New Madrid on the loop above and to the northwest of Island No. 10. Though he was unable to cross the river because of Confederate gunboats, he planted batteries on the west bank as far south as Tiptonville (on the opposite bank, fifteen miles down the river from New Madrid), and by them prevented Confederate transports from taking up supplies. On the 16th Foote's mortar boats took position and, opening fire, compelled several regiments on the island to change the location of their camp. Next day, at noon, the gunboats joined in an attack on the uppermost fort on the Tennessee shore, but kept at a safe distance of 2000 yards or more. Throughout the siege Foote was cautious. He well knew that if his gunboats were disabled, they would not be carried out of action by the current as at Henry and Donelson, but would be swept immediately under the enemy's guns. Further, he had to take into consideration that there was a Confederate fleet stationed below the island near Fort Pillow, reported to be not less powerful than his own; for if several of his boats should be lost, the Confederate fleet might capture the rest, and, steaming up the river, strike a heavy blow at Cairo.

The bombardment of the 16th and 17th, as of the days following, annoyed the enemy, at times temporarily silencing certain of the batteries, but seems to have done little injury. A rifle gun on the *St. Louis* burst during the engagement of the 17th, killing two and wounding thirteen, probably a much greater loss than the Confederates suffered from the combined fire of gunboats and mortars. The mortars, as Foote later observed, lacked effectiveness because the forts were widely separated and presented a small target. The Confederate position, indeed, was too strong to be captured by direct attack, even if the Union fleet had been increased to two or three times its size. On the island were four batteries mounting twenty-three guns, on the Tennessee shore six batteries with thirty-two guns; and there was, besides, a floating battery moored near the middle of the island reported as carrying nine or ten 9-inch guns.

While the flotilla continued to bombard the forts during the latter half of March, General Pope was digging a canal to cut off the loop on which were all the fortifications; by means of this on April 4 he was able to take his light transports from above the Confederate works to New Madrid without passing Island No. 10. The gunboats, however, drew too much water to pass through the canal, and until Pope had gunboats to protect his troops in crossing from Missouri to Tennessee, he could not attack from the rear the Confederate works just opposite Island No. 10.

On March 20 Foote held a council of war and considered running the batteries with part of his squadron. All of his officers with the exception of Commander Walke opposed the plan. The risk was undeniably great, yet so urgent was the need of a gunboat to co-operate with the army below New Madrid, that on March 30 Foote ordered Commander Walke, who was eagerly waiting for permission, to prepare for the perilous enterprise.

Meanwhile, an expedition, consisting of fifty men from the squadron and the same number from the army under the command of Colonel Roberts, performed a hazardous service. Late in the evening of April 1, the party, in five boats, crept down the river, keeping close under the shadow of the Kentucky shore towards the nearest battery, known as "No. 1 Fort." Taking the greatest care to avoid discovery, the men had come within ten yards

The Carondelet Passes the Batteries 303

before the sentinels at the guns saw them and gave the alarm. Landing with great quickness, the Union force met with no resistance, and having spiked every gun, returned without losing a man.

This exploit was especially timely for the Union forces, as they were about to send a gunboat down the river. They gained another advantage three days later, when the fleet, by their fire, managed to cut loose the floating battery, which had been an important defense of the island. As the current was strong, the Confederates were not able to secure the battery till it had drifted three miles below.

On the 4th of April, Walke announced to Foote that his vessel, the *Carondelet*, was ready to run the blockade. He had made use of some clever expedients to protect her from the enemy's fire. Around the boilers and engine room he had placed a barricade of heavy timber and loose iron. The parts of the sides without iron plating he had strengthened with bales of hay, lumber, and chain-cables; and to her port quarter had lashed a coal barge as an added safeguard to the magazine and shell rooms. The upper deck he had covered with lumber, cord wood, coal bags, chain-cables, and hawsers. And around the pilot house he had coiled cables and ropes from twelve to eighteen inches thick.[8]

The plan was to run the batteries that evening, though conditions were not altogether favorable, for the afternoon indicated that a clear night was to follow. However, at sunset the sky became hazy, and at ten o'clock, when the *Carondelet* got under way, a thunder storm was about to break—conditions decidedly more promising.

During the first half mile everything went well, and

---

[8] Walke's own account of the preparations and the exploit is to be found in his *Scenes and Reminiscences*, p. 120 ff.; also in *Battles and Leaders*, i, 441 ff.

the *Carondelet,* with her lights covered, was running so silently that there was hope that she might pass the batteries unobserved. But just as she came abreast the first, her flues caught fire, and, blazing up, disclosed her position. The flames were quickly checked, but five rockets, followed by a cannon shot from Fort No. 2, showed that the alarm had been given. Since the only course of safety for the Union vessel then lay in quick action, Walke crowded on steam and made all haste to pass the batteries.

The thunder storm now burst with great violence, and vivid flashes of lightning showed the hurried movements of the Confederates as they were running to their guns and charging them. Soon, with the heavy crashes of thunder and the torrents of rain were mingled the roar of the cannon and the fall of shot and musket balls. In order to avoid needless exposure, the men of the *Carondelet* were for the most part under cover. But Commander Walke, First Master Hoel (the chief pilot), and Wilson and Gilmore (the two leadsmen at the bow) kept their stations on deck through this double storm, exhibiting splendid coolness and courage.

It was difficult to keep the *Carondelet* with the cumbersome coal barge on the course because of the rapid current. And once, after an unusually long pause between the flashes of lightning, a timely illumination showed the pilot that he was running on a bar right under the enemy's guns. His prompt command, "Hard-a-port!" saved the boat. The Confederates fired at almost the same moment, but they either did not sufficiently depress their guns or were firing without taking aim, for their shot had no effect. The *Carondelet* was subjected for thirty minutes to an almost uninterrupted fire of the batteries on the Tennessee shore, besides one at the head of the island; and when she had passed these, there was still the floating battery three miles below to reckon with. A light burning

The Capture of Island No. 10

on its deck showed that the Confederates were there awaiting the gunboat. The *Carondelet* was not prepared to engage it, for in running past the forts everything on her decks and in her hold had been arranged with the idea of protection. Therefore, bearing over to the Missouri shore, she slipped by, being fired on only six or eight times. About midnight she arrived at New Madrid, and was joyfully welcomed by the forces of General Pope.

It seems almost incredible that in passing the gantlet of six forts and more than fifty guns the *Carondelet* should have escaped all injury. Not only had most of the Union officers believed that the project was too hazardous to justify attempting it, but the Confederates manning the forts had been confident that it was impossible of execution. The risk was unquestionably somewhat overestimated, for two days later the *Pittsburg* repeated the exploit. However, this does not detract from the courage of Walke and his men.

"The passage of the *Carondelet*," remarks Mahan, "was not only one of the most daring and dramatic events of the war; it was also the death-blow to the Confederate defense of this position." Events followed in rapid succession. On April 6 General Granger accompanied Commander Walke in the *Carondelet* in making a reconnoissance of the fortifications on the Tennessee shore down to Tiptonville. Before their return the Union force stopped to engage one of the works, and, having silenced it, landed and spiked the guns. On the 7th the *Carondelet* and the *Pittsburg* took in succession the Confederate batteries on the east bank of the river and enabled Pope's army to cross in safety. Already the Confederates had become convinced that it was impossible to hold Island No. 10 much longer, and most of their force had withdrawn, leaving but a hundred artillerymen, who surrendered the forts to Flag-Officer Foote late in the evening of

April 7. But the Confederates' retreat had begun too late. Because of the impassable swamp on the east, their only road to safety was by way of Tiptonville; and when Pope with great celerity threw his army across the river, he captured the entire force. In this move of the Union army the *Carondelet* and the *Pittsburg* had been absolutely essential, and Pope recognized them as having an important part in his success. The number of prisoners taken by Pope and Foote together was 7273. Pope writes in his report of April 9, "Three generals, seven colonels, seven regiments, several battalions of infantry, five companies of artillery, over 100 heavy siege guns, twenty-four pieces of field artillery, an immense quantity of ammunition and supplies, and several thousand stand of small arms, a great number of tents, horses, wagons, etc., have fallen into our hands. Before abandoning Island No. 10, the enemy sank the gunboat *Grampus* and six of his transports. These last I am raising and expect to have ready for service in a few days. The famous floating battery was scuttled and turned adrift, with all her guns aboard. She was captured and run aground in shoal water by our forces at New Madrid." [9]

While the gunboats on the Mississippi were co-operating with Pope to such advantage, the *Tyler* and the *Lexington* on the Tennessee River were rendering service not less important to Grant at Pittsburg Landing. On April 6 General A. S. Johnston had unexpectedly fallen upon the Union army, and in a fiercely contested battle lasting all day had driven the Federal troops from their camp, half way to the river. In the afternoon the fighting was especially determined on the Union army's left wing, which Johnston attempted to turn so as to get possession of the landing and the transports. General Hurlbut,

---

[9] *Army War Records*, viii, 78.

commanding this wing, was so hard pressed that he felt that without reinforcements he could not hold out for more than an hour longer. Then it was that the *Tyler*, by a rapid and well-directed fire, not only silenced the hostile batteries, but checked the Confederate advance. Later in the afternoon the *Tyler* and the *Lexington* shelled the Confederate batteries three-quarters of a mile above the landing, and silenced them in thirty minutes. At 5.30 the enemy, almost everywhere victorious, had succeeded in gaining a position on the Union left, but the gunboats, with the Federal field batteries, drove them back in confusion. Early that evening the advance of Buell's army, from Nashville, came to the support of the shattered left wing. A disastrous defeat had been averted, and the battle of Pittsburg Landing, or Shiloh, renewed on the following day, ended in victory.

The Capture of Fort Pillow and Memphis

Four days after the surrender of Island No. 10, Flag-Officer Foote started down the river, and, aside from one slight skirmish, met with no opposition until he reached Fort Pillow, eighty miles below New Madrid on the Tennessee side. Here General Pope joined him with 20,000 troops, and though Fort Pillow was a strong position, the combined force would have captured it at an early date, had not Pope almost immediately been withdrawn by Halleck with all but 1500 of his army.

Among the enemies the squadron had to meet was the so-called River Defense Fleet. This was composed of river steamboats, which, strengthened by iron casings at their bows and by an improvised protection for their boilers and engines, were to serve as rams. The commanders were Mississippi River captains and pilots, supposed to be under the military chief of department, but not subject to orders from any naval officers. Farragut was destined to meet some of this fleet below New Orleans; and eight vessels of this class were now lying under the guns of Fort Pillow.

On May 9, Captain C. H. Davis took temporary command of the squadron, relieving Flag-Officer Foote, who was in need of rest and was troubled by a wound received at Fort Donelson. The next morning the Confederate rams made a sudden attack upon the *Cincinnati*, which, with a mortar boat, had moved down to bombard the fort. There was a difficulty in signaling, and as a result only four of the seven Union gunboats took part in the fight. The Confederates succeeded in ramming two of the gunboats so that they had to be run ashore to avoid sinking; on the other hand, three of the Confederate rams were disabled.

The Confederates had shown considerable dash and spirit as they made the attack, and the injuries they received were of such a character as to admit of speedy repair. However, this was the only time the River Defense Fleet ever performed any service of special value. Their lack of organization rendered them incapable of vigorous and sustained action.

The bombardment of Fort Pillow continued until the night of June 4, when it was evacuated. Next morning the squadron steamed down to Memphis and engaged the Confederate rams before the city. These were eight in number, and to oppose them Davis had five gunboats and two rams. A one-sided engagement followed, in which the Confederates lost four of their boats, in return disabling only slightly one of the Union rams. The other four Confederate vessels then fled down the river; however, they were pursued, and in a running battle one was destroyed and two were captured. On the same day the city of Memphis surrendered; so that when Farragut,

Results of the Western Campaign 309

who had already captured New Orleans, brought his fleet up the river and passed the fortifications of Vicksburg, Davis was able to join forces with him.

During four months the army and navy, co-operating on the western rivers, had broken the Confederate line of defense along the southern border of Kentucky, and had pierced the second line at Corinth, Mississippi (near Pittsburg Landing). They had also captured all of the fortifications on the Mississippi down to Vicksburg. Thus they had saved Kentucky for the Union, and had largely retaken Tennessee.

The battles at Fort Donelson and Shiloh were the first great defeats that the Confederate land forces had received, and served to weaken the confidence in their armies, which the South had come to believe were invincible. The people of the North were in danger of entertaining the same view, especially as McClellan, with the superior Army of the Potomac, was meeting with reverse after reverse in the Peninsula Campaign. The successes won by Grant and Foote in the West, almost at the same time, afforded a striking contrast, and served to keep the North from discouragement.

XIX

OPERATIONS ON THE LOWER MISSISSIPPI

Passing the Forts Below New Orleans

SCARCELY had the Department received news of the success of the expedition against Port Royal, when Assistant Secretary Fox was planning another expedition for the capture of New Orleans.

New Orleans was the largest city in the Confederacy; its population in 1860 was 168,675, more than twice that of Richmond and Charleston combined. It was also the richest city, and, being the natural commercial centre for Louisiana and Texas, was forwarding great quantities of food supplies to the Confederate armies.

The general opinion of the North, as well as of the South, was that any attack on New Orleans would be by a slow advance down the Mississippi. But Mr. Fox, who knew the lower Mississippi from having taken an ocean steamer under his command up to New Orleans, believed that it was within the power of the navy, operating from the Gulf, to capture the city.

Strongly impressed with his project, Mr. Fox arranged for a conference at which, besides the Cabinet officers, General McClellan and Commander David D. Porter were present. Porter unhesitatingly expressed his confidence in the plan; the others showed some doubt, yet gave their assent.

To command the expedition, the Department, after some hesitation, agreed on a captain comparatively unknown—David Glasgow Farragut, the choice of Mr. Fox. This officer, born near Knoxville, Tennessee, in 1801,

David G. Farragut

was but nine years and five months old when he was appointed midshipman in the navy. As has been narrated in previous chapters, he had seen active service in the War of 1812, had taken part in suppressing the West Indian pirates, and had engaged in the Mexican War. But none of these operations had given him a chance to show his extraordinary abilities, and at the age of nearly sixty-one he was unrecognized.

At the outbreak of the Civil War, Farragut was awaiting orders in Norfolk, Virginia, which for forty years had been his home. There was no wavering in his allegiance. On the secession of Virginia he immediately left for the North and applied for a command. The Government kept him waiting for several months, for after several unhappy experiences it had grown suspicious of Southerners. However, the sacrifice made by Farragut did not altogether escape notice: it was the spirit that he had shown in so promptly leaving his State and in volunteering for service that caught the attention of Mr. Fox. This argued, in the latter's opinion, "great superiority of character, clear perception of duty, and firm resolution in the performing of it."

When Farragut was called to Washington in December, 1861, and was informed of the expedition planned, he said without hesitation that it would succeed, and he manifested almost a boyish enthusiasm on learning that he was to command it.[1] He was to have even more ships than he said were required. The expedition was to be purely naval, and the responsibility for success or failure would rest on the naval commander. Nevertheless, the co-operation of the army to hold whatever the navy

---

[1] Montgomery Blair, Postmaster-General in Lincoln's Cabinet, was present at the first interview between Farragut and Fox, and gives a highly interesting report, to be found in *The United Service*, 1881, p. 39.

captured was guaranteed, and accordingly 18,000 troops under Major-General Butler were sent later.

In the latter part of February, 1862, Farragut arrived at the mouth of the Mississippi. He had come in the *Hartford*, which he continued to make his flagship. She was a sloop of war with auxiliary steam power capable of propelling her eight knots an hour. She was a new ship, having sailed on her first cruise to China in 1859. Although rated a sloop of war, she had a greater tonnage, and was more formidable, than the ordinary ship-of-the-line of the War of 1812. Farragut believed in introducing a gun wherever there was a place, and the *Hartford*, with twenty-two 9-inch Dahlgren guns, had twice as heavy an armament as many a cruiser of her size.

After the *Hartford* had joined the blockading squadron in the Gulf, two months of preparation followed. To get the large ships over the bars before the Passes at the mouth of the Mississippi was an undertaking that required resourcefulness and patience; thus it was two weeks' work to drag the *Pensacola* through the mud and into the deep water inside. Finally, on April 7, Farragut had his fleet in the river and ready for active operations. It included, not counting the boats in the mortar flotilla under Commander Porter, seven steam sloops of war, one large side-wheel ship-of-war, and nine gunboats. These seventeen vessels were armed with 154 cannon.

To oppose the progress of this force, the Confederates had two powerful forts, eighty miles below New Orleans and twenty miles above the head of the Passes. Fort St. Philip, mounting forty-two guns, was on the left bank (as one goes down the river), and being at a bend in the river it could not only command the river front but rake approaching ships; Fort Jackson, mounting fifty-eight guns, was lower down on the right bank, and was the stronger of the two. But, according to Mahan, about

Preparations 313

half of the guns of the forts were obsolete 24-pounders, for the Confederates were so imbued with the idea that any attempt to seize the Mississippi must be made from the north, that they had given no heed to the warnings of army and navy officers at New Orleans. Besides the forts the Confederates had a flotilla of fifteen gunboats, two of them ironclad rams, and had stretched across the river under the guns of Fort Jackson two heavy chains supported by a series of hulks.

On April 18 Porter's mortar boats took a position about 3000 yards below Fort Jackson, and began to bombard the forts. If Farragut had been consulted by the Department, he would have declined the assistance of the mortar boats, for he had little confidence in their power to reduce a strong fortification. However, he gave them opportunity to do their utmost. For six days and nights the mortars poured forth an unremitting fire mainly on Fort Jackson, throwing nearly 6000 shells. The aim seems to have been good, yet the damage done to the forts was but trifling.

When the mortars had kept up their fire for three days without appreciable effect, Farragut felt that it was time to bring the ships into action. Accordingly, on the night of the 20th he sent his fleet-captain, Henry H. Bell, with two gunboats, to destroy the barrier of logs and schooners joined by chains stretched across the river. The men worked under the fire of the forts, and were greatly embarrassed when one of the gunboats ran aground. Still they succeeded in making an aperture sufficiently wide for the largest ship to pass through.

Then followed two days spent in preparing the ships to run the forts. Each vessel was trimmed a few inches by the head, so that if she touched bottom she would not swing down river. Sheet cables were stopped up and down on the sides in line with the engines; and hammocks, coal, and bags of sand were piled up to protect the boilers from shot coming from forward or aft. Some of the commanders had the hulls of their ships rubbed with mud to make them less visible at night, and one had his decks whitewashed to make guns and ammunition more easily seen and handled. In the afternoon previous to the attack, Farragut visited each ship to make sure that the commanding officer had all in readiness and understood the orders. Though Farragut is popularly known for his quickness and power in action, he was no less remarkable for the wisdom and thoroughness of his preparation.

Two o'clock in the morning, April 24, 1862, was the time set for the attacking ships to get under way. They were to advance in two columns; one was to take a course well to the right and attack Fort St. Philip, the other, to the left, and attack Fort Jackson. The original plan of having the two columns advance side by side was later changed; and the column on the right, which consisted of the First Division, three ships of war, one side-wheeler, and four gunboats, led by Captain Bailey in the *Cayuga*, was to precede the column on the left, which consisted of the Second Division, three sloops of war under Flag-Officer Farragut, and the Third Division, one sloop and five gunboats under Captain Bell. This change made the fleet weaker by being less compact, but more than compensated for the disadvantage by reducing the danger of collision when the ships were passing the narrow opening in the chain-barrier.

At the appointed hour, two red lights displayed from the flagship gave the signal to the commanders to get under way. In a few minutes the clink-clank of the anchor chains was heard throughout the fleet, but because of various little delays, it was not until 3.30 that the First Division reached the barrier. The *Cayuga* was nearly

Passing the Forts below New Orleans

abreast the forts before the Confederates opened fire. Not strong enough to deal with her powerful foes, she sped along; but the sloop *Pensacola*, which followed, carried twenty-three heavy guns, and as she passed Fort St. Philip steamed slowly, frequently stopping to return the fire. Meanwhile the mortar flotilla had moved forward so as to shell both forts.

Twenty-five minutes after the *Cayuga* had begun the attack, the *Hartford*, leading the Second Division, had passed the barrier and was opening with her bow guns on Fort Jackson. The darkness and smoke, together with the terrific fire from the forts, made it difficult for the Union ships to keep their course or to distinguish friend from foe. Suddenly, out of the gloom and confusion, Farragut saw a fire-raft coming directly for his ship. The helm of the *Hartford* was put over in order to avoid the raft, whereupon the ship grounded on a shoal near Fort St. Philip. Under the heavy fire of the forts she was in a trying position; and what was far worse, a Confederate tugboat, till then unnoticed, was pushing the fire-raft down upon her. In an instant the port quarter of the *Hartford* was a mass of flames, which were licking the paint and rising half way to the tops. It was one of those moments that are full of destiny, but Farragut was equal to the crisis. His quiet self-possession reassured his men, and each with alacrity did his part in carrying out the orders. The ship's guns drove off the tug, and kept playing on the forts; the well-organized fire company, by great exertion, put out the flames; the engines backed the ship off the shoal, and again she headed up the river.[2]

The *Brooklyn*, Captain Craven, which followed the *Hartford*, also had some grim experiences. In the dark-

[2] Farragut's report will be found in the *Naval War Records*, xviii, 155.

ness and blinding smoke, Craven lost sight of the *Hartford*, and suddenly found his vessel running over one of the hulks that carried the chain-barrier.

"For a few moments," writes Captain Craven, "I was entangled and fell athwart the stream, our bow grazing the shore on the left bank of the river. While in this situation I received a pretty severe fire from Fort St. Philip. Immediately after the ship had been extricated from the rafts, her head was turned up stream, and a few minutes thereafter she was feebly butted by the celebrated ram *Manassas*. The latter came butting into our starboard gangway, first firing from her trap-door, when within about ten feet of the ship, directly towards our smokestack, her shot entering about five feet above the water line and lodging in the sand-bags which protected our steam drum. I had discovered this queer-looking gentleman, while forcing my way over the barricade, lying close to the bank, and when he made his appearance the second time, I was so close to him that he had not an opportunity to get up his full speed, and his efforts to damage me were completely frustrated, our chain armor proving a perfect protection to our sides. He soon slid off and disappeared in the darkness. A few moments thereafter, being all the time under a raking fire from Fort Jackson, I was attacked by a large rebel steamer. Our port broadside, at the short distance of only fifty or sixty yards, completely finished him, setting him on fire almost instantaneously.

"Still groping my way in the dark, or under the black cloud of smoke from the fire-raft, I suddenly found myself abreast of St. Philip, and so close that the leadsman in the starboard chains gave the soundings 'Thirteen feet, sir.' As we could bring all our guns to bear, for a few brief moments we poured in grape and canister, and I had the satisfaction of completely silencing that work before I left it—my men in the tops witnessing, in the flashes of their bursting shrapnel, the enemy running like sheep for more comfortable quarters.

"After passing the forts, we engaged several of the enemy's gunboats. . . . This ship was under fire about one hour and a half."[3]

The fight was by no means ended for the ships of the First Division when they had passed the forts, for, awaiting them, the Confederates had a flotilla of thirteen gunboats, besides two ironclad rams. The *Cayuga*, as has been told, had made it her chief business to get safely by the batteries of St. Philip, while the *Pensacola* had slowed down to engage them. As the *Mississippi* and the *Oneida*, which came next, had kept their positions in the column, the *Cayuga* emerged from the smoke to find herself unsupported.

"After passing the last battery and thinking we were clear," writes Lieutenant George H. Perkins, of the *Cayuga*, who was acting as pilot, "I looked back for some of our vessels, and my heart jumped into my mouth, when I found I could not see a single one. I thought they all must have been sunk by the forts. Then looking ahead I saw eleven of the enemy's gunboats coming down upon us, and it seemed as if we were 'gone' sure. Three of these made a dash to board us, but a heavy charge from our 11-inch gun settled the *Governor Moore*, which was one of them. A ram, the *Manassas*, in attempting to butt us, just missed our stern, and we soon settled the third fellow's 'hash.' Just then some of our gunboats which had passed the forts came up, and then all sorts of things happened. There was the wildest excitement all around. The *Varuna* fired a broadside into us, instead of the enemy. Another of our gunboats attacked one of the

---

[3] *Naval War Records*, xviii, 182.

Cayuga's prizes—I shouted out, 'Don't fire into that ship, she has surrendered!' Three of the enemy's ships had surrendered to us before any other of our vessels appeared; but when they did come up we all pitched in, and settled the eleven rebel vessels in about twenty minutes."[4]

The *Varuna*, the fifth vessel of the First Division, was the only Union ship to be lost. She had passed through the Confederate flotilla, firing right and left. Then, seeing ahead a small steamer that was fleeing, she started in pursuit. She had, however, been observed by Beverly Kennon, formerly of the United States Navy, now in command of the *Governor Moore*. Convinced that he could do nothing against the larger ships, he left the mêlée and went in pursuit. Displaying signal lanterns such as he had noticed the Union ships were showing, he was almost upon the *Varuna* before he was recognized. He then fired two destructive shells from his bow gun, and when the *Varuna's* helm was put hard-a-port so as to bring her guns to bear, he rammed. The *Varuna* was a few minutes later struck also by the Confederate gunboat *Stonewall Jackson*, and in a sinking condition she was headed for the shore. But her guns, with those of the *Cayuga*, had in the meantime disabled the *Moore*, causing the latter to drop out of the action; and as the *Varuna*, which had settled on the bank, continued to pour shot into her, setting her afire, the Confederate gunboat surrendered to the *Oneida*, which had just come up.

The *Itasca*, the *Winona*, and the *Kennebec*, of the Third Division, following at the end of the procession, had not the support of the heavy ships, and did not succeed in passing the forts. The Confederates, though

---

[4] Alden, *George Hamilton Perkins*, pp. 118, 119.

The Capture of New Orleans

driven from many of their guns by the fire of the fleet, had quickly returned, and just as day was breaking, gave all of their attention to these small vessels. The *Itasca* received a shot through her boiler, disabling her so that she was compelled to drift back. The *Winona* and the *Kennebec* became entangled in the chain-barrier, and when they freed themselves and attempted to proceed, they found the concentrated fire of the forts too much for them.

THE CAPTURE OF NEW ORLEANS

When Farragut collected his forces at Quarantine, five miles above the forts, he had thirteen vessels. Believing the time had come when he could co-operate with the army, he sent a messenger to General Butler and also to Commander Porter. The *Wissahickon* and the *Kineo* were left behind to guard the landing of the troops, should they come by way of the Quarantine Bayou, as now they could with safety. With the rest of the fleet Farragut then slowly steamed towards New Orleans.

About 10.30 the following morning the ships reached the English Turn, five miles below New Orleans, the spot where the British attack had been repulsed in 1815. Here the fleet was fired upon from some new earthworks erected on the lines of the old, but the ships as they drew abreast quickly silenced the shore batteries.

"All the morning," writes Farragut, "I had seen abundant evidence of the panic which had seized the people of New Orleans. Cotton-loaded ships on fire came floating down, and working implements of every kind, such as are used in shipyards; the destruction of property was awful. . . . The levee of New Orleans was one scene of desolation; ships, steamers, cotton, coal, etc., were all in one common blaze, and our ingenuity was much taxed to avoid the floating conflagration. . . .

"We now passed up to the city and anchored immediately in front of it, and I sent Captain Bailey on shore to demand the surrender of it from the authorities, to which the mayor replied that the city was under martial law, and that he had no authority. General Lovell, who was present, stated that he should deliver up nothing but, in order to free the city from embarrassment, he would restore the city authorities and retire with his troops, which he did."[5]

The mayor, in the further correspondence, continued to make evasive replies, which soon became a heavy tax on Farragut's patience. The State flag of Louisiana was still flying from the city hall. It might be some time before troops could be brought up to occupy the city. Farragut had the city helpless under his guns, but since he did not wish to destroy property or take the lives of women and children, he was in an awkward position. However, the Union commander, simple and direct, as he ever was, proved himself a statesman as well as a warrior; he gained his point by insistence. The United States flag was raised from the city hall and the government buildings, and the municipal officers acknowledged the authority of the National forces.

On the evening of the 29th Captain Bailey brought the welcome news that Forts Jackson and St. Philip had surrendered. There had not been the necessity of immediate capitulation; yet, as New Orleans was the source of supplies, the capture of the city made that of the forts, sooner or later, inevitable. The end was hastened by a mutiny which broke out in the forts, where a considerable proportion of the defenders are said to have been foreigners.

Running past the forts below New Orleans was an

---

[5] *Naval War Records,* xviii, 158.

The Capture of New Orleans

exploit of surprising boldness. Previous to its accomplishment several officers had disapproved of Farragut's plan. They thought it bad policy to cut loose from the base of supplies, and doubted whether it were possible for wooden ships to pass two such powerful forts. The Confederates also had the utmost confidence in their forts, and, believing that they could annihilate any fleet coming within reach of their guns, had been slow in preparing other defenses.

Two other modes of operation had been suggested by Commander Porter: an attack by the fleet, with reduction of the forts before the fleet went farther; and a combined attack by the fleet and the troops. Farragut favored neither plan, because of the delay it was sure to involve. To postpone decisive action was to give the Confederates opportunity for strengthening their defenses; besides, ammunition for his mortars was running low. He was not averse to profiting by the assistance of the army, but he believed a joint movement could be made from above the forts much better than from below.

Previous to the engagement, large stories had been circulating concerning the Confederate ironclads *Manassas, Louisiana,* and *Mississippi;* and if Farragut had been more leisurely in his attack, he might have found that the tales were not so greatly exaggerated. The *Mississippi,* being unfinished, was burned at New Orleans on his approach; and the *Louisiana,* which had been brought down to assist the forts, proved ineffective because her engines had not yet been put into working condition. The gunboats above the forts, commanded with two exceptions by captains of Mississippi steamboats, belonged to the River Defense Fleet, another part of which Foote and Davis were engaging at Fort Pillow and Memphis. They made but a weak, ill-organized fight, although they would undoubtedly have caused greater destruction had their foes acted with more deliberation. Farragut plainly had a strong grasp of the situation, and recognized the principle that to increase the vigor of the attack is to lessen the risk involved.

FROM NEW ORLEANS TO VICKSBURG

The Department, impressed by Farragut's exploits at New Orleans, believed there was nothing to prevent the navy from quickly gaining entire control of the Mississippi. Flag-Officer Davis, who with his fleet was above Memphis, was ordered to move down the river; and Flag-Officer Farragut was similarly ordered to move up the river. The two forces, having cleared the river of all obstructions, were to combine.

It was a simple matter for Farragut to send forward one of his smaller vessels and secure the submission of Baton Rouge and Natchez. Vicksburg, however, defiantly refused to surrender. Consequently, as soon as he was able, Farragut came up with his fleet, and was joined by 1500 troops under Colonel Williams. A combined attack was considered, but the strong position of the batteries, some of them near the level of the river and others on a cliff 200 feet above, as well as Vicksburg's excellent railroad connections, by which the Confederates could secure an overpowering force of troops almost at an hour's notice, made it evident that the Union forces could do little. Williams' troops had come with only a few days' rations, supplies were short also on the ships, and the river was beginning to fall. These reasons seemed to Farragut sufficient for taking his fleet without delay down the river to New Orleans.

The Department, however, was still determined to clear the Mississippi, and ordered the ships back to Vicksburg. Farragut obeyed as soon as he was able to secure coal and supplies, but with none of the confidence and enthusiasm with which he had entered upon the operations against New Orleans. It was now June, and he was apprehensive lest in navigating the Mississippi 500 miles from its mouth with sea-going ships, such as the *Hartford*, some of his fleet might be caught in the mud, when their capture by the enemy would be easy. The ships were constantly running into snags, which, as Farragut wrote Secretary Welles, were "more destructive to our vessels than the enemy's shot." Also, their engines were showing signs of wear under the hard service, in which opportunities for rest and overhauling were lacking. And not the least of the difficulties was that of bringing coal and provisions up the river to the fleet. Confederate sharpshooters on the banks were constantly picking off the crews; masked batteries sprang up like mushrooms and made it impossible for the supply ships to move with safety except when attended by gunboats, which could not be sent without weakening the force at Vicksburg.

When all was ready, Porter opened with his mortars and bombarded the forts of Vicksburg for two days. Then Farragut decided to run past the batteries, and, as the Department had requested, join Davis' fleet above. Forming his fleet in two columns, the gunboats and lighter vessels to the left, away from the shore batteries, he weighed anchor at two o'clock on the morning of June 28, and at four was engaging the works.

"The *Hartford*," writes Farragut, "fired slowly and deliberately and with fine effect—far surpassing my expectations in reaching the summit batteries. The rebels were soon silenced by the combined efforts of the fleet and of the flotilla [the mortar boats], and at times did not reply at all for several minutes, and then again at times replied with but a single gun. . . .

"The Department will perceive, from this report, that

the forts can be *passed*, and *we have done it*, and *can do it again as often as may be required* of us. It will not, however, be an easy matter for us to do more than silence the batteries for a time, as long as the enemy has a large force behind the hills to prevent our landing and holding the place."[6]

At six o'clock Farragut met Lieutenant-Colonel Ellet with a division of Davis' fleet, and anchored. Seven of his ships had succeeded in passing Vicksburg; but the *Brooklyn*, the *Katahdin*, and the *Kennebec*, which brought up the rear of the two columns, became separated from the rest of the fleet, and after enduring a heavy fire, retired below the town.

Farragut had now carried out his order to the letter; he had cleared the river, at least temporarily, and had joined the upper fleet. In reality he had accomplished little, as he was well aware. Williams, who had accompanied him with 3000 troops in transports, was unable to attack the heights of Vicksburg. The Confederates, having lost Island No. 10 and Memphis, were massing to defend the position they had still in their possession. The troops which the Government had intended that General Halleck should send to co-operate with the ships, he was unable to furnish. The Department, at length recognizing the true state of affairs, ordered Farragut to return to New Orleans. As he was about to obey, there occurred an incident which occasioned him much chagrin.

Upon the capture of Memphis the Confederates had saved the ironclad *Arkansas*, then under construction, by hurrying her up the Yazoo River. The Yazoo flows into the Mississippi near Vicksburg, and only four miles below its mouth the combined fleets of Farragut and Davis had been at anchor since July 1.

---

[6] *Naval War Records*, xviii, 609, 610.

The Career of the Arkansas 325

On July 15 Davis, at Farragut's suggestion, sent Colonel Ellet with three vessels to learn what he might of the *Arkansas*. When Ellet had gone six miles up the Yazoo, he met the *Arkansas* coming down. A running battle ensued in which the light Union ironclad *Carondelet* doggedly clung to her enemy, but got rather the worst of it. The unarmored *Tyler*, after firing a few shots, sped down the river to give warning to the fleet.

The ships were all at anchor with fires banked, and it was impossible for them to get steam up before the *Arkansas* appeared and was running the gauntlet for Vicksburg. The *Carondelet's* fire had already riddled the smokestack of the *Arkansas* and reduced her speed to one knot. But, aided by the current, the Confederate ram passed down the line, and, though receiving a terrific pounding, she suffered no vital injury, and reached Vicksburg.

At once Farragut resolved to follow her up and destroy her under the guns of the town. Early that evening he took his ships down the river and past the forts. But as the *Arkansas*, when hidden by darkness, had been moved by the Confederates to a protected position, she escaped.

The last of July, Farragut got his ships back to New Orleans, and none too soon, for a large number of the officers and men were sick with malaria. He was, however, still troubled that the *Arkansas* remained uncaptured. His anxiety was relieved on August 6, when, in an attack which the Confederates made on Baton Rouge, the *Arkansas* dropped down the river to lend her assistance. Her engines as usual were working badly, and when the *Essex*, Commander W. D. Porter, dashed forward to engage her, the Confederates set fire to the ram and withdrew.

Nothing further of importance was done by the ships on the Mississippi during the remainder of 1862. Meanwhile, the Confederates were preparing to make a desperate resistance at Vicksburg, and had begun to fortify another strong position, at Port Hudson, twelve miles north of Baton Rouge.

In October, 1862, David D. Porter was chosen to command the Mississippi squadron, still operating above Vicksburg. He succeeded to the post which, with its onerous duties, had worn out Foote and Davis. Previous to this time his dash and brilliant strategy had never had opportunity for full exercise, because of his subordinate rank. But Lincoln divined his latent power, and, passing over eighty officers higher in rank, made him acting rear-admiral, and gave him the squadron.

Early in January, 1863, Porter co-operated with McClernand in an expedition directed against Arkansas Post, a stronghold on the left bank of the Arkansas River, fifty miles from its mouth. Here in a two days' battle most of the fighting was done by the gunboats, which succeeded in silencing the batteries. And it was Admiral Porter who, just as McClernand's army had finally secured a favorable position for assault, received the surrender of the fort with its garrison of 6000 men. As a result of this victory the fleet and transports above Vicksburg were secure from all molestation from the Arkansas and White Rivers.

When, in January, 1863, Grant took command in person of the operations against Vicksburg he promptly sought out Porter. In the long and arduous campaign that followed, the co-operation between the forces ashore and those afloat was remarkable for its heartiness and for the absence of friction. Of this General Grant says, "The navy under Porter was all it could be during the entire campaign. Without its assistance the campaign could not have been successfully made with twice the number of men engaged. It could not have been made at all in the way it was, with any number of men, without such assistance. The most perfect harmony reigned between the two arms of the service. There never was a request made, that I am aware of, either of the flag-officer or any of his subordinates, that was not promptly complied with."[7] While the details of Porter's service are too complex even for a general account, it should be noted that it was by the passing of Vicksburg by a large part of Porter's squadron that the Union army was enabled to cross the river below in safety, and suddenly to attack the Confederate fortifications from the south and east. Grant conducted in person the brilliant campaign that followed, and captured Vicksburg on July 4, 1863.

A half year previous to the surrender of Vicksburg, while Grant and Porter were still above the city, Farragut had proposed to Banks, who had relieved Butler in command of troops at New Orleans, that the army and the navy should make a joint attack on Port Hudson. Because of the lack of preparation on the part of the army, the attack did not take place until March 14, 1863. Even then it was almost entirely the work of the navy, and was chiefly an attempt to get seven ships above Port Hudson, where they were very much needed. The fortifications at this point were now so formidable, as Farragut was well aware, that this was an extremely hazardous undertaking. Only the two ships leading the column, the *Hartford* and the *Albatross*, succeeded in passing the batteries. The *Mississippi*, running aground under the works, had to be fired to prevent her falling into the possession of the enemy. The other four ships suffered so severely from the enemy's guns that they were obliged to retire.

Small though his force was above Port Hudson, Farra-

---

[7] *Memoirs*, i, 574.

gut was able in large part to accomplish his purpose. He intermittently patrolled the Mississippi from Port Hudson to Vicksburg—as yet Porter had been able to send only two of his squadron below Vicksburg, the *Queen of the West* and the *Indianola,* and these had been captured. Farragut also blockaded the Red River, and by cutting off supplies to Vicksburg and Port Hudson very materially assisted in their downfall.

RESULTS

The importance of the naval operations on the Mississippi in 1862 and 1863 is not likely to be overestimated. At their termination, with the river in Union control, the Confederacy was split in two. The rich and fertile States of Louisiana, Arkansas, and Texas could no longer forward supplies across the Mississippi to the armies fighting in Virginia and elsewhere. The Confederate States that were more particularly the seat of war could furnish little, and armies without food and clothing are doomed.

The capture of New Orleans had still another very important result. It deterred France from action hostile to the United States. Louis Napoleon had already suggested to England the advisability of recognizing the Confederate States; and just as Farragut was about to open fire on Forts Jackson and St. Philip, Napoleon was conferring with Mr. Lindsay, a member of the British Parliament and a Southern sympathizer. "Mr. Lindsay spoke of the Federal blockade as being ineffectual, and not in accordance with the fourth article of the Congress of Paris, and mentioned facts in support of his opinion." The Emperor fully concurred in Mr. Lindsay's opinion, and said that "he had from the first considered the restoration of the Union impossible, and for that reason had deprecated the continuance of a contest which could not lead to any other result than separation." Moreover, he assured Mr. Lindsay that "he would at once dispatch a formidable fleet to the mouth of the Mississippi, if England would send an equal force, and that they would demand free egress and ingress for their merchantmen with their cargoes of goods, and supplies of cotton which were essential to the world."[8] When the Northern troops were in possession of New Orleans, the Government was very willing that the city's commerce should again be renewed, but to have abandoned the blockade of the Confederate ports would have been fatal to a successful termination of the war.

---

[8] *North American Review,* cxxix, 346.

XX

BATTLE OF MOBILE BAY

HAD Farragut been free after the capture of New Orleans to choose the next point of attack, instead of making two futile expeditions to Vicksburg in the spring and summer of 1862, he would have moved against Mobile. At that time its capture would have been an easy matter for the fleet under his command. Two years later, when the Department ordered the attack, the undertaking was of much greater magnitude, for the Confederates had vastly strengthened the defenses.

On the surrender of Port Hudson, July, 1863, Farragut turned over to Porter the command of all the Mississippi above New Orleans, and on August 1 sailed for New York. He needed rest, and the *Hartford,* the *Brooklyn,* and the *Richmond* required extensive overhauling. With both objects attained, the admiral and his ships returned in January, 1864, to take a further part in the blockade of the Gulf.

After the fall of New Orleans, Mobile became the Confederates' most important port for the shipment of cotton. Its situation near the head of a bay thirty miles long, with two large rivers flowing into the bay, and with a railroad system well developed, made its retention by the Confederates of great importance. For nearly two years previous to Farragut's return in 1864, the general blockade had been regarded as technically effective. Still, it constantly happened that the swift blockade runners, creeping along the shore on a dark night, would make a bold dash and gain the protection of the forts command-

Defenses of Mobile

ing the entrance to the bay before the Union ships could come up with them.

These forts were, in the order of their strength and importance, Morgan, Gaines, and Powell. Fort Morgan, on the east side of the main channel at the southern end of Mobile Point, was a pentagonal, bastioned work, with a full scarp wall of brick, four feet and eight inches thick. It mounted eighty-six guns and had a garrison of 640 men. As the channel passed close under its guns, it was an admirable defense to the bay. Fort Gaines was on Dauphin Island, three miles to the northwest of Morgan. And Fort Powell was six miles farther in the same direction, commanding one of the passes navigable for small steamers only. Since neither Gaines nor Powell had any part in the battle about to be described, they will not be considered further. On the flats to the south and east of Gaines, a long row of piles had been driven to prevent the passage of small boats, and where the piles ended, a double row of torpedoes had been planted toward Morgan.

Further to strengthen the forts, the Confederates had ready, some months before Farragut could make his attack, the ironclad *Tennessee*, built on the general lines of the *Merrimac*. Though not so long as the latter, the *Tennessee* had a somewhat heavier armor, and also had an advantage in her shallow draft of fourteen feet. Her beak and her powerful battery of four 6-inch and two 7-inch rifles made her a dangerous foe to the wooden ships; indeed, she was commonly regarded as the most powerful ship afloat. Supporting the *Tennessee* were three wooden gunboats, which were reported to Farragut by refugees and deserters also as ironclads.

After making a reconnoissance on arriving off Mobile, Farragut informed the Department of the need of an ironclad and of troops to make a successful attack upon the forts. It was not until the last of July that troops could be sent, and not until the 4th of August that the four monitors assigned him had all arrived. On the 5th of August, 1864, Farragut proceeded to the attack.

He had made careful preparations for passing the forts, similar to those in the operations below New Orleans; and since a large proportion of his fourteen wooden ships were only of the gunboat class, he resorted to the expedient tried at Port Hudson of having his ships proceed in pairs; on the port side of each of the heavy vessels was lashed a light vessel, the latter being thus protected from the fire of Fort Morgan. The fight was to be the most desperate one that Farragut had engaged in since he was a boy on the *Essex;* he seemed to know this in advance, and there is a deep seriousness, almost melancholy, not characteristic of the admiral, that appears in a letter written August 4:[1]

"MY DEAREST WIFE: I write and leave this letter for you. I am going into Mobile Bay in the morning, if God is my leader, as I hope He is, and in Him I place my trust. If He thinks it is the proper place for me to die, I am ready to submit to His will, in that as all other things. . . .

"Your devoted and affectionate husband, who never for one moment forgot his love, duty, or fidelity to you, his devoted and best of wives,

"D. G. FARRAGUT."

There were two favoring conditions that he desired in making the attack: a flood tide, and a westerly wind to blow the smoke of the guns from the ships upon Fort Morgan. Early Friday morning, August 5, he had both.

Long before daylight Farragut had given orders for the ships to be ready to advance. At 5.30, while sipping

---

[1] Loyall Farragut, *Life of Farragut*, p. 405.

Farragut's Preparations

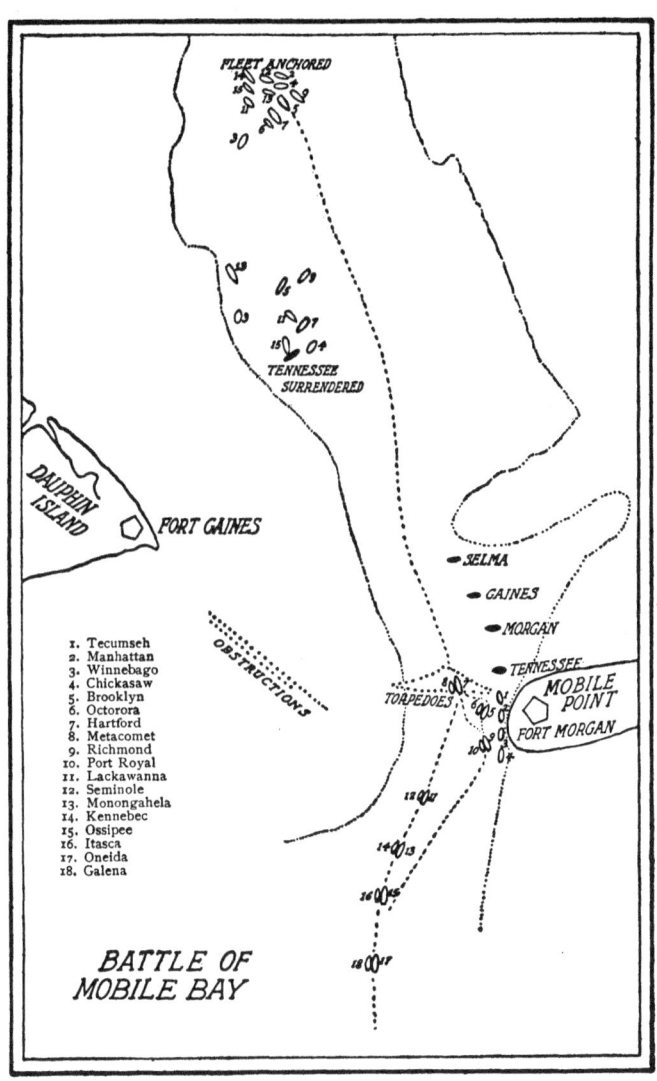

BATTLE OF MOBILE BAY

a cup of tea at the conclusion of breakfast, he turned to his fleet-captain and quietly said, "Well, Drayton, we might as well get under way." In a minute there came back answering signals from the expectant captains, and the ships, lashed in couples, took their assigned positions.

The column was led by the *Brooklyn*, Captain James Alden, and the *Octorora*, Lieutenant-Commander Charles Green. Following them came the flagship *Hartford*, Captain Percival Drayton, and the *Metacomet*, Lieutenant-Commander James E. Jouett. Since the ships would be subject to a raking fire on approaching Fort Morgan, and could bring but very few guns into action until abreast the fort, the monitors *Tecumseh, Manhattan, Winnebago*, and *Chickasaw*, which could fire in any direction, were to form a column to starboard and in advance of the ships, engaging the fort to protect the ships' approach. That the fleet might demoralize the gunners in Fort Morgan by a hot fire of grape and shrapnel, the vessels were to pass close to the fort, to the east of a certain red buoy. It was said that the buoy marked the limit of the line of torpedoes, so that this order had a double reason.

The *Tecumseh*, Commander T. A. M. Craven, opened the battle, firing the first shot at 6.47.[2] Meanwhile, the Confederate vessels *Tennessee, Morgan, Gaines*, and *Selma* had emerged from behind the fort, and had taken position in echelon across the channel, with their port batteries toward the advancing fleet; the *Tennessee* was the farthest to the left, and rested a little to the westward of the red buoy. The ram had been designated by Farragut as the antagonist especially of the *Tecumseh* and *Manhattan*, and Craven was all eagerness to engage her. Accordingly, after his first fire, Craven loaded the

---

[2] For Farragut's report of the battle, see the *Naval War Records*, xxi, 405 ff.

guns each with sixty pounds of powder and a steel shot, and held them in readiness.

Fort Morgan had opened on the approaching ships shortly after seven, and for half an hour was raking them while they could answer only with their bow-chasers. At the end of that time, the *Brooklyn* and the *Hartford*, drawing abreast of the fort, brought their broadsides into action, and Farragut, from his station in the port main rigging, saw the gunners driven from the barbette and water batteries. But his satisfaction was of short duration; suddenly all went wrong.

Commander Craven, in the *Tecumseh*, was about 300 yards in advance and to starboard of the *Brooklyn*, and as he approached the red buoy, remarked to his pilot, "The admiral ordered me to go inside [to the east of] that buoy, but it must be a mistake."[3] Just at that moment the *Tennessee* moved slightly forward and to the west. Craven, in his doubt as to the course and in his eagerness to grapple with the enemy, put on full speed and made directly for the ram. This led him slightly to the west of the buoy.

The bow gun of the *Tennessee* was heavily loaded to meet the monitor, and the attention of onlookers was

---

[3] From Farragut's notes on the battle, quoted by his son (*Life of Farragut*, p. 422). Immediately after this the admiral added, "He ran just his breadth of beam too far westward, struck a torpedo, and went down in two minutes." There is, however, a lack of agreement in the reports of various officers as to just where the *Tecumseh* ran on the torpedo. This is important, for on it hinges the question, did Craven disobey the admiral's orders? Mr. Julian M. Spencer, who, as first lieutenant on the *Morgan*, was an eye-witness of the disaster, says, in a statement made to the authors, "The *Tecumseh* was well to the east of the red buoy. Craven did not strike the line of torpedoes, but he must have run upon a torpedo that was adrift and in the ship-channel. This I am positive of, not only because I saw the *Tecumseh* when she

eagerly directed towards the ironclads about to engage each other, when suddenly a muffled roar was heard; the *Tecumseh* careened violently, and then settled so quickly that 113 men out of a complement of 135 were carried down with her. A torpedo had exploded under her turret, and within less than two minutes nothing but eddies marked where the large sea-going monitor had been. Commander Craven was among the lost. It is related by Mr. Collins, the pilot, who was with him in the conning tower when the explosion occurred, that as both instinctively turned to the ladder, the only means of escape, Craven drew back, saying, " After you, pilot." The commander's noble courtesy cost him his life.[4]

Captain Alden, in the *Brooklyn*, leading the column of wooden ships, was a close spectator of the disaster. At this time, or slightly earlier, his lookout reported torpedo-buoys, almost under his bows. Alden at once backed his engines, and then stopped. He was signaled by the admiral to go forward, but he either did not see the signal or, with the torpedoes ahead and the monitors close to starboard, did not know how to obey, for he remained inactive. Meanwhile, the other ships were coming on, and the column was in danger of becoming hope-

---

sank, but also because it was what the other officers of the *Morgan* remarked when we talked over the fight afterwards in the wardroom." Supporting this view, at least in part, is a letter of Captain J. W. Whiting, of the Confederate Army (quoted in the *Naval War Records*, xxi, 598): " I was on duty at Fort Morgan when the enemy's fleet entered the bay on the morning of August 5, and saw the monitor *Tecumseh* when she went down. I am of the opinion that she sank before reaching the line of torpedoes. This opinion is entertained by such other of the officers of the fort as witnessed the sinking, and by the pilots on lookout duty, and privates who had been detailed to assist in planting the torpedoes."

[4] Narrated in Parker's *Battle of Mobile Bay*, p. 27.

lessly entangled right under the guns of Fort Morgan. Already the defenders, seeing the confusion, were firing with increased vigor.

Admiral Farragut, from the rigging of the *Hartford*, had witnessed the destruction of the monitor. He had also seen the *Brooklyn* stop and back, though he did not know the reason why. On his starboard bow were the *Brooklyn* and the *Octorora* athwart the channel, on his starboard beam were the monitors *Winnebago* and *Chickasaw*, while the fleet was rapidly massing together, so that in a minute more even retreat would be impossible. It was, as Mahan terms it, "the supreme moment of his life." On a right and immediate decision depended the crowning victory of his long naval career. An error would mean colossal defeat, of terrible costliness to the Union, and a tragic ending to all his years of preparation and his brilliant exploits on the Mississippi. "In later days, Farragut told that in the confusion of these moments, feeling that all his plans had been thwarted, he was at a loss whether to advance or retreat. In this extremity the devout spirit that ruled his life, and so constantly appears in his correspondence, impelled him to appeal to Heaven for guidance, and he offered up this prayer: 'O God, who created man and gave him reason, direct me what to do. Shall I go on?' 'And it seemed,' said the admiral, 'as if in answer a voice commanded, Go on.' "[5]

Since the signal to the *Brooklyn*, to go ahead, had produced no effect, Farragut decided to take the lead himself. And as he could not take the safe course to starboard, he determined to pass to port. Ordering the *Hartford* to drive her engine forward, and the *Metacomet*, lashed alongside, to back hers, he twisted short around,

---

[5] Mahan, *Admiral Farragut*, p. 277.

and, passing the stern of the *Brooklyn*, made directly for the line of torpedoes. There came from the *Brooklyn* a warning cry of torpedoes ahead.

"Damn the torpedoes!" shouted the admiral, intent only on his high purpose. "Four bells! Captain Drayton, go ahead! Jouett, full speed!" The *Hartford* and *Metacomet* crossed the line of torpedoes, and men on board said they heard some of the primers snap, but no torpedo exploded. The *Brooklyn* and *Octorora* followed in their wake, and the column straightened out as by magic.

Meanwhile Farragut had not been forgetful of the few survivors of the *Tecumseh*, still struggling near where the monitor had sunk, but directed Jouett to send a boat. Acting Ensign Henry C. Nields, a mere boy, had charge of the boat and pulled within a few hundred yards of the fort, where he was exposed to the fire of both foes and friends. He rescued ten men, and rowing back to the fleet, succeeded in reaching the *Oneida*, where he remained till the end of the battle.

When the leading ships had passed beyond the danger of the torpedoes, they found the Confederate squadron awaiting them. The three wooden gunboats slowly retreated, firing as they went, and doing considerable damage to the *Hartford*, which for fifteen minutes was obliged to endure their fire, and because of the narrow channel could not bring her guns into action. Admiral Buchanan, who was commanding the *Tennessee*, made a dash at the *Hartford*, but the latter, which was much quicker, easily eluded the ram, and after returning her fire, continued up the bay. Then Buchanan gave his attention successively to the *Brooklyn*, the *Richmond*, and the *Lackawanna*, exchanging shots with each, but causing no serious damage. The *Monongahela* attempted to ram the *Tennessee*, but succeeded in giving her only a glancing blow.

Passing Fort Morgan

By this time the *Hartford* had reached a position where she could bring her guns to bear on the three gunboats that had been annoying her; she then quickly drove them off, and so damaged the *Gaines* that the latter was with difficulty kept afloat till she had reached Fort Morgan. Meanwhile the *Metacomet* was pursuing the *Selma*, and succeeded in capturing her. The *Morgan*, and a little later also the *Tennessee*, took refuge under the guns of the fort.

Shortly after eight o'clock, the three Union monitors and all fourteen of Farragut's wooden ships had safely passed the fort, with comparatively little injury except to the *Oneida*. This vessel, which occupied an exposed position at the end of the column, received a shot from Fort Morgan that penetrated her boilers and completely disabled her. Here the wisdom of Farragut's sending the ships in couples became apparent. The *Oneida's* consort, the *Galena*, aided by the tide, brought her through, and into the bay beyond.

As the Union vessels one by one reached a position four miles above Fort Morgan, where there was a large pocket, they were directed to anchor. Soon the stewards had breakfast preparing, and officers and men were relaxing after the intense strain. Farragut, on the poop of the *Hartford*, was talking with his fleet-captain, Drayton, who observed that although the engagement was ended they still had their strongest foe, the *Tennessee*, to meet again. The same thought had been in Farragut's mind, and he had resolved to go himself on the *Manhattan*, with the other monitors, to attack the ram that evening under the fort; he planned to board her, taking advantage of the darkness to compel the Confederate gunners, if they fired, to shoot at friend as well as at foe. But it proved unnecessary to resort to this desperate measure, for at 8.45 A.M., before all his vessels had anchored, it was reported that the *Tennessee* was coming out, and later that she was heading for the Union flagship.

One cannot but admire the daring of Admiral Buchanan in thus boldly advancing in broad daylight, single-handed, to engage an entire fleet. But his act was nothing less than recklessness, and by it he threw away the evident advantages he possessed. With his heavy rifled guns, of much greater range than the smooth-bores forming the chief part of the Union ships' batteries, he could have hammered at the wooden ships from a distance, dealing destruction and receiving no injury in return. If the fleet should have attempted to attack the ram, he could have retreated to the fort, or, choosing a position in shallow water, have prevented Farragut from using his heavier vessels. The *Tennessee* was too slow to be effective as a ram, so that she had little to gain by action at close quarters. Thus Buchanan, steaming into the midst of the Union fleet, where the water was deep and the channel broad, was offering battle on terms most advantageous to his enemies.

Mess-gear on the Union vessels was hurriedly put away, and preparations were made for another engagement. The stronger wooden ships were ordered to attack "not only with their guns, but bows on at full speed." Dr. Palmer, the fleet-surgeon, who, in going his rounds, happened to be just leaving the flagship in his launch, was dispatched by Farragut with orders for the monitors to attack.

The Union ironclads had already shown themselves slow and difficult to maneuver, and it was the wooden *Monongahela*, which had not yet come to anchor, that began the second engagement. She struck the *Tennessee* a blow that carried away her own iron prow and cut-water (already weakened by the attempt to ram when passing the fort), but did no injury to the Confederate. The

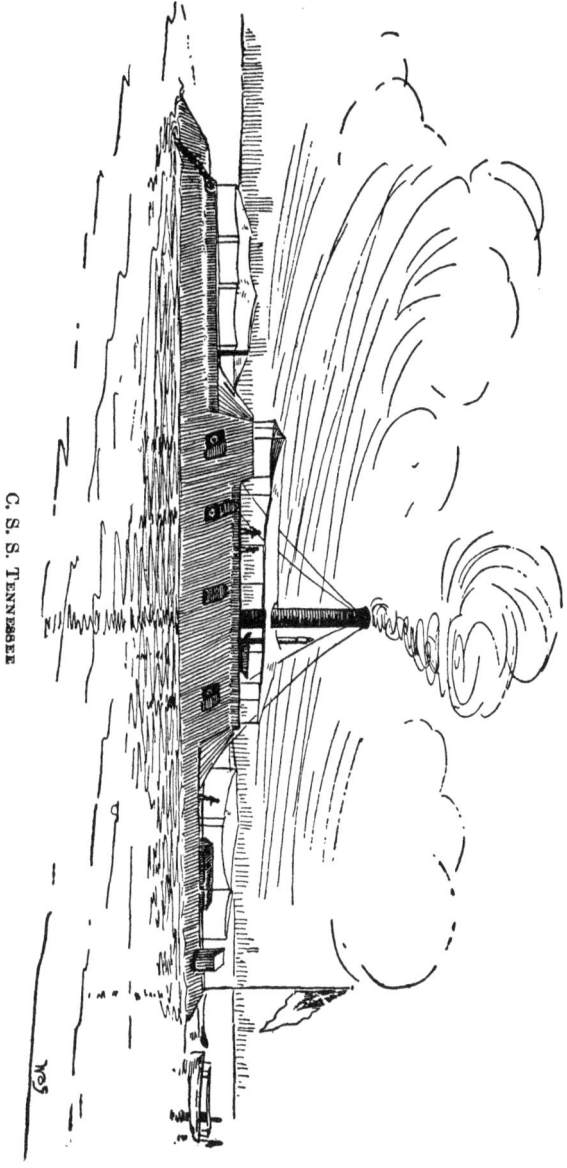

C. S. S. Tennessee

Lackawanna followed close after, and struck the *Tennessee* at full speed. Again it was the attacking ship that suffered, for though her stem was crushed to the plank ends above and below the water line, the only perceptible effect on the *Tennessee* was to give her a heavy list. The *Lackawanna* received two destructive shells through her bows, but, in return, on separating, fired a 9-inch shell that destroyed one of her enemy's port shutters, driving the fragments into the casemate.

The *Hartford* was the third vessel to strike the ram. The blow, however, was but a glancing one, for the Confederate had turned towards the Union flagship on her approach. As the *Hartford* scraped past, she fired her entire port broadside of 9-inch guns, but the shot bounded off with no effect. The *Tennessee* in reply was able to fire only one shell, but this, passing through the berth deck of the *Hartford,* killed five men and wounded eight. When the two vessels came together, Admiral Farragut, who had been standing on the quarter-deck, jumped on the rail, holding to the port mizzen rigging, just above the ram. His flag lieutenant, Watson, fearful for his safety, passed a rope around him and secured it to the rigging—this had been done also on entering the bay, when Captain Drayton, seeing the admiral in the main rigging near the top, ordered Quartermaster Knowles thus to protect him from a fall.

Both the *Hartford* and the *Lackawanna* now made a circuit to get into position to charge again on the ram, but while thus maneuvering, the *Lackawanna* came crashing into the flagship just forward of the mizzenmast, breaking two ports into one, dismounting a Dahlgren gun, and cutting the hull down within two feet of the water. In a moment Farragut was climbing over the side to see the extent of the damage. "Immediately," says Captain Drayton, "there was a general cry all round, 'Get the

The Fight with the Tennessee 343

admiral out of the ship!' and the whole interest of every one near was, that he should be in a place of safety.'' Farragut, however, had no intention of leaving the *Hartford*, and when he discovered that she would still float, he repeated his orders to make for the ram. But again there was confusion in the maneuvers, and the flagship narrowly escaped being rammed a second time by the *Lackawanna*.

In the meantime the monitors had approached and were attacking the ram. One gun of the *Manhattan* was disabled, but with the other she planted a 15-inch shot that penetrated the armor and woodwork of the casemate, and was held only by the netting inside. The turrets of the *Winnebago* would not turn, and her guns could be fired only by pointing the ship; in consequence, her effectiveness was much lessened. But the double-turreted monitor *Chickasaw*, brilliantly handled by Lieutenant-Commander Perkins (the youngest of Farragut's captains), secured a position under the stern of the *Tennessee*, and there she stuck, as the Confederate pilot said later, "like a leech."

On the *Tennessee*, throughout the engagement, Admiral Buchanan superintended the handling of the guns. After the collision with the *Hartford*, the engineer reported that the ram was leaking rapidly, whereupon the Confederate admiral sent word to Commander J. D. Johnston, in the pilot house, to steer for Fort Morgan. Then it was that the *Chickasaw* secured her position under the stern and so annoyed the ram.

The wheel chains of the *Tennessee*, which by a colossal blunder in construction lay exposed on the deck, were carried away. Next, a port cover was struck by an 11-inch shot from the *Chickasaw*; the impact instantly killed a machinist who was working there, and threw iron splinters which mortally wounded one of the gunners and broke

Buchanan's leg above the knee. Johnston, to whom Buchanan then gave over the command, did his utmost to save the vessel, but he could do very little. The relieving tackles by which he was steering the ship were shot away, and the tiller was unshipped from the rudder head. The smokestack, riddled by shot, had fallen over when the *Tennessee* was struck by the wooden vessels, and the steam was going down rapidly. Two quarter ports intended for the after gun had been so jammed that they could not be removed, and two of the broadside port covers had been entirely unshipped by the fire of the fleet. Because of these injuries it happened that in the last half hour of the fight, that is, following the collision with the *Hartford*, the *Tennessee* was unable to fire a shot. During this period the *Chickasaw* had kept up a persistent pounding from her position under the stern, never more than fifty yards away, and had fired fifty-two 11-inch shot. Of the monitor's fire Johnston remarks in his report, "the shot were fairly raining upon the after end of the shield, which was now so thoroughly shattered that in a few moments it would have fallen and exposed the gun deck to a raking fire of shell and grape." [6]

The *Tennessee* lay helpless as a log, and Buchanan, recognizing her condition, said to Johnston, who had sought him out on the berth deck, "Do the best you can, sir, and when all is done, surrender." The *Ossipee* was now charging down at full speed, and the *Hartford*, the *Monongahela*, and the *Lackawanna* were seeking another opportunity to ram. Convinced that the *Tennessee* was nothing more than a target for the Union ships, Johnston went out on the casemate and hauled down her colors, shortly afterwards reappearing and hoisting a white flag.

---

[6] Buchanan's and Johnston's reports will be found in the *Naval War Records*, xxi, 576–581.

The Capture of the Forts

LeRoy, of the *Ossipee*, at once attempted to stop his ship, but the momentum carried him on, and he struck the ram on her starboard quarter. The blow, however, did no harm.

The engagement ended at ten o'clock, having lasted three hours and a quarter, with a half hour's intermission. The losses of the Union fleet were large, amounting to fifty-two killed and 170 wounded. The *Hartford* suffered far more severely than any other ship; twenty-five of the killed, or nearly one-half of the entire number, were of her crew. This was because for several minutes she had endured the concentrated fire of the Confederate gunboats without being able to reply, and also twice had entered into close action with the *Tennessee*. The fire of the Confederate ships did far more damage than that of Fort Morgan. When the men drowned in the *Tecumseh* are included, the total Union loss mounts to 335. That of the Confederate fleet was in comparison very small, ten killed and sixteen wounded.

On the afternoon of the same day, August 5, the *Chickasaw* shelled Fort Powell and compelled its evacuation during the night. The following day she attacked Fort Gaines, and, assisting the army, induced that work to capitulate on August 7. Fort Morgan had defiantly refused to surrender, and held out several days longer. When, however, heavy siege guns and the whole fleet, including the three monitors and the captured *Tennessee*, opened on it, resistance soon became impossible; the defenders endured the bombardment for one day, and on the next, August 23, surrendered.

Farragut, having now complete control of the bay, could seal the port to blockade runners, and had accomplished all that he had contemplated. It was not his purpose to attempt the capture of the city of Mobile—of questionable advantage when it was taken. An army of 20,000 to 30,000 men, he estimated, would be required for this, and almost as many to hold it; only the lighter-draft monitors and the gunboats would be able in the shallow water to lend their co-operation. Consequently he was content to clear the lower bay of torpedoes and remain there quietly for several months.

As we consider the importance of the battle of Mobile Bay, it is evident that the perfecting of the blockade in the Gulf States, accomplished by the capture of the forts and the possession of the bay, was of great moment. More than that, Farragut's victory came at a political crisis, and, because it was opportune, strongly affected a decision of vital consequence to the republic.

Near the close of summer, 1864, the friends of Lincoln, looking forward to the election of the following November, had become greatly alarmed. Reliable reports from Illinois, Indiana, and Pennsylvania indicated that those States were strongly opposed to the administration and its policies. They were tired of war. And the platform adopted by the Democratic party at its national convention—in substance, resolved, that the war is a failure—indicated what kind of policy was likely to be substituted if Lincoln were not re-elected. But the battle of Mobile Bay and Sherman's capture of Atlanta, which followed shortly after and gave it a cumulative force, put a new aspect upon the war. As Seward, in a brief speech at Washington, said, "Sherman and Farragut have knocked the bottom out of the Chicago [Democratic] nominations." In September, Sheridan won his brilliant successes at Winchester and Fisher's Hill. The political campaign was now prosecuted with vigor. Lincoln's adherents had little need to argue; they had but to point to recent events. On November 8, when the election took place, the people gave Lincoln 212 electoral votes to his opponent's twenty-one. "In spite of burdensome taxa-

Farragut Honored

tion, weariness of war, and mourning in every household, they had decided on this election day of 1864 to finish the work they had begun."[7]

After his exploits in Mobile Bay, Farragut had been ordered to command the expedition planned against Fort Fisher. But his long service in the Gulf States had been unusually severe; any man, no matter how young, must have felt the strain, and Farragut, who was past sixty-three, could not go on indefinitely. Accordingly, the command of the expedition was given to Admiral Porter, and Farragut was ordered north. His arrival in New York City, December, 1864, was an occasion for universal rejoicing. A committee of municipal officers and representative citizens waited on him, inviting him to make New York City his home, and accompanying their invitation with a gift of $50,000. The same month the Government showed its appreciation by creating for him the grade of vice-admiral. In July, 1866, Congress passed an act making him admiral, an honor which it had never conferred before, and has but twice since. The following year, when commanding the European squadron, he was received with marked attention by the crowned heads of Europe, and everywhere was greeted "with the enthusiasm and distinguished consideration that were aroused among naval officers by the presence of the man who had bestowed upon their profession a lustre unequalled by any other deeds of that generation."[8]

---

[7] Rhodes, *History of the United States*, iv, 539.
[8] Mahan, *Admiral Farragut*, p. 298.

XXI

THE WAR ON ALBEMARLE SOUND

IMPORTANCE OF ALBEMARLE SOUND

DURING the winter of 1861–62, following up the successes at Hatteras and Pamlico Sound, the North had taken measures to gain control of Albemarle Sound. This step was necessary for several reasons: the Confederates found this sound a refuge from which to prey upon coastwise commerce; the North needed harbors in Southern territory for repair shops and coaling stations; numerous rivers penetrating the heart of the Confederacy flow into this sound, and on their banks are many important towns; two railroads and four canals formed excellent means of communication, and, most important of all, Norfolk might be severed from her main sources of supply in the rear, and troops might thus co-operate in the attacks on this important city. Furthermore, the control of Albemarle Sound threatened the Norfolk Navy Yard, and made imminent the cutting off of Norfolk from Richmond and the severing of railroad communication between these cities and the States farther south. The South, after the loss of Pamlico Sound, made strenuous efforts to fortify Roanoke Island, commanding the entrance to Albemarle Sound, but the scant forces under General Wise and the small fleet of Captain Lynch proved inadequate.

Early in January, 1862, 12,000 troops under General Burnside, and a large but nondescript naval force, consisting mainly of river steamers, ferry-boats, and tug-boats, under Flag-Officer Goldsborough and Commander Rowan, sailed for Albemarle Sound. The army and navy, co-operating most harmoniously, captured the Confederate forts and garrisons on Roanoke Island, February 8. They next took possession of Elizabeth City and the Pasquotank River, which commanded the approach to the Dismal

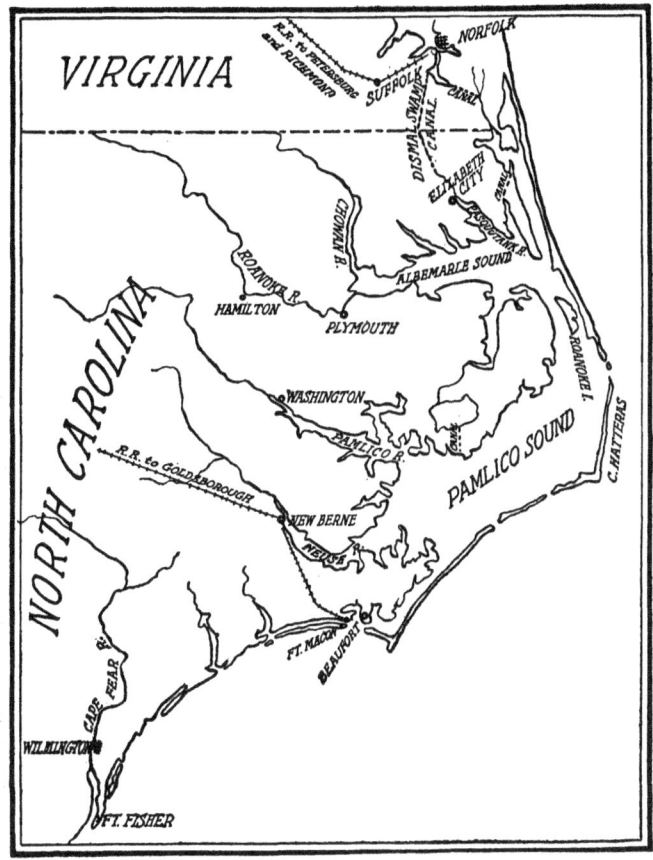

ALBEMARLE AND PAMLICO SOUNDS

Swamp Canal to Norfolk. Having gained control of the sound, the Union forces steamed up the Neuse River, and, in spite of the fact that New Berne was protected by forts and barricades of sunken vessels and iron-pointed piles, captured the town, at that time the second commercial city in North Carolina. This was on March 14; and when, a month and a half later, the Union forces had taken Fort Macon, Federal control of the sounds and the adjacent rivers was virtually complete.

THE RAM ALBEMARLE

The Confederates, feeling keenly the loss of their power on the sounds, made two abortive attempts, on March 14, 1863, and on January 30, 1864, to recapture New Berne. Moreover, the attempts made by the Southern Government to build ironclads on the rivers emptying into the sounds kept the Union forces busy in making incursions up the streams to the towns of Washington, Plymouth, and Hamilton. Notwithstanding the Northern fleet and army in these waters, Captain Cooke and Gilbert Elliott, early in 1863, managed to lay, at Edward's Ferry on the Roanoke River, the keel of a ram, the *Albemarle*. Cooke, who, by reason of his zeal, gained the name "ironmonger captain," ransacked the adjacent country for iron, and by the spring of 1864 launched and armed a vessel that threatened for a time to destroy the wooden Union fleet, and restore the sounds to Southern control.

The *Albemarle* was 122 feet in length, with a beam of forty-five feet and a draft of eight feet. She was built of massive pine timbers, dovetailed, and covered with four-inch planking. On her deck was an octagonal shield, or casemate, sixty feet long, with faces sloping so as to make projectiles glance off. This casemate was also of very heavy timber covered with planking, and was sheathed in two layers of two-inch iron. The ram of the *Albemarle* was of solid oak, plated with heavy iron, and tapering to an edge. The ironclad had two engines, each of 200 horsepower, to drive her twin screws. Her armament consisted of two 100-pound Armstrong guns, mounted one in the bow and the other in the stern; and the casemate was so pierced that these guns on pivots could be used on either broadside, or as quarter guns.

On the morning of April 18, 1864, the *Albemarle* started down the Roanoke to co-operate with General Hoke, who had on the previous day begun an assault on Plymouth. As the ram could not be steered in the swift current, she proceeded down stream stern foremost, with chains dragging from the bow. Forges and sledge hammers were still at work completing the armor of the casemate. "The never-failing Cooke had started his voyage in a floating workshop. . . .On the turtleback numerous stages were suspended, thronged with sailors wielding sledge hammers. Upon the pilot house stood Captain Cooke, giving directions. Some of the crew were being exercised at one of the big guns. 'Drive in spike number ten!' sang out the commander. 'On nut below and screw up! Serve vent and sponge! Load with cartridge!' was the next command. 'Drive in number eleven, port side—so! On nut and screw up hard! Load with shell—Prime!' And in this seeming babel of words the floating monster glided by on her trial trip and into action."[1]

The ram made her way safely over the obstructions of old sunken vessels, piles, and torpedoes placed in the river near Warren's Neck to prevent her co-operation in an attack on Plymouth. Early on the morning of the 19th, Captain Cooke saw, farther down the stream, two Union gunboats, the *Miami* and the *Southfield*, coming up to intercept him. These vessels, under the command of Lieutenant Flusser, had been lashed together, by means of long spars and chains festooned between them, with the

---

[1] Quoted in Maclay, *History of the United States Navy*, ii, 525.

object of seizing the ram as in a vise and then pounding her to pieces by means of their heavy 9-inch guns and rifled 100-pounders. But Cooke was on his guard; he hugged the shore until nearly abreast of the Union vessels, then turning suddenly toward mid-stream, with throttles wide open he passed the bow of the *Miami*, and plunged the heavy ram into the *Southfield's* starboard side, sinking her instantly. The ram's sharp beak was held and her bow submerged by the *Southfield*. As the water poured into the *Albemarle's* ports, it looked for a moment as if she, too, were doomed. But when the Union vessel rolled heavily on her side in the shallow water, she released her hold of Cooke's ironclad, which was rapidly filling from the forward ports.

Lieutenant Flusser on the *Miami* at once opened with his heavy guns, and he himself fired a shell with a ten-second fuse, which, on rebounding from the ram's slanting sides, exploded and killed him. The *Miami's* crew, seeing that their projectiles were glancing off harmlessly like so many pebbles, now attempted to board, but the *Albemarle's* deck was quickly crowded with men ready to thwart this attempt. Hereupon the Union vessel, a fast side-wheeler, without receiving a blow, made good her escape. The *Albemarle* kept up a steady fire the rest of the day into the forts defending Plymouth, and on April 20, General Wessells, with 1500 Union soldiers, surrendered to the Confederates under General Hoke.

On May 5, the *Albemarle*, accompanied by the *Bombshell*, captured at Plymouth, and the transport *Cotton Plant*, emerged from the Roanoke River to attack Captain Melancton Smith's "pasteboard fleet," consisting of the double-enders *Mattabesett*, *Sassacus*, *Wyalusing*, and *Miami*, the ferryboat *Commodore Hull*, and the gunboats *Whitehead* and *Ceres*. The Union commander had been preparing for the inevitable conflict as best he could. He

Attack on Smith's Fleet

had equipped the *Miami* with a torpedo, and a strong net with which to foul the ram's propellers. His plan of attack was to take advantage of the double-enders' quick maneuvering qualities, approach the enemy as near as possible without endangering the side-wheels, discharge his powerful guns, and then quickly return for a similar circuit.

The *Albemarle* opened the battle at long range with a well-aimed shot at the *Mattabesett*, which cut away her rails and spars and wounded six men at the guns. But as the *Albemarle* then attempted to ram, the Union ship skilfully avoided her. Like a pack of wolves attacking a stag, Captain Smith's fleet surrounded the ironclad. The firing from the Union vessels was rapid, but had no effect on the ram's iron sides; even the 100-pound shot from the pivot-rifles glanced harmlessly off. All attempts, also, to send shot through the ports of the ram, or to find vulnerable spots on her, proved futile. At this juncture Captain Roe's ship, the *Sassacus*, whose prow had a three-ton bronze beak, backed slowly; then, with waste and oil thrown on her fires, the Union vessel sprang at the iron monster. "All hands lie down," was the order as the frail vessel crashed into the ram, careening the ironclad and hurling her crew off their feet. At the same moment a shell from the *Albemarle* tore through the *Sassacus*. A second shot exploded the double-ender's boiler. Mingled with the cries of agony from the scalded and frantic men was heard the rattle of small arms as the crew of the *Sassacus*, with pistols, muskets, and hand-grenades, repelled the boarders. During this time the other vessels, except the *Miami*, could not or did not make any attempt to come to close quarters, owing partly to a signal, given by mistake, that the *Wyalusing* was sinking. An attempt of the *Miami* to use her torpedo, owing to her poor maneuvering, failed. In the gathering darkness, the *Albemarle* retreated up the river; the muzzle of one of her guns was cracked, her tiller disabled, and her smokestack riddled.

The ram's object in thus giving battle to the Union fleet in order to co-operate with the Confederate land forces in an attack on New Berne had failed. On May 24, the *Albemarle* again appeared, this time at the mouth of the Roanoke to drag for torpedoes laid there for her destruction. From this date until October 27 she lay in "inglorious inactivity" at Plymouth. Meanwhile Captain Cooke, by reason of illness, was superseded by Lieutenant Warley. The existence of the ram continued, in spite of her inaction, to be a grave menace to the Union fleet, and consequently to the control of the sounds.

LIEUTENANT CUSHING PLANS TO DESTROY THE RAM

In this crisis Lieutenant William B. Cushing, then only twenty-one years old, made a suggestion to the Navy Department to destroy the *Albemarle* by torpedoes. This young man had on several previous occasions been remarkably successful in dare-devil adventures. In November, 1862, he made a successful raid in the *Ellis* up New River Inlet, N. C. The following January, with twenty-five men, he captured an earthwork at Little River. In February, 1864, in the Cape Fear River, Cushing boldly entered the Confederate lines and captured one of General Hebert's staff officers. In a cutter, with fifteen men, the following June, he made a reconnoissance near Wilmington, N. C., preliminary to destroying the ironclad *Raleigh*, captured the mail from the fort orderly, and ascertained that the *Raleigh*, retreating up Cape Fear River after an attack on a Union fleet, had "broken her back" on a bar. Thereupon Cushing, with remarkable skill, having eluded a large force of guard boats, returned safely to his vessel without the loss of a man. To such a youngster the Department readily entrusted the destruction of the *Albemarle*.

Cushing was sent to New York to select suitable vessels for his "torpedo-boats," and chose two boats built for picket duty. "They were open launches, about thirty feet in length, with small engines, and propelled by a screw. A 12-pounder howitzer was fitted to the bow of each, and a boom was rigged out some fourteen feet in length, swinging by a goose-neck hinge to the bluff of the bow. A topping lift, carried to a stanchion inboard, raised or lowered it, and the torpedo was fitted into an iron slide at the end. This was intended to be detached from the boom by means of a heel-jigger leading inboard, and to be exploded by another line, connected with a pin which held a grape shot over a nipple and cap."[2]

Torpedoes in the Civil War

Various forms of early torpedoes or submarine mines had been invented by Bushnell during the Revolution, and by Robert Fulton during the War of 1812, but the first successful mechanisms for submarine explosion came into use during the Civil War, in the course of which about twenty-eight vessels were either sunk or seriously injured by such devices. The ingenious machines included such classes as frame torpedoes, floating or buoyant torpedoes, electric torpedoes, spar torpedoes made fast to the early forms of torpedo-boats, and submarines or "Davids," as the Goliath slayers were called. Under the general term of torpedoes were included even such infernal machines as the coal torpedoes, irregular cast-iron shells filled with powder, painted to resemble coal, and surreptitiously hidden in coal heaps intended for

---

[2] Cushing, *Battles and Leaders of the Civil War*, iv, 634.

Union vessels; another form was a clockwork device with a harmless-looking exterior intended to be carried aboard ship and exploded at the time set. Numerous forms of mines were planted in rivers and bays to destroy vessels, which frequently provided themselves with nets and guard boats to fend these off.

The Confederates were the first to adopt the new weapon. In spite of considerable opposition even in the South to what was regarded as an inhuman mode of warfare, the Southern Government established in October, 1862, a torpedo bureau in its Navy Department. In 1863 one of its "cigar-shaped torpedo-boats" made an attack off Charleston on the *New Ironsides*, and failed only because of the Union vessel's great thickness of iron and timber. Another form of these "Davids," on February 17, 1864, sank in four minutes the heavily armed steam sloop of war *Housatonic*, also off Charleston. This torpedo-boat had been a submarine, but after suffocating three crews in attempts at submersion, it made its final and only successful attack on the surface, when its crew perished with the *Housatonic*.

Of the spar torpedo there were various forms that had been successfullly used in the war. The type adopted by Cushing was the invention of Engineer Lay of the navy. It consisted of a copper cylinder at the bottom of which was a cone containing a fulminate cap. Within the cylinder was a tube running the whole length, in the end of which a grape shot, held up by a trigger pin, was so arranged that by a slight pull the pin was withdrawn and the grape fell on the cap in the cone and exploded a charge of from fifty to seventy pounds of powder in the space between the outer cylinder and the tube. In the upper part of the apparatus was an air chamber that enabled the torpedo, when detached from the spar, to float in an upright position. In handling such a complex

Cushing Destroys the Albemarle

mechanism the most delicate touch was required. The torpedo-boat had to stop just at the right place to give free play for lowering the spar under the overhang of the vessel. Cushing, as he used the torpedo against the

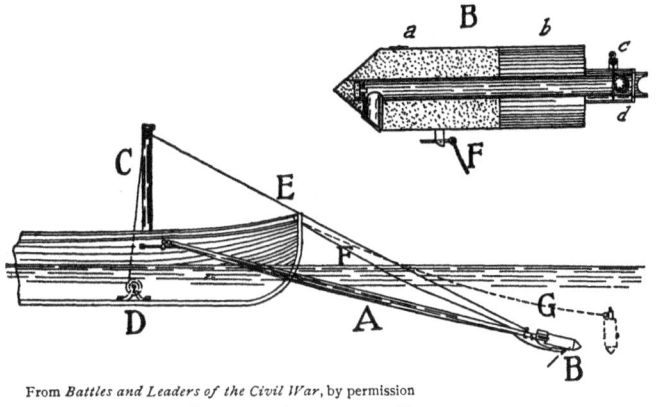

From *Battles and Leaders of the Civil War*, by permission
CUSHING'S LAUNCH AND TORPEDO

A, Spar. *B*, Torpedo. *C*, Stanchion. *D*, Windlass. *E*, Topping Lift. *F*, Heel-Jigger. *G*, Trigger Line. *a*, Powder Chamber. *b*, Air Chamber. *c*, Pin holding Grape Shot in place and attached to Trigger Line *G*. *d*, Grape Shot.

Albemarle, had attached to his person four lines: the detaching lanyard, the trigger line, and two cords running respectively to the engineer's wrist and ankle to direct the movements of the launch.[3]

THE DESTRUCTION OF THE ALBEMARLE

On the way southward, through the canals to Chesapeake Bay and thence to Norfolk, Cushing had lost one of his picket boats. With the other, after many adventures in passing through hostile country, he finally reached the Union fleet anchored off the mouth of Roanoke River.

[3] *Submarine Warfare,* by Lieut.-Commander J. S. Barnes, U. S. N., gives a brief but excellent history of early forms of torpedoes.

The young officer then disclosed his plan to his crew, and gave them the chance to avoid the hazardous undertaking, but they volunteered to a man.

The *Albemarle,* protected by several thousand soldiers deployed in the surrounding country, was moored at Plymouth, eight miles from the mouth of the river. A mile below the town was the wreck of the *Southfield,* on whose hurricane deck a guard was stationed to give warning of the approach of danger. The ram, according to her commander, Captain Warley, had a crew of only sixty,—"too small to keep an armed watch on deck at night and do picketing besides."

On the dark and slightly rainy night of October 27, 1864, Cushing started up the river and passed the wreck of the *Southfield* unobserved. His own very interesting account of his adventures that night and the next day is in part as follows:

"We passed within thirty feet of the pickets without discovery, and neared the vessel. I now thought that it might be better to board her, and 'take her alive,' having in the two boats twenty men well armed with revolvers, cutlasses, and hand-grenades. To be sure, there were ten times our number on the ship, and thousands nearby; but a surprise is everything, and I thought if her fasts were cut at the instant of boarding, we might overcome those on board, take her into the stream, and use her iron sides to protect us afterward from the forts. Knowing the town, I concluded to land at the lower wharf, creep around, and suddenly dash aboard from the bank; but just as I was sheering in close to the wharf a hail came, sharp and quick, from the ironclad, and in an instant was repeated. I at once directed the cutter to cast off, and go down to capture the guard left in our rear, and, ordering all steam, went at the dark mountain of iron in front of us. A heavy fire was at once opened upon us, not only from the ship, but from men stationed on the shore. This did not disable us, and we neared them rapidly. A large fire now blazed upon the bank, and by its light I discovered the unfortunate fact that there was a circle of logs around the *Albemarle*, boomed well out from her side, with the very intention of preventing the action of torpedoes. To examine them more closely, I ran alongside until amidships, received the enemy's fire, and sheered off for the purpose of turning, a hundred yards away, and going at the booms squarely, at right angles, trusting to their having been long enough in the water to have become slimy—in which case my boat, under full headway, would bump up against them and slip over into the pen with the ram. This was my only chance of success, and once over the obstruction my boat would never get out again. As I turned, the whole back of my coat was torn off by buckshot, and the sole of my shoe was carried away. The fire was very severe.

"In a lull of the firing, the captain hailed us, again demanding what boat it was. All my men gave comical answers, and mine was a dose of canister from the howitzer. In another instant we had struck the logs and were over, with the headway nearly gone, slowly forging up under the enemy's quarter port. Ten feet from us the muzzle of a rifle gun looked into our faces, and every word of command on board was distinctly heard.

"My clothing was perforated with bullets as I stood in the bow, the heel-jigger in my right hand and the exploding line in the left. We were near enough then, and I ordered the boom lowered until the forward motion of the launch carried the torpedo under the ram's overhang. A strong pull of the detaching-line, a moment's waiting for the torpedo to rise under the hull, and I hauled in the left hand just cut by a bullet.

"The explosion took place at the same instant that

100 pounds of grape, at ten feet range, crashed among us, and the dense mass of water thrown out by the torpedo came down with choking weight upon us.[4]

Cushing's Escape

"Twice refusing to surrender, I commanded the men to save themselves; and throwing off sword, revolver, shoes, and coat, struck out from my disabled and sinking boat into the river. It was cold, long after the frosts, and the water chilled the blood, while the whole surface of the stream was plowed up by grape and musketry, and my nearest friends, the fleet, were twelve miles away; but anything was better than to fall into the enemy's hands, so I swam for the opposite shore. As I neared it a man [Samuel Higgins, fireman], one of my crew, gave a great gurgling yell and went down.

"The Confederates were out in boats, picking up my men; and one of the boats, attracted by the sound, pulled in my direction. I heard my own name mentioned, but was not seen. I now 'struck out' down the stream, and was soon far enough away again to attempt landing. This time, as I struggled to reach the bank, I heard a groan in the river behind me, and, although very much exhausted, concluded to turn and give all the aid in my power to the officer or seaman who had bravely shared the danger with me.

"Swimming in the night, with eye at the level of the water, one can have no idea of distance, and labors, as I did, under the discouraging thought that no headway is made. But if I were to drown that night, I had at least an opportunity of dying while struggling to aid another.

---

[4] Captain Warley, of the *Albemarle*, states that the launch was at this time "so close that the gun could not be depressed enough to reach her." *Battles and Leaders*, iv, 642.

The swimmer proved to be Acting Master's Mate Woodman, who said that he could swim no longer. Knocking his cap from his head, I used my right arm to sustain him, and ordered him to strike out. For ten minutes at least, I think, he managed to keep afloat, when his physical force being completely gone, he sank like a stone.

"Again alone upon the water, I directed my course toward the town side of the river, not making much headway, as my strokes were now very feeble, my clothes being soaked and heavy, and little chop-seas splashing with choking persistence into my mouth every time I gasped for breath. Still there was a determination not to sink, a will not to give up, and I kept up a sort of mechanical motion long after my bodily force was in fact expended. At last, and not a moment too soon, I touched the soft mud, and in the excitement of the first shock I half raised my body and made one step forward; then fell, and remained half in the mud and half in the water until daylight, unable even to crawl on hands and knees, nearly frozen, with my brain in a whirl, but with one thing strong in me—the fixed determination to escape.

"As day dawned I found myself in a point of swamp that enters the suburbs of Plymouth, and not forty yards from one of the forts. The sun came out bright and warm, proving a most cheering visitant, and giving me back a good portion of the strength of which I had been deprived before. Its light showed me the town swarming with soldiers and sailors, who moved about excitedly, as if angry at some sudden shock. It was a source of satisfaction to me to know that I had pulled the wire that set all these figures moving, but as I had no desire of being discovered, my first object was to get into a dry fringe of rushes that edged the swamp; but to do this required me to pass over thirty or forty feet of open ground, right under the eye of a sentinel who walked the parapet.

"Watching until he turned for a moment, I made a dash across the space, but was only half way over when he again turned, and forced me to drop down right between two paths, and almost entirely unshielded. Perhaps I was unobserved because of the mud that covered me and made me blend with the earth; at all events the soldier continued his tramp for some time, while I, flat on my back, lay awaiting another chance for action. Soon a party of four men came down the path on my right, two of them being officers, and passed so close to me as almost to tread upon my arm. They were conversing upon the events of the previous night, and were wondering 'how it was done,' entirely unaware of the presence of one who could give them the information. This proved to me the necessity of regaining the swamp, which I did by sinking my heels and elbows into the earth and forcing my body, inch by inch, toward it. For five hours then, with bare feet, head, and hands, I made my way where I venture to say none ever did before, until I came at last to a clear place, where I might rest upon solid ground.

. . . A working-party of soldiers was in the opening, engaged in sinking some schooners in the river to obstruct the channel. I passed twenty yards in their rear through a corn furrow, and gained some woods below. Here I encountered a negro, and after serving out to him twenty dollars in greenbacks and some texts of Scripture (two powerful arguments with an old darkey), I had confidence enough in his fidelity to send him into town for news of the ram.

"When he returned, and there was no longer doubt that she had gone down, I went on again, and plunged into a swamp so thick that I had only the sun for a guide and could not see ten feet in advance. About two o'clock in the afternoon I came out from the dense mass of reeds upon the bank of one of the deep, narrow streams that abound there, and right opposite to the only road in the vicinity. It seemed providential, for, thirty yards above or below, I never should have seen the road, and might have struggled on until, worn out and starved, I should find a never-to-be-discovered grave. As it was, my fortune had led me to where a picket party of seven soldiers were posted, having a little flat-bottomed, square-ended skiff toggled to the root of a cypress tree that squirmed like a snake in the inky water. Watching them until they went back a few yards to eat, I crept into the stream and swam over, keeping the big tree between myself and them, and making for the skiff. Gaining the bank, I quietly cast loose the boat and floated behind it some thirty yards around the first bend, where I got in and pulled away as only a man could when his liberty was at stake.

"Hour after hour I paddled, never ceasing for a moment, first on one side, then on the other, while sunshine passed into twilight, and that was swallowed up in thick darkness only relieved by the few faint star rays that penetrated the heavy swamp curtain on either side. At last I reached the mouth of the Roanoke, and found the open sound before me. My frail boat could not have lived in the ordinary sea there, but it chanced to be very calm, leaving only a slight swell, which was, however, sufficient to influence my boat, so that I was forced to paddle all upon one side to keep her on the intended course.

"After steering by a star for perhaps two hours for where I thought the fleet might be, I at length discovered one of the vessels, and after a long time got within hail. My 'Ship ahoy!' was given with the last of my strength, and I fell powerless, with a splash, into the water in the bottom of my boat, and waited results. I had pulled every minute for ten successive hours, and for four my body had been 'asleep,' with the exception of my arms and brain. The picket-vessel, *Valley City,* upon hearing the hail, at once got under way, at the same time lowering boats and taking precaution against torpedoes. It was some time before they would pick me up, being convinced that I was the rebel conductor of an infernal machine, and that Lieutenant Cushing had died the night before. At last I was on board, had imbibed a little brandy and water, and was on my way to the flagship.

"As soon as it became known that I had returned, rockets were thrown up and all hands were called to cheer ship; and when I announced success, all the commanding officers were summoned on board to deliberate upon a plan of attack. In the morning I was well again in every way, with the exception of hands and feet, and had the pleasure of exchanging shots with the batteries that I had inspected the day before. I was sent in the *Valley City* to report to Admiral Porter at Hampton Roads, and soon after Plymouth and the whole district of the Albemarle, deprived of the ironclad's protection, fell an easy prey to Commander Macomb and our fleet."[5]

The *Albemarle* had sunk instantly at her moorings. Of Cushing's crew, he himself and Houghton escaped, Higgins and Woodman were drowned, and the remaining eleven men were captured.

For his brave deed, than which, as Captain Warley said, "a more gallant thing was not done during the war," Cushing received substantial recognition. He was given a vote of thanks by Congress, and although not yet twenty-two was promoted to the rank of lieutenant-commander.

---

[5] *Battles and Leaders*, iv, 634, ff.

XXII

ACTIONS IN FOREIGN WATERS

THE WYOMING AT SHIMONOSÉKI

WHILE the Federal Navy was using the utmost of its resources in tightening the line of blockade, in opening the Mississippi, and in capturing harbor defenses, the activity of Confederate commerce-destroyers made it necessary to detach several cruisers to hunt them down in foreign waters. One of these Federal cruisers, the screw-sloop *Wyoming*, Commander David McDougal, was ordered to the Pacific in pursuit of the Confederate steamship *Alabama*. As the *Alabama's* business was to destroy commerce rather than to engage a man-of-war, she avoided meeting the Federal vessel.

After a fruitless search for the *Alabama,* Commander McDougal, early in the summer of 1863, arrived on the Japanese coast. There he received a dispatch from the American minister to the effect that the guns of the *Wyoming* were greatly needed to protect American lives and property at Yokohama. McDougal went thither at once and made his vessel a refuge for American residents until safe quarters could be found for them on shore. The American commander found himself face to face with a wholly unexpected situation. At that time Japan was on the verge of a civil war which, like the Boxer rebellion in 1900, represented a determined effort on the part of the rebels to expel the "foreign devils" from the nation.

This disturbance was the sequel of Perry's mission to Japan. In 1858, the Japanese prime minister signed the completed treaty establishing commercial and diplomatic relations with the United States, but this act of amity five years later precipitated civil war in Japan. Although for 250 years Japan had been at peace, the embers of rebellion had long been smoldering, and the act that admitted the foreigner only fanned them into open blaze. The trouble at bottom was that the "Shogun," or "Tycoon"—the viceroy of Japan—had become all-powerful; while the Mikado himself, because of a policy of seclusion that had been forced on him, had become only a figurehead. Since the treaty with America had been signed under the authority of the Tycoon, the rebels took up arms in a double cause of patriotism, to restore the Mikado to his old-time authority and to expel the foreigner.

The insurgents represented some of the most warlike elements of the population, especially the great clans of Choshiu and Satsuma, which surrounded the Mikado at Kioto, and proclaimed his throne the seat of authority. They persuaded him to issue an edict setting June 25, 1863, as the date on which all foreigners should be expelled. The Tycoon, who was bound by treaty to the United States and other powers, was helpless. He sent in his resignation, but the Mikado refused to accept it, and left the viceroy to get out of his predicament as best he could.

The chief of the Choshiu clan proceeded at once to fortify the straits of Shimonoséki, the gateway to the inland sea of Japan, and to make war on his own account. On the 11th of July, McDougal received the news that an American steamer, the *Pembroke*, had been fired on without warning in the straits, and, according to the report, had been sunk with all on board. At this time McDougal was under orders to return to America, but realizing that the situation called for prompt action on his part, he weighed anchor and on the evening of the 15th arrived off the eastern end of the straits.

At this point the inland sea narrows down to a channel about three miles in length, and varies from one-half mile to a mile in width. The town of Shimonoséki lies at the foot of high bluffs which overlook the channel.[1] Through this the tides run like a mill race, over sunken rocks and shoals that have long made the place famous for shipwrecks.

It was here that the *Pembroke,* while she awaited a pilot and the turn of the tide, had been fired on. As a matter of fact, she came off with small injury, but others were not so fortunate. A French dispatch boat was attacked shortly after the *Pembroke* and narrowly escaped sinking in mid-channel. Her commander reported his experience to Captain Casembroot of the Dutch steam frigate *Medusa* of 16 guns. On account of the long-standing friendship between the Dutch and the Japanese, Casembroot went to Shimonoséki with the expectation of making peace; but hardly was the *Medusa* in the channel when she was under heavy fire. Before she could get away she had been hulled thirty-one times, and had lost four killed and five wounded. A day or two later, a French gunboat was hulled three times as she dashed past the batteries at full speed, and a Satsuma vessel, which was mistaken for a foreigner, was sent to the bottom. It was evident that the Japanese knew how to handle their guns, and had the range of the channel.

At five o'clock on the morning of the 16th, the *Wyoming* got under way. Her entry into the straits was announced by signal guns on shore, and as soon as she came in range she was fired upon by the batteries. She made no reply, however, until she reached the narrowest part of the straits. At that point the larger shore batteries concentrated their fire; beyond, in more open water

---

[1] For map of Japan, see p. 228.

lay three armed merchantmen, all heavily manned, and with their crews yelling defiance. These ships were the bark *Daniel Webster,* the brig *Lanrick,* and the steamer *Lancefield,* all, oddly enough, American vessels which had been purchased by the Choshiu clansmen. In the land batteries, too, were five 8-inch Dahlgren guns which had recently been presented to Japan by the United States. The bark lay anchored close to the town on the northern shore, the brig was about fifty yards outside and a little beyond, while the steamer lay further ahead and outside, that is, nearer mid-channel. As McDougal approached the narrows, he noticed a line of stakes which he rightly guessed had been used by the Japanese to gauge their aim. Accordingly, he avoided the middle of the channel and steered close under the batteries. This shrewdness probably was the salvation of the *Wyoming,* for the batteries at once opened a tremendous cannonade which would have sunk a dozen vessels in mid-channel, but which only tore through her rigging. She soon cleared the narrows and bore out into the open water where her guns could reply.

Commander McDougal then gave orders to " go in between those vessels and take the steamer." The Yokohama pilots [2] protested loudly, but the American had made up his mind to take the chances of shallow water and headed for the three ships. At this moment a fresh battery of four guns opened a raking fire, but the *Wyoming* answered with a single shell so accurately aimed that it tore the entire battery to pieces. Dashing ahead, she passed abreast the bark and the brig at close quarters and exchanged broadsides with both. The firing was so close that the long guns of the *Wyoming* seemed almost to touch the muzzles of the enemy, and it

---

[2] These pilots had been furnished by the Tycoon's government.

was in these few minutes at close quarters that the greater part of the American loss occurred. The forward gun division suffered most on account of its exposed position, sustaining, in fact, all the casualties of the day except three. The Japanese handled their guns so rapidly that the brig alone managed to pour three broadsides into the *Wyoming.* On the latter every gun was served to the utmost and every shot told on the hulls of the enemy.

Passing on, McDougal rounded the bow of the steamer and maneuvered for a fighting position. The brig was already settling, but the *Daniel Webster,* in spite of the great holes in her side, still kept up a steady fire, and six land batteries now reopened with the *Wyoming* as a fair target. The steamer, meanwhile, weighed anchor and, moving to the opposite side, seemed to be getting ready to ram the American. At this critical moment the rushing tides sent the *Wyoming's* bow aground, but after some minutes her engines succeeded in backing her off.

Then, ignoring the shore batteries and the *Daniel Webster,* McDougal opened fire with his two 11-inch Dahlgren pivot guns on the steamer *Lancefield.* Both shells took effect in her hull; another from the forward pivot tore through her boiler, and in a cloud of smoke and steam the vessel went down. Meanwhile, the bark *Daniel Webster* had been firing as fast as the guns could be loaded, and the six shore batteries were a continuous line of smoke and flame. McDougal now trained his guns to reply. In a few minutes the bark was wrecked, and then one shore battery after another was silenced. When satisfied that he had destroyed every thing within range, he turned and steamed slowly back. On his return he was practically unmolested.

This action had lasted one hour and ten minutes, in the course of which the *Wyoming* had been hulled ten times, her rigging had been badly cut, her smokestack perforated, and she had lost five killed and seven wounded. The battle had been won by the coolness and nerve of the American commander, and a fine feature of the story is that while most of the *Wyoming's* crew had never before been under fire, even when the ship was aground and the pilots were paralyzed with terror the bluejackets stood by their guns like veterans. Those were the days, too, when a white man caught by the insurgents endured the unspeakable death of the "torture cage," and the men knew that their commander had ordered that if the ship became helpless by grounding or by shot she was to be blown up with all on board.

A few days after McDougal's exploit a heavy French frigate with a gunboat entered the straits and destroyed what was left of the batteries by landing a force of marines. Some months later, however, the clansmen rebuilt their forts and succeeded in closing the straits for fifteen months. Finally, a large allied fleet put an end to the uprising and restored safety to the foreigner in Japan. But no other operation impressed the insurgents with the same respect as the attack of the *Wyoming*, singlehanded, against their entire force.

The Dutch captain who had taken his punishment without accomplishing anything in return, was knighted on his arrival in Holland, and all his crew received medals. McDougal, on the other hand, got no promotion and not even contemporary fame among his countrymen, for 1863 was the crucial year of the Civil War, and his exploit in far-away Japan was lost in the roar of battles at home. As Roosevelt once said of this fight, "Had that action taken place at any other time than during the Civil War, its fame would have echoed all over the world."[3]

---

[3] Quoted by E. S. Maclay, *A History of the United States Navy* ii, 396.

THE ALABAMA AND THE KEARSARGE

The Confederate sloop of war *Alabama*, which Commander McDougal failed to meet in the Pacific, had, in the course of two years, practically banished American merchantmen from the ocean. Built like her sister ships, *Florida*, *Georgia*, and *Shenandoah*, in the dockyards of Liverpool, she was from the first suspected of being a vessel of war designed for the Confederacy; and the United States minister, Adams, was so energetic in pressing on Lord Russell his evidence of her destination that even the British authorities, pro-Confederate as they were, reluctantly issued orders to restrain her from getting to sea.

As the Confederate agents learned of these orders in advance, the *Alabama* was hastily taken out (July 29, 1862) on a "trial spin" in the Mersey, from which she never returned. Instead, she steamed to the secluded port of Praya in Terceira, one of the Azores. There she was met by the bark *Agrippina* from London, carrying a cargo of ammunition, coal, and supplies of various sorts, which was transferred to the *Alabama*. Scarcely was this done when the steamer *Bahama* from Liverpool arrived with the future officers of the *Alabama*—including Captain Semmes—thirty of her crew, and $100,000 in money. Considerable difficulty was experienced in fitting out the *Alabama* in the Azores on account of the evident purpose for which she was intended, but under cover of various excuses to the Portuguese officials, the work went on rapidly. On August 24, after gaining the open sea, Captain Semmes summoned his crew and announced to them the character of his ship and of the cruise he intended to make. Then he lowered the English ensign, hoisted the Confederate colors, and read aloud his commission from

President Davis. With that formality the *Alabama* began her career.

After a few minutes of deliberation, eighty-five of the crew who had shipped in the *Alabama* at Liverpool stepped to the capstan and signed the articles as seamen in the Confederacy. Among them were many English man-of-warsmen, who were the bone and sinew of the crew. The rest of the complement—except the southern coast-pilots who came with the *Bahama*—was made up later by volunteers from the crews of the prizes.

Of the officers, Master's-mate Fullam, Assistant Surgeon Llewellyn, and Fourth Lieutenant Low also were Englishmen; Fullam and Low were at the time of their enlistment members of the Royal Naval Reserve. It was due to the latter's superb seamanship that the *Alabama* was saved from foundering during a hurricane early in her career. The remaining watch officers, the captain, and the surgeon were from the Southern States.

Captain Semmes, like most of the Confederate naval officers, had received his training in the "old navy," in which he had risen to the grade of commander. He was captain of the *Somers* at the time she foundered off Vera Cruz during the Mexican War, but had been honorably acquitted of blame by the subsequent court-martial. His first command under the Confederacy was the *Sumter*, a converted packet steamer; but this, after a brief though successful cruise, he was forced to abandon at Gibraltar, where it had been blockaded by Federal vessels. His second command, the one with which his name is chiefly associated, was the *Alabama*. This vessel, rated as a "screw-sloop," was 220 feet long, thirty-two feet in beam, and eighteen feet from deck to keelson. She carried two horizontal engines of 300 horsepower each, and bunkers holding coal sufficient for eighteen days' steaming. In order to economize his coal supply, Semmes cruised

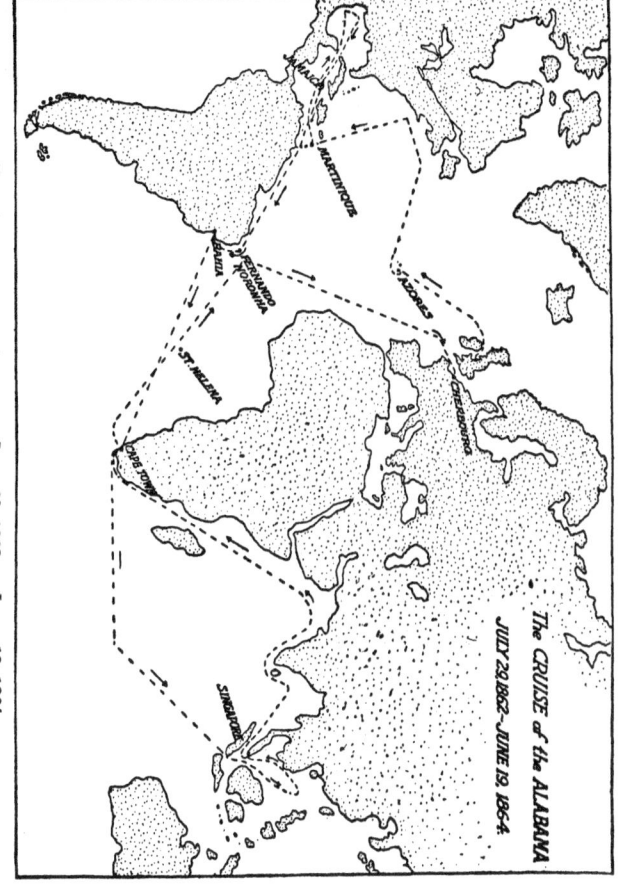

The Cruise of the Alabama, July 29, 1862 to June 19, 1864

most of the time only with his sails. The *Alabama* was rigged as a barkentine, and proved a good traveller under canvas. She had a device by which her propeller could be quickly detached from the shaft and hoisted so as not to retard her progress while under sail.

Captain Semmes did not have far to seek for his first prizes. After capturing and burning nine American merchantmen in the vicinity of the Azores, he steered across the Atlantic, taking in all twenty prizes before he headed toward the West Indies for fresh coal. At one time he took a ship within 200 miles of New York, and though searched for by Federal war vessels, managed to keep out of sight. While he was at Martinique, coaling from the *Agrippina,* which met him by appointment, he was blockaded by the *San Jacinto,* Commander Ronckendorff, but two nights later Semmes escaped to sea unobserved. From the West Indies he sailed to the Gulf; and, hoping to intercept some Federal transports that he knew were due at Galveston, he laid his course for that point. While off Galveston he lured away one of the blockading squadron, the *Hatteras,* a converted paddle-wheel river boat, and sank her, getting away again before the other vessels could come to the rescue. From this point Semmes began a slow cruise, along the Brazilian coast, round the Cape of Good Hope, to the East Indies. There he remained seven months; then, eluding the *Wyoming,* he returned round the Cape.

On June 11, 1864, the *Alabama* entered the harbor of Cherbourg for fresh coal and general overhauling. Since the day she went into commission, August 24, 1862, she had been on one continuous cruise, covering about 75,000 miles, during which she had burnt fifty-seven merchantmen and released a large number on ransom bond. The total valuation of these vessels reached a high figure, but the loss to American commerce was far more serious because the ships that were not captured were sold or kept in port, and the American carrying trade was turned over to British bottoms. By the time the *Alabama* entered Cherbourg practically all American shipping, save the Arctic whalers, had been annihilated or driven to cover, and even the whaling fleet was soon afterwards destroyed by the *Shenandoah*.

The amount of damage inflicted by the *Shenandoah* came within half a million of the sum represented by the work of the *Alabama*, but since the depredations of the former in the whaling fleet took place after June, 1865—when the war had been ended two months—her cruise, as an act of hostility, was worse than useless. While the damage inflicted by these two vessels more than doubled that of the ten other Confederate cruisers combined, it is necessary to bear in mind that there were these others as well, operating with varying degrees of success, but on a comparatively insignificant scale.[4] Like the *Alabama* and the *Shenandoah*, the most efficient of these minor commerce-destroyers were built to order or purchased on the Clyde, and some of them never saw the Southern coast during their entire career. The extraordinary success of Captain Semmes was due to the diligent study he had made of trade routes during his brief cruise on the *Sumter*, and his careful system of time-calculation, by which he would remain in one vicinity just long enough for news of his whereabouts to start a Union man-of-war after him, and then shift to another cruising ground.

The wholesale destruction of defenseless merchantmen naturally aroused the bitterest feeling in the North against Captain Semmes, and, it might be added, he reciprocated

---

[4] The following are the names of these cruisers, given in the order of the amount of damage inflicted by each: *Florida, Tallahassee, Georgia, Chickamauga, Sumter, Nashville, Retribution, Jeff. Davis, Sallie* and *Boston*.

the sentiment. He was referred to as a "pirate," not only by loyal newspapers, but also by Secretary Welles and the President, and there was much high talk of hanging the captain and crew of the *Alabama* at the yardarm if they ever were caught. As a matter of fact, if Semmes was a pirate so also was Paul Jones, David Porter, or any other commissioned officer of any government who has attacked the commerce of his enemy. As a recognized belligerent power, the Confederacy could commission vessels entitled to all the privileges of a man-of-war, among which the destruction of the enemy's shipping could certainly be included. The irregularity of burning his prizes instead of sending them to a Confederate prize court was forced on Semmes by the existence of the blockade, which made it impossible for a prize to reach a Confederate port. Semmes, who was a lawyer as well as a naval officer, examined the ship's papers himself, and constituted himself in all cases the prize court. He conducted his cruise with extraordinary skill, and it is not too much to say that Semmes with the *Alabama* injured the United States more than did all the rest of the Confederate Navy put together.

As soon as the *Alabama* arrived at Cherbourg, the United States minister to France telegraphed the fact to Commander Winslow of the United States sloop *Kearsarge*, then lying at Flushing, Holland. Three days after the arrival of the *Alabama* the *Kearsarge* appeared off the port. Winslow came in close enough to send a boat ashore, but did not anchor, for fear the "twenty-four hour rule" might be applied to allow the *Alabama* to escape. Then for five days the *Kearsarge* maintained a patient blockade, steaming back and forth just outside the breakwater, waiting for the *Alabama* to come out. Semmes had asked permission to use the naval dock at Cherbourg for a stay of two months, during which he had intended

The Kearsarge and the Alabama 377

to give his ship a thorough overhauling; but this request was denied as being incompatible with the position of France as a neutral. Hitherto Semmes had very properly refused to fight the *San Jacinto,* the *Wyoming,* the *Vanderbilt,* and the other cruisers sent after him; but at Cherbourg the French naval officers gave him emphatically to understand that the conduct of the *Kearsarge* was a "challenge" which no "man of honor" could decline.[5] This made it virtually impossible for one like Semmes to avoid a combat, in which, as he must have realized, he had little to gain and everything to lose. The North could have readily made good the loss of the *Kearsarge* with any one of a number of cruisers in European waters, but the South could not replace a sunken *Alabama.* Having applied for and received permission from Commodore Samuel Barron, the Confederate officer in charge of naval matters abroad, Semmes forwarded to Commander Winslow through the United States consul a note to the effect that if the *Kearsarge* would wait, the *Alabama* would come out and fight as soon as she could get her coal on board. On Saturday, he announced that on the next day he would go out to fight the *Kearsarge.* The sentiment in France was overwhelmingly in favor of the Confederate vessel, although the officials of Cherbourg were scrupulous in observing the laws of neutrality.

By ten o'clock in the morning of the 19th the preparations on the *Alabama* were complete, and shortly afterward she got under way. As she left the harbor she was escorted by the French ironclad *Couronne,* which stood by to see that the action took place outside the marine league. As soon as Commander Winslow of the *Kearsarge* saw his antagonist coming out to meet him, he sent his crew to quarters and headed out to sea, in order to draw

---

[5] *Harper's Magazine,* Nov. 1910, p. 873 ff.

her a safe distance from neutral waters. The *Couronne*, after accompanying the *Alabama* beyond the three mile limit, returned to port; but an English steam yacht, the *Deerhound*, which had also followed the men-of-war, kept on her course in order to be a spectator of the coming fight.

When the *Kearsarge* had led the way about seven miles off the coast, she turned to meet her enemy. The following details of the engagement are from the narrative of Lieutenant Sinclair of the *Alabama*:[6]

"The *Kearsarge* suddenly turned her head inshore and steamed toward us, both ships being at this time about seven or eight miles from the shore. When at about one mile distant from us, she seemed from her sheer-off with helm to have chosen this distance for her attack. We had not yet perceived that the *Kearsarge* had the speed of us. We opened the engagement with our entire starboard battery, the writer's 32-pounder of the port side having been shifted to the spare port, giving us six guns in broadside; and the shift caused the ship to list to starboard about two feet, by the way, quite an advantage, exposing so much less surface to the enemy, but somewhat retarding our speed. The *Kearsarge* had pivoted to starboard also; and both ships with helms a-port fought out the engagement, circling around a common centre, and gradually approaching each other. The enemy replied soon after our opening; but at the distance her pivot shell-guns were at a disadvantage, not having the long range of our pivot guns, and hence requiring judgment in guessing the distance and determining the proper elevation. Our pivots could easily reach by richochet, indeed by point-blank firing, so at this stage of the action and with a smooth sea, we had the advantage.

---

[6] Sinclair, *Two Years on the Alabama*, p. 267, ff.

"The battle was now on in earnest; and after about fifteen minutes' fighting, we lodged a 110-pound percussion-shell in her quarter near her screw; but it failed to explode, though causing some temporary excitement and anxiety on board the enemy, most likely by the concussion of the blow. We found her soon after seeking closer quarters (which she was fully able to do, having discovered her superiority in speed), finding it judicious to close so that her 11-inch pivots could do full duty at point-blank range. We now ourselves noted the advantage in speed possessed by our enemy; and Semmes felt her pulse, as to whether very close quarters would be agreeable, by sheering towards her to close the distance; but she had evidently reached the point wished for to fight out the remainder of the action, and demonstrated it by sheering off and resuming a [course] parallel to us. Semmes would have chosen to bring about yard-arm quarters, fouling, and boarding, relying upon the superior physique of his crew to overbalance the superiority in numbers; but this was frustrated, though several times attempted, the desire on our part being quite apparent. We had therefore to accept the situation, and make the best of it we could, to this end directing our fire to the midship section of our enemy, and alternating our battery, with solid shot and shell, the former to pierce, if possible, the cable chain-armor, the latter for general execution.

" Up to the time of shortening the first distance assumed, our ship received no damage of any account, and the enemy none that we could discover, the shot in the quarter working no serious harm to the *Kearsarge*. At the distance we were now fighting (point-blank range), the effects of the 11-inch guns were severely felt, and the little hurt done the enemy clearly proved the unserviceableness of our powder, observed at the commencement of the action.

"The boarding tactics of Semmes having been frustrated, and we unable to pierce the enemy's hull with our fire, nothing could place victory with us but some unforeseen and lucky turn. At this period of the action our spanker-gaff was shot away, bringing our colors to the deck; but apparently this was not observed by the *Kearsarge,* as her fire did not halt at all. We could see the splinters flying off from the armor covering of our enemy; but no penetration occurred, the shot or shell rebounding from her side. Our colors were immediately hoisted to the mizzenmast-head. The enemy having now the range, and being able with her superior speed to hold it at ease, had us well in hand, and the fire from her was deliberate and hot. Our bulwarks were soon shot away in sections; and the after-pivot gun was disabled on its port side, losing in killed and wounded all but the compressor-man. The quarter-deck 32-pounder of this division was now secured, and the crew sent to man the pivot gun. The spar deck was by this time being rapidly torn up by shell bursting on the between-decks, interfering with working our battery; and the compartments below it had all been knocked into one. The *Alabama* was making water fast, showing severe punishment; but still the report came from the engine room that the ship was being kept free to the safety-point. She also had now become dull in response to her helm, and the sail-trimmers were ordered out to loose the head-sails to pay her head off. We were making a desperate but forlorn resistance, which was soon culminated by the death blow. An 11-inch shell entered us at the water line, in the wake of the writer's gun, and passing on, exploded in the engine room, in its passage throwing a volume of water on board, hiding for a moment the guns of this division. Our ship trembled from stem to stern with the blow. Semmes at once sent for the engineer on watch, who reported the fires out, and

The Kearsarge and the Alabama 381

water beyond the control of the pumps. We had previously been aware that our ship was whipped, and fore-and-aft sail was set in endeavor to reach the French coast; the enemy then moved inshore of us, but did not attempt

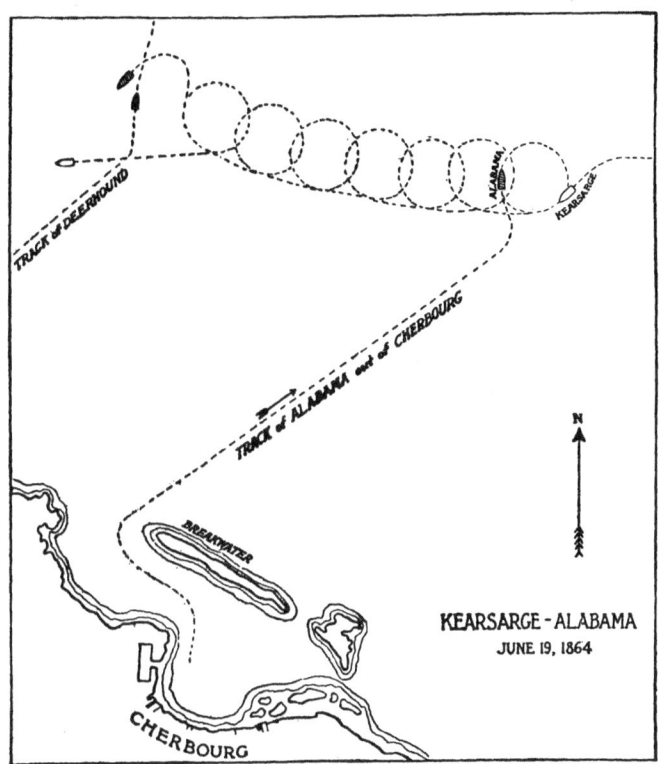

DRAWN FROM THE DIAGRAM SUBMITTED TO THE SECRETARY OF THE NAVY BY COMMANDER WINSLOW

to close any nearer, simply steaming to secure the shore-side and await events.

"It being now apparent that the *Alabama* could not float longer, the colors were hauled down, and the pipe given, 'All hands save yourselves.' Our waist-boats had been shot to pieces, leaving us but two quarter-boats, and one of them much damaged. The wounded were dispatched in one of them to the enemy in charge of an officer, and this done we awaited developments. The *Kearsarge* evidently failed at once to discover our surrender, for she continued her fire after our colors had been struck—perhaps from the difficulty of noting the absence of a flag with so much white in it, in the powder smoke. But be the reason what it may, a naval officer, a gentleman by birth and education, would certainly not be guilty of firing on a surrendered foe; hence we may dismiss the matter as an undoubted accident.

"The *Kearsarge* was at this time about 300 yards from us, screw still and vessel motionless, awaiting our boat with the wounded. The yacht was steaming full power towards us both. In the meantime the two vessels were slowly parting, the *Alabama* drifting with her fore-and-aft sails set to the light air. . . .

"The *Deerhound* approached the *Kearsarge* and was requested by Captain Winslow to assist in saving life; and then, scarcely coming to a full stop, turned to us, at the same time lowering all her boats, the *Kearsarge* doing the same. The officers and crew of our ship were now leaving at will, discipline and rule being temporarily at an end. The ship was settling to her spar deck, and her wounded spars were staggering in the 'steps,' held only by the rigging. The decks presented a woeful appearance, torn up in innumerable holes, and air-bubbles rising and bursting, producing a sound as though the boat were in agony. . . . The *Alabama's* final plunge was a remarkable freak. She shot up out of the water bow first, and descended on the same line, carrying away with her plunge two of her masts, and making a whirlpool of considerable size and strength."

The loss of the *Alabama* in this engagement amounted

to twenty-six killed or drowned and twenty wounded, three mortally. The wounded were brought to the *Kearsarge*, and her boats picked up fifty prisoners more. Nine escaped to Cherbourg on a French pilot boat and forty-two were carried to Southampton on the *Deerhound*.[7]

Captain Semmes, who had been wounded in the arm by a fragment of shell, was kept afloat by his first lieutenant, Kell, until both were picked up by one of the *Deerhound's* boats. Master's-mate Fullam, who brought the first boat load of wounded to the *Kearsarge*, was sent back under parole in order that he might assist in the rescue of the drowning crew. Before this task was finished, he, too, made for the *Deerhound*. In a few minutes the yacht, instead of returning with the prisoners to the *Kearsarge* as Winslow expected, put on full speed for Southampton.

The reception of Captain Semmes and his officers in England was most enthusiastic. A few newspapers, like the London *Daily News*, took the opposite side, and referred to the hero of the hour as a "runaway smuggler" and "nimble-footed buccaneer," but these were rare exceptions. This general cordiality on the part of the English is not surprising in view of the fact that the welcome accorded to the *Alabama* in the ports of the British empire had invariably been so hearty as to strain to the breaking point all pretense of neutrality. The reasons were that the ship was a product of a British shipyard, manned chiefly by a British crew, and numbering British officers in the wardroom; and in less than two years she had driven from the seas England's most formidable commercial rival.

Scarcely was the defeated captain on English soil before he wrote to the press, opening a controversy re-

---

[7] Figures from Ellicott's *Life of Winslow*.

markable for the violence of its contradictions. In the first place he charged the Federal captain with lack of "chivalry" in hanging chains over the sides amidships to protect the engines. To Semmes this was a sly "Yankee" trick, constituting the *Kearsarge* ironclad, while she was rated only as a wooden ship. If he had known this circumstance, he declared, he would never have risked the *Alabama* in such unequal combat. The idea had been suggested to Winslow the year before by his able executive, Lieutenant-Commander Thornton, who had seen the device used by Farragut during the passage of the defenses of New Orleans. The idea had been put into effect at once as a special protection to the engines when the coal bunkers were empty, as was the case when the *Kearsarge* fought the *Alabama,* and it attracted no little attention in European ports. Lieutenant Sinclair, who must have known his commander's statements to the contrary, says in half a dozen places that the chain protection of the *Kearsarge* was a matter of common knowledge on the *Alabama.* He adds, "Winslow for protecting his ship with chain armor should, in the humble judgment of the writer, submitted with diffidence, be accounted as simply using proper prudence in the direct line of duty. He had not given, accepted, or declined a challenge. But it was his duty to fight if he could and to win. *Semmes knew all about it* and could have adopted the same scheme. It was not his election to do so." [8]

The more serious charge that Semmes brought against Winslow was that of inhumanity. He declared that Winslow had fired into a surrendered ship, and was criminally negligent in the rescue of the *Alabama's* crew. These statements provoked equally scathing countercharges from Winslow and his officers. According to them, after the *Alabama* surrendered she fired two guns

---

[8] *Two Years on the Alabama,* p. 273.

The Controversy

at the *Kearsarge.* Furious at this breach of the flag of truce, Winslow opened fire again till he was assured of the *Alabama's* surrender. Surgeon Brown of the *Kearsarge* fully corroborated Winslow's account, adding that he was informed by the prisoners that two of their junior officers "swore they would never surrender, and in a mutinous spirit rushed to the two port guns and opened fire on the *Kearsarge.*"[9] This Lieutenant Kell of the *Alabama* emphatically denied, and so the question of fact must always stand in doubt.[10] As to the dilatory rescue of prisoners, Surgeon Brown gave as his opinion that Winslow would have done better to run alongside the sinking *Alabama* than to lie some 400 yards away. However, Winslow's asking the *Deerhound* to save lives, and allowing Fullam's boat to return, together with the fact that his own uninjured boats were immediately called away, clear him of the charge of inhumanity. The difficulty with the *Kearsarge's* boats lay in the fact that only two were uninjured—the sailing launch and the second cutter—and these were the least accessible.

In the North, as well as among the officers of the *Kearsarge*, indignation was kindled by the conduct of Semmes in escaping to an English vessel after his surrender to the *Kearsarge*, and by the conduct of the *Deerhound* in running away with the prisoners. For thus allowing the yacht to get away, Winslow was, in many quarters, sharply criticised. The only justification of Semmes's conduct lies in his belief that the Federal ship had already broken faith by firing on a surrendered vessel, and that fact relieved him of all obligations. Second Lieutenant Joseph Wilson of the *Alabama*, however, refused to go aboard the *Deerhound*, and was the only officer to surrender his sword to Commander Winslow. For

---

[9] *Battles and Leaders of the Civil War*, iv, 619.
[10] *Ibid.*, p. 610.

this he was released on parole by Winslow with a special letter of recommendation which gave him a speedy exchange. This conduct makes a sharp contrast with that of Fullam, which is inexcusable.

As to the *Deerhound,* the Federal commander should have known that once his prisoners were on her decks they were on neutral territory, and could neither be touched by him nor surrendered by her captain. Any attempt to take them by force would have been only a repetition of the *Trent* blunder. The case of the *Deerhound* led subsequently to special rulings in international law covering the services of neutral vessels in saving the drowning. To-day, in the same situation, the *Deerhound* would be obliged to give up the rescued men to the victorious commander.

The *Kearsarge* in this engagement had a broadside of five guns to her opponent's six, but the Federal battery was heavier at the point-blank range in which the greater part of the action was fought. The conclusive victory, however, was due rather to the great superiority in the gunnery of the *Kearsarge*. The *Alabama's* crew fired three broadsides to the *Kearsarge's* one, but this rapidity seems to have contributed to the wildness of the Confederate fire.[11] Only one dangerous wound was inflicted, a 100-pound shell that lodged in the stern post of the *Kearsarge,* but failed to explode. Two shots were deflected by the chains that hung over the side, but according to the testimony of the Federal officers, even if these shots had penetrated they would have cleared the engines and boilers. Eleven other shot or shell pierced the hull, most of them through the bulwarks. The rest of the shot seem to have gone high, for three boats were de-

---

[11] Lieutenants Kell and Sinclair attributed the ineffectiveness of the *Alabama's* fire to damaged powder, a circumstance which Kell says he did not discover in the careful overhauling of ammunition made by him prior to the battle.

stroyed, the smokestack was badly perforated, and the rigging was considerably cut. On the other hand, the guns of the *Kearsarge* were handled deliberately and with such precision that the *Alabama* was literally shot to pieces.

The newspaper warfare over this battle was not its most important sequel. In September, 1872, the "Geneva Tribunal," which had convened as a board of arbitration on the claims of the United States against Great Britain, found the defendant guilty of a violation of neutrality in that she had permitted Confederate men-of-war to be built, bought or equipped in her ports, and awarded to the plaintiff $15,500,000 for the value of ships and cargoes destroyed by the *Alabama, Shenandoah,* and *Florida.* This sum was increased by interest to about $16,000,000.

The theory, which is still widely held, that the *Alabama* was responsible for the disappearance of the American merchant marine after the war cannot be maintained. Though she and her consorts drove practically all American ships to cover, they captured only five per cent of the whole number, and only thirty-two per cent were sold or transferred temporarily to neutral hands.[12] Under normal conditions, the American carrying trade ought to have revived after the Civil War as it had done after the War of 1812. The reason it did not revive is to be found in changed economic conditions brought about, at least in part, by an increased tariff, which made it impossible to build and man ships as cheaply as our commercial rivals, and by the laws of navigation, which forbade the purchase of foreign vessels for use under the American flag. These measures operated severely against the merchant marine and drove American capital from ships into railroads, factories, and mines.

---

[12] Figures from " A Memorandum of the Admiralty to the Royal Commission on the Supply of Food and Raw Materials to the War," quoted by Thursfield, *Nelson and Other Naval Sketches,* p. 306.

XXIII

THE BLOCKADE AND THE END OF THE WAR

THE BLOCKADE

THE blockade of the entire Southern coast, the beginning of which has been described in Chapter XV, was in part prompted by the proclamation of President Davis, April 17, 1861, calling for privateers to prey on the commerce of the Northern States. In respect to both the blockade and privateering, the United States, although not a signatory to the Declaration of Paris of 1856, was considerably affected by it. In this compact the great powers of Europe had defined a blockade to be binding only when it had been made effectual (thus refusing to recognize "paper blockades"); and they had agreed not to resort to privateering. To make Europe respect the blockade, therefore, the North was obliged to put forth prodigious efforts to close the Southern ports; and yet, since the United States had not signed the Declaration of Paris, the North was precluded from objecting to the South's resorting to that last hope of a country without a navy—privateering. Furthermore, as a nation does not blockade its own ports, the adoption of this mode of warfare against the South put the Union in an anomalous position. In spite of the efforts of the administration at Washington at the beginning to regard the closure of ports in the nature of an embargo, or "domestic municipal duty," Europe could not so consider it, and hence the proclamation of a blockade left England no alternative except to recognize the South as a belligerent. This England did in a proclamation of neutrality on May 13; but she declined to go beyond this, and refused to recog-

David D. Porter

nize the Confederate States as a sovereign power. To make the blockade effective, therefore, so as to avoid European intervention, the small navy of the United States had before it an enormous task; for by "effective," within the meaning of the law of nations, was understood that there must be "evident danger in entering or leaving port." In spite of the greatness of the undertaking, this blockade was legally effective after being in operation six months. Furthermore, by the capture of one Southern port after another, the cordon was drawn so tight that it became gradually a military occupation.

In accordance with President Davis' proclamation, letters of marque were issued to owners of private vessels. As the North had a commerce ranking second in the world at that time, this was a means of striking the Union in its most vulnerable point; on the other hand, the South had no commerce on which the North could retaliate. The later stringency of the blockade, and the nondescript character of the letters of marque, caused the gradual dying out of this mode of warfare—not, however, before considerable damage had been done on the unsuspecting trading vessels of the North.

The first privateer to be captured, the *Savannah*, brought up anew the question of the status of the Confederacy. The crew of this vessel were tried for treason, on the ground that they were levying war against their own country. Moreover, the North maintained that an insurgent's man-of-war was, in the eyes of international law, a pirate. The crew of the *Savannah* were kept in prison for several months, but no further penalty was applied. The South had threatened to treat a like number of army prisoners in its hands in the same way that the Federal Government dealt with the *Savannah's* crew. Lincoln had from the first been in favor of a liberal policy, and the insurrection had assumed such proportions that it would have been impossible to regard a whole section of the country as guilty of treason. No real justification could be given for imprisoning privateersmen as pirates, and on February 16, 1862, they were put on the same footing as army prisoners.

The blockade began at Hampton Roads, which was nearest to both centres of government. The only serious attempt to break it at this point was made by the *Merrimac*. The other two lines of blockade were on the Atlantic and the Gulf coasts. In the Gulf the capture of New Orleans, the principal commercial city in that quarter, made the task less difficult than along the Atlantic, and as the plans of operation of the two squadrons were very similar, we can gain sufficient idea of the operations of the blockaders by considering only the work of the Atlantic squadron.

The duties of this squadron proved so difficult that it was divided early in the war between two squadrons: the North Atlantic, under Goldsborough, and later under Porter; and the South Atlantic, successively under DuPont and Dahlgren. The task of these squadrons was arduous for several reasons: the Atlantic seaboard from the Carolinas to Florida, with its numerous inlets and sand bars, has practically a double coast line; several friendly ports not far away, particularly Nassau and the small towns of the Bermudas, gave the blockade-runners a convenient market for the cotton so much needed by British manufacturers; furthermore, specially designed steam blockade-runners, connecting the three important commercial centres, Wilmington, Charleston, and Savannah with Nassau and Europe, kept the squadron always on the *qui vive*.

This remarkable type of vessel, the blockade-runner, had no armament to speak of, nor was it intended to make any resistance. It was presumably a merchantman.

The South, not being a manufacturing community, had to import munitions, and to pay for military stores it had to send abroad its one great staple, cotton. To effect this exchange and to elude the Federal ships, the blockade-runners early in the war came into being. As the cordon of Northern vessels grew more taut, there was an increasing need in the South for ships whose main points were speed, stowage space, and invisibility. "The typical blockade-runner of 1863–64 was a long, low side-wheel steamer of from 400 to 600 tons, with a slight frame, sharp and narrow, its length perhaps nine times its beam. It had feathering paddles, and one or two raking telescopic funnels, which might be lowered close to the deck. The hull rose only a few feet out of the water, and was painted a dull gray, or lead color. . . . Its spars were two short lower-masts, with no yards, and only a small crow's-nest on the foremast. The deck forward was constructed in the form known as 'turtle-back' to enable the vessel to go through a heavy sea. Anthracite coal, which made no smoke, was burned in the furnaces. . . . When running in, all lights were put out; the binnacle and fire-room hatch were carefully covered, and steam was blown off under water."[1]

The blockading squadrons had to be eternally vigilant, with steam up night and day, to catch these vessels, which frequently made fifteen knots. Some of the Northern ships cruised in wide circuits in the neighborhood of Nassau and the Bermudas, where they were often more successful than nearer home; the unsuspecting blockade-runner was thus at times caught off his guard. To circumvent the vigilant Northern fleets, the steamers, with their cargoes of "hardware," the innocent name under which they listed the arms and ammunition in their holds, prac-

---

[1] Soley, *The Blockade and Cruisers*, p. 156.

tised every ruse to avoid capture. When the beacon lights on the coast were extinguished, these craft made their dash for port, guided by signal fires, or by the lights on the blockading fleet. If the squadron commander, discovering this, kept a light only on the flagship, or on a different blockader every night, the information was carried with remarkable speed to Nassau, and the next runner was ready for the new order of things. At one time an order was issued that a vessel, discovering a steamer slipping in under cover of darkness, should fire a gun in the direction the pursued was taking, in order to give a clue of the whereabouts of the chase. A few days afterwards blockade-runners were equipped with rockets to be shot off at right angles to the intended course. Wilkinson, in his interesting *Narrative of a Blockade-Runner,* describes another device frequently used by the pursued vessel. The engineer was ordered to make a black smoke; at the moment when the lookout with his glass gave the word that the pursuer in the gathering twilight was just out of sight, the dampers were closed, and the runner sped away in a different direction, leaving the Union vessel to chase a shadow. The start from Nassau or the ports in the Bermudas was made when there would be a high tide and no moonlight for the run into port. If very hard pressed, the pursued vessel might run ashore, where a nearby battery could cover the landing of the cargo, though the vessel might be sacrificed.

Many of the blockade-runners were owned by companies financed by Southern and British investors. Even the Confederate Government shared in the business. Suitable vessels were bought in England, and were put in command of naval officers of the Southern Government. One of these owned by the Government was the famous *R. E. Lee,* a Clyde-built side-wheel steamer, which, under the able Captain Wilkinson, ran the blockade successively twenty-one times within a year. Indeed, this vessel and the *Kate* made trips as regularly as a packet. The traffic became so profitable that even officers of the British Navy condescended to take command, under assumed names, for ships often paid as high as £1000 to their captains for the round trip from a Southern port to Nassau. With cotton at four pence a pound in Wilmington, and two shillings a pound in Liverpool, these captains could gain sufficient to retire on after six months' service. The companies engaged in this lucrative trade could afford to lose a vessel after two successful trips.

The strictness of the blockade and the occupation of one Southern port after another eventually put an end to this trade. During the war the blockading fleets captured or destroyed 1150 vessels, with their cargoes, aggregating in value $30,000,000.

OPERATIONS BEFORE CHARLESTON

After the capture of Port Royal, DuPont had directed his energy to making the blockade—especially of Charleston—thoroughly effective. The able Assistant Secretary of the Navy, Fox, who had the greatest faith in monitors, hurried as many of these " marvelous vessels " to DuPont as he could, and ordered the latter to capture Charleston.

This city was well defended by a large army under Beauregard, by numerous forts, by ironclads, and by mines, to say nothing of the natural defenses of sand bars, which kept the blockading fleet well outside and gave the shallow draft blockade-runners an opportunity to make their dashes through the inlets. Moreover, the harbor was a veritable *cul de sac*, from which there was little chance of escape for vessels of any type once caught inside.

The Confederates made several attempts to break the

blockade on the South Atlantic coast, which kept DuPont's attention too much occupied to risk the loss of vessels in premature attempts on Charleston. In January, 1863, the ironclad rams *Chicora* and *Palmetto State* emerged early one morning from Charleston harbor and inflicted signal damage on the wooden gunboats *Mercedita* and *Keystone State,* before the scattered blockaders could close in on the rams. In this affair there seems, on the Union side, to have been a lack of co-operation and of rapid communication by signal; for the dispersed ships took the sally of the rams for one of the frequent attempts of blockade-runners, and when they came up the Confederate vessels were retreating to the cover of the forts. As a result of this attack Beauregard, by proclamation, declared that the blockade of Charleston was raised, a statement which was soon proved untrue.

Admiral DuPont determined to test the new monitors before he made his attempt on Charleston. These vessels were still largely an experiment, and the commander of the squadron was by no means so sure of their endurance against powerful forts as was the Assistant Secretary of the Navy. With this object in view, DuPont sent, in February, 1863, the *Montauk* to test her powers against Fort McAllister. At this time the *Nashville,* a Confederate cruiser, was lying in the Great Ogeechee River behind the fort. With her cargo of cotton, she had been trying for some time to slip through the blockade. Captain Worden, of the *Montauk,* found that he could bear the fire of the earthwork with little damage to his vessel, but he noticed also that he did no harm to the fort. Moreover, as the *Nashville* had retreated up the river, he could not get within striking distance of her. Worden kept a close watch, however, and on the evening of February 27, after a careful reconnoissance, he discovered that the *Nashville* was aground. Waiting until daylight, that he might see better, he planted his ironclad under the guns of Fort McAllister, and coolly dropped his 11-inch and 15-inch shells with fatal precision upon the *Nashville;* in a few minutes the cruiser was in flames, and later blew up. The *Montauk,* under the concentrated fire of the fort, had been hit only five times, and retreated unharmed from her target practice. On her way out, however, she struck a torpedo, which caused a serious leak, necessitating her running on a mud flat for temporary repairs. She was able later to rejoin the fleet.

Shortly afterwards three monitors were sent to make a further test against the same fort. In these attacks the vessels did little damage to the fort, and the admiral wrote to the Department, ''Whatever degree of impenetrability they might have, there was no corresponding quality of destructiveness against forts.''

Under Department coercion, however, Admiral DuPont, with the *New Ironsides* [2] and his seven monitors, made an attack on Charleston on April 7, 1863. The channel was not deep enough for vessels of the draft of the *Ironsides;* moreover, there was continual danger from the torpedoes at the entrance to the harbor. After an hour's fighting under these difficulties, DuPont withdrew his ships to ascertain the damage received, with the purpose of renewing the battle next day, if after consultation with his captains he felt the risk was not foolhardy. The ironclad *Keokuk,* which had been stationed nearest to Fort Sumter, had been struck ninety times, nineteen shot

---

[2] The *New Ironsides* was a ship-rigged armor-clad, the most powerful vessel in the Northern Navy. Over her heavy oak framework she had four inches of armor. With her engines of 1800 horsepower and her sails she could make eleven knots. Her armament consisted of sixteen 11-inch Dahlgren guns and of two 200-pounder Parrott rifles.

penetrating her below the water line. Both her turrets were pierced in many places. She sank the following morning. The other vessels had been struck in a degree corresponding to their proximity to the forts. The defenses of Charleston, on the other hand, seemed practically intact.

In spite of another proclamation of General Beauregard that the blockade of Charleston was raised as a result of the battle of April 7, Admiral DuPont quickly repaired his vessels and kept the cordon of ships around the harbor. General Gilmore, a Federal engineer of great ability, succeeded in landing troops at Morris Island, and thus enabled the fleet to operate closer in shore and render blockade-running more difficult than before.

At this time information came to the fleet that the powerful ram *Atlanta* and other Confederate ironclads at Savannah were about to leave Wilmington River for Warsaw Sound to break up the blockade in this vicinity. The *Atlanta,* formerly the *Fingal,* a Clyde-built iron steamer, had been transformed into a ram. The usual heavy-timbered casemate covered with four inches of iron had been superposed on the razed deck. Brooke rifles were so placed in the casemate as to be fired either laterally or fore-and-aft. Admiral DuPont dispatched two monitors, the *Weehawken,* Captain John Rodgers, and the *Nahant,* Captain Downes, to intercept the *Atlanta.*

Early on the morning of June 17, 1863, Captain Rodgers discovered the ram coming down the river. With the cool deliberation that characterized him, Rodgers let the ram open fire and approach to within 300 yards of the *Weehawken.* Then he discharged his huge Dahlgren smooth-bores. The first four shot struck with terrific effect. The very first missile, a 15-inch cored shot, penetrated the armor. Just fifteen minutes after the *Wee-*

Fall of Charleston

hawken opened, the *Atlanta* hauled down her colors. The *Nahant* did not get a chance to take part in the contest.

Captain Rodgers was an excellent disciplinarian, and by much practice had made his men skilled marksmen. On the other hand, the *Atlanta* had a new crew, and went into battle in great hurry and disorder. Of the eight shot which she fired, none hit. The result showed also that in the contest between armor and guns, some improvement had been made in penetrating power since the day when the first *Monitor* tried to pierce the *Merrimac*.

Admiral DuPont decided not to renew the attack on Charleston without the co-operation of a large land force. The admiral, earlier in his career, had shown no compunction in attacking, even with wooden vessels, Port Royal, but on that occasion he could pass the forts and attack them from the rear. On account of his decision not to make another attempt on Charleston, the Assistant Secretary of the Navy ordered Admiral Dahlgren to the command of the South Atlantic squadron; the latter relieved DuPont on July 6, 1863.

Admiral Dahlgren soon realized that much was expected of him. He was told that Charleston must be taken. Yet his judgment coincided with his predecessor's; and when, goaded by official pressure and newspaper attacks, he called in October a council of war, finding that his officers thought as he did, he decided not to attack Charleston with his present force. The city was finally taken sixteen months later in just the way that DuPont had urged, by a powerful army operating from the rear. General Hardee, who had escaped from Savannah before the capture of that city by Sherman, had assumed command of the Confederate forces at Charleston. Hemmed in here by Sherman's army, he was compelled to evacuate on February 18, 1865.

CAPTURE OF FORT FISHER

We have seen in a former chapter that the North Atlantic squadron under Goldsborough wrested the control of the North Carolina sounds from the Confederates and destroyed the *Albemarle*, the greatest menace to the blockade in these waters. After Goldsborough was relieved, Admiral Lee took command and brought the squadron to a still higher degree of efficiency. In October, 1864, Admiral David D. Porter succeeded Lee and began preparations for the capture of Fort Fisher.

The possession of this earthwork, commanding "the last gateway between the Confederate States and the outside world," was of the utmost importance to the North to end the long-drawn-out agony of the war. It defended the approach to Wilmington, N. C., on which the starving, ill-clad, and poorly equipped remnant of Lee's army depended for its supplies of food, clothing, and ammunition, brought by blockade-runners from Nassau. The stores of flour in Virginia were exhausted; bread was three dollars (Confederate currency) a loaf in Richmond, and Lee's army was on half-rations. Meat, too, was very scarce, and the soldiers often eked out their scanty fare with rats, muskrats, etc. Lee had informed Colonel Lamb, the commander of Fort Fisher, that if Wilmington was lost, his troops would have to fall back from Richmond. The importance of Wilmington to the Confederates may be inferred from the fact that "between October 26, 1864, and January, 1865, 8,632,000 lbs. of meat, 1,507,000 lbs. of lead, 1,933,000 lbs. of saltpetre, 546,000 pairs of shoes, 316,000 pairs of blankets, half a million pounds of coffee, 69,000 rifles, and 43 cannon were obtained through this port from the outer world, while cotton sufficient to pay for these purchases was exported."[3]

---

[3] *Cambridge Modern History*, vii, 557. Figures taken from the report of the Confederate Secretary of the Treasury.

Fort Fisher and Wilmington 399

On December 20, 1864, the largest fleet hitherto assembled under the Union flag, commanded by Admiral Porter, and accompanied by 6500 troops under General Butler, arrived off Fort Fisher. The armada consisted of nearly sixty vessels, five of which were ironclads; the powerful *New Ironsides* and the four monitors, *Monadnock, Canonicus, Saugus,* and *Mahopac*. In Porter's fleet were also our largest steam-frigates, *Minnesota, Colorado,* and *Wabash*.

Fort Fisher was situated at the southern extremity of a narrow tongue of land, called Federal Point. The earthwork was in the shape of a right angle, the vertex of which pointed northeast. One leg of this angle extended westward across the peninsula from the ocean to Cape Fear River, and the other ran southward along the sea-shore. Hence the fort had a land face and a sea face. It was the best-constructed earthwork known, and had the most recent ideas adopted in its structure. The parapets were twenty-five feet thick. Heavy traverses had been constructed to protect the gunners against enfilading fire, and there were numerous bomb-proof chambers. On the land face twenty heavy guns were mounted, and on the sea face twenty-four, all in barbette, and among these guns, which ranged from six to ten inches, were columbiads, Brooke, and Blakely rifles, a 150-pounder Armstrong, and some mortars. Moreover, in front of the land face was a high palisade of logs pierced for musketry, and farther out, a network of subterranean torpedoes was set as a defense against infantry. The defenders of this great work, however, had many difficulties to overcome. The walls of the fort were so massive that soldiers in the gun chambers could not see the approach immediately in front for a hundred feet. Hence they had to expose themselves on the parapet to make a reconnoissance of an attack at close quarters. To defend the huge work,

Colonel Lamb had only 1900 men. His supply of ammunition was also small; he had not over 3600 shot and shell for his forty-four heavy guns and three mortars, and only thirteen shells for his 150-pounder Armstrong.

On the night of December 23, the *Louisiana,* an old Union gunboat, loaded with powder, was sent in close to the fort and exploded by means of a clockwork device. This preliminary attempt to destroy the earthwork proved an utter failure. The next day the Federal fleet in four great lines made the attack. The first line bombarded the land face; the ironclads, which constituted a separate unit, anchored farther inshore to concentrate their fire on the bastion at the northeast salient; lines numbers two and three attacked the sea face; and the reserve line was to land troops, cover landings, and carry dispatches. The ships kept up the bombardment all day of the 24th. The next day, Christmas, the troops landed, but General Butler, after a reconnoissance, declared that "the place could not be carried by assault, as it was left substantially unimpaired by the navy fire." To the great dissatisfaction of Porter and Grant, the first attack on Fort Fisher proved "an ignominious failure." The fleet had suffered little damage from the fort's fire, but the bursting of 100-pounder Parrott rifles on five of the Union vessels had killed sixteen men and wounded many others.

General Grant, at the request of the Secretary of the Navy, immediately sent, in Butler's stead, General Terry, an officer of great decision. On January 13, the fleet, in formation like that of the previous attack, renewed the bombardment of Fort Fisher. Line number one shelled the woods to the north of the land face to clear the way, and by afternoon 6000 troops, with twelve days' provisions, were landed. The fleet's fire continued night and day. The vessels aimed with deliberation, making the guns of the fort their targets. Notwithstanding this

Second Attack on Fort Fisher

slow shooting, the naval fire of the fleet's 600 guns, Colonel Lamb tells us, amounted often to two shots per second, while the gunners in the fort, being compelled to husband their ammunition, were ordered to fire each piece only once every half hour. In the interim of firing, the gunners took refuge in the bomb-proofs, but the bursting of the 11- and 15-inch shells from the *New Ironsides* and the monitors, to say nothing of the countless shot from the other vessels, was doing terrible execution in the little garrison. Colonel Lamb had appealed in vain to General Bragg for reinforcements.

General Terry was meanwhile entrenching himself two miles north of the fort. All day of the 14th and the following night the fleet kept up the relentless fire on the earthwork, especially on the land face, with the purpose of making the attack for the troops as easy as possible. The network of torpedoes had been cut to pieces by the navy gunners. Admiral Porter and General Terry had prearranged the final plan of assault. At a signal from the troops, the fleet was to change the direction of its fire, and a detachment of sailors and marines was to attack the sea face, while the soldiers were to attempt to scale the parapets at the western end of the land face.

On the morning of the 15th, the navy gunners, who had had ample practice to get accurate range, renewed the storm of shot and shell, and by noon there was but one serviceable heavy gun left on the land face. By three in the afternoon the signal came from General Terry, and at the blast of the whistles of fifty vessels, the direction of the navy fire was changed to the higher parts of the earthwork. The detachment of sailors and marines, armed only with cutlasses and revolvers, advanced along a half-mile of sand dunes, exposed to the rifles of the defenders, and to the enfilading fire of grape and shells from the guns of the fort. The 2000 sailors, in three divisions,

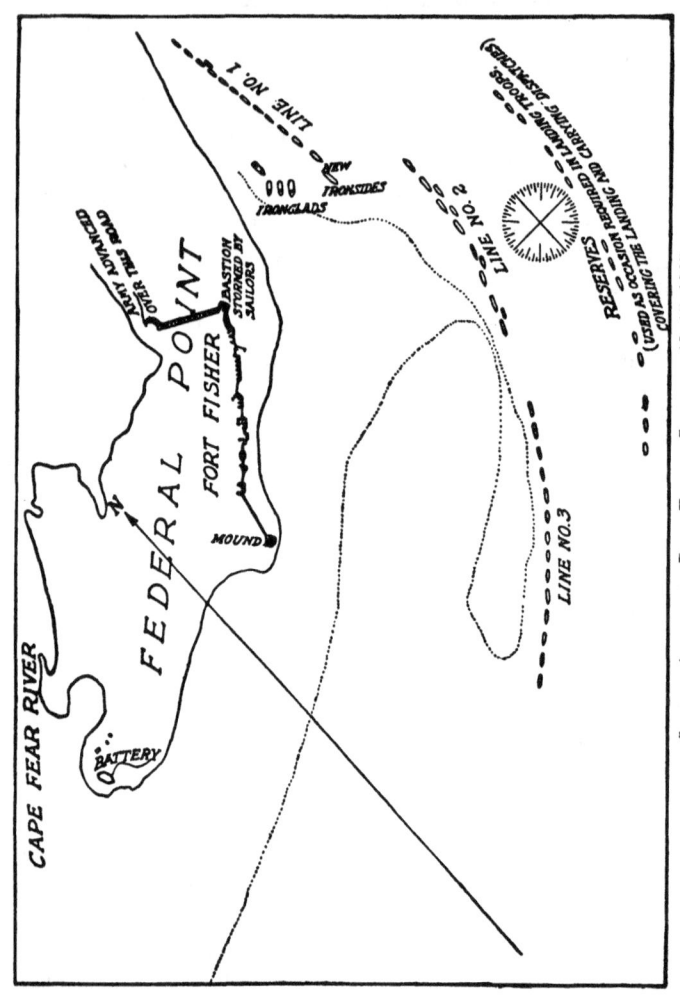

Second Attack on Fort Fisher, January 13–15, 1865

under Lieutenant-Commander Breese, acted as a diversion, and thus helped toward the success of the troops. But, although the bluejackets showed magnificent courage, yet in their exposed positions, with no means of throwing up entrenchments, they were foredoomed to failure in their attack. The navy lost 300 killed and wounded in this assault.

Meanwhile the troops were taking one traverse after another on the land face. The accurate fire, especially of the *Ironsides*, prepared the way for the capture by the soldiers of each new traverse to the eastward. Under the cover of night, the disorganized companies of sailors and marines emerged from their shelters behind sand dunes, and crept around the northeast salient to join the soldiers in their attack. The Confederates were compelled to abandon the bastion, and then one traverse after another on the sea face. Colonel Lamb and his handful of men, having fought to the last ditch, surrendered at ten o'clock on the night of the 15th.

The capture of Fort Fisher had cost the Federal army 691 men, and the navy 309, killed, wounded, and missing, but the results were worth while. The fall of Fort Fisher opened the way for General Schofield, who now joined Terry and assumed command, to capture Wilmington a few weeks later. Of this event, Scharf, the Confederate historian, says: " The fall of Wilmington was the severest blow to the Confederate cause which it could receive from the loss of any port. It was far more injurious than the capture of Charleston, and, but for the moral effect, even more hurtful than the evacuation of Richmond. With Wilmington open, the supplies that reached the Confederate armies would have enabled them to maintain an unequal contest for years; but with the fall of Fort Fisher the constant stream of supplies was effectually cut off." In March, Schofield joined Sherman, who was marching up through the Carolinas. In April Lee retreated from Richmond to meet his fate at Appomattox.

The surrender of Lee at Appomattox practically ended the war. After the capture of Mobile, which took place contemporaneously with Grant's victory over Lee, the Confederate troops and ships in Alabama retreated up the Tombigbee River. On May 4, Commander Farrand, in charge of the Confederate naval forces in this State, made a proposal to give up all the vessels under him. "On the 10th of May the formal surrender took place, and the insurgent navy ceased to be an organization. . . . On the second of June, Galveston was surrendered, and the supremacy of the Government was once more established on the entire coast, from Maine to and including Texas.

"Immediately after the fall of Fort Fisher and the capture of Wilmington, measures were taken for the gradual reduction of the naval forces employed on the duties of blockade. The recovery of Charleston, Mobile, and Galveston justified a still further diminution, and as these events occurred, measures were promptly taken to reduce the squadrons and economize expenses."[4] Finally, by a series of proclamations of President Andrew Johnson, made from May 22 to August 29, 1865, the blockade of Southern ports was gradually ended.

What the Navy Accomplished

The importance of the control of the sea was strikingly exemplified in the Civil War. For the reason that the Union navy had this control it often exercised a shaping influence in events. Its work consisted of both

---

[4] *Report of the Secretary of the Navy*, December, 1865, pp. viii, ix.

what it accomplished and what it prevented the Confederate navy from accomplishing.

The great achievements of the navy were the blockade of the Confederate coast and the splitting of the Confederacy into two parts by taking the Mississippi River. Both of these operations were essential for the shutting off of munitions and supplies from the Confederate armies fighting in the east. The war was primarily a land fight, and the greatest campaigns were aimed at Richmond. The heart of the Confederacy was in Virginia, and when the navy stopped the flow of the life currents, one by one, the heart was no longer nourished, and the end came.

Further the importance of the control of the sea was shown in what the North, with its organized naval force, prevented the South, with no organization at the beginning, from doing. The South had an ambitious building program, and the *Merrimac, Albemarle, Mississippi, Manassas,* and *Tennessee* (which were only a part of this program), crude though they were, at various times made the North tremble. If the South could have brought in the necessary materials and ship builders, these and other craft might have changed the character of the blockade. So strong was the Southern army, and so well adapted was their territory for defense, that without the blockade we can only speculate as to how long the war would have lasted and what would have been its outcome.

While it remains true that the Civil War was primarily a military war, still the army received great help from the navy, and vice versa. The Mississippi could probably not have been opened without Farragut's help, and, on the other hand, the navy needed a Sherman to bring about the capture of Charleston.

XXIV

THE NAVY IN THE YEARS OF PEACE

The Period of Naval Decay

In the brief period since 1850, the United States Navy had been revolutionized. The wooden frigates of other days were supplanted in this short interval by ironclads propelled by steam. So great was this sudden change that it has been aptly said that the sailor of the Invincible Armada would have been more at home on a frigate in 1840, than the "marline spike seaman" of the middle of the nineteenth century was in the new types of ships that came into being during the Civil War. In other words, three centuries had not effected such great changes as had the brief quarter of a century ending in 1865.

These revolutionary changes were mainly the invention of rifled guns, the heavy smooth-bores of Dahlgren, and the torpedo; the introduction of ironclads; and the application of steam to ships of war. Of all these changes, perhaps the greatest was the supplanting of sail by steam. This made possible the revival of the ram, which had gone out after the oar-galleys were succeeded by sailing vessels. The first forms of steam ships, the side-wheelers, were exceedingly vulnerable; but a great advance was made by the invention of the screw-propeller, which permitted the defense of the machinery by submersion and by armor-plating on the sides. And, as every new mode of defense leads to new means of offense, the torpedo was devised for use against the under-water body, the only vulnerable part of this latest type of ironclad. Thus began the race, still going on, between armor and ordnance.

But, as far as the United States was concerned, the

The Protected Cruiser *Olympia* The Screw-Sloop *Hartford* The Frigate *Santee*
THREE HISTORIC SHIPS FORMERLY AT THE NAVAL ACADEMY

The Period of Naval Decay 407

development in the science of naval warfare that had been so rapid during the Civil War ceased abruptly with its close. The nation, weary of the tremendous burden of armies and fleets, demanded a wholesale reduction in the military establishment. The general opinion was that the chances of a conflict with any European nation were remote, and since ships and men had been forthcoming in sufficient numbers to crush the forces of secession in the greatest civil war in history, there would be time enough to raise armies and build fleets when another war came.

For the reduction of the navy at this time there were also special reasons. An inventory of the ships made after the war showed that most of them were unfit because of faulty design, the use of unseasoned timber, and hurried construction. Common sense demanded the weeding out of these, and the few vessels that remained Congress regarded as sufficient for a peace footing, with the addition of four new monitors. These monitors, however, were built in the style prevailing during the Civil War, with wooden hulls heavily plated with iron; and by 1874 they had rotted so badly that they were ordered broken up and rebuilt in iron. Congress subsequently stopped the work of reconstruction, and for twenty years the United States had not a single armored ship. During the administration of President Hayes our navy was inferior to that of any European nation; even Chile's two ironclads, if properly handled, would have been more than a match for all our ships combined. The most discouraging feature of the situation was that the navy at this time seemed to be without friends at Washington, and the country at large was wholly indifferent to its needs. All naval appropriations that could be got out of Congress were designed to keep existing ships in re air, and much of this money was wasted because the congressmen were more interested in "making business" for their constituencies than in repairing the ships. The Navy Department, in order to have any men-of-war at all, was forced to rebuild ships under the old names, paying for them out of the proceeds from the sale of condemned hulks and out of the appropriation for "repairs."

One excuse can be offered for the attitude of Congress towards the navy. After the Civil War, changes in naval construction followed each other with such bewildering rapidity that naval constructors and line officers held the most divergent opinions as to the types of ship worth building, the amount of sail power to be retained, the kind of engines, the use of steel or iron, the amount of armor plate, etc. Naturally, this utter lack of agreement among the experts made Congress unwilling to appropriate money for new vessels which might prove costly blunders.

The year 1881, when Garfield succeeded to the Presidency, marks the lowest point to which the navy has ever sunk since the days when the United States had to pay a ransom to Algiers. Out of the 140 vessels on the navy list in 1881, twenty-five were tugs, and only a few of the rest in condition to make a cruise. Not a single ship was fit for warfare. An engraving published in 1881 pictured the "Fleet" being reviewed by the President, a pathetic attempt to put the best face possible on our miserable ships. This group represented the best dozen vessels in the navy at that time; they were all built of wood, and included not only the side-wheel steamer *Powhatan*, a relic of the forties, but also the ancient frigate *Constitution!* And the batteries mounted by these ships were chiefly smooth-bores left over from the Civil War. No wonder that an American captain in those days was ashamed to take his ship to European waters!

If the year 1881 represent the lowest ebb in the American Navy, it marks also the turning of the tide. The policy of trusting to luck in our relations with foreign nations began to lose favor. Long before this the weakness of our navy had been felt during the strained relations with Great Britain arising from the Alabama Claims shortly after the war, and again when war with Spain seemed imminent over the *Virginius* affair in 1873. And when, in 1880, France laid hands on the Isthmus of Panama without any regard for the Monroe Doctrine, it began to dawn on the Americans that European nations laughed at the demands of our State Department when backed by nothing better than a few, rotting, wooden hulls mounting antiquated guns.

THE BIRTH OF THE NEW NAVY

The first step toward a new navy was taken by Secretary Hunt, with the approval of President Garfield, in the appointment of an advisory board to prepare a report on the needs of the navy. President Arthur, in his first annual message (1881), declared his policy in regard to the navy in the following words, "I cannot too strongly urge upon you my conviction that every consideration of national safety, economy, and honor imperatively demands a thorough rehabilitation of the navy." Although he was hampered by the reluctance of Congress, President Arthur succeeded in beginning the regeneration of the American Navy.

The advisory board, mentioned above, recommended the construction of thirty-eight unarmored cruisers, five rams, five torpedo gunboats, ten cruising torpedo-boats, and ten harbor torpedo-boats. The smaller vessels were to be all of steel, and of the cruisers it was recommended that eighteen should be of steel and twenty of wood. Strange as it seems now, the minority members of the board, including three naval constructors and Chief Engineer Isherwood—the great engineer of the Civil

War—opposed the use of steel and recommended iron, largely on the ground that we had no plants capable of producing the steel required. The new market, however, created new plants to meet its needs, and the decision of the majority resulted in the rapid development of one of the greatest American industries, the manufacture of steel.

Congress was now willing to do something to better the navy, but not prepared for the ambitious program recommended by the Advisory Board. The House Naval Committee accepted the decision on steel as "the only proper material for the construction of vessels of war," and urged the building of two cruisers capable of an average speed of fifteen knots, four cruisers capable of a speed of fourteen knots, and one ram. It ignored the torpedo-boats and recommended only one ram because it regarded the type as experimental.

The House Committee had thus made a sweeping reduction of the number of ships called for by the Board, but Congress was not willing to go even as far as the Committee. The act of August 5, 1882, called for only "two steam cruising vessels of war . . . to be constructed of steel of domestic manufacture: . . . said vessels to be provided with full sail power and full steam power." Then Congress neglected to make any appropriation for them! The only effective clause of this act was a provision appointing a second advisory board. This board promptly recommended five vessels, one of about 4000 tons, three of about 2500 tons, all of steel, and one iron dispatch boat of 1500 tons.

The act of March 3, 1883, provided for these ships with the exception of one of the smaller cruisers. These four, the first of the "white squadron," were the *Chicago*, the *Boston*, the *Atlanta*, and the *Dolphin*. In the same year, to put an end to the practice of rebuilding old ships out of money for "repairs," Congress prohibited the repairing of any wooden vessel when it amounted to twenty per cent of the cost of building a new one. This action instantly dropped forty-six ships from the naval list. Later on the figure was changed from twenty to ten per cent, and the patchwork policy was definitely abandoned.

The decay of the navy after the Civil War had resulted in the lack of facilities in this country for the manufacture of steel plates or of modern ordnance. American inventors of guns, like Hotchkiss, for example, had been compelled to go abroad to sell their patents. When in 1885 the Government was ready to mount modern guns on the warships, it had to get the forgings and castings abroad. In five years, however, by the creation of a home market for ships and guns, manufacturing plants were developed in America capable of turning out the highest types of large calibre and machine guns, as well as every other requisite for the construction of a modern battleship.

Four more vessels were ordered in 1885, the cruisers *Newark* and *Charleston*, and the gunboats *Yorktown* and *Petrel*. The *Charleston* was the first of our men-of-war to abandon sail power and to use only military masts. The following year Congress ordered the completion of the four monitors, work on which had been suspended twelve years before, and the construction of one other. These were the *Miantonomoh, Amphitrite, Monadnock, Terror*, and *Monterey*. With each succeeding year thereafter, new vessels were added. In 1890 the Government took a long stride forward in naval construction; hitherto there were no ships larger than cruisers, but in this year Congress authorized three first-class battleships—the *Indiana*, the *Massachusetts*, and the *Oregon*. Eight years later our successes in the War with Spain gave the navy a tremendous impetus, which has since put the United States for the first time in the front rank among the naval powers of the world.

THE NAVY IN POLAR EXPLORATION

The years of peace have afforded splendid instances of heroism in the service of polar exploration, which are well worthy to rank with the more famous deeds of war. The record begins with the year 1837, when an expedition was fitted out for "maritime observation" in the South Pacific and Antarctic. So much quarrelling marked the organization of the expedition that several officers in turn declined to accept the command. Finally it was given to a junior officer, Lieutenant Charles Wilkes, U. S. N., noted later for his connection with the "*Trent* affair." The squadron consisted of five small ships ranging from 780 to 96 tons, " wretchedly prepared for an extended voyage, and especially unsuited for Antarctic navigation."[1] However, what his expedition lacked in equipment, Wilkes very nearly made up by his resourcefulness, persistence, and courage. It was not until further exploration was a physical impossibility that he reluctantly turned his ice-shattered squadron home.[2] The most important result of his voyage of three years and ten months was conclusive evidence as to the existence of the Antarctic continent, which had been a matter of speculation. The next naval expedition and all subsequent ones were sent to the Arctic.

In the spring of 1845 Captain Sir John Franklin, of the British Navy, set sail with two ships to discover the Northwest Passage. The last message received from him

---

[1] Greely, *Handbook of Arctic Discoveries*, p. 289.
[2] One of his vessels was lost with all on board.

The Search for Franklin 413

by the Admiralty was dated the following July, and although the squadron was fitted out with supplies for three years, as time went by with no word whatever from the party, anxiety deepened, and one relief expedition after another was dispatched. In 1850 American sympathy was represented by a squadron of two ships under Lieutenant E. J. De Haven, U. S. N. The expenses of the enterprise were shared by private subscription, headed by Mr. Grinnell of New York, and by the Government. The American vessels entered northern waters almost at the same time as those of English relief parties. No clues except a few graves of the Franklin party were discovered. In August Lieutenant De Haven decided to return, but a succession of gales, combined with severe cold, caught his ships before he could reach clear water. The two vessels were frozen into the ice pack, and drifted helplessly with the currents. The imprisonment lasted over eight months, and all the while the two vessels were in daily peril of being crushed. The life on board was made almost unendurable by the strain of constant danger, the monotony, the privations, and the fearful cold, against which there was no adequate protection. For 1050 miles the ships were carried by the drift before the midsummer sun released them from their prison of ice. During the northerly drift of the floe, De Haven discovered Murdaugh Island and the wide plateau to which he gave the name "Grinnell Land." His ships were so weakened by the strain they had undergone, that he abandoned the idea of continuing the search for the Franklin party, and sailed for the United States, reaching New York on September 30, 1851.

The next expedition had for its aim the discovery of the Pole. In the summer of 1879 a party left San Francisco in the steamer *Jeannette*, Lieutenant-Commander

G. W. De Long, U. S. N., commanding. It was organized by James Gordon Bennett, proprietor of the New York *Herald,* with the co-operation of the Government. It was known that the Japanese current splits in Behring Strait, sending one branch to the west coast of North America, and the other into the Arctic Ocean in a northeasterly direction. Before this time no polar explorers had ever set out by way of Behring Strait, and the idea of the *Jeannette* party was to try to reach the Pole by following this northeasterly branch of the Japanese current. The first voyage, however, was to be more of a preliminary or experimental nature than of an actual dash for the Pole.

The *Jeannette* early encountered ice floes, which crowded her off her intended course. Finally, De Long decided to winter at Wrangell Land, then supposed to be part of a huge Arctic continent. By September 6, the vessel was wedged and frozen solidly into a floe and carried to the northwest of Wrangell Land, which proved to be only a small island. All winter she drifted with the ice, in imminent danger of being crushed. Once she certainly would have foundered but for the skill of her chief engineer, G. W. Melville. Summer did not bring the party their expected release, and still another year dragged by in the icy prison, with only sickness to vary the fearful monotony of their existence. Finally, on June 12, 1881, the long-threatened disaster fell—the *Jeannette* was sunk by the ice, leaving her people stranded on the floes in mid ocean. To add to the hardships of their situation, two of the officers and three of the men were sick, provisions were scanty, and the clothing of the entire party was so worn that many a march had to be made over the snow and ice with bare feet.

There was one chance of escape, and that was to reach the settlements on the Lena delta, 500 miles away. To this end De Long and his men laid their course, partly by boat and partly by sledge. Unluckily, at the outset they had against them the northerly drift of the ice floes, which carried them twenty-eight miles in the opposite direction, to the northernmost point ever reached in that sea, before they could make any gains to the southward.

On September 12, exactly three months after their desperate retreat began, the three boats of the expedition were separated by a violent gale, just off the Lena delta. Melville, commanding the whale boat, entered a mouth of the Lena and succeeded, with his nine men, in reaching a Siberian village on its banks, after fearful sufferings. The second cutter, commanded by Lieutenant Chipp, evidently foundered, for nothing was ever heard or seen of it or its crew after the night of the storm. The first cutter, under Commander De Long, with the surgeon and twelve men, succeeded in entering the Lena delta, and struggled southwards.

It was the fate of this party not to meet any of the natives of the region or to know of villages nearby which might have proved their salvation. They were soon facing death from starvation. De Long, remaining with his sick and dying, dispatched his two strongest seamen to hasten up the course of the Lena and bring relief. By the end of October these men managed to reach a village, more dead than alive. They gave one of the natives a pencil message to be taken with quickest dispatch to the nearest Russian official, thence to be forwarded to St. Petersburg; but the native, having heard that another American—Melville—was in the neighborhood, carried the dispatch to him.

This was the first word Melville had heard from his shipmates, and although the early winter had set in, and his feet and legs were still in such condition from frostbite that he was unable to stand, he organized a sledging outfit and made the journey to the village where the two survivors were. Thence, with these two seamen and some native guides, he started north to find De Long and his men. At various points along the river he found records left by De Long, but was baffled by the fact that De Long had, toward the end of his march, crossed on the ice to the opposite banks. The search was blocked by a furious snowstorm on November 14, and Melville narrowly missed giving his own life in the vain quest.

As early as possible the following spring he renewed his search, and on the 23d of March, 1882, he came upon the bodies of De Long and his men. The last entry in the commander's diary was October 30, 1881, recording briefly the death of two and the approaching end of a third in the party. Probably by the first of November the last man had died of starvation.

Meanwhile, in 1881, a party under Lieutenant A. W. Greely, U. S. A., had gone north for three years of exploration and scientific observation in Grinnell Land. A store ship was to be sent them in 1882, and another in 1883. As it happened, the first supply ship was unable, on account of ice, to reach either Fort Conger or Lady Franklin Bay, and instead of leaving the supplies in a "cache" on shore, returned to the United States with everything on board. The second vessel was sunk by the ice, its crew returning on the steamer *Yantic* which accompanied it. The failure of these two expeditions made the situation of the Greely party critical. While Congress wasted valuable time in quarrels over the necessary appropriation, Secretary Chandler took the responsibility on himself of purchasing two Scotch whalers, the *Bear* and the *Thetis*, and fitting them out to undertake the rescue at the earliest practicable moment in the summer of 1884. Queen Victoria gracefully repaid the American efforts for the relief of

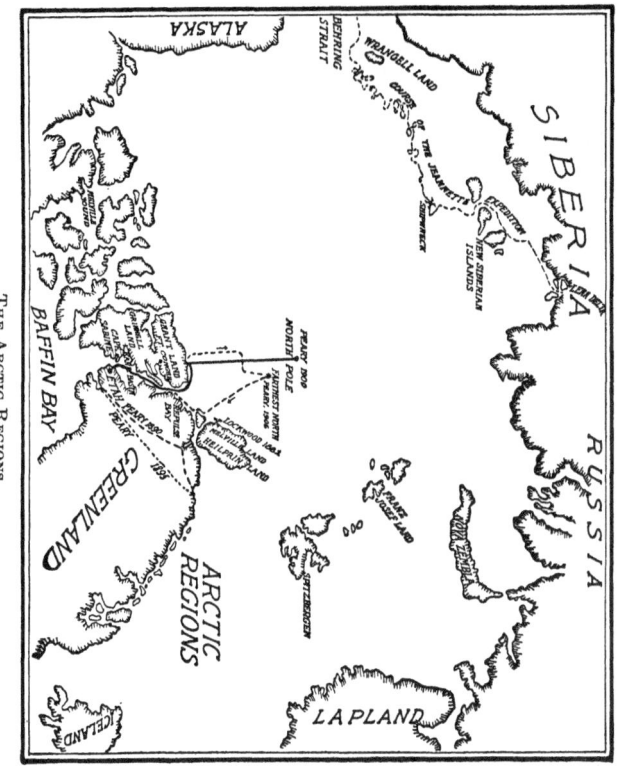

THE ARCTIC REGIONS

the Franklin party by contributing the *Alert,* a ship especially designed for polar service and regarded as the stoutest wooden vessel afloat. The squadron of three vessels was placed under Commander W. S. Schley, who conducted the relief with the most praiseworthy skill and dispatch. On June 22, 1884, they discovered the survivors of the Greely party, including Lieutenant Greely himself, in a tent on Cape Sabine, and conveyed them to the ships, with the greatest difficulty, during a violent gale. These survivors were almost at the point of death from starvation, but all except one recovered on the return voyage to the United States. The indomitable Melville had returned from Siberia just in time to go north again with the Schley expedition, and was one of the first to clasp hands with Lieutenant Greely in the tent on Cape Sabine.

The conquest of the Pole was at last accomplished by an officer of the American Navy after a siege of twenty-three years. In 1886, Civil Engineer Robert E. Peary, U. S. N., made a reconnoissance of the Greenland ice cap. In 1891–2 he discovered and named Melville Land and Heilprin Land, lying beyond Greenland, and by the same expedition he determined the insularity of Greenland. The ten years between 1892 and 1902 were spent in exploration. In the expedition of 1898–1902 Peary attained a new ''farthest north'' for the western hemisphere.[3] His expedition of 1905–1909, with the *Roosevelt,* was crowned with success. On April 6, 1909, the climax of all northern exploration was reached, and the American flag was unfurled at the North Pole. The attainment of this point revealed the fact that the supposed Polar continent did

---

[3] Till then the farthest north had been a point reached by Lieutenant Lockwood, U. S. A., a member of the Greely expedition.

not exist, and that the pole was only a point in the ice-covered Arctic sea.

Peary's success was the logical outcome of his years of preparation. Every expedition heretofore had been defective in important details of planning and equipment. Peary made the most of the experience of each voyage. He established the most practicable route to the Pole, he invented his own sledge to meet the local conditions, and, in short, reduced, detail by detail, the whole problem of Arctic exploration to a science.

DIPLOMATIC SERVICES OF NAVAL OFFICERS

The exploit of Commodore Matthew C. Perry, in 1854, in opening the trade of Japan to the world, thus inducing the "Hermit Nation" to take her rightful place in the family of nations, is probably the greatest feat of the kind in the history of the world. But it is by no means the only instance of the navy's being called on to act in a diplomatic capacity.

In the famous letter of Paul Jones to the Marine Committee (September, 1775), defining the duties of the naval officer, occurs this passage: "The naval officer should be familiar with the principles of international law. . . . He should also be conversant with the usages of diplomacy and capable of maintaining, if called upon, a dignified and judicious diplomatic correspondence; because it often happens that sudden emergencies in foreign waters make him the diplomatic as well as military representative of his country, and in such cases he may have to act without opportunity of consulting civic or ministerial superiors at home, and such action may easily involve the portentous issue of peace or war between great powers." The introduction of cables and wireless plants has in nowise lessened this service, for, seemingly, instructions that leave the conduct of affairs, often of the most delicate and important nature, to the "discretion and sound judgment" of the senior naval officer present, are issued as frequently as in the earlier period of our history. A reading between the lines of some of the paragraphs of the navy blue book is enough to show the extent and nature of the mental equipment required for the successful performance of the trying duties that so often confront the officer in times of peace. For instance, the commander-in-chief of a naval force, in the absence of a diplomatic or consular officer of the United States at a foreign port has authority—

(*a*) To exercise the powers of a consul in relation to mariners of the United States;

(*b*) To communicate or remonstrate with foreign civil authorities as may be necessary;

(*c*) To urge upon citizens of the United States the necessity of abstaining from participation in political controversies or violations of the *laws of neutrality.*

"On occasions where injury to the United States or to citizens thereof is committed or threatened, in violation of the *principles of international law or treaty rights,* he shall . . . take such steps as the gravity of the case demands. . . . The responsibility of any action taken by a naval force, however, rests wholly upon the commanding officer thereof."

"Although due weight should be given to the opinions and advice of the consular and diplomatic representatives of the United States, a commanding officer is solely and entirely responsible to his own immediate superior for all official acts in the administration of his command."

"The use of force against a foreign and friendly state, or against anyone within the territories thereof, is illegal. The right to self-preservation, however, is a right which belongs to states as well as to individuals, and in the case of states it includes the protection of the state, its honor, and its possessions, and the lives and property of its citizens against arbitrary violence, actual or impending, whereby the state or its citizens may suffer irreparable injury. The conditions calling for the application of the right of self-preservation can not be defined beforehand, *but must be left to the sound judgment of responsible officers, who are to perform their duties in this respect with all possible care and forbearance.*"

"He shall exercise great care that all under his command scrupulously respect the territorial authority of foreign civilized nations in amity with the United States."

"So far as lies within their power, commanders-in-chief and captains of ships shall protect all merchant vessels of the United States in lawful occupations, and advance the commercial interests of this country, *always acting in accordance with international law and treaty obligations.*"

Two prominent things are noted in the above: first, the requirement of a thorough knowledge of international law and various treaty provisions; second, the insistence upon the responsibility remaining, in all circumstances, with the naval officer—a responsibility not lessened by advice from diplomats, nor removed by general instructions from the Government. The officer must decide, and quickly, grave questions that may involve peace or war.

That the confidence reposed in the abilities of officers by both the Navy and State departments has not been misplaced, is shown by many instances of fine work done by naval officers in various ports of the world.

President Cleveland, in one of his annual messages, wrote: " It appearing at an early state of the Brazilian insurrection that its course would call for unusual watchfulness on the part of the Government, our naval force in the harbor of Rio de Janeiro was strengthened. Our firm attitude of neutrality was maintained to the end. The insurgents received no encouragement of eventual asylum from our commanders." Again, in the same message it is reported that " our naval commanders at the scene of disturbances in Bluefields, Nicaragua, by their constant exhibition of firmness and good judgment, contributed largely to the prevention of more serious consequences and to the restoration of quiet and order. . . . Although the practice of asylum is not favored by this Government, yet in view of the imminent peril which threatened the fugitives, and solely from considerations of humanity, they were afforded shelter by our naval commander."

An event in which readiness in dealing with a critical situation was strikingly shown, occurred in the Brazilian insurrection of 1894. The Brazilian Navy was in possession of the revolutionists, who held the bay of Rio de Janeiro, where much interference was made with the movements of peaceful merchantmen. Saldanha da Gama, the rebel leader, threatened to fire on any ship that should go to the piers to discharge its cargo; and merchantmen, despite the fact that yellow fever was decimating their crews, were obliged to lie out in the bay and await the end of the war.

Such was the condition of affairs when Rear-Admiral A. E. K. Benham, U. S. N., arrived. He at once told the American captains to go to the piers and trust him to protect them from harm. Inspirited by this promise, Captain Blackford, of the bark *Amy*, and two other captains, gave notice on Sunday, January 29, 1894, that they would take their ships in to the wharves on the following morning. Da Gama, hearing of this, made proclamation that he would fire on any vessel that ventured to do so, and a conflict seemed impending. The commanders of the war-vessels of other nations looked

Diplomatic Services

anxiously to see if the American admiral would hold fast to his position. Day had hardly dawned before active preparations were visible on the small American squadron, which was soon cleared for action, the cruiser *Detroit* taking a station from which she could command two of Da Gama's vessels, the *Guanabara* and the *Trajano*.

When the *Detroit* reached her station, the *Amy* began to warp in towards her pier. From the *Guanabara* came a warning musket shot. In an instant more a ball from the *Detroit* hurtled across the bow of the Brazilian, followed by another that struck her side. These were in the way of admonition. Seeing a couple of tugs maneuvering as if with purpose to ram his vessel, Commander Brownson took the *Detroit* in between the two Brazilian warships, and occupied a position that would have enabled him to sink them and their tugs at the same time.

This decisive action ended the affair. No further shot came from a Brazilian gun, and the *Amy*, followed by the other two vessels, made her way unharmed to the wharves.

President McKinley's message of December, 1898, contained the following: "A menacing rupture between Costa Rica and Nicaragua was happily composed by the signature of a convention between the parties, the act being negotiated and signed on board the United States steamer *Alert*, then lying in Central American waters. It is believed that the good offices of the commander of that vessel contributed largely toward this gratifying outcome." Another incident involving the navy is referred to in the same message: "Pending the consideration of the treaty providing for the annexation of the Hawaiian Islands, I directed the U. S. S. *Philadelphia* to convey Rear-Admiral Miller to Honolulu, and intrusted to his hands an important legislative act, to be delivered to the President of the Hawaiian Republic, with whom the admiral and the minister were authorized to make appropriate arrangements for transferring the sovereignty of the islands to the United States."

That Admiral Dewey's valuable services did not end with the battle of Manila Bay is shown by the words of the Secretary of the Navy on the occasion of the presentation of a sword, the nation's gift, October 3, 1899: "Later [after the battle], by your display of large powers of administration, by your poise and prudence, and by your great discretion, not only in act but also in word, you proved yourself a great representative citizen of the United States, as well as already its great naval hero."

Finally, President McKinley, in 1899, wrote: "The habitual readiness of the navy for every emergency has won the confidence and admiration of the country. The officers have shown peculiar adaptation for the performance of new and delicate duties which our recent war has imposed."

Thus ministers, secretaries, and presidents acknowledge the indebtedness of the country to the services of naval officers in the preservation of order, the settlement of difficult problems, and the upholding of the country's honor.

A survey of the general work of officers other than that directly connected with the preparation and conduct of war is arrested at once by the name of Rear-Admiral A. T. Mahan. Uniting as he does the professional knowledge of the naval officer with the endowment of the scholar and historian, he stands unique, and enjoys a reputation as an expert in naval matters even higher in Germany and England than in the United States. "It is a mere truism," writes a British naval authority, "to say that Captain Mahan has taught all serious students of naval warfare in two worlds how to think rightly on the prob-

Special Duties

lems it presents. The phrase 'sea power,' as applied, though not invented, by him, is one of those happy inspirations of genius which flash the light of philosophy on a whole department of human action."[4]

In the field of science, no other officer in the nineteenth century rendered to the world a service equal to that of Commander Matthew Fontaine Maury, "Pathfinder of the Seas." Maury in the 40's, being in charge of the Depot of Charts and Instruments (the predecessor of the United States Naval Observatory), conceived the idea of collating the data available in the numberless old log books stored in the Navy Department. These he supplemented with observations made at his request several times each day by ships in the navy and by merchant ships, American and foreign. From such materials he drew definite conclusions in regard to winds and currents, the paths of storms (showing the season when they might be expected and the locality), the shortest routes between the great shipping ports, etc. The results were published and distributed, commonly without charge. In 1853 at his prompting an international congress met at Brussels, attended by representatives of ten great nations, and he secured a world-wide coöperation in his work. Maury's charts, with modifications that bring them up to date, continue to the present time, and for making ocean travel safe and expeditious they are indispensable.

[4] Thursfield, *Nelson and Other Naval Studies*, p. 82.

XXV

WAR WITH SPAIN: THE BATTLE OF MANILA BAY

Causes of the War

THE intervention of the United States on behalf of Cuba, against the mother country Spain, was the logical result of many years of misrule in the island. The unwise and sometimes cruel governors were responsible for constant insurrections, which provoked filibustering on the part of American sympathizers and caused almost incessant friction between our country and Spain. In 1854 the seizure of the American ship *Black Warrior,* on a charge of violating the custom-house regulations, seriously menaced our peace. Again, in 1869, the seizure and long detention of the American steamer *Colonel Lloyd Aspinwall,* on the apparently unfounded charge of landing arms for the insurgents, excited public feeling. And in 1873, when the Spaniards captured the filibuster *Virginius* (claiming American registry) and summarily shot several Americans in her crew, there was a burst of indignation throughout the United States. In each case war was averted by Spain's making a tardy reparation, but the settlement served only to postpone the final conflict.

In 1876 General Campos was sent to Cuba. Adopting a conciliatory tone, he brought peace to the island, which lasted from 1878 to 1895. Then an insurrection occurred which he was unable to suppress. He resigned, in consequence, and was succeeded by General Weyler in February, 1896. This governor determined to rule with an iron hand. He decreed the death penalty for numerous petty offenses, and by his reconcentration policy

Copyrighted, 1903, by Clinedinst, Washington
GEORGE DEWEY

Causes of the Spanish-American War

huddled the people into the cities so that plantations were left uncultivated. Cuba now entered upon a terrible era of famine and desolation. President Cleveland offered, through Secretary Olney, to help Spain in bringing peace to the island, but the offer was refused. Relief, in the form of food and supplies, was sent to Cuba by our Government and by charitable associations. Weyler was recalled in October, 1897, and the new Spanish ministry under Sagasta sent General Blanco, an honest but weak governor, to bring order out of chaos. Blanco offered autonomy to the Cubans, but could not induce the insurgent leaders to listen to him. The good intentions of Spain came too late.

The distress in the island became greater. Consul-General Lee reported to Washington, in May, 1897, that from 600 to 800 Americans were among the destitute. President McKinley made a public appeal for funds, which resulted in contributions amounting to $200,000. The American Red Cross Society took charge of the relief work. Meanwhile, Congress was from time to time debating whether or not to recognize Cuba as a belligerent, or even as an independent state. In our country at large, the activity of Cuban agents and sympathizers in the United States, and the inflammatory editorials of certain of our newspapers, increased the popular feeling against Spain. Moreover, affairs in Havana had assumed so threatening an aspect that Consul Lee feared for the safety of our citizens in that city. Hence the battleship *Maine*, which had been lying for some time at Key West in readiness for an emergency call, was sent to Havana, where she arrived on January 25, 1898.

A succession of events followed that had an important bearing in fanning into flame the smoldering fires of war. On February 9, 1898, a private letter, written by the Spanish minister at Washington to the editor of a

Madrid newspaper, had, through theft in the Havana post office, come into the hands of the insurgents. In this communication the diplomatist had declared that Sagasta's policy of conciliation was "a loss of time and a step in the wrong direction." Commenting on a message of President McKinley, he had characterized the American executive as "weak and catering to the mob," and had used other objectionable language. The publication of this letter aroused the wrath of the American people. Instead of peremptorily recalling her representative, Spain allowed him to resign, and sent another in his place. This scant reparation for a serious offense did not help matters. To cap the climax, a few days later the people of the United States were horrified to hear of the blowing up of one of their finest battleships in Cuban waters.

On February 15, 1898, the *Maine*, after an uneventful three weeks at Havana, was lying in apparent security moored to a buoy 500 yards from the arsenal; about 200 yards distant lay the Ward Line steamer *City of Washington*, and a little farther off the Spanish cruiser *Alphonso XII*. At 9.45 that evening, without the slightest warning, there was an explosion under the keel of the *Maine*, so violent as to shake the whole water front of the city, put out the adjacent electric lights, and throw down many telephone poles. The unfortunate ship had been wrecked in a moment's time, and her total destruction followed in a great flame that shot up from her magazines, illuminating the whole harbor, and showing to the hurrying people on shore the locality of the disaster.

All of the officers but two were saved, but of the ship's company of 353 men only forty-eight escaped uninjured, and the number of the dead in the end reached 266.

A naval court of inquiry entered upon an exhaustive investigation of the affair, sending down divers to examine the hull of the *Maine,* then fast sinking into the mud of Havana harbor. These divers found evidence that the cause of the explosion had been external, the bottom of the hull having been driven upward to the level of the gun deck. The decision of the court was that, in its opinion, "the *Maine* was destroyed by a submarine mine, which caused the partial explosion of two or more of her magazines."

A hasty investigation made subsequently by the Spanish authorities led to the opposite verdict, that the cause of the disaster was internal, and that the destruction of the *Maine* was due to the explosion of her own magazines. But this decision had no effect on American public opinion.

The real causes of the war were the conditions in Cuba and the long-standing wrongs to our trade and citizens. But, as is often the case in wars, the great causes lie dormant until some acute crisis, as in this case the destruction of the *Maine,* stretches public patience to the breaking point. General Woodford, the American minister to Spain, was advised to defer decisive action regarding the unfortunate event, in order to give the United States a brief interval to prepare the navy, and especially the army, for the threatening war.

Events Preceding Hostilities

On the 9th of March, both Houses of Congress, by a unanimous vote, appropriated fifty million dollars "for the national defense to be expended at the discretion of the President." That this was none too soon was disclosed when the application of the fund was undertaken. Our coasts were practically undefended. Our navy needed large provision for increased ammunition and supplies, and even for additional ships to cope with any sudden attack from the navy of Spain.

The battleship *Oregon*, which was on the Pacific coast at the time of the destruction of the *Maine*, was at once put into drydock. She was of little use in the Pacific and would make a great addition to the Atlantic naval strength in case of war. Her famous trip of 15,000 miles around the Horn, begun on March 6, caused the Washington authorities considerable alarm. The *Oregon* learned of the existence of war on April 30, when she reached Rio de Janeiro. As the destination of a Spanish fleet under Admiral Cervera was a matter of conjecture, Captain Charles E. Clark had considerable anxiety lest his vessel, deemed so essential to our needs on the Atlantic coast, should be caught by a whole squadron. On May 25, however, with his ship in excellent condition, he reached the coast of Florida. But we have been anticipating the events that culminated in war.

The proposals of Spain to the Cuban people, offering autonomy and other measures of relief, had been rejected by the Cubans, and the insurrection continued. Whereupon President McKinley, seeing no prospect of a change, sent a special message to Congress on April 11, 1898: "The war in Cuba is of such a nature that short of subjugation or extermination a final military victory for either side seems impracticable. The alternative lies in the physical exhaustion of the one or the other, or perhaps of both. The prospect of such a protraction and conclusion of the present strife is a contingency hardly to be contemplated with equanimity by the civilized world, and least of all by the United States, affected and injured as we are, deeply and intimately, by its very existence.

"The only hope of relief and repose from a condition which can no longer be endured is the enforced pacification of Cuba. In the name of humanity, in the name of

Events Preceding Hostilities 431

civilization, in behalf of endangered American interests which give us the right and duty to speak and to act, the war in Cuba must stop.

"I ask the Congress to authorize and empower the President to take measures to secure a full and final termination of hostilities between the Government of Spain and the people of Cuba, and to secure in the island the establishment of a stable government, capable of maintaining order and observing its international obligations, insuring peace and tranquillity, and to use the military and naval forces of the United States as may be necessary for these purposes."

The response of Congress to this message was, on the 19th of April, by a vote of 42 to 35 in the Senate and 311 to 6 in the House of Representatives, the passage of a joint resolution declaring—"First, That the people of the Island of Cuba are, and of right ought to be, free and independent. Second, That it is the duty of the United States to demand, and the Government of the United States does hereby demand, that the Government of Spain at once relinquish its authority and government in the island of Cuba and withdraw its land and naval forces from Cuba and Cuban waters. Third, That the President of the United States be, and he hereby is, directed and empowered to use the entire land and naval forces of the United States, and to call into the actual service of the United States, the militia of the several States, to such an extent as may be necessary to carry these resolutions into effect. Fourth, That the United States hereby disclaims any disposition or intention to exercise sovereignty, jurisdiction, or control over said island except for the pacification thereof, and asserts its determination when that is accomplished to leave the government and control of the island to its people."

In accordance with this joint resolution, President

McKinley immediately forwarded, on April 20, to General Woodford an ultimatum to which a "full and satisfactory response" was required by noon of April 23. The Spanish minister at Washington, on hearing of this joint resolution and the instructions to Woodford, at once demanded his passport. On April 21, before our minister at Madrid could deliver the ultimatum, he was informed by the Spanish Government that diplomatic relations between the countries were at an end.

Meanwhile Rear-Admiral Sicard, commanding the North Atlantic Squadron, had kept his men busy for two months at target practice, in anticipation of war, and had brought his command to a high standard of efficiency. During this time he kept his squadron off Key West in order to be near Cuba in case of a declaration of war. On April 21, on account of ill health, he was relieved by Captain William T. Sampson, now made an acting rear-admiral. Sampson was at once ordered to proceed to Cuba to institute a blockade of the north coast of the island for a distance ranging between forty miles west of Havana and fifty miles east of that city. He was also to blockade on the south side of Cuba the port of Cienfuegos, which had railroad communication with the capital. This blockade was published to the world next day, April 22, by President McKinley's proclamation. On April 25, an act declared that war between the United States and Spain existed and had existed from and including April 21. A Spanish fleet, which had been mobilized at the Cape Verde Islands under Admiral Cervera, left this rendezvous on April 29 for unknown parts. Two days later came Admiral Dewey's crushing blow to the power of Spain in the East, which relieved the military tension somewhat on the Atlantic coast. In this rapid sequence of events the United States, in the early days of the war, played an extremely cautious game. This country

Comparison of Naval Forces 433

credited Spain with ample preparations for a war that had been threatening for some months. The inefficiency of the Castilian Government and its military weakness became apparent only after the first moves in the great game had been made.

On paper the naval strength of Spain was greater than that of the United States. It was said at the beginning of hostilities that Spanish warships in commission numbered 137, to eighty-six in the American service. But such figures are deceptive. The United States had, besides vessels of less tonnage, six armored ships of 8000 tons or more. In this number were the four first-class battleships *Iowa, Indiana, Massachusetts,* and *Oregon,* each of which was of 10,000 tons or more. Spain had nothing equal to these. The flower of the Castilian Navy consisted of nine armored men-of-war, ranging from 6840 to 9900 tons. The rest of the Spanish Navy comprised, for the most part, old iron and wooden ships.[1] But the disparity between the figures on paper and the real facts was not known even among some leading Spanish officials. Lieutenant Jose Muller y Tejeiro, the second in command of the naval forces of the Province of Santiago, says, if we may anticipate: "No one wanted to believe that they [Cervera's ships] were the only ones that Spain was going to send, since they were called the 'first division,' and at least two more divisions were expected. The only ones who had no illusions, who knew what to expect, who were acquainted with the true condition of affairs, were those who had arrived in the ships. From the admiral down to the last midshipman, they knew perfectly well that there were no more fleets, no more divisions, no more vessels, and that these six ships (if the destroyers may be

---

[1] These figures were taken from Brassey, *Naval Annual,* 1898, pp. 332, 340. Compare also the *Naval Pocket Book,* p. 750, and Titherington, *History of the Spanish-American War,* pp. 99–100.

regarded as such) were all that could be counted on to oppose the American fleet."[2]

· Since this was not a matter of common knowledge, the American Navy made its preparations to meet a superior foe. It is greatly to the credit of the United States, as it is to the discredit of Spain, that the former was ready for the emergency and the latter was not. At the first real intimation of war, the officers at Key West drilled their crews night and day, especially at target practice, while the Spaniards let the valuable time between February and April slip by in procrastination. Hence, if it be said that the enemy had to fight against great odds, we may answer that the disgrace of Spain was all the greater. Besides, American officers at the beginning of hostilities had no idea of the weakness of the Spanish Navy, or if they did, they acted as if the enemy's paper statements were truths.

THE WAR IN THE PHILIPPINES

An encounter had taken place April 27, at Matanzas, Cuba, where a detachment of the blockading squadron shelled the harbor forts, but the first engagement of importance occurred four days later in the Philippines, a colonial possession of Spain since the days of Magellan. As in Cuba, the rule of Spain in the East was a long story of misgovernment and rebellion. In 1896 a formidable revolt broke out, and Blanco, the captain-general at Manila, did not succeed in suppressing it. Other Spanish generals followed Blanco with similar lack of success, and early in 1898 General Basilio Augustin was put in command of the Spanish forces in the Philippines. Meanwhile the leader of the Filipinos, Aguinaldo, opened nego-

---

[2] Tejeiro, *Battles and Capitulation of Santiago de Cuba*, published by the Office of Naval Intelligence, War Notes, No. 1, p. 28.

Dewey in the East 435

tiations with the United States through the American consul at Singapore; the insurrection in these islands, in the end, however, served only to complicate the problem for the United States.

Commodore Dewey, with his squadron consisting of the *Olympia,* flagship, the *Baltimore,* the *Boston,* the *Raleigh,* the *Concord,* the *Petrel,* and the *McCulloch,* was lying in the cosmopolitan harbor of Hong Kong, when, on April 24, he was notified by the Navy Department of the beginning of war, and was ordered to proceed at once to the Philippine Islands and to capture or destroy the enemy's vessels.

Dewey had not been idle while lying in this neutral port. For weeks he had been preparing for the threatening conflict. He had dismantled the unserviceable *Monocacy,* a wooden vessel, and had distributed her crew among his other men-of-war. He purchased, right at hand, two ships of considerable size—the *Zafiro* and *Nanshan*—loaded them with coal and provisions, and also filled the bunkers of all his other vessels with coal. And, finally, he dressed his white squadron in a war-coat of drab.

As the law of nations allows belligerents a stay of only twenty-four hours in a neutral port after war has been declared, Dewey was requested by the British Government to leave Hong Kong. He therefore withdrew to Mirs Bay, about thirty miles distant. As the latter port is in Chinese territory, and as China had not at this time announced her position of neutrality, the American commodore could take refuge here until he had completed his preparations. From Mirs Bay, on April 27, he set forth upon his quest for the Spanish fleet.

On arriving at the Philippines, Dewey sent his scouts into every harbor and inlet likely to be tenanted by the enemy. Subig Bay, where it was half hoped the Spanish admiral would be found, was empty of war vessels. Still skirting the Luzon coast, Dewey's ships arrived off the entrance to Manila Bay at midnight, April 30.

With an opening on the China Sea to the westward, the Bay of Manila is in shape not unlike a vast balloon. In this entrance, ideally placed by nature to guard the approach to Spain's richest spot in her Oriental colonies, tower the islands of Corregidor and Caballo. Twenty-six miles to the northeast lies the city of Manila, the commercial centre of the vast Philippine group.

Ten miles to the south and west of Manila is Cavite, on an arm of land which points outward, completely sheltering a large sheet of water, where the Spanish Admiral Montojo had anchored his fleet. Cavite was the seat of Spanish naval activity in the East. It contained a dock, an arsenal, and a marine railway.

Dewey's hardihood in entering hostile waters during the hours of darkness will be best understood when it is remembered that throughout the Eastern seas it was the belief that the defenses of Manila were impregnable, so ample had been the precaution of Spain. Strong testimony to Dewey's heroism is the fact that he went to his work anticipating all the dangers that his own skill, prudence, and scientific knowledge could suggest. He naturally supposed that Spain's chief city in the East was prepared for such an onset as he meditated. He gave his enemy credit for the plans of defense that he himself would have adopted, had their positions been reversed. Before entering Manila Bay, he called his captains together and made known his plan of operations. The ships were to slip past the islands and into the bay under cover of the darkness, and when inside they were to engage the enemy wherever found.

THE BATTLE OF MANILA BAY

With all lights extinguished, on a night of misty darkness, the commodore led the way, followed by the remainder of the line. When the lights of Corregidor were plainly visible, and while under the very sweep of its guns, "All hands" was called and coffee served. The fleet was passing without challenge, when suddenly a shower of sparks from the *McCulloch's* funnel was followed by the boom of a gun from the enemy, then another, and still a third. To this last the *Boston* and the *McCulloch* replied. The flashing and booming from the island continued for a few minutes longer—then silence.

The perils of torpedoes and mines still remained to the groping vessels; the possibility of being rammed by the Spanish fleet was present in every mind, yet Dewey's squadron kept on. Afterward, an officer, in analyzing the sensations of that time, said: "This invisible fleet ahead was a test out of which no man came without a sigh of relief. It is a hard thing to whisper an order, I know, so perhaps it is not to be wondered at that there should have been a break or vibration in men's voices as they passed the necessary word from mouth to mouth. We were all keyed up, but it was not long before the fighting string in every man's heart was twanging and singing like a taut bow."

After safely anchoring his supply ships out of range, Dewey led his fleet in a circle to the eastward to meet the Spanish admiral, who had aligned his ships at Cavite with the intention of compelling a standing fight.

Admiral Dewey reported under date of May 4, 1898: "The squadron then proceeded to the attack. The flagship *Olympia*, under my personal direction, led, followed at a distance by the *Baltimore, Raleigh, Petrel, Concord,* and *Boston,* in the order named, which forma-

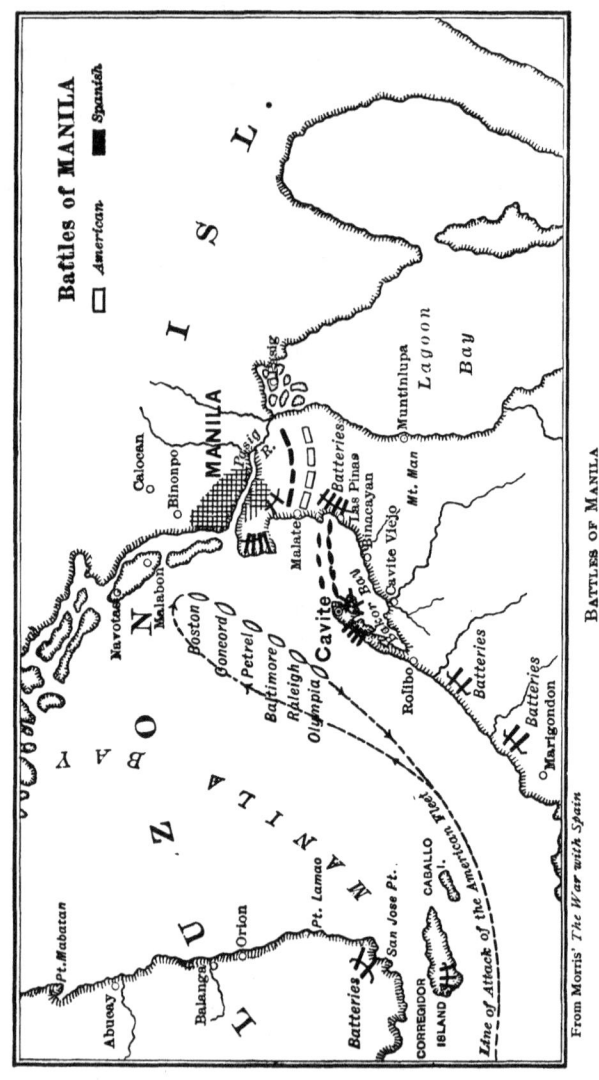

BATTLES OF MANILA

The Battle of Manila Bay 439

tion was maintained throughout the action. The squadron opened fire at 5.41 A.M.''

The enemy had been firing without effect at the Americans for half an hour before Commodore Dewey had his vessels in the formation he desired. At the end of this time he turned to the captain of the *Olympia* and said, "You may fire when you are ready, Gridley!" Almost simultaneously with the quietly uttered permission to return the enemy's fire, the roar of the *Olympia's* guns sounded as the flagship presented her side to the line of fire, and each ship in turn took up the refrain. Dewey's plan was to begin firing when at a range of 5000 yards, to pass the Spanish ships, gradually lessening the range to 2000 yards, and then to countermarch in a line approximately parallel to that of the enemy's fleet. His vessels would thus turn an alternate side in firing, enabling every battery to come into play in succession, thereby easing the strain on each. Such a plan was not counted upon by the Spanish admiral, who had anticipated a combat ship to ship, and it reflects the highest credit upon Dewey's strategy.

Again referring to the American commodore's account of the action, we find: "The enemy's fire was vigorous, but generally ineffective. Early in the engagement two launches put out towards the *Olympia* with the apparent intention of using torpedoes. One was sunk, and the other disabled by our fire and beached, before an opportunity was had to fire torpedoes. At 7.00 A.M. the Spanish flagship, *Reina Cristina,* made a desperate attempt to leave the line and came out to engage at short range, but was received with such a galling fire, the entire battery of the *Olympia* being concentrated upon her, that she was barely able to return to the shelter of the point. The fires started in her by our shells at this time were not extinguished until she sank.

"The three batteries at Manila had kept up a continuous report from the beginning of the engagement, which fire was not returned by this squadron. The first of these batteries was situated on the south mole head, at the entrance to the Pasig River. The second was on the south bastion of the walled city of Manila, and the third at Malate, about one and a half miles farther south. At this point I sent a message to the Governor-General to the effect that if the batteries did not cease firing, the city would be shelled. This had the effect of silencing them."

Admiral Montojo's report gives the following view from the Spanish side: "Although we recognized the hopelessness of fighting the American ships, we were busy returning their fire. The *Reina Cristina* was hit repeatedly. Shortly after 6.30 o'clock I observed fire forward. Our steering gear was damaged, rendering the vessel unmanageable, and we were being subjected to a terrible hail of shot and shell. The engines were struck. We estimated we had seventy hits about our hull and superstructure. The boilers were not hit, but the pipe to the condenser was destroyed. A few minutes later, I observed the after part on fire. A shell from the Americans had penetrated and burst with deadly effect, killing many of our men. The flag lieutenant said to me: 'The ship is in flames. It is impossible to stay on the *Cristina* any longer.' He signaled to the gunboat *Isla de Cuba,* and I and my staff were transferred, and my flag was hoisted on her. My flagship was now one mass of flames; I ordered away all the boats I could to save the crew."

Commodore Dewey, continuing his report, says: "At 7.35 I ceased firing and withdrew the squadron for breakfast. At 11.16 A.M. [the squadron] returned to the attack. By this time the Spanish flagship, and almost the entire Spanish fleet, were in flames. At 12.30 P.M. the squadron

The Battle of Manila Bay

ceased firing, the batteries being silenced, and the ships sunk, burned, or deserted. At 12.40 P.M. the squadron returned and anchored off Manila, the *Petrel* being left behind to complete the destruction of the smaller gunboats that were behind the point of Cavite. This duty was performed by Commander E. P. Wood in the most expeditious and complete manner possible."

Says an eye-witness of the battle, "Every ship in the Spanish fleet, with one exception, fought valiantly; but to the *Don Antonio de Ulloa* and her commander, Robion, should be given the palm for that form of desperate courage and spirit which leads a man to die fighting. The flagship and the *Boston* were the executioners. Under their shells the *Ulloa* was soon burning in half a dozen places, but her fighting crew gave no sign of surrender. Shot after shot struck her hull until it was riddled like a sieve. Shell after shell struck her upper works, but there were no signs of surrender. The main deck crew escaped, but the captain and his officers clung to the wreck. On the lower deck the gun crews stuck to their posts like the heroes they were. . . . Her commander nailed the Spanish ensign to what was left of the mast, and the *Don Antonio de Ulloa* went down, not only with her colors flying, but also with her lower guns still roaring defiance."

Having completed his work of destruction, Dewey now turned to a task of mercy—that of caring for the wounded. These he established in hospitals on shore. To Admiral Montojo he sent the following message: "I have pleasure in clasping your hand and offering my congratulations on the gallant manner in which you fought."

Of the annihilated Spanish squadron, the *Reina Cristina*, a steel cruiser of 3500 tons, built in 1886, was the only vessel that might be considered formidable. The *Isla de Cuba* and the *Isla de Luzon* were small cruisers of 1030 tons each, and the *Don Antonio de Ulloa* and the *Don Juan de Austria* were old iron ships in need of repairs. The *Castilla*, of 3342 tons, was a wooden relic of older days. She rapidly became, under the fire of the American vessels, a burning slaughter house. Montojo should have dismantled her and mounted her guns ashore. Besides these vessels, the Spaniards had two gunboats, the *General Lezo* and the *Marques del Duero*, of 500 tons each, two transports, the *Manila* and *Isla de Mindanao*, and four little torpedo boats. "In offensive and defensive power the squadron was far inferior to Dewey's fine quartette of cruisers, but it had a great advantage in position, fighting in its own waters, where it knew the ranges, and had the aid of batteries on shore."[3]

According to Admiral Montojo's report, the enemy lost 381 killed and wounded. The damage done to the American squadron was inconsiderable. Several of the vessels were struck, and even penetrated, but the slight injuries admitted of speedy repairs, and the squadron was soon after the battle in as good condition as before. There were none killed, and only seven men very slightly wounded.

Although Dewey had a more powerful force than the Spanish, he had the disadvantage of advancing into strange waters, where, for all he knew, torpedoes and mines were laid. He had also the shore batteries to contend against, which made the opposing weight of metal more than equal to his. "The Spanish admiral," says a contemporary journal, "though he must have been aware that the American squadron was somewhere in the vicinity, could not bring himself to believe that the American commodore would have the audacity to steam into a mined harbor in the night time, with forts on both sides,

---

[3] Titherington, *History of the Spanish-American War*, p. 136.

The Battle of Manila Bay

and the Spanish squadron ready to receive him. But Dewey took the chances, and his being beforehand was half the victory. Many men, equally as brave in action, would have delayed to reconnoitre, and thereby have given time for the enemy to make additional preparations to receive him."

Some of the qualities of character that contributed to Dewey's success were referred to soon after the war by one who knew him well: "Dewey has been a life-long *student of everything connected with the sea.* He is a constant reader, but in his studies he seldom goes outside of nautical science, or some collateral branch, such as naval history. He made a study of harbors, too, and is a thorough geographer. I attribute his success at Manila in part to his knowledge of the harbor. He undoubtedly knew just what he was doing and where he was going when he made that midnight dash which seems to be so amazing to people who don't know him."

Although Dewey had seized the cable connecting the Philippine Islands with the rest of the world, he was prevented from using it by Spain's contract with the company at Hong Kong. Hence he had to send dispatch boats back and forth to Hong Kong to communicate with Washington. During the battle, the Spanish general Augustin had sent a dispatch to his home Government which gave the impression that the victory was Spain's, and this was the only news the Americans had until May 7, when Dewey's cablegram, sent from Hong Kong, told a different story. This was received with great joy in the United States, and immediately upon its arrival the Secretary of the Navy congratulated Commodore Dewey upon the overwhelming victory. He also communicated to the American commander that the President had appointed him an acting rear-admiral. Congress shortly after passed a resolution giving the victor a vote of thanks and a sword.

As a result of the battle, Dewey was in possession of the arsenal at Cavite, and of the fort on Corregidor, but he decided not to bombard the defenses nearer the city until he had troops to hold what the navy might capture. He was also short of ammunition. In answer to his request for supplies and troops, the Washington authorities at once dispatched the cruiser *Charleston*, loaded with ammunition, and on May 11 the War Department put General Merritt in command of the new Philippine army corps to be organized immediately. The *Charleston* was ordered to capture *en route* the Spanish island Guam, a task which it easily accomplished. The first instalment of troops arrived at Manila on June 30, the same day that the *Charleston* reached her destination. Of the monitors *Monterey* and *Monadnock*, which had also been dispatched on the long journey across the Pacific, the former arrived in time for the bombardment of the Philippine capital, which will be taken up in a later chapter.

Dewey's victory of May 1 destroyed Spain's power in the East. Its completeness everywhere caused surprise, and not only aroused tremendous enthusiasm for the navy at home, but strongly impressed Europe with the growth of American sea power. The victory gave promise of a speedy conclusion of the war.

XXVI

THE WEST INDIAN CAMPAIGN

THE BLOCKADE OF CUBA

THE orders to Sampson of April 21 had definitely forbidden, for the present, an attack on Havana, which had been considered by the captains of his fleet. There were no troops ready to hold what ground the navy might gain. Also, it was of the greatest moment to save the vessels under Sampson's command for the more important work of destroying Spain's naval force. But according to these orders his chief duty for the time being was to institute a blockade. This at once isolated the Spanish army in Cuba, and forced upon Spain a counter naval move, unless she were willing to abandon her most important insular possession in the West Indies. Since the holding of Cuba was the issue of the war, Spain would naturally make every effort to relieve her army in the island.

The United States rightly directed the energy of the navy in the first days to the blockade of Cuba. Some writers maintain that the seizure of private property at sea is a relic of barbarism, and should be tolerated no more than such seizure by troops on land. But if the end can be attained without bloodshed; if, for instance, by a siege on land a garrison can be starved into submission, why waste unnecessarily the lives of men? The blockade, says Mahan, "is the most scientific warfare, because the least sanguinary, and because, like the highest strategy, it is directed against the communications—the resources—not the persons of the enemy. It has been the glory of sea-power that its ends are attained by draining men of their dollars instead of their blood."[1]

The blockade was effective from the very beginning. All told, the United States Navy took about fifty-six prizes during the war, while the Spanish captured but one, the *Saranac*, a seizure which was subsequently declared illegal. To avoid any possible conflict with neutral governments regarding the closure of Cuban ports, the United States limited the parts of the island to be blockaded so that there could be no doubt raised as regards effectiveness of blockade.

In the threatening state of affairs just prior to the breaking out of hostilities, and during the early days of the war, there had been some time to mobilize the vessels on the Atlantic coast. Rear-Admiral Sampson's command comprised two main divisions: his own, with its base at Key West, within easy reach of Cuba; and Commodore Schley's "flying squadron," assembled at Newport News in readiness to meet any move of the Spanish fleet under Cervera, who was lying at St. Vincent in the Cape Verde Islands. Also a "northern patrol squadron," under Commodore Howell, was hurriedly organized to protect the coast from Delaware northward. Gradually, as the weakness of Spain's military power and the destination of Cervera's fleet became more apparent, the fears of the coast cities were allayed, and the vessels of Howell's squadron were, one by one, withdrawn to aid in the blockade of Cuba.

SEARCH FOR CERVERA'S SQUADRON

As stated in the last chapter, Admiral Cervera left the Cape Verde Islands on April 29, for an unknown destination. As early as February 12, 1898, he had written to

---

[1] Mahan, *Lessons of the War with Spain*, p. 106.

Movements of Cervera and Sampson 447

the Minister of Marine, asking for information regarding the distribution and movements of United States ships, their bases of supplies, charts and plans of the possible theatre of war, and the objective of his fleet in the event of hostilities. "I cannot help thinking," writes the admiral, " of a possible war with the United States, and I believe it would be expedient if I were given all available information." He then enumerated some of the matters on which he sought enlightenment, and continued, "If I had information on these matters, I could go ahead and study, and see just what is best to be done, and if the critical day should arrive, we could enter without vacillation upon the course we are to follow." The reply to this reasonable and pathetic request was vague and unpractical. Again and again Admiral Cervera wrote for information and instructions, and as often he was put off by the incapacity or ignorance of the Minister of Marine. Finally, the orders above mentioned were issued, and Cervera sailed westward with a squadron consisting of the cruisers, *Maria Teresa* (flagship), *Cristobal Colon*, *Vizcaya* and *Almirante Oquendo*, and the three torpedo-boat destroyers, *Furor, Pluton*, and *Terror*.

Immediately upon hearing the news, Secretary Long informed Sampson of Cervera's departure and suggested the West Indies as his probable destination. At the same time, the *Harvard, St. Louis*, and *Yale*, vessels that had been taken into the navy from the merchant marine, were sent as scouts to cruise off Martinique, Guadeloupe, and Porto Rico, to bring back word of the first appearance of the Spaniards. The strategists at Washington assumed quite naturally that the probable objective of Cervera was Porto Rico; this Spanish possession, lying nearest to the enemy's sources of supplies, would be an excellent stopping place for coaling and for further operations at Cuba or against the Atlantic coast. As the vessels of

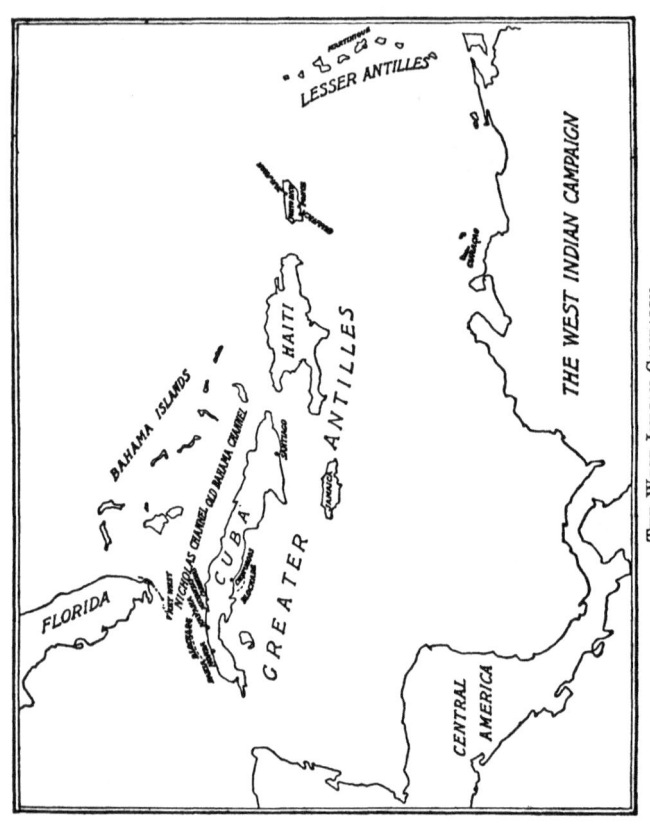

THE WEST INDIAN CAMPAIGN

Movements of Cervera and Sampson 449

Cervera's squadron were credited with great speed, they were expected to arrive in West Indian waters about May 8. To intercept him, Sampson left his naval base, Key West, on May 4, but on account of the slowness of the monitors *Terror* and *Amphitrite*, he did not reach San Juan, Porto Rico, until early in the morning of May 12. At once he began a bombardment of the forts defending the city, but as daylight dawned, it became clear that Cervera was not in the harbor. The American fleet, having ascertained the strength of the defenses of San Juan, then turned backward unscathed to its other duty, the blockade of Cuba. Doubtless Sampson could have forced the surrender of San Juan, but, without troops to hold the city, he would have had to keep his fleet at Porto Rico, at the risk of not destroying the enemy's fleet, and to the neglect of the blockade.

The first American vessel to get any news of the movements of the enemy's squadron was the *Harvard*, which on May 11 learned that the *Furor* had that day called at Fort de France. But the *Harvard* was detained at St. Pierre by rumors that the enemy were lying in wait for her outside. As a matter of fact, Cervera was at this time making for Curacao. As soon as it became clear that the Spanish fleet was in the southeastern part of the Caribbean, Secretary Long, surmising that the real destination must be Cuba, ordered Schley to proceed to Key West, and on the same day, May 15, he sent the swift scouts *Minneapolis, St. Paul,* and *Harvard* to follow Cervera. Sampson, meanwhile, had left his squadron off the north coast of Cuba, and hurried in the *New York* to Key West, where he met Schley on May 18. On the morning of the 19th, Schley, with his squadron, proceeded to Cienfuegos, at the very hour when Cervera entered Santiago. On nearing his destination, Schley noticed volumes of smoke arising from behind the high forts that screened the entrance to the harbor, and hence he inferred that the enemy's fleet must be here. The signal corps had, meanwhile, sent the news of the arrival of Cervera at Santiago, but there was considerable doubt in which of the two harbors the enemy was really hidden. This uncertainty entailed considerable delay. Only after thorough confirmation of the Santiago report, and after a reconnoissance at Cienfuegos, did Commodore Schley start, on May 24, for Santiago. As it was thought that Cervera would try to reach Havana, Admiral Sampson did not dare leave the north coast of Cuba until he felt sure that Cervera was bottled up at Santiago. After coaling some of his vessels, Sampson on May 29 withdrew the main part of his force from the blockade of Havana, and hastened to Santiago.

All this shows that despite the weakness of Cervera's squadron, the Spaniards had a great advantage in so far as they prevented concentration of power on the part of the Americans at any one spot. This is only one of the many illustrations in history of what naval strategists call the advantage of a "fleet in being"; that is, a fleet at large, not itself in command of the sea, but sufficiently strong to deny that command to the other side. As long as the Spanish fleet was "in being," especially as its destination was unknown, it threatened not only the military operations in Cuba but the entire coast of the United States.

On his arrival Commodore Schley instituted a blockade of Santiago, after having definitely assured himself that the enemy were in the bay. On May 31 he bombarded the forts guarding the entrance, but without material result. It was evident that well-ordered land operations were indispensable to hold what the navy might gain.

Admiral Sampson, shortly after his arrival early in June, formulated a careful and complete plan of blockade of Santiago. A mile from the Morro he placed three steam launches as picket boats. Outside of these he stationed the smaller vessels of the fleet, and three or four miles from shore he arranged his battleships and cruisers in a semicircle. At night a battleship approached to the middle line and kept its searchlight steadily on the harbor entrance, while a sister ship lay close by to answer any fire from the enemy.

On June 6 Sampson bombarded the Morro, Fort Aguadores, and Socapa. The fleet fired in all about 2000 shots. The batteries were frequently hit and lost three men killed and forty wounded. As the forts were so much above sea level, many of the shells passed over them and did considerable damage in the village on Smith Key. It was by these high shots that the *Reina Mercedes,* which was lying in the harbor, was injured; she was struck thirty-five times and was twice set on fire. The reply of the Spanish batteries was feeble; the *Massachusetts* was hit once, but the other vessels of Sampson's fleet were unscathed.

Meanwhile, on the night of June 3, Naval Constructor Hobson, aided by seven volunteers, had attempted to block the narrow outlet from Santiago harbor by sinking the collier *Merrimac* in the channel, under a fierce fire from the shore batteries. All the men escaped with their lives, as by a miracle, but fell into the hands of the Spaniards. It is most gratifying to note that the bravery of this little band of heroes was cordially appreciated by the Spanish admiral, who sent a flag of truce to notify Admiral Sampson of their safety, and to compliment them on their daring act. They were subsequently exchanged, July 7.

On June 7, the cutting of the last Cuban cable isolated the island. Thereafter the invasion was vigorously prosecuted. Three days later, under a heavy protecting fire, a landing force of 600 marines from the *Oregon, Marble-*

head, and *Yankee,* was effected in Guantanamo Bay, where it had been determined to establish a naval station. This important and essential port was taken from the enemy after severe fighting by the marines, who were the first organized force of the United States to land in Cuba.

The position thus won was held in spite of desperate attempts to dislodge our troops. By June 16 additional forces of marines had been landed and strongly intrenched. On June 22 the advance of the invading army under Major-General Shafter made at Daiquiri, about fifteen miles east of Santiago, a landing which was accomplished under great difficulties, but with dispatch. On June 23 the movement against Santiago was begun. On the 24th the first serious engagement took place. By nightfall ground within five miles of Santiago was won, and this advantage was steadily increased. On July 1 a severe battle took place, our forces gaining the outworks of Santiago; on the 2d El Caney and San Juan were taken after a desperate charge, and the investment of the city was completed. The navy co-operated by shelling the town and the coast forts.

The Battle of Santiago

On the third of July, the day following this success of our land forces, occurred the decisive contest of the war. The line of blockading ships at this time formed a long arc about the harbor entrance, lying at distances varying from one and a half to two miles off shore. The squadron ranged from east to west in the following order: the *Indiana, New York, Oregon, Iowa, Texas,* and *Brooklyn.* Shortly before nine o'clock on the morning of the 3d, the flagship *New York* left her place between the *Indiana* and the *Oregon* to go four miles east of her station in order that Admiral Sampson might confer in

The Battle of Santiago 453

person with General Shafter. With the flagship were the converted yacht *Hist* and the torpedo-boat *Ericsson*. The auxiliary *Gloucester*, formerly the yacht *Corsair*, lay slightly to the east of the *Indiana* and closer to the harbor; while to the west of the *Brooklyn* lay the gunboat *Vixen*.

About forty minutes after the *New York* left her station, the prow of a Spanish cruiser was discovered heading out of the harbor, and at the same instant several of the American ships hoisted the signal, "Enemy's ships escaping." "General quarters" was sounded throughout the squadron, the men sprang to the guns, and forced draft was applied to the furnaces in the effort to get up enough steam to close in upon the Spanish squadron before it could escape. The Spanish column, headed by the flagship, left the harbor mouth in the following order: *Infanta Maria Teresa*, *Vizcaya*, *Cristobal Colon*, and *Almirante Oquendo*. As soon as the *Maria Teresa* cleared the harbor, she turned sharply to the west, followed by the rest of the line, all under full speed.

The *New York*, lying so far to the eastward, could take no part in the early stages of the action, though her engines were taxed to the limit in the effort to get within range. As soon as the enemy was sighted, she flew the admiral's signal, "Close in toward harbor entrance and attack vessels," but the other ships of the squadron, owing to the complete preparation that had been made for every emergency, needed no orders to begin the engagement. In a few minutes the Spanish cruisers, with their running start, had swung past the blockading line, and the battle became a chase, in which the *Texas* and the *Brooklyn* had the advantage of position.

Meanwhile, Lieutenant-Commander Wainwright of the *Gloucester*, as soon as he saw the enemy heading west, steamed directly toward the Spanish vessels and opened fire upon them with his light guns. Then, anticipating the appearance of the two torpedo-boat destroyers, *Pluton* and *Furor,* he slowed down, giving his ship a heavy head of steam, so that when the destroyers appeared at the end of the column, he dashed for them at full speed and opened fire at close quarters. The *Gloucester* was entirely unprotected, and had a battery inferior in weight to that of either of the destroyers. In a few minutes the leading destroyer, the *Pluton,* turned and ran upon the beach, where a moment later she was broken in two by an explosion. The *Furor* kept going a few minutes longer, though in evident distress, hounded by the guns of the *Gloucester* and the secondary battery of the *Indiana.* Finally, a shot from the approaching *New York* sent her to the bottom in deep water. It should be added that during this plucky attack at close quarters, the *Gloucester* was under the fire of the Socapa shore battery as well as that of the destroyers, but it is an astonishing fact that she was not hit once by either.

Hardly had the cruisers turned westward before they began to show the effect of the American guns. In about fifteen minutes the *Maria Teresa* caught fire, and in less than three-quarters of an hour from the time she was sighted in the harbor entrance, she turned and ran ashore in flames. Five minutes later, the *Oquendo* also was beached in the same condition. The *Colon,* the fastest vessel in the two squadrons, now passed the *Vizcaya* and forged ahead, beyond the range of the leading American ships. Shortly before the *Maria Teresa* had run aground she made a desperate effort to ram the *Brooklyn.* The latter, which was heading toward the approaching *Teresa,* suddenly ported her helm and made a wide turn to the south off shore. She then resumed a course parallel to that of the Spanish column, though at a greater range. The *Brooklyn* thus avoided being rammed but, by putting the helm to port instead of to starboard, she lost ground in

The Battle of Santiago

pursuit and nearly collided with the *Texas*. This much-discussed maneuver was due, according to Commodore Schley's testimony before the Senate Committee, to a desire to avoid blanketing the fire of the other American vessels.

At about eleven o'clock the *Vizcaya* also was set on fire, and was compelled to turn and run ashore. At this time the speedy *Colon*, the only remaining vessel of the Spanish squadron, was six miles ahead of the *Brooklyn* and the *Oregon*. In the pursuit the latter vessel had outstripped and passed both the *Iowa* and the *Texas* and taken second place. As the *Colon* was supposed to have a speed of twenty knots, she seemed to have an excellent chance of escape.

Sampson now detailed the slower vessels to remain behind to attend to the rescue of prisoners, and with the *New York* joined the *Brooklyn, Vixen, Oregon,* and *Texas* in the chase. By the end of an hour it was evident that the *Colon*, for some reason, was not able to keep up her spurt, and that the American ships were gaining. About one o'clock the *Oregon* dropped a 13-inch shell just ahead of the Spaniard, and fifteen minutes later, though practically uninjured, the latter fired a gun to leeward, lowered her colors, and ran ashore. After striking on the beach, her crew treacherously opened the sea valves and sank her. This incident completed the destruction of Admiral Cervera's fleet.

The following extract from Admiral Sampson's report of the battle bears gratifying testimony to the efforts of the American officers and men in the work of rescue:

"When about ten miles west of Santiago the *Indiana* had been signaled to go back to the harbor entrance, and at Acerraderos the *Iowa* was signaled to 'resume blockading station.' The *Iowa*, assisted by the *Ericsson* and the *Hist*, took off the crew of the *Vizcaya*, while the *Harvard* and the *Gloucester* rescued those of the *Infanta*

Maria Teresa and the *Almirante Oquendo*. This rescue of prisoners, including the wounded from the burning Spanish vessels, was the occasion of some of the most daring and gallant conduct of the day. The ships were burning fore and aft, their guns and reserve ammunition were exploding, and it was not known at what moment the fire would reach the main magazine. In addition to this, a heavy surf was running just inside of the Spanish ships. But no risk deterred our officers and men until their work of humanity was complete.''[2]

The number of prisoners amounted to 1300, including the Spanish admiral. According to the latter's estimate, some 600 Spaniards were killed. On the American side but one man was killed (on the *Brooklyn*), and one man was seriously wounded. Although some of our ships were repeatedly struck, not one was seriously injured; and the *Oregon, Indiana, Gloucester, Vixen,* and *New York* were untouched.

A comparison of forces at the battle of Santiago shows that the advantage lay with the Americans. Cervera's four cruisers were modern steel vessels, three of 7000 tons, and one of 6840 tons. Besides these he had two destroyers.[3] On the other hand, Sampson had four battleships of more than 10,000 tons, besides two armored cruisers upward of 8000 tons and a small converted yacht.

COMMENTS ON THE BATTLE

Commander Jacobsen, of the German Navy, made the following suggestive comments on the disastrous attempt of Cervera's fleet:

''There was only one chance for the success of the

---

[2] Goode, *With Sampson Through the War*, p. 299.

[3] Admiral Cervera had to leave his third destroyer, the *Terror*, at Martinique.

Comments on the Battle 457

sortie. It should have been made at night in scattered formation. After a personal investigation of the locality, it is my opinion that it is entirely practicable for a fleet to leave Santiago harbor at night. The wreck of the *Merrimac* did not constitute an obstruction. The dark nights at the time of the new moon about the middle of June would have been best suited for the enterprise. The vessels should have steered different courses, previously determined, with orders not to fight except when compelled to do so by the immediate vicinity of a hostile ship or when there was no possibility of escaping the enemy in the darkness. A rendezvous should have been fixed for the next day, where the ships that succeeded in escaping were to assemble.

"If the fleet did not dare to attempt a night sortie, and was nevertheless compelled to leave the harbor in obedience to orders, then the ships should have been headed straight at the enemy. All weapons, including the torpedo and the ram, should have been used. A bold attack in close formation was the only chance of success against the superior hostile fighting forces, who would hardly have found time to form their lines."[4]

In connection with the views of Commander Jacobsen, it is interesting to note that at conferences called on board the Spanish flagship in Santiago harbor on May 26 and June 8, to consider the advisability and means of a sortie, the chief of staff, Captain Bustamente, and Captain Concas of the *Maria Teresa*, voted in favor of an immediate sortie at night, in which the vessels should scatter and create as much confusion in the blockading squadron as possible, in much the same manner as that suggested by the German officer. The other officers of

---

[4] Jacobsen, *Sketches from the Spanish-American War*, Office of Naval Intelligence, War Notes, No. iv, pp. 17, 18.

the squadron, including the admiral, voted against the sortie.

Commander Jacobsen mentions among the lessons to be learned from this battle the following: the abolition of all woodwork and of unprotected torpedo tubes; better protection for gun crews and for fire extinguishing apparatus against shell fire; the greatest possible simplicity in gun mechanism, and the greatest possible rapidity of fire; good speed of ships under normal conditions; and thorough training of crews in all branches of the service.[5]

The capitulation of Santiago followed very shortly after the destruction of the Spanish fleet. The city had been closely besieged by land, and the entrance of our ships into the harbor had cut off all relief on that side. On the 17th General Shafter occupied the city. The capitulation embraced the entire eastern end of Cuba. The number of Spanish soldiers surrendered was 22,000, all of whom were subsequently conveyed to Spain at the charge of the United States.

OCCUPATION OF PORTO RICO

With the fall of Santiago, the occupation of Porto Rico became the next strategic necessity. General Miles had previously been assigned to organize an expedition for that purpose. Fortunately he was already at Santiago, where he had arrived on the 11th of July with reinforcements for General Shafter's army. With these troops, consisting of 3415 infantry and artillery, two companies of engineers, and one company of the Signal Corps, General Miles left Guantanamo on July 21, having nine transports convoyed by a squadron under Captain Higginson. The expedition landed at Guanica, Porto Rico, July 25, which port was entered with little opposi-

---

[5] Jacobsen, *Sketches from the Spanish-American War*, Office of Naval Intelligence, War Notes, No. iv, p. 18.

tion. From here two of the ships went to San Juan and thence to Fajardo and Ponce. On July 27 the major-general commanding entered Ponce, one of the most important ports of the island, from which place he thereafter directed operations for the capture of the island.

The campaign, which met with no serious resistance, was now prosecuted with great vigor, and by the 12th of August much of Porto Rico was in our possession, and the acquisition of the remainder was only a matter of a short time. At most of the points in the island our troops were enthusiastically welcomed.

CONCLUSION OF THE WAR

With the catastrophe of Santiago, Spain's efforts upon the ocean virtually ceased. A spasmodic attempt toward the end of June to send her Mediterranean fleet under Admiral Camara to relieve Manila was abandoned, the expedition being recalled after it had passed through the Suez Canal.

The last scene of the war was enacted at Manila, its starting place. On August 13, after a brief assault upon the works by the land forces, in which the squadron assisted, the capital surrendered unconditionally. The casualties were comparatively few. By this the conquest of the Philippine Islands, virtually accomplished when the Spanish capacity for resistance was destroyed by Admiral Dewey's victory of the 1st of May, was formally sealed.

The total casualties in the American Navy in killed and wounded during the war were: killed, seventeen; wounded, sixty-seven; died as result of wounds, one; invalided from service, six; total, ninety-one. Among the number of American killed was Ensign Worth Bagley, who lost his life on the torpedo-boat *Winslow* in its attack on May 11, on some batteries at Cardenas, Cuba. On the other hand, the Spaniards had at least 1000 killed and wounded; this is a conservative estimate, as Cervera reported 600 and Montojo 381 killed and wounded in the two great battles. This disparity in casualties was caused by the greater accuracy of Dewey's and Sampson's gunnery. Even if we admit that the American weight of metal was fifty per cent greater than the Spanish—a conservative estimate—it nevertheless remains true that the hits were out of all proportion to the respective numbers of guns, or respective weight of metal thrown. For instance, at Santiago the United States vessels made about 123 hits to thirty-five of the Spaniards,[6] and the latter were mostly by small projectiles that did little or no damage. With such a difference, the enemy might have had a much larger number of ships and guns, with the victory still on the side of the United States.

It is noteworthy, further, that while the American Navy was engaged in two great battles, besides difficult and perilous undertakings in blockade and bombardment, and transported more than 50,000 troops to the scenes of action, it did not lose a gun or a ship, and the crew of the *Merrimac* were the only prisoners captured by the Spaniards during the war.

THE PEACE TREATY

The annihilation of Admiral Cervera's fleet, followed by the capitulation of Santiago, brought to the Spanish Government a realizing sense of the hopelessness of continuing a struggle now become wholly unequal; and overtures of peace were made through the French ambassador,

---

[6] Figures compiled by the *Scientific American*, from the official report of the Survey Board, quoted by Spears, *Our Navy in the War with Spain*, p. 341.

The Treaty of Peace

who had acted as the friendly representative of Spanish interests during the war. On the afternoon of August 12, M. Cambon, as the plenipotentiary of Spain, and our Secretary of State, as the plenipotentiary of the United States, signed a protocol which suspended hostilities.

The protocol was followed by the treaty of peace between the United States of America and the kingdom of Spain, signed at Paris, December 10, 1898, and ratified and proclaimed at Washington, April 11, 1899. It was, in brief, as follows:

Article I. Spain relinquishes all claim of sovereignty over and title to Cuba.

Article II. Spain cedes to the United States the island of Porto Rico and other islands now under Spanish sovereignty in the West Indies, and the island of Guam in the Marianas or Ladrones.

Article III. Spain cedes to the United States the archipelago known as the Philippine Islands. The United States will pay to Spain the sum of twenty million dollars ($20,000,000) within three months after the exchange of the ratifications of the present treaty.

XXVII

EMERGENCE OF THE UNITED STATES AS A WORLD POWER

The Philippine Insurrection

Spain's defeat and humiliation was so unexpected as to startle the more conservative European peoples; but America's new responsibilities, together with the sudden access of power, also came without warning and bewildered the people of the western hemisphere. The question, what should be done with the colonies wrested from Spain, was indeed a formidable one. It was not for territory that the United States had gone to war, and many leading citizens expressed the fear that we were departing from our early traditions and inclining towards "imperialism." Especially over the Philippines there were antagonistic views. Though far from satisfying all, the President and Congress decided that, since the islands could not be returned or sold or left to shift for themselves, they must be held at least for a period, and that the first step was to establish law and order.

Immediately after the destruction of the Spanish fleet in Manila Bay, the great powers had displayed a lively interest in the islands, as evidenced by the German, English, and French warships dispatched to Manila. Japan was also represented. Had Dewey not been firm in upholding the rights of the victorious belligerent, as recognized by international law, he might have been embarrassed by the German force, which was steadily increased until it was stronger than his own. It was not merely the presence of their ships; the German officers,

Courtesy of Navy Recruiting Bureau, New York

U. S. S. PALOS IN THE YANGTZE AT ICHANG, CHINA

disregarding the blockade Dewey had established, even went so far as to land provisions for the Spaniards. Finally Dewey sent his flag lieutenant, Thomas M. Brumby, to inform Rear-Admiral von Diederich of this "extraordinary disregard of the usual courtesies of naval intercourse" and to tell him that "if he wants a fight he can have it right now." [1]

It was afterwards related that the German admiral sought out Captain Chichester, the senior English officer there, to induce him to join in opposing Dewey; but he obtained in reply a sharp refusal because "this American admiral is so deadly right in all that he has done."

On the 26th of May, that is, three to four weeks after the battle, Secretary Long cabled Dewey, warning him not to enter into any "political alliances with the insurgents;" and when General Merritt sailed from San Francisco with an army to complete the work of the navy, he carried with him instructions not to recognize Aguinaldo but to set up a provisional government. Already the army of insurgents were strongly intrenched about Manila, and it remained only for a slight collision (February 4, 1899) between the two forces to supply the match that ignited the conflagration.

The population of the Philippines was about twice that of the American colonies at the time of the Revolution. But it was but a slight resistance that they could offer in open conflict to the American Army, which grew to more than 54,000 in number.[2]

The difficulty lay rather in the character of the country. The Philippine Islands have a land area equal to that of the New England states and New York combined. From north to south, if superimposed upon the eastern United States, they would extend from Narragansett

---

[1] *The New American Navy*, ii, 111, 112.
[2] Secretary of War, *Annual Report*, 1900, i, part iv, 560.

Bay to Key West, and their coast line, 11,000 miles, is greater than that of continental United States, excluding Alaska. Thus, even if the difficulties of the terrain, the mountains, the marshes, and the dense tropical forests, are passed over, the army had a hard problem to face and could not put down a general insurrection without the coöperation of the navy. This was given with the same decision and promptness that had brought the initial success.

When fighting began between the two armies in and about Manila, the ships steamed in close to the shore and shelled the insurgents' trenches north and south of the city. A week later the navy landed a force at Iloilo, Panay, and occupied that important seaport until the army took it over.[3]

Sailors and marines landing at Olongapo, Subig Bay, destroyed a heavy rifled gun, mounted there by insurgents. Captain B. H. McCalla, commanding the *Newark*, in December, 1899, compelled the surrender of the northern provinces of Luzon, Cagayan, and Isabela, turning them over to the army. In February, 1901, when General Funston set out on the expedition to Isabela that resulted in the capture of Aguinaldo, the gunboat *Vicksburg*, Commander E. B. Barry, rendered important assitance. Meanwhile there was constant patrolling of islands that were the especial sources of trouble, thus cutting off war supplies that came from Hong Kong and Chinese ports. Also the ships were engaged in making surveys and correcting charts, which were needed for merchant vessels just as much as for war ships. The cruiser *Charleston* showed the need and the danger, for she struck on an uncharted reef and was lost. As the rivers and inlets were often too shallow to permit sea going ships to enter, a mosquito fleet of seventeen gunboats, four taken by

---

[3] Long, *The New American Navy*, ii, 115.

Dewey at Manila Bay and thirteen acquired by purchase from the Spaniards, was organized. They were commanded for the most part by ensigns or naval cadets, and rendered efficient service.

All open resistance to American forces was ended nine months after the beginning of the insurrection. But guerilla warfare following, two years more were required to stamp this out. Finally, determined efforts began to tell, and insurgent leaders having been for the most part captured, the islands one by one gave up the struggle. Then ensued an era of unprecedented progress.

THE SAMOAN TROUBLE

Dewey's victory in the Far East had at once given us a new interest in the Pacific. Hawaii, occupying a position of the greatest strategic importance at the "cross roads of the Pacific," had five years before asked to be joined to the United States, and on July 7, 1898, she was annexed by a joint resolution of Congress. Guam, and the tiny Wake and Midway Islands were occupied during the war, and became American territory.

In 1898, Samoa, which had been governed for nine years by the natives, under the control of England, Germany, and the United States, was the scene of factional strife over the choice of a new king. The law said that when the natives could not agree on such a question they should refer it to the chief justice of the island court. Mr. W. L. Chambers, an American citizen, who held that office, on being appealed to, gave a decision that was impartial and fair. The trouble would probably then have ended, had not the German consul secretly encouraged the losing faction. Guards became necessary to protect the English and American consulates in Apia, the chief city of Samoa.

An act of heroism occurred when an expedition was

organized with sixty-one Americans under Lieutenant P. V. Lansdale, U.S.N., and sixty-three British under Lieutenant A. H. Freeman, R.N. They marched against Vailele, near Apia, where ammunition and supplies had been stored. Not encountering any opposition, they destroyed the camp; but on the return march they were ambushed by an overwhelming force of natives. Lansdale was shot below the knee so that he could not walk, and Ordinary Seaman N. E. Edsall, who came to his assistance, was mortally wounded. The American and British forces happened to be so scattered that they were unable to make an effective resistance, and slowly gave way. But Ensign Monaghan, after doing his utmost to remove Lieutenant Lansdale to a place of safety, seized a rifle from a disabled man, and "stood steadfast by his wounded superior and friend—one brave man against a score of savages. . . . He died in a heroic performance of duty." [4] Lieutenants Lansdale and Freeman were both among the killed.

To settle the trouble a commission, with representatives from England, Germany, and the United States, visited the islands in one of our warships. As a result of their negotiations, the tripartite control of the islands ended. Germany was granted the largest islands to the west, England having ceded her claims in exchange for concessions elsewhere, and the United States was granted Tutuila and five other small islands to the east. This arrangement lasted till the World War, when New Zealand seized the German islands, her retention of them as a mandate being later established by the Treaty of Versailles.

The advantage to the United States in these small islands (the total area of her share is about fifty-eight

---

[4] Report of Captain Edwin White, quoted by Long, *The New American Navy*, ii, 125.

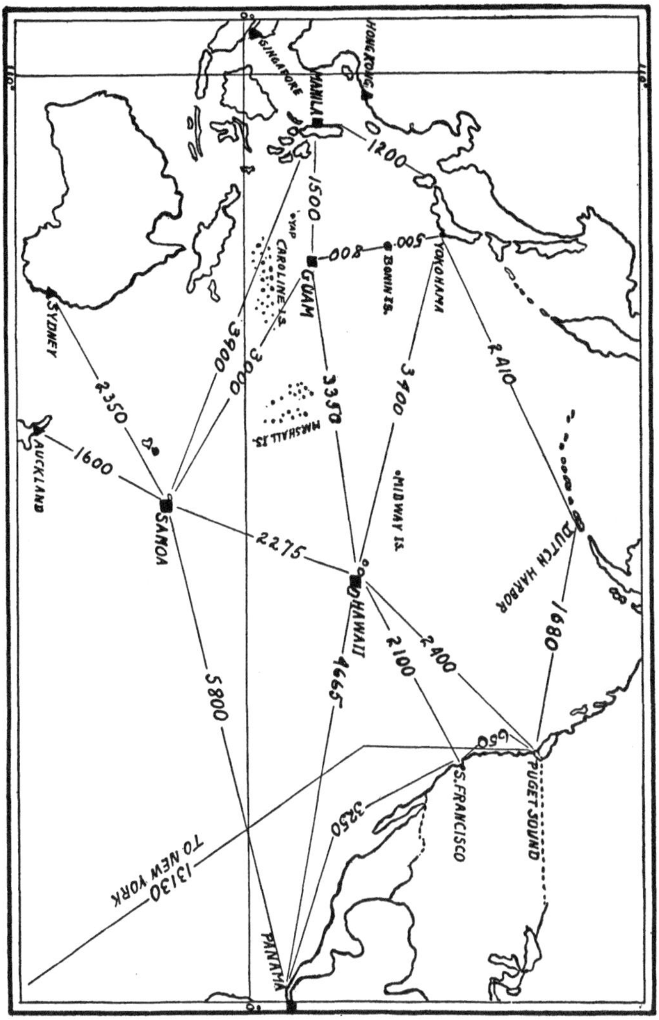

The Samoan Trouble

America's Strategic Position in the Pacific

square miles) lies in the possession of a coaling station at Pago Pago, Tutuila, one of the finest harbors in all the Pacific, and of great strategic importance. It is about 4200 miles from San Francisco, 2275 from Hawaii, 1600 from Auckland, and 2350 from Sydney.

When our country assumed sovereignty over the islands in 1900, with the written consent of the native chiefs the Government appointed a naval officer as governor. This method of administration, as at Guam, is the system that still is in operation.

The Boxer Rebellion

While the uprisings just described were being met, trouble was brewing in China. This great country had been suffering from the rapacity of the western powers and there was much ground for believing that her dismemberment was near. Thus when Secretary Hay in 1899 addressed a note to Great Britain asking her to join in maintaining the "open door" policy so that all nations might carry on their commerce on equal terms even within the "spheres of influence or interest," it was timely. Great Britain assented, provided that the other powers concerned would agree. Like answers were obtained from Germany and Russia, and in time from Japan, France, and Italy. Hay then followed these notes by one addressed to the several nations, giving a résumé of the negotiations and concluding that, since each nation had "accepted the declaration suggested by the United States concerning foreign trade in China," he considered the assent as no longer provisional, but "as final and definitive."

The Chinese, however, already alarmed, were fostering a movement, secretly favored by the reactionary Empress Dowager, to drive out all foreigners. To accomplish this they organized the society of the "I-Ho Ch'uan,"

The Boxer Rebellion 469

or "Fist of Righteous Harmony," popularly known as the "Boxers."

Disorder and acts of violence in 1900 were widespread. Mission stations in various places were attacked and destroyed. Toward the last of May, our minister in Peking, E. H. Conger, believing that the Boxer movement was threatening to become an open rebellion, telegraphed Admiral Kempff, then at Taku in his flagship *Newark,* that the American legation needed a strong guard. Marines were dispatched and reached the capital just in time, for only a few days later all railroad communications were cut off, and the foreign legations were in a state of siege. The situation soon was so serious that, when the consuls and naval officers of the several nations at Tientsin could agree on no plan for relieving the legations at Peking, Captain B. H. McCalla, U.S.N., in command of 112 officers and men, proposed to set out at once for Peking, even if his force should have to act alone. This decisive utterance had a good effect, and the British, Japanese, Austrian, and Italian officers joined with McCalla. Eventually the Germans, French, and Russians added their detachments. The whole force, amounting to 2066 officers and men, was commanded by Vice-Admiral Seymour of the British Navy. They succeeded in reaching Langfang, forty miles from Peking, on June 13, without great difficulty. Meanwhile the Imperial forces had joined with the Boxers and had cut the railroad communications in their rear. The railroad to Peking had also been destroyed. Lacking food supplies and ammunition, and threatened by an enormous host of Boxers and Imperial troops, the council of senior officers decided to fall back to Tientsin. On the return march, which was made not without considerable fighting, the most dangerous position, that of advance guard, was given to the American sailors. Captain McCalla was wounded three times, but he held to his post till the force reached Tientsin. Seven hundred allied troops remained here and were soon besieged by several thousand Boxers.

It then became imperative to hurry forward men and supplies from Taku to Tientsin. The railway between these points, on being abandoned, had been plundered by Boxers and roving bands, and in places had been destroyed. To an American naval officer, with a force of bluejackets, was given the task of putting the miserably equipped single-track system into commission, and of operating it. It was new work for our sailors, but in a few weeks they transported 13,000 troops, besides horses, ammunition, provisions, and water.

Grave anxiety had in the meantime prevailed throughout the western nations for the safety of their people in China. It was commonly believed that all the ministers in Peking had perished. Large reinforcements of men and ships had been sent to China or were on their way, and the threat of dismemberment of the Empire was more grave than ever before. But Secretary Hay met the crisis; writing to the European Powers, he stated "the purpose of the United States to be the relief and protection of American interests," and "reiterated the principles of Chinese territorial and administrative entity, protection of treaty rights, and preservation of the 'open door.'" The stand taken by the United States influencing the other nations, the dissolution of China did not take place.

On the arrival of adequate reinforcements, another international expedition was organized, and on August 14 it entered Peking. It was none too soon, for, since June 19, when Baron von Ketteler, the German minister, was killed, the besieged had been subjected to many fierce attacks. Our marines had intrenched themselves on the ancient city wall near the American legation, and there made a brave defense. Twice they were driven from their position, but both times they succeeded in retaking it.

President McKinley during the time of hostilities had made it very clear to Minister Wu in Washington and to the viceroys in southern China (who throughout were helpful) that the United States was fighting not the Imperial Government, but a large group of excited and rebellious fanatics. Thus it was not strange that Prince Ch'ing should at the conclusion have written to our minister in Peking, "I was profoundly impressed with the justice and great friendliness of the American Government, and wish to express our sincere thanks."

The western nations affected required China to pay large indemnities. The United States, however, in May, 1908, decided to remit to the Imperial Government the balance still due, which was about $12,000,000, or one-half. Whereupon China announced, in accordance with a suggestion made by the United States, that she would use the money to send selected students to American schools and universities. It is to be hoped that China will ever have reason to look on America as her best friend.

INFLUENCE IN FOREIGN AFFAIRS

Roosevelt, during his second term, showed himself much interested in foreign affairs. The first occasion was the Russo-Japanese War (1904–1905). In the encroachments upon Chinese territory Russia had been the worst offender, and Roosevelt had let Japan know, previous to the war, on which side his sympathies lay. When hostilities began, he used his influence, by addressing notes to the powers, (1) to keep Germany and France out of the conflict, that is, to keep it from becoming a world war, and (2) to localize the theater of operations, that is, to keep the war from spreading over China. When Japan had won her decisive victory at Tsushima, it was Roosevelt that she asked to mediate, as the head of a great neutral power, in offering peace. The treaty conference, which was held in Portsmouth, New Hampshire, seemed unable to agree on satisfactory terms. In fact it was about to break up when Roosevelt came forward and outlined what he thought would be a just settlement. This led to further deliberation, and the terms which he had proposed were what the two nations accepted. Undoubtedly Roosevelt had saved the situation and had spared the belligerent countries the heavy sacrifices incident to many months of further warfare. For his service he was much lauded throughout Europe.

Roosevelt added to American prestige also in quite another affair. At the time of the war just mentioned, Germany taking advantage of Russian preoccupation, acted towards France, the ally of Russia, in an arbitrary manner that was bitterly resented. This occurred as the Kaiser actively interested himself in the affairs of Morocco, which France by agreement with certain countries had assumed a protectorate over, a year or more previous. The Kaiser now intervened with "terrible brusqueness." In the negotiations that followed Roosevelt took a leading part and, working in conjunction with others, induced the Kaiser to modify his demands. Thus a conflict which might have approximated almost the magnitude of that of 1914 was averted.

Although these two achivements of President Roosevelt belong primarily to diplomatic history, they also bear a relation to the development of our navy. It was not a matter of accident nor merely because of his superabundant vigor that Roosevelt should have been the first president to take such an important part in world affairs. The United States had become a world power, and she had a navy. Roosevelt was known as one who believed in a strong navy and who would not hesitate to use it, if necessity arose.

CRUISE OF THE BATTLE FLEET

The issue of the Russo-Japanese War was still undecided when certain newspapers tending towards sensationalism began talking of the "yellow peril." There admittedly was commercial rivalry between Japan and the United States, and later something of sensitiveness on the part of Japan that her subjects should not be placed on a parity with other aliens. This to most people seemed an insufficient cause for war, but there was something ominous in the air, perhaps a lack of confidence on both sides. Even the conservative admitted that there was a growing dread, which though it might be foolish and unreasonable, constituted a menace.

In December, 1907, President Roosevelt reviewed at Hampton Roads the "Battle Fleet" consisting of sixteen battleships, all commissioned since the Spanish-American War, and six destroyers. They were starting for San Francisco, going around the Horn, setting out on a voyage which because of its length many regarded as impracticable and ill advised. Scarcely had Roosevelt returned to Washington when he announced that the trip to San Francisco was only a part of their cruise, for from California they would go to our insular possessions and return home by the Suez Canal. Though on a gigantic scale, this was to be a practice cruise. As Roosevelt wrote in his *Autobiography,* "It seemed to me evident that such a voyage would greatly benefit the navy itself; would arouse popular interest in and enthusiasm for the navy; and would make foreign nations accept as a matter of course that our fleet should from time to time be gathered in the

Pacific, just as from time to time it was gathered in the Atlantic." [5]

There were additional reasons, not given to the public, revealed in a letter Roosevelt wrote to Secretary Root: "I am more concerned over the Japanese situation than almost any other. Thank Heaven we have the navy in good shape. It is high time that it should go on a cruise around the world. In the first place I think it will have a pacific effect to show it can be done; and in the next place, after talking thoroughly over the situation with the naval board, I became convinced that it was absolutely necessary for us to try in time of peace to see just what we could do in the way of putting a big battle fleet in the Pacific and not make the experiment in time of war."

High naval authorities in Germany and Italy told Roosevelt later that they had expected hostilities with Japan to begin when the ships passed the Straits of Magellan. Instead, invitations came, not only from New Zealand and Australia, but also from Japan and China that the fleet should make them a friendly visit. These countries then all began to make plans for elaborate entertainment.

The voyage of the Battle Fleet, covering 46,000 sea miles, proved most uneventful so far as martial adventure is considered. But when the ships returned after an absence of fourteen months the benefits resulting from the cruise at once became apparent to those who had taken part in it. The fleet had found itself, the men had got the "sea habit," and the vast aggregation had become a unit in a sense such as had not been realized before. The fleet had been self-sustaining in the matter of repairs, and despite its long absence from the navy yards, had come back in the best of condition. New standards in steam engineering had been established, with economy

---

[5] P. 548.

in coal consumption and increased radius of action. Officers and men had obtained daily practice in technical work of all kinds; they had profited from the unusual opportunities of maneuvering, and had improved in gunnery.[6] The cruise also brought home some needs of the navy, especially the lack of colliers.

The relations with Japan, as well as with all the countries visited, were improved. Roosevelt in his enthusiasm wrote: "The most noteworthy incident of the cruise was the reception given to our fleet in Japan. In courtesy and good breeding, the Japanese can certainly teach much to the nations of the Western world." [7]

CUBA AND THE CARIBBEAN

The second sphere of influence which the Spanish-American War pointed the way to, though marked by no international affair comparable with that of maintaining the integrity of China, still has been of wide significance. In the eighteenth and nineteenth centuries, England had commonly kept a squadron at her West Indian Station. But when the threat of her German rival required concentration in the Home Fleet, she seemed very ready to turn over to the United States the responsibility of patrolling the Caribbean.

The first duty of the United States when Spain had left Cuba was to put that country firmly on her feet. That she might be saved from foreign exploitation there was an agreement made with her commonly known as the Platt Amendment, which was passed by both houses of Congress (March 2, 1901), and was incorporated by Cuba into her constitution. This contained among others the following provisions:

---
[6] Based on the statement of Admiral Sperry, quoted in Brassey's *Naval Annual*, 1909, p. 35.

[7] *Autobiography*, p. 553.

"I. That the government of Cuba shall never enter into any treaty or other compact with any foreign power which will impair or tend to impair the independence of Cuba . . . .

"III. That the government of Cuba consents that the United States may exercise the right to intervene for the preservation of Cuban independence, maintenance of a government adequate for the protection of life, property, and individual liberty, and for discharging the obligaitons with respect to Cuba imposed by the treaty of Paris on the United States, now to be assumed and undertaken by the government of Cuba."

An election having been held in December, 1901, all United States troops were withdrawn the following May. But when an insurrection occurred after an election in 1906, and the Cuban Congress could not or would not handle the difficulty, the United States intervened to save the island from anarchy. It was not, however, for annexation, which many feared would be the outcome; and in January, 1909, our forces were again withdrawn. Two years later opposing factions were raising a storm, and intervention three times seemed imminent. In 1916 an election once more caused trouble and United States marines were landed in Santiago to protect American life and property. But the Cuban president then succeeded in restoring order without our assistance. Thus the army and navy, working with the State Department, have been instrumental in maintaining peace and order in the new republic.

What has been done for Cuba differs only in degree from the assistance rendered to other states in the Caribbean. This work was practically a necessity after the United States in 1903 decided to build an Isthmian canal. From that time on the United States was an interested party. An uprising in countries neighboring upon the canal meant a loss possibly of life, certainly of property, to the citizens of foreign nations concerned, for which the latter would be likely to demand substantial reparation. To secure this reparation they might resort to force and temporarily or permanently obtain a foothold in the unruly country. Such a procedure would make additional protection necessary for the Isthmian canal and might rob the United States of her unique position in the Western Hemisphere.

For these and like reasons the United States has established what amounts to a political or financial protectorate over several of the Caribbean countries, as will be discussed later. To make unnecessary the use of force, periodic visits from our warships to the countries concerned have been deemed advisable.

NAVAL PROGRESS UP TO THE WORLD WAR

After every great war there has always been a cry to do away with armaments, and beginning with the Revolution, the rule has been on the termination of hostilities to decrease the naval establishment both in men and ships. The Spanish-American war stands out as the conspicuous exception. Instead of there being a decline, the new navy went forward with leaps and bounds. There were two reasons why the American people turned from their traditional policy of keeping the naval establishment at a minimum: (1) we had acquired extensive insular possessions, some far removed, and there was need of a navy to look after them; (2) President Roosevelt, a student of naval affairs, was a warm supporter of the navy, and in keeping with his policies required an adequate force to make the United States a power among the nations. During his second administration, there was a spirit of uneasiness, of dread, felt round the world.

All the countries were preparing—for what, they did not know—and the spirit was contagious.

It was the battleship that showed the most marked development during the period between the Spanish-American and the World War. Mahan had taught that capital ships are the strength of a fighting force, and it was to them that the United State devoted her attention. The strongest units of the United States Navy of 1898, the *Indiana, Oregon,* and *Massachusetts* (authorized in 1890 and launched in 1893), were of 10,250 tons displacement, with moderate speed (designed speed, 16 knots), low freeboard, small normal coal supply (400 tons), heavy armament, and armor giving strong protection. They were built when the idea prevailed that the chief duty of the navy was to defend our coasts. Their seagoing qualities were unsatisfactory, their low freeboard in heavy weather causing general wetness and impairing the efficiency of the forward heavy and intermediate batteries. The territorial expansion that followed as a result of the Spanish-American War required our ships to render their chief service commonly in waters far from home ports. Thus a navy for coast defense was no longer adequate, and soon the naval policy of the United States had to conform largely to that of the leading European nations. Accordingly the *Virginia* class, authorized in 1899 and launched in 1904, possessed greater speed, increased length, and a high freeboard They carried four submerged torpedo tubes, and showed a rapid development in the application of electricity.

In 1906 the British launched the *Dreadnought,* and she so plainly outclassed all previous battleships as to make them virtually obsolete.[8]

---
[3] "While the *Dreadnought* affected injuriously the value of seven British vessels then under construction, it relegated to the background forty-one ships then building for the seven other great Powers of the world." Hurd, *Our Navy,* p. 191.

This type has, as its characteristics, simplicity and concentration of power. There are batteries of heaviest guns available (all of one size) and light torpedo defense guns, but nothing between. The speed, which is considerably higher, permits strategical and tactical concentration of gun power. The unusually heavy guns enable them to penetrate heavy armor and reach the vitals of the enemy. Their effectiveness was greatly increased at the time of the first *Dreadnought* by improvement in ballistics and in the accuracy of gun fire—due in the English Navy to Captain Percy Scott. "Spotting" at this time was in its early infancy.[9]

The United States quickly followed, and the *Michigan* and *South Carolina* were built with no intermediate batteries. Then came the *Utah* and *Florida* (21,800 tons displacement, speed 21 knots), and we had some of the units of our present navy. The *Nevada* (1914) showed the advantage of the exclusive use of oil fuel. The *New Mexico* (1916—32,000 tons, 21 knots, twelve 14-inch guns) had as her new feature, tried for the first time on a warship, the electric drive for the main propulsion; and this, proving successful, was adopted as standard in American battleships.

The cast iron shot of Civil War days had long ago

---

[9] Japan, Germany, and Italy had been working on the same problem, and, though the *Dreadnought* was the first of its type, each nation claimed credit for originating the idea. The British writer Jane, remarks, however, that the claims of the United States Navy "rest on a stronger basis," for the *South Carolina* type with "all big guns in the center line, all bearing on either broadside, was a distinct advance and novelty." He says, further, that, since the actual date of laying down goes for nothing, inasmuch as ships are designed and authorized long before work on them commences, "a strong body of opinion will always credit the United States with being the first navy that adopted the 'all big-gun idea.'" Jane, *The British Battle Fleet*, pp. 326, 327.

given way to forged-steel, elongated, pointed shells, capable of piercing armor, and carrying a charge of high explosive Black powder had been replaced by smokeless powder, because the energy of the latter was four or five times as great as that of old-time gunpowder, and the more gradual production of gas gave more uniform pressure in the bore and a higher velocity to the projectile; and withal, it produced much less smoke, always confusing to gun pointers and those controlling gun fire.

In only one other type of warship did the United States keep pace with her rivals, and that was the destroyer. Our navy of 1898 included eighteen torpedo boats, but though suggesting great possibilities for harfor defense they had never demonstrated their value.[10] Already there had been evolved the effectual enemy of the torpedo boat, the torpedo boat destroyer, which was superior in seaworthiness, speed, and armament. Because of greater size, its cruising radius (dependent on fuel capacity) was enormously increased, and it could accompany the fleet and take part in maneuvers. At the beginning of the Great War (1914) we had about fifty destroyers, which though less than half of those in either the British or the German Navy, were a strong force, one that with the addition of those building was to bring great credit to our navy.

The two entirely new types of warship developed during this period were the submarine and the aeroplane.

The pioneer in the development of the modern submarine, in the United States, was Mr. John P. Holland. Engineers in England and France were making progress, but they owed much to him. His first submarine, built in 1877, was a crude one-man boat with a petroleum motor.

---

[10] "In the war with Spain torpedoes were much more dangerous to those who attempted to use them than to their enemy." Brassey, *Naval Annual*, 1899, p. 112.

Naval Progress up to the World War 481

Later ones were also unsatisfactory, but each embodied some improvement, until in 1899 he built the first to be accepted by the navy. This was propelled by a gasoline engine on the surface and an electric motor when submerged. Holland was the first to use an internal combustion engine in conjunction with a storage battery and electric motor, and this feature was the chief cause of his success. But even at the time of the Russo-Japanese War (1904–1905), the submarine had not reached the point of development that rendered either belligerent willing to try it in actual service. Its real usefulness began with 1907–1912, when the Diesel engine, burning heavy oil, was introduced. In the later developments the United States Navy for some time did much less than either England or Germany, and was considerably behind those countries as we entered the World War.

The aeroplane and its development has almost the same story. The Wright brothers of Dayton, Ohio, were the first of any county to make a successful flight with a heavier-than-air machine, which they accomplished in December, 1903, when they flew for fifty-nine seconds going very nearly a mile. Two years later, by incessant labor, they had improved their machine so that in a flight of eighteen minutes they covered ten miles. However, it was the French, who had for years been studying the possibilities of balloons and dirigibles, that were the first to take up aviation for military purposes on a large scale.

The first practicable seaplane (1911) was the invention of another American, Glenn H. Curtiss. In 1914 he produced a flying boat double the size of those previously made, named the *America*. She flew thirteen hours at a speed of about fifty knots, which was equal to that made by the best land aeroplanes of that time. Though she never was tried for a trans-Atlantic flight (for which she had been designed), it was the *America* type that was used by the British for patrol service over the North Sea.

The Great War began the last of July, 1914. At once the submarine, aeroplane, and every type of ship that could be quickly built was so rapidly developed both in structural features and in operation that the United States within a few months seemed hopelessly out of the race. Actual use in war is so stimulating to naval progress that our officers, observing from far and near, felt that we had almost everything yet to learn. Very soon, however, the prospect of being drawn into the maelstrom quickened our naval service and preparations were begun on an extended scale.

Courtesy of Navy Recruiting Bureau, New York

DIVISION OF BATTLESHIPS AT FORCE BATTLE PRACTICE

XXVIII
THE WORLD WAR

THE RIGHTS OF NEUTRALS IGNORED

AMERICA joined in the war against Germany, April 6, 1917. The events leading up to this decision went back two years and more. Both England and Germany had disregarded neutral rights. International law, with new conditions arising, had been set aside or had been changed to meet those conditions. At the hands of either belligerent American communications suffered. England's offense consisted in intercepting articles, consigned not only to Germany, but to countries neighboring upon her, from which they might be forwarded to her; also England greatly extended the classes of contraband. Germany's offense consisted in destroying merchantmen engaged in commerce with England and France, without exercising the right of visit and search, commonly without warning and often without making any effort to save passengers and crew. The first class of offenses caused irritation, but the trouble was only of money. In some cases compensation was made at the time; in others it bade fair to be settled by claims made after the war. The second class of offenses caused deep indignation. Among the people lost were American citizens, women and children as well as men, and for their lives there could be no compensation. Germany was said to be waging war against humanity.

A conspicuous example of this kind of warfare, a success that was to prove unfortunate for Germany, was the sinking of the *Lusitania*. On May 7, 1915, without the slightest warning that ship was torpedoed off the Irish coast. She sank in eighteen minutes, and with her were lost 1153 men, women, and children, of whom 114 were citizens of the United States. Some people of our country were for an immediate declaration of war, but President Wilson bent his efforts to gaining a repudiation of the act, coupled with the promise of respecting in the future the rules of cruiser warfare. Although there were two further lapses that occasioned sharp notes, Germany was kept from unrestricted submarine warfare until February 1, 1917. Then diplomatic relations between the United States and Germany were severed, and when news came that three American ships had been sunk, an extra session of Congress was called and war was declared.

General Character of the War

From a naval point of view the World War was a conflict of two blockades. Great Britain, since the beginning of hostilities, had been so superior on the surface as to enforce a long distance blockade that prevented ships from the west entering or leaving German ports. Occasionally German warships slipped out, but it was only for short runs or raids, from which they returned after a few hours. Germany, on the other hand, had a force of undersea craft that came and went at pleasure, encircling the British Isles and sailing about the French coast. They sank so many merchantmen as to make hazardous the carrying of cargoes to the Allied countries. Though many ships eluded them, the large number lost seriously interfered with the Allies' prosecution of the war, and in 1917 the menace was becoming worse.

Thus when the United States joined the Allies, if the surface blockade could be maintained and avenues from the United States to the Allies be kept open, our vast resources in men and war supplies of all kinds would eventually insure victory. On the other hand, if the undersea craft, with the increased force then available, could prevent men and supplies from reaching England and France, they felt confident of a result favorable to them.

THE NAVAL SITUATION, APRIL, 1917

Three days after the declaration of war there arrived in England the naval representative of the United States, Admiral W. S. Sims, who had been sent when the break with Germany was inevitable, in order that he might get in touch with the British Admiralty and acquaint the Navy Department with the situation. He kept this position throughout the war, his duty for the most part being in London with his office near the Admiralty. When American naval forces were sent to join the British, French, and Italian, he was made "Commander of the U. S. Naval Forces Operating in European Waters."

It was plain to him that the United States had not entered the war merely to be on the winning side. The prospects for the Allies in April, 1917, were bleak enough. Germany was making the unrestricted submarine campaign terribly effective, and in this month alone her boats sank 900,000 tons. This was out of all proportion to what the overworked British shipyards could do in making good the losses by building, and there was no disguising the truth that at this rate England would be isolated and starved out by the early fall.

There had been published many lurid accounts of the destruction of German submarines. . Many of them originated with eye witnesses who had seen oil slicks and wreckage of some kind or other, making them believe that a U-boat had been destroyed. Yet the Admiralty intelligence reports gave conclusive evidence of only fifty-four German submarines having been destroyed since the beginning of hostilities, and the German shipyards were now turning out new boats at the rate of three a week.

All the facts at their disposal the British put before Admiral Sims, and he and the American ambassador, Walter Hines Page, reported to Washington the critical situation. In conclusion, Sims said, "Briefly stated, I consider that at the present moment we are losing the war."

Our army had promptly undertaken the task of organizing and training overseas forces, but it was plain that the process would take time, and there was the problem of transporting them to France. To make the United States at once effective, however, two kinds of assistance were possible: sending of destroyers and forwarding of supplies, both munitions and food. To this the United States promptly gave itself.

The Destroyers First on the Scene

From 1914 Great Britain had been sending a constant procession of troop and supply ships to France, and not a single one had been sacrificed to the U-boats. This showed plainly the power of the destroyers, which always served as escorts. But the undersea craft, carefully avoiding them near Dover, operated almost at will in the entrance to the English Channel, St. George's Channel, and Bristol Channel. In these waters only occasionally did a destroyer appear, for the British had not a sufficient force to patrol them.

Thus to overcome the German submarine blockade American destroyers were essential. The Navy Department had surmised this even before Admiral Sims's urgent messages were received. A division was dispatched the instant it was ready, and on the fourth of May, less than a month after war had been declared, six American destroyers, under Commander J. K. Taussig, steamed into

THE RETURN OF THE MAYFLOWER

Painting by B. F. Gribble. Courtesy of the U. S. Naval Academy

The Destroyers First on the Scene 487

Queenstown. No newspaper had announced their coming, but the whole city was out to welcome them. Their presence had the greatest significance to the Allies. Even more important than the increase of force was the visible evidence that the United States had entered the war and was taking her part. The moving pictures photographed at the time were soon shown all over England; prefacing this with the story of a few Englishmen who in 1620 went to North America to found a state based on justice and liberty, they emphasized this home-coming three centuries later to fight for justice and liberty by calling it "The Return of the Mayflower."

Admiral Bayly, R.N., the commanding officer at Queenstown to whom Commander Taussig and his associates hastened to report, was known to be a man of few words, but the response which he elicited became famous in British as well as American annals.

"After acknowledging the introduction, Bayly's first words were these: 'Captain Taussig, at what time will your vessels be ready for the sea?' Taussig replied, 'I shall be ready when fueled.' The admiral then asked, 'Do you require any repairs?' [meaning, dockyard work]. Taussig answered, 'No sir.' The admiral's third and last question was, 'Do you require any stores?' [meaning dry provisions]. Taussig answered, 'No sir! Each vessel now has on board sufficient stores to last for seventy days.' The admiral concluded the interview with these instructions: 'You will take four days' rest. Good Morning.' "[1]

The grim Admiral Bayly, who was a lion in action, when he found that his new force were as bold and efficient in deeds as in words, became enthusiastically devoted to them, and their relations were most cordial throughout.

On the 17th of May the second division of six de-

---

[1] *Naval Institute Proceedings*, December, 1922, vol. 48, p. 2036.

stroyers arrived, and another division appeared nearly every week thereafter until the fifth of July, when thirty-four destroyers were at Queenstown, the number that continued there until the end of the war.

Certain areas for patrol were assigned to the American force and a definite routine was established: six days of patrol, followed by two days in port; once a month, five days off for boiler cleaning and overhaul.

It was hard, wearing duty for the destroyer force; and only by constant vigilance was there safety for those intrusted to their charge as well as for themselves. There were repeated S.O.S. calls from ships attacked by U-boats, and the destroyers had to rush off to their rescue. There were boat loads of survivors to pick up and bring in. There were convoys to meet and escort through the danger zone. Occasionally they sighted a periscope, and by quick firers, ramming, and depth charges they hunted the hunter. The last of these three methods of attack, a new type of mine, was invented as America entered the war, and possessed great possibilities. If the submarine by delay disclosed even its approximate position, a mine, adjusted to explode at a certain depth, was dropped overboard (or projected by the Y-gun) from a destroyer, and it gave a frightful shock, in many cases causing serious damage.

On an October morning as some destroyers were escorting a convoy of British ships to the east coast of England, they received a radio message from the American steamer *J. L. Luckenback* calling for help, for she was being shelled by a submarine. Though the position she gave was ninety miles away, the *Nicholson* went at once to her assistance. The *Luckenback,* being an armed merchantman, was by her guns keeping the submarine at a distance, but as the latter outranged her, it had the game seemingly in its own hands. Yet when the *Nicholson* radioed,

The Destroyers First on the Scene 489

"Do not surrender!" there came back the spirited answer, "Never." As the *Nicholson* appeared, the American merchantman, though crippled and on fire, was still fighting. The destroyer by her prompt response saved her and brought her to England with the convoy.

At other times the destroyers were not so successful. The *Cassin* while on patrol was herself torpedoed, a torpedo striking the stern. She was kept afloat, however, and as the submarine appeared on the surface to complete its work it was driven away by the destroyer's guns. A storm followed, but the *Cassin* succeeded in weathering it, and when help arrived, after much labor she was towed into port.

The most satisfactory engagement any of our destroyers had was that of the *Fanning,* Lieutenant A. S. Carpender, with the *U-58* on the afternoon of November 17, 1917. It occurred while, with the *Nicholson,* she was escorting a convoy of eight British merchantmen ten miles out from Queenstown. A vigilant coxswain espied the top of a periscope only 400 yards distant and ahead, slowly making toward the path of the convoy—the submarine in excellent position for firing. The torpedo was never discharged, however, for before the periscope went under it revealed the *Fanning* working up to a speed of twenty knots and charging down.

Reaching the spot where the periscope had disappeared and going slightly ahead of the estimated position of the U-boat, the *Fanning* dropped a depth charge and then continued on the turn she was making. The *Nicholson,* having also circled about, was approaching so as to join the *Fanning* in laying a depth-charge barrage around their quarry. As she neared the spot where the depth charge had been dropped, her officers saw a bow and conning tower emerging; they released a depth charge alongside when they passed, and followed this by three shots from their stern gun. A minute later the conning tower opened and the officers and crew began crawling out, each one, with hands up, calling "Kamerad" to show he wished to surrender. Under cover of the *Nicholson's* guns, the *Fanning* approached, and as the bow of the submarine settled and the stern rose, the destroyer succeeded in picking up all but one of the German force, four officers and thirty-five men. While the prisoners were being taken on board, a chief pharmacist's mate and a coxswain of the *Fanning* jumped into the icy water to save a German sailor who was drowning. They succeeded in getting him on board, but efforts to resuscitate him were unavailing. Later it was learned from the commanding officer of the *U-58,* that the first depth charge (dropped by the *Fanning*) had wrecked his motors, had put the diving rudders out of commission, and broken the oil leads. When the submarine, utterly unmanageable, had sunk to a depth of 200 feet, the officers had blown the tanks and come to the surface; in the choice between a horrible death on the bottom and surrender, they preferred the latter.

In order to increase the number of small boats hunting submarines, the Navy Department accepted several large pleasure yachts which their owners offered. Also a new type was developed, the subchaser, 110 feet long and of 60 tons displacement. Some 400 of these were turned out by the shipyards in eighteen months, and 170 were dispatched to Queenstown, Brest, Gibraltar, and Corfu. We used, further, coast guard boats, gunboats, and old-time torpedo boats brought from the Philippines. Living conditions on these tiny craft were often grim enough, but they kept at sea no matter what was the weather. Although the larger number of their officers and crew were college men, new to the service, never having made an ocean voyage before, they made a splendid record.

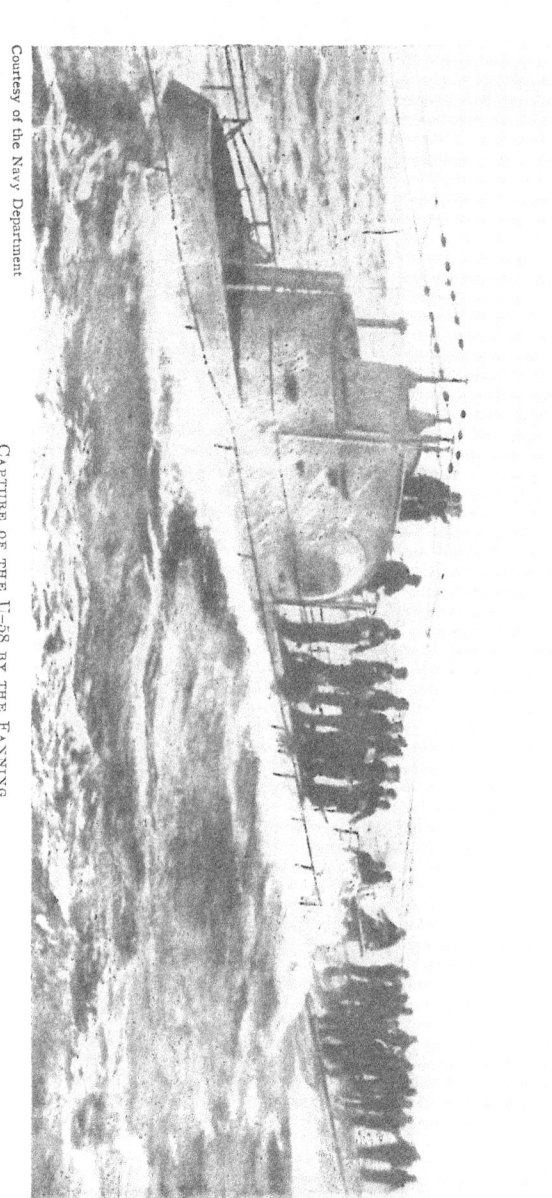

Courtesy of the Navy Department

CAPTURE OF THE U-58 BY THE FANNING

The little yacht *Christabel* won high honors. While protecting a British merchantman that had fallen behind her convoy, off the coast of southern France, she had an engagement with a submarine that hovered about attempting to sink the ship. A depth charge dropped where the periscope had disappeared brought up all kinds of débris followed by quantities of heavy black oil. A day or two later the *UC-56*, battered and bruised, crawled into the Spanish port of Santander, so badly damaged that she was interned for the rest of the war.

Thirty-six of the subchasers, which had steamed all the way from New London to Greece, 6000 miles, were based on Corfu. Under the command of Captain C. P. Nelson, they were very efficient in the patrol of the Straits of Otranto, where the Adriatic narrows down to forty miles. By their listening devices they became skillful in trailing submarines and they caused great disquiet by dropping depth bombs.

Early in October, 1918, Captain Nelson with twelve chasers was asked to coöperate with the British and Italian light cruisers in an attack on the Austrian base at Durazzo.

"It's going to be a real party, boys," was Nelson's remark as he appeared after conferring with Commodore W. A. H. Kelly of the British Navy. And it was with a spirit emulating that shown by Decatur in his exploits in the Mediterranean one hundred years before that our force entered the affair.

The subchasers had as their mission the screening of the cruisers from submarine attack, while the latter shelled the city, destroyed the shipping, and demolished military storehouses. Austrian batteries opened upon the small boats and the missiles fell all about them, but they held calmly to their work. At length one of the subchasers detected the presence of a U-boat making towards the British cruisers, and changed its course to meet it.

The second subchaser in the division following the new lead, its skipper caught a glimpse of a periscope. Smashing the periscope with a well-aimed shot, he dashed forward and began dropping depth charges, in which sport a third chaser also joined. One bomb evidently hit its mark, for steel plates and other wreckage were blown into the air. The first chaser was found with her engine broken down, but she announced that before this happened she had discharged eight depth charges, bringing up masses of oil and seven pieces of metal plate.

Durazzo was ruined as a military base, but not an American in this exploit was injured.[2]

The Transport Service

The raising and equipping of an army of two millions in the short time at our disposal was a great achievement. But that is a chapter of military history. It is the transportation of this army to France that belongs to naval annals.

The British plan of escorting troop and cargo ships across the Channel proving successful was adopted by our forces, and was put into operation for the protection of shipping bound for England and western Europe, whether from the United States or from Africa and Gibraltar. It slowed down the carriers by twenty per cent., but what did that matter if it made them safe—a result which in time was very largely accomplished.

For the United States to send what the Balfour Mission representing England and the Joffre Mission representing France implored of the President, it was seen that a vast flotilla would be required, and accordingly the United States Shipping Board and the Emergency Fleet Corporation were created. Ships were procured

---

[2] Sims, *Victory at Sea*, pp. 233–239.

from every possible source. German merchant ships and interned warships lying in our harbors were overhauled and repaired for American service. American vessels in the coast trade were taken over, old shipyards were enlarged, and others newly established worked with feverish intensity, turning out craft of every kind. Of naval transports at the beginning we had only two, but this number during the war was increased to forty-eight. As escorts to the convoys while crossing the Atlantic, twenty-four cruisers were secured, some from the Atlantic Fleet, some from those on special assignments, and some from those out of commission.[3]

The large and faster cruisers were used to escort troop convoys, and the smaller vessels to escort cargo convoys.

The duty of this deep-sea escort, which guarded the ships from destruction by German raiders as well as from attack by cruising U-boats, was indeed a strenuous one. "Theirs was the constant and unceasing toil, in summer and winter.... Seven days of rest in port, then out again, mothering liners and pot-bellied merchant ships loaded with their invaluable cargo. The hard part of it was that they rarely sighted land on the other side, but met the escorting destroyers far out from shore, where they had to turn around to buck the heavy nor'westers and so for home again, only to coal, have a little run on the avenue, a look at the movies, then back again with another convoy."[4]

The record they made was an enviable one. Not a troopship nor a single American soldier sent across by the United States Naval Transport Service was lost going over.[5] The ships did not have quite the same immu-

---

[3] Gleaves, *History of the Transport Service*, p. 28.
[4] Ibid., p. 154.
[5] *Report of Secretary of Navy*, 1918, p. 27; Gleaves, *History of the Transport Service*, p. 29.

nity returning, since five were torpedoed, three being lost, but two in spite of injuries making port. Every effort was made to protect the empty ships, but when it was necessary with the limited number of destroyers to choose between a heavily loaded convoy going over and empty ships returning, reason sent the escorts to the former.

The submarine blockade which Germany had counted on to prevent America's taking any appreciable part in the war was overcome by two lines of operations. The first was the use of every available means of protection— such as has been described. The second was the careful routing of the convoys. Trip after trip was made without a lookout's sighting any U-boat. None was seen, for the ships had been directed in lanes where there was no enemy. This was the work of one or two officers in the convoy room in Brest or in London.

In this room, from which no secrets issued, for practically no one beyond a very few officers of the staff were admitted, a huge chart of the Atlantic Ocean filled a side of the wall. The position of every convoy was marked and its progress was indicated. Similarly the position of practically every German submarine was marked, surrounded by a circle equal to its estimated cruising radius during the day or since the time when last reported. These circles were the danger zones to be avoided. To those unfamiliar with the methods of the convoy room it seemed strange that its officers could obtain such definite information about the U-boats. In the first place, whenever a ship sighted a submarine, or was attacked, it promptly sent a radio message reporting the fact with longitude and latitude. Second, whenever a U-boat opened up with its radio, the different stations quickly recognized it and with their direction-finders determined its position. The Allied submarines, destroyers, and convoys were cautioned not to use their radio except when absolutely necessary; but the German submarines were much given to talking, commonly getting into communication about the same hour every evening and often talking at other times. By patient observation, supplemented by information gained by the British intelligence office, the identity and habits of U-boats in certain areas were learned. Some of them had as their chief mission the laying of mines, others rarely used anything but torpedoes in attack, and others made a considerable use of their guns, staying out longer by holding their torpedoes in reserve. The number of torpedoes they commonly carried was known; so if the data collected on a particular submarine showed that these had all been fired, one could be rather sure that it would soon be returning to port. Many a time when the routing officer in the convoy room saw peril for an approaching convoy, because, if it kept on its course, it would on the following day or night enter the circle where a U-boat was operating, he radioed to the convoy, sending it off on a wide detour or directing it to a different port. Thus it was that convoys arrived without sighting an enemy, in truth without having been within striking distance.

Of the vast American army overseas at the time of the Armistice 46¼ per cent. had been carried in United States ships; or in figures given by the Secretary of the Navy, 924,578 of our troops in Europe, November 1, 1918, had made the passage in United States naval convoys under the escort of United States cruisers and destroyers.[6] Beginning with spring, 1918, when men were so much needed in France, they were transported at the rate of 10,000 a day, together with food supplies required for soldiers and civilians of all nationalities,

---

[6] Gleaves, *History of the Transport Service*, p. 25; *Report of Secretary of Navy*, 1918, p. 27.

and war munitions. Within ten months after work had begun in organizing the transportation service, the Secretary of the Navy estimated, a vessel manned by an American naval crew, carrying subsistence and equipment for the American Expeditionary Forces, was leaving an American port on an average of every five hours.[7] At the head of the transport service and working indefatigably with his corps of assistants was Vice-Admiral Albert Gleaves. Its success was due in a very large degree to him and to Vice-Admiral Henry B. Wilson, our naval representative in France and the officer in charge of the naval base at Brest.

It was Admiral Wilson who had the problem of circumventing the U-boats operating in the Bay of Biscay and of safeguarding the two million soldiers sent to France, when they had reached the danger zone. This he did through the convoy room at Brest and by means of the large force of destroyers, yachts, and other auxiliary craft under his command. The receiving and unloading of troop- and cargo-ships was also his responsibility; and their quick return was due in a large degree to his constant supervision and tireless energy.

AMERICAN BATTLESHIPS ASSIST IN MAINTAINING SURFACE BLOCKADE

Grand Admiral von Tirpitz, who for the first two years of the war (previous to America's entry) was the minister who had charge of the German Navy, records that even as early as August 19, 1914, he remarked to the chancellor of the German empire, "The decision of the war turns exclusively on whether Germany or England can hold out the longer;" and he observed to the chief of the naval staff, "The English fleet and England are Germany's most dangerous enemy."

---

[7] *Report of Secretary of Navy*, 1918, p. 20.

Work of the Battleships 497

Whatever we may think of von Tirpitz's conduct of the war, his estimate of the situation was correct. It was the British Navy and more particularly the battleships and battle cruisers of the British Grand Fleet that were the backbone of the blockade, and the blockade was one of the two or possibly three great factors that brought Germany's downfall.

The superiority of the Grand Fleet was such that the German High Seas Fleet never sought a general engagement, and with sound strategy pinned its hopes of success on the expectation of surprising and crushing detached squadrons or units, until it had reduced this superiority. Consequently the activities of the High Seas Fleet (aside from Jutland when the general engagement came from a meeting unintended on the part of the Germans) consisted of raids and short runs with a home port near for a safe return. Had the Grand Fleet even momentarily neglected its vigilant watch, swarms of raiders might have dashed out, attacking the troop and cargo convoys bound for France, and defeating every means used by the Allies to overcome the submarine blockade. When the United States began sending its large convoys overseas, there was fear that Germany, taking a desperate chance, might send out even a battle cruiser and cause consternation in America as well as wild rejoicing in Germany by destroying a whole convoy. It was to guard against such a disaster that three of our fastest and strongest battleships, the *Nevada, Oklahoma,* and *Utah,* under Rear-Admiral T. S. Rodgers, were dispatched to Bantry Bay, southwest Ireland, whence they might be ready to meet any raider. Perhaps it was the knowledge of this precaution that prevented an attack.

Previous to the stationing of these ships in Ireland, Battleship Division No. 9 of the United States Atlantic Fleet had been sent to Scapa Flow to be combined with the Grand Fleet. The constant sea service of the latter required that strong units frequently drop out for overhaul. That the British numerical superiority might still be maintained, as well as to strengthen the morale by this visible evidence of our participation in the war, the division just mentioned consisting of five battleships, the *New York* (Captain C. F. Hughes), the *Wyoming* (Captain H. A. Wiley), the *Texas* (Captain Victor Blue), the *Florida* (Captain Thomas Washington), and the *Delaware* (Captain A. H. Scales), under Rear-Admiral Hugh Rodman, joined the British at Scapa Flow, December 6, 1917. From that date until the end of the war it constituted the Sixth Battle Squadron of the Grand Fleet.

Every navy has its own codes, its own system of signals, and its own system of tactics. The Sixth Battle Squadron promptly began to study and to adopt British ways. To simplify the process, with each American was paired a British dreadnought, which should accompany her in all maneuvers and act as her mentor. So quick was the assimilation that in four days the new squadron went out for maneuvers, taking its assigned position in the fleet.

It was not the contacts with the enemy but the constant vigilance that made this duty a severe one. The fleet, studying not to make its movements too regular, for the most part alternated between Scapa Flow in the Orkneys and Rosyth in the Firth of Forth. Some recreation was planned for the personnel, but it was necessarily limited when every ship, no matter how recent had been its patrol, must be ready to put to sea at four hours' notice. The winter nights in the northern latitude were long and the waters were cold and stormy. But cheerfulness and optimism were the prevailing note, and the only real grumbling was because the enemy would not come out and give the battleships a chance. Our force, however, found their service not without thrills. Some of the thrills came from the maneuvers and others from attacks by the U-boats.

In one of the frequent patrols, as the fleet steamed out of Rosyth on an afternoon, they ran into a blinding snow storm. The *Delaware,* which happened that day to be the last battleship in the column, lost touch with the other ships when the fog buoy, trailing along from the ship she followed, carried away. After that there was no alternative but strictly to follow sailing orders, which prescribed the course and included two right-angle turns. An anxious night for the skipper and his officers followed, but not only did they not collide with any of the other units, but they sighted none. When dawn came and the weather, clearing, lifted the veil, it disclosed to them just one ship in sight, the flagship of Admiral Sir David Beatty, who seeing them suddenly appear, trained his guns on them and demanded the recognition signal. During the night they had steamed through the entire fleet to a position close to their flagship, which was supposed to be leading the column.

The Germans plainly cherished hopes of bolstering up their morale by sinking one of the American dreadnoughts, and singled them out for repeated attacks. In February, 1918, when the *Florida* and *Delaware* were escorting a convoy off the coast of Norway, a U-boat discharged four torpedoes at the former and two at the latter, but the battleships by quick turns avoided them all, and destroyers drove off the assailant. On a later day, in Pentland Firth, the skipper of the *New York,* seeing a suspicious object, changed his course, and then discovering that it was a U-boat, headed for it at full speed. Officers felt a blow on their starboard quarter, followed by a second blow. When the *New York* was examined, it was found that two blades of her propellers had been broken off. The submarine was not seen again and it was believed that it had sunk to rise no more.

Shortly after this, the dreadnought being on her way to be refitted, a U-boat attacked her and fired in quick succession three torpedoes, all passing ahead. Because of her damaged propellers she was making at the time but twelve knots; it may have been this that caused the U-boat wrongly to estimate her progress and to miss her.

Meanwhile the various squadrons in home waters had been brought together and organized in the Atlantic Fleet, of which Admiral Henry T. Mayo was in command. He went abroad during the first months of the war to make a comprehensive study of conditions there. In the Atlantic Fleet there was constant drilling and fullest preparation for war service. German U-boats, as a matter of fact, did come to the American coast in 1918, sinking with a mine the cruiser *San Diego* and shelling or torpedoing several small merchant vessels. If disaster had come to the British Grand Fleet, the United States had ready a strong reserve for immediate service.

Admiral Benson, as Chief of Naval Operations, had the duty of organizing the vast resources of the navy and coördinating our forces at home and abroad. His was an office of the very first importance, for all naval operations, big or little, had to be directed from it. He went to Europe near the beginning and the close of hostilities that he might visit the Allied navies and confer with the naval leaders as to the most effective prosecution of the war.

In Washington, at the heart of activities, was the Secretary of the Navy, Josephus Daniels. Closely in touch with the varied work of the navy, he was indefatigable in representing its needs to Congress and securing the colossal appropriations required. Early and late he was at his desk; he personally attended to a huge volume of naval business, and yet he was always ready to listen to the request of the humblest sailor.

XXIX

THE WORLD WAR (CONTINUED)

American Submarines and Aircraft

WE HAVE considered the fight made by the several kinds of surface craft to enforce the surface blockade of Germany and to break up the under sea blockade with which that country was retaliating. There remains for discussion the fight made also by our submarines and aircraft.

In neither of these types was our navy strong. Our submarines, such as we had, were small and designed, like our early battleships and torpedo boats of the Spanish-American War period, mainly for harbor defense. They lacked necessary comforts and they were years behind those of leading European powers. Further, the navy as a whole had little confidence in them. Of aircraft we had next to none, with a correspondingly small personnel trained in flying.

Yet the experience of the Allies had plainly showed the value of both of these services for scouting and for offensive operations. Since America was determined to prosecute the war in every possible way, the Navy Department decided to send what was available and to build extensively.

It was in October, 1917, that one submarine flotilla set out for the Azores, and two months later that another went to the British Isles. The latter could not have chosen a worse season for crossing, encountering gale after gale, some rising to the proportions of a hurricane. But the boats, seven in number, eventually reached Bantry Bay, Ireland, and there after undergoing a brief period of instruction from selected British submarine officers they began regular patrol duty. Certain areas were assigned to them in St. George's Channel, Bristol Channel, and in waters to the south and west of Ireland, in all of which shipping was crowded and the U-boats had wrought havoc.

The U-boats found the submarine of their opponents hard to contend with when their own attention was focused on commerce destruction. As they were out for long cruises they had to be saving in use of their storage batteries. Therefore generally they had to run on the surface using their Diesel engines. Thus if an Allied submarine approached submerged, since they themselves were low in the water, they were in as great danger of surprise as were the merchant ships from them. Confronted by such a peril, they acted like the merchant ships; they planned to give the hostile submarine a wide berth. The result was that the U-boats tended to operate farther and farther out at sea, where the chances of success were decidedly less.

Our submarines, designated as the AL-boats, might well have been satisfied if this result had been their only service. But they were constantly seeking to destroy one of their foe. The exploit of the *AL-2,* Lieutenant Paul F. Foster, is one that deserves especial notice.

The *AL-2,* while running awash on her way to Bantry Bay near the close of an eight-day patrol, changed her course to investigate a suspicious looking object that had been sighted in the dim distance. As she approached, a torpedo exploded only sixty feet away and a periscope appeared for a moment. But, for a reason that can only be conjectured—perhaps because the torpedo had boomeranged, striking the ship that fired it—it did not harm the *AL-2,* and it did injure the U-boat. The skipper of the *AL-2,* at once grasping the situation, ordered a quick dive and circled around to ram the U-boat. He passed so near that through his hull he could hear the propellers, but he did not strike. Quickly the propellers stopped, and though the *AL-2* searched for hours the officers detected no further sign of their enemy. It is very likely that the U-boat in order to avoid the *AL-2* had dived, whereas if she had remained on the surface she might have been saved. The one thing certain is that the British Admiralty three months later published confidential reports secured by their intelligence officers in Germany, showing that the *UB-65,* which had been reported operating off Fastnet, Ireland, on the day of this occurrence, had never been heard from since. On receipt of this intelligence, the Admiralty credited the sinking of the *UB-65* by indirect action, to the *AL-2*.[1]

Considering next the work of the aviation service, one is struck with how little they had to begin with and how quickly they expanded. A year previous to hostilities a Yale University aviation unit had begun training under the leadership of Trubee Davison and this volunteer unit formed an important nucleus. The aviators were the first of our forces to land in France, seven officers and one hundred and twenty-two men arriving at St. Nazaire on the 5th of June, 1917.

Soon American naval aircraft stations were building all along the western coast of France, areas were charted off and each station was assigned one of them for patrolling. At the conclusion of hostilities we had four kite balloon stations, eighteen seaplane stations, three dirigible stations, and five bombing plane stations.[2]

And this was as nothing in comparison with the huge plant that was under construction at Pauillac and else-

---

[1] Alden, "American Submarine Operations in the War." *Naval Institute Proceedings*, vol. xlvi, pp. 1035–1040.

[2] *Report of Secretary of the Navy*, 1918, p. 12.

where. American equipment was lacking; nevertheless our men saw action and they made their presence felt. The Northern Bombing Group, commanded by Captain David C. Hanrahan, U. S. Navy, included 305 officers and 2000 enlisted men working with 112 planes. They gave their attention to bombing the submarine bases at Zeebrugge and Ostend. The greatest single service of the aircraft, however, was the escorting of convoys that were approaching or leaving French ports. From their lofty positions they increased the means of picking up craft in the distance. Often they saw lurking U-boats, even though submerged. When unequal themselves to engaging the enemy, they accomplished their purpose by directing a destroyer to where a depth charge might prove effective.

Figures show how active was this branch of our service. The American naval forces in the war zone under the command of Captains H. I. Cone and T. T. Craven had forty-four stations and made more than 5600 war flights.

The Northern Mine Barrage

The United States had entered the war resolved to make use of every device that would help to defeat the U-boats. Nine days after hostilities began the Bureau of Ordnance put forward a scheme that was staggering in its immensity. This was the bottling up of the German craft in the North Sea, by laying a mine barrage from Norway to the Orkneys, a distance of 230 miles (about the same as from New York to Washington), where the water attains a depth of 1100 feet.

The British had already sealed the southern entrance leading to the English Channel, and during the two years and a half had planted 30,000 mines in the Bight of

The Northern Mine Barrage 505

Heligoland. In 1917 they were using 7000 a month, and this was very nearly the limit of their capacity in production.

There was thus a challenge and to this the Bureau of Ordnance applied itself. Soon its chief, Rear-Admiral Ralph Earle, was able to submit to the Navy Department and the British Admiralty a new type of mine, very greatly improved, the combined work of Commander S. P. Fullinwider, Lieutenant-Commander T. S. Wilkinson, and Mr. Ralph A. Browne. An adjustable anchoring device permitted it to be planted at any depth, and a long antenna, consisting of a thin copper cable attached to a float a few feet below the surface, was so delicate in its mechanism that the touching of this by a metallic substance, as the hull of a boat, was sufficient to produce an electric current and explode the charge. Thus there was a danger for a submarine crossing the mine field either on the surface or to a depth of 240 feet.

When the period of study, conference, experimentation, and improvement was concluded there came the extensive organization required for production. No factory in America had the machinery or capacity for turning mines out in the numbers required. There was the safeguarding the secret, further, by distributing the work. Five hundred and forty contractors and sub-contractors were involved in this great project. A base was established on the James River; later two bases were established on the east coast of Scotland, with Rear-Admiral Joseph Strauss, U. S. Navy, in command of the whole operation overseas.

It was on the 8th of June, 1918, that ten American mine layers commanded by Captain R. R. Belknap slipped out, attended by destroyers and screened by battleships, which got between them and the German coast, to plant forty-seven miles of mines. Twelve other such expeditions, coming at regular intervals through the summer and early fall, were necessary to complete the undertaking. The barrage was the combined work of Great Britain, and the United States. Altogether 70,263 mines were planted, and of these the Yankee Mining Squadron planted 56,611. The width of the barrage was fifteen to thirty-five miles. So it took a submarine on the surface from one to three hours to pass through the danger zone, submerged from three to six hours.

In June, almost immediately after the first planting, a U-boat badly damaged by a mine exploding nearby crawled into a Norwegian port and had to be interned for the remainder of the war. Other disasters followed, and when a U-boat which had been talking very glibly over her radio became suddenly silent as it reached the barrage, the inference was that something had happened. At the conclusion of the war German sources revealed that, on account of the barrage, seventeen [3] of their submarines had been lost or damaged to such an extent as to be no longer serviceable.

The indirect results were probably still more important. The one to six hours spent in passing through the mine field were nerve racking to the last degree and broke down many a man's morale.

Had the war continued another year, American mine planting on a much larger scale would have occurred in other waters, including the Mediterranean. The knowledge of America's vast resources and the lavish manner in which she employed them in her enterprises brought Germany to a realization of the fact that she was near defeat.

---

[3] These figures are taken from Admiral Earle's statement in *Makers of Naval Tradition*, p. 311.

NAVAL OPERATIONS ON LAND

The United States Navy, though its natural element is the sea, has never hesitated when there has been opportunity to fight also on land.

A second large project of the Bureau of Ordnance, also put forward by Rear-Admiral Ralph Earle, was constructing mounted railway batteries of a size beyond anything ever before attempted, sending them to France, and operating them on the battle front.

There were certain 14-inch guns designed for battle cruisers which had been authorized, but which the war had delayed the building of. The proposal of the Bureau of Ordnance was that these huge rifles should be mounted, not on permanent artillery bases of concrete or steel, which were slow of construction and often when battle came were not where they were most needed, but on mobile and independent mounts—that is, on especially designed railway cars.

As in the case of the mine barrage, the work was advanced with the utmost expedition. By the middle of August, 1918, five of these monsters, under the command of Rear-Admiral C. P. Plunkett, were moving on the railways of France, and manned by navy crews were ready to go into action. For each gun there was a train of fourteen cars making the equipment and operation of the great piece complete, one or more cars being devoted to each of the following: armored magazine, machineshop, crane, radio, kitchen, and berths. These cars as well as the mounts were all designed and contracted for by the Bureau of Ordnance.

The first action in which they took part was near Laon, September 16. At once their great power was perceived. They had a range of thirty miles and could fire behind the enemy lines, reaching points hitherto out of reach of Allied artillery. They saw service with our army also in several later engagements. Of their performance Admiral Earle remarked, "By their fire the German railway lines were disrupted, especially at their most important junctions of Montmédy, Longuyon, and Conflans; and ammunition dumps supposed to be immune from damage were destroyed in the areas well back of the firing lines." [4]

The Marine Corps, established in 1798, almost immediately after the creation of the Navy Department, has had a history to be proud of, but it was in the last five months of the World War that it won its brightest laurels. At Chateau Thierry, Belleau Wood, in the offensive near Soissons, in the battle for the St. Mihiel salient, and in the capture of Blanc Mont Ridge near Rheims, the marines fought with a courage, a desperation, and an endurance that could not be surpassed. Their first engagement coming at a critical moment in the war, their service was out of all proportion to the number engaged, in the turning of the great German offensive into a retreat. The severity of their fighting was shown by the casualty lists; out of 8,000 men engaged they lost 1600 killed and 2513 wounded, that is, more than one-half.[5] Even a general account of their battles would be beyond the scope of this book, and as they were serving with the army under the command of General Pershing it is commonly treated in military history.

THE SURRENDER

Early on the 21st of November, 1918, the Grand Fleet arriving at a rendezvous forty miles east of May Island, which guards the entrance to the Firth of Forth, was drawn up in two long columns six miles apart to await

---

[4] *Makers of Naval Tradition*, p. 313.
[5] *Report of Secretary of Navy*, 1918, p. 103.

the German High Seas Fleet. The American Sixth Battle Squadron occupying a place about the middle of the northern column was thus present at the closing scene of the great drama. A British light cruiser had guided the German ships to the meeting place where was Admiral Sir David Beatty on the *Queen Elizabeth,* waiting to receive the surrender. Then, led by the *Queen Elizabeth,* the High Seas Fleet steamed down the long lane; first, five battle cruisers in single column, three cables apart, and nine ponderous dreadnoughts; then three miles astern of the last battleship, six light cruisers, as before three cables apart; and, last, three miles astern of the rear light cruiser, fifty destroyers arranged in five groups.[6]

When the German fleet had reached a point where it was enveloped by the two columns, the Allied ships countermarched, turning outward, and escorted it to its anchorage. The German colors were still flying from the gaff. Near sunset Beatty gave his famous signal, "The German flag is to be hauled down at 3.57 to-day, and is not to be hoisted again without permission."

The victory had been won, and America had taken part during the last year or year and a half in almost every phase of the struggle. It would be folly to magnify what our forces did, and not to be profoundly grateful to our Allies, who threw larger numbers into the struggle and bore the brunt of fighting for a much longer period. On the other hand, it would be untrue to our dead and living if we failed to recognize their remarkable adaptability and spirit of coöperation, their thoroughness, and their eagerness as they threw all into the conflict.

---

[6] Under the terms of the Armistice the Germans were to surrender ten battleships, six battle cruisers, eight light cruisers, fifty destroyers, and all submarines. The submarines had surrendered previous to the great day off the Firth of Forth, and a few of the other types were surrendered elsewhere.

Admiral Scheer, the redoubtable leader of the High Seas Fleet at Jutland and the one in charge of German naval affairs at the close, in a volume published a year after the war,[7] though with a curious logic depreciating what the British and American forces accomplished, nevertheless admits the general undermining of the German morale. He tells of the High Seas Fleet weakened in the effort to send out old and new U-boats. He tells of the U-boats becoming ineffective because of the better submarine defense and the loss of experienced U-boat captains. He tells of the plan cherished by German naval leaders, when their government, recognizing the inevitable, was making overtures for peace, of sending out the High Seas Fleet to give battle. Theirs was a forlorn and desperate hope, but not even the glory of dying in battle was granted them. When orders were given to get under way, October 29, 1918, the fleet mutinied. And the disaffection spread with great rapidity throughout northern Germany.

The end came quickly, for German morale had crumbled. The tireless American destroyers, yachts, sub-chasers, aeroplanes, and mine-planters, the unending line of men, munitions, and supplies of every kind pouring from America, increasing instead of diminishing, when added to one side of a scale that for months and years had been balancing almost even, were of unquestioned weight in deciding the issue.

---

[7] *Germany's High Seas Fleet in the World War.*

XXX

THE NAVY AND AMERICAN FOREIGN POLICY

ISOLATION ENDED

IF THE United States had an important part in the war, not less was her presence felt in the Peace Congress that met in Paris, January, 1919, to prepare the treaty that should be offered to the defeated Central Powers. President Wilson departed from all tradition by himself going as the head of the American commission, and though he was far from dominating the Congress he did succeed in writing into the treaty the world-famous document known as the Covenant of the League of Nations. The United States for many reasons has not become a member of the League, although in several of its activities, such as have the betterment of social and economic conditions for their aim, our country is actively coöperating. What is especially significant in this is that the American policy of isolation, adhered to for over a century, is ended. Although this country is not disposed to meddle in European politics, it is profoundly interested in the people of the various countries, as has been shown in innumerable ways since the World War.

America, "in getting back to normalcy" (to use a favorite expression of President Harding's), could not return quite to her old way of looking at things. During the war her economic position had changed. The money center of the world had moved from London to New York. The lavish expenditures connected with every phase of military operations had involved the spending of more than one million dollars an hour for the eighteen months we were fighting, and had left us with a national debt amounting to twenty-five billions; yet the total national wealth had greatly increased and savings banks showed how general was the individual prosperity. The United States had developed markets in countries where heretofore England, Germany, or Italy had been the ones chiefly interested. And our manufacturing plants had been enlarged by the war needs to the point where they must look to foreign markets or face large losses. Therefore aside from the humanitarian instinct, which was genuine, we had reason to be interested in the recovery of the war-stricken nations and also in the welfare of others.

The navy similarly in a double service, humanitarian and commercial, has been actively engaged.

There was a stormy period in the Mediterranean before peace was to prevail. Since Rear-Admiral Mark L. Bristol was in command of our forces at Constantinople in August, 1919, when fighting supposedly was over, he was appointed High Commissioner of the United States—a position he filled with such general acceptance he has held it continuously since, now for eight years. His duties have been largely of a diplomatic character. In the early years of this service, having two cruisers and a detachment of destroyers under his command, he was of the greatest assistance to the Red Cross, the Near East Relief, the Food Administration (which rendered aid to starving Russian peasants), and to American commercial enterprises. His command rescued tens of thousands of fugitives fleeing before the Bolsheviks when Wrangel's offensive collapsed in Southern Russia; and it saved no less than 262,000 Greeks and Armenians, when the Greek army routed by the Turks fell back upon Smyrna, and the Christian population in that region was utterly panic stricken. So just and efficient was this naval diplomat's management of affairs that he obtained great influence with the Turks. At the treaty-making conference of Lausanne, 1923, Admiral Bristol was one of the American representatives; and when Turkey and the western powers were unable to agree, it was he who saved the conference from breaking up without result.

The Dawes Commission (1924) was evidence of America's interest in the rapprochement of France and Germany, aiming to save both those countries from economic ruin. Not without significance, however, at that time and since has been the stationing of a naval force in European waters; in the summer it visited ports in northern waters—English, French, Danish, etc.; and in the winter visited ports in the Mediterranean—Spanish, Italian, Greek, Algerian, Egyptian, etc. The duty of the vice-admiral commanding this squadron (at present made up of a light cruiser and destroyers) is, except in case of an emergency, largely diplomatic. His itinerary is made out long in advance and submitted to the State Department for approval. He not only visits the seaports, but often leaving his flagship goes inland to a national capital to represent his country at court or elsewhere. Many times it has happened that the presence of American officers and ships has served to safeguard American lives and property and has been stimulating to our commerce.

THE NAVY AFTER THE WAR

Following the Armistice and the treaty-making conference, there was no longer need of a navy expanded to such enormous proportions: it had reached a total in November, 1918, of nearly one-half million men, about ten times as large as the navy of 1913. Reductions in personnel soon began, and by 1922 there remained only 86,000 enlisted men (the force authorized by Congress), and 20 per cent. less than the 5700 officers required. A service that could expand so rapidly and be efficient, and return to the normal without disintegration shows unusual adaptability.

From the supreme test which war means our forces emerged with increased confidence. It was not merely because of the praise abroad and at home; it was rather because of the consciousness that in the emergency they had done the work, and even where material had been inadequate they had gone ahead, their initiative and resolution largely compensating for what was lacking in equipment.

A quickening of activity and interest was especially felt in the submarines and airships.

The experience of our submarines operating about the Azores and the British Isles showed that these little craft, miserably uncomfortable though they were, could keep at sea in all weathers. Also it emphasized the need of large modern submarines. Three " fleet " submarines were authorized in the early period of the war and three more during the later period. When the last of these had been completed in 1925, they constitabuted, with the ninety-three coastal submarines also authorized during the war, a force that compares favorably with that of other navies. The AL-boats sent to Bantry Bay, 1918, were of about 450 gross tons, surface displacement, and had a maximum speed of fourteen knots; the fleet submarines of the V-class are of 2164 tons and have a surface speed of twenty-one knots; their cruising radius is 10,000 miles at eleven knots. As their name implies, they are designed to accompany the fleet; by reason of their speed they can keep up with fast battleships.

There is considerable official reticence regarding the submarine service, as its success is largely dependent on surprise. But the exploits of the aeroplane can hardly be other than blazoned in the sky. The naval advance in this field during the ten years following 1917 would in itself fill a volume. We shall attempt scarcely more than to enumerate the outstanding exploits.

It was the United States Navy that made the first flight across the Atlantic. In 1917–1918 among the planes building were some Navy-Curtis (NC) flying boats, of superior size and strength, being designed for war service off the French coast. The Armistice came about as the first was completed. But in May, 1919, three of these NC-boats set out from Far Rockaway, Long Island, for Plymouth, England, their schedule calling for flights, first to Newfoundland, then to the Azores, then to Portugal, and then to England. Sixty destroyers were stationed at intervals between the continents to guide the boats on their course, and to render assistance if needed. Two of the flying boats, lost in the fog when approaching the Azores, alighted in the rough sea, and although their crews reached safety the planes were so damaged that their flight ended there. The *NC-4*, Commander A. C. Read, made the harbor of Horta, in spite of the fog, and in two weeks more had completed without mishap the other jumps, making the whole trip from New York to England in less than seventy-one flight hours.

In 1922–1923 unusual circumstances provided a large number of naval vessels to be scrapped, among them a German dreadnought, several American pre-dreadnoughts, and an American super-dreadnought that had been launched but not entirely completed. These the Government devoted to a series of tests made by the Aviation Service so that they might try their skill in landing bombs on or near the warships, and observe the destructive power of these agents against obsolete and modern types. The results though instructive were not altogether convincing. Certain bombs, it is true, were highly destructive, but though the ships were for the most part stationary targets, only a few bombs hit their mark.

What would have resulted if the ships had been under way and had kept the airships at a safe altitude by their anti-aircraft guns was not at all certain.

The record of the *NC-4* was surpassed in 1924 when two U. S. Army planes made a flight around the world, 26,000 miles in 365 flight hours. The navy actively coöperated by sending cruisers and destroyers to various points, establishing bases, giving information about weather conditions, and standing by in case of emergency.

The navy had also become interested in the possibilities of the dirigible. In May, 1923, the *Shenandoah* was launched, 680 feet long, and soon had visited the more important cities of the northeast. In October of the next year she flew to the Pacific and back, crossing the Rockies twice and making a flight of 8100 miles without accident. During the same month the *ZR-3,* 658 feet long, flew to New York from Germany (where she had been built for the United States), and on being rechristened the *Los Angeles* was taken into the navy. In September, 1925, the *Shenandoah,* after having flown 30,000 miles, came to a tragic end. She was caught in a violent squall, which twisted her about and finally tore her apart. The captain, Lieutenant-Commander Zachary Lansdowne, and thirteen of the crew in the stern, crashing to earth, lost their lives. The bow floating on, however, was safely landed by the navigating officer; with him twenty-five of the ship's company with an army observer were saved.

At the time that the *Shenandoah* was making her ill-fated trip, the airplane *PN-9 No. 1,* Commander John Rodgers, was being searched for on the wide Pacific. She had left San Francisco for a flight of 2100 miles to Hawaii. Again destroyers and tenders were stationed at intervals along the route. All went well for 1700 miles, when the gasoline was exhausted and the air men entirely missed the tender from which they thought to refuel. So suddenly did their power give out that they did not have opportunity to radio a message informing the watchers of their position and plight. For nine days they drifted, or crept along under such kind of rig as they could extemporize. After thus cruising 400 miles they made the island of Kauai. When ten miles from its dangerous coast they were sighted by a patrolling submarine, which towed them in.

The last flight which we shall mention was that of Lieutenant-Commander Richard E. Byrd, U. S. Navy (Ret.), in 1926, from Kings Bay, Spitzbergen, to the North Pole. The fact that two other aeronautic expeditions were aiming that spring for the same goal and that the veteran Norwegian explorer Amundsen was in charge of one of them, also based on Kings Bay, gave additional excitement as of a race. It was at 12.30 A.M. on the ninth of May that Lieutenant-Commander Byrd with one companion rose from the ground and laid his course for the Pole. All went well until he was within an hour of it, when he detected an oil leak in the tank connected with the right-hand motor. The idea was suggested of landing on their skiis to make repairs. But Byrd was opposed to this, fearing that if they landed on the rough ice, they would never rise again. Next they considered turning back. Instead, Byrd decided to take the chances and push on to the Pole. This they flew over at 9.02 A.M., Greenwich time. After going a few miles beyond they circled about, gazing down on the great expanse of ribbed ice that stretched in every direction. After taking some still and motion pictures of the scene, they headed for Kings Bay again. Fortunately the oil, being of a heavy type, flowed slowly so that the motor connected with the leaking tank was still running smoothly as they returned to their base. They had made a total flight of 1545 statute miles. As Doctor Grosvenor, President of the National Geographic Society remarked, Peary in the conquest of the Pole was absent from civilization 400 days; Byrd left his friends in the morning and returned in the evening.

The most sweeping change in naval policy since the war consists in the maintenance of both an Atlantic and a Pacific Fleet. The importance of having a force in the Pacific had been recognized by Roosevelt, and he had sent the so-called Battle Fleet to California and then around the world. But a division of the fleet at that time was not regarded with favor by naval strategists because of the weakness that would exist for either part that could not quickly be supported by the other. The stationing of a fleet on both coasts was made practicable, however, by the construction of the Panama Canal, long urged by Mahan, and not less important for unified naval protection than for the extension of commerce. The two fleets are now frequently merged into one for extensive maneuvers.

A marked trend in this period, closely related to naval policy, is to be found in the emphasis placed on the education of officers and enlisted men; the Naval War College, the Naval Postgraduate School, the Naval Academy, the special schools, the courses organized for reserve officers in selected universities, and the courses offered to enlisted men on board ship and at shore stations, have all taken on a new importance.

The American Merchant Marine

One of the lessons brought home by the war was that a merchant marine is an extremely important auxiliary to the navy. Our shipping during the latter part of the nineteenth century and the early twentieth had suffered a sad decline. Although our foreign trade had enormously increased from 1880 to 1914, our vessels engaged in this had actually decreased. "One and one-quarter million tons were registered for the foreign trade in 1880, while only a little over a million tons were so registered in 1914." [1] In the World War America had to have ships if she was going to do her part; besides, shipping then was profitable. With the gigantic shipbuilding program of the Emergency Fleet Corporation, there was launched in 1919 over three and a half million tons. By this great effort we had that year a merchant marine second only to that of Great Britain and considerably larger than Germany's had ever been. What the United States had registered for foreign trade was nearly ten times what she had similarly registered, June 30, 1914.

We finally had a merchant marine, but when peace came and all the countries attempted to restore their old time carrying trade, our economists discovered that since production had long been decreased there were not more than two-thirds of the cargoes to be transported; also that operating costs had increased threefold. This meant that ships sailed without full cargoes; as a result, freight rates, which had been towering, came down with a crash. The Shipping Board sought to sell its ships to American purchasers, but many companies, organized at this time to purchase or build steamships, were confronted with failure. In consequence the Shipping Board has been obliged to continue operating a considerable number of its ships, though the policy of the Government is that as opportunity offers they shall be transferred to private ownership.

The best statement of the national policy in regard to our shipping was that formulated by Congress in the Merchant Marine Act of 1920:

---

[1] Herrick, *History of Commerce and Industry*, p. 537.

"That it is necessary for the national defense and for the proper growth of its foreign and domestic commerce that the United States shall have a merchant marine of the best equipped and most suitable types of vessels sufficient to carry the greater portion of its commerce and serve as a naval or military auxiliary in time of war or national emergency, ultimately to be owned and operated privately by citizens of the United States; and it is hereby declared to be the policy of the United States to do whatever may be necessary to develop and encourage the maintenance of such a merchant marine."

We still have a large merchant marine, but the part of it that is engaged in foreign trade is obliged to contend with unfavorable economic conditions such as proved a heavy handicap at the beginning of the century. In competition with the lower cost of building in foreign countries and still more the lower operating expenses when the ships sail under foreign flags, American mercantile companies find it hard to secure a return on their investment. An exception is found in the coast trade between American ports and the trade on the Great Lakes. By law, only American shipping may participate; so there is no competition.

Then how shall a way be found to maintain our foreign shipping, which is necessary for the extension of American commerce in distant countries and for the highly valued reserve that a merchant marine furnishes for the navy? The problem still awaits a solution.

THE WASHINGTON CONFERENCE

Had the United States Navy completed the building program authorized and begun during the World War, she would have had by 1925 the strongest navy in the world.

But in this competition there was the imposing of burdens which had been found so well nigh intolerable in Europe and which it was hoped the war had shown the folly of. Further, with the clash of interests in the Pacific there were all kinds of prophecies of war between the United States and Japan, in which even England might become involved. Many who were more calm in their analysis, nevertheless, pointed out that we were entering upon the same kind of rivalry as had brought the conflict between the Allies and the Central Powers. It was to avoid all these evils, real and imaginary, that the United States invited the following powers to meet with her at a conference in Washington: the British Empire, France, Italy, Belgium, Holland, Portugal, Japan, and China.

The conference opened on Armistice Day, 1921. Secretary Hughes, who presided, with a directness characteristic of America, at once put his country's proposal before the delegates: it provided that no less than sixty-six capital ships, completed or undergoing construction, in the navies of the five powers, they should scrap, and then take a ten-year naval holiday. To make his proposal specific he proceeded to name the ships that each nation would sacrifice. Thus the tonnage of the United States and Great Britain as the plan was finally elaborated was not to exceed 525,000 each, of Japan 315,000, and of France and Italy 175,000 each. This would reduce their forces to the approximate ratios of 5:5: 3:1¾: 1¾. As one writer remarks of this proposal of Hughes, "He destroyed more British vessels in five minutes than the German navy had done in any battle of the war." [2]

However, the United States offered to scrap more of

---

[2] Adams, *A History of the Foreign Policy of the United States*, p. 420.

her force than would be required of all the others put together.[3] For a while Japan objected because of the position of inferiority assigned her, but finally assented when the United States agreed not to fortify further any of her possessions in the Orient. As Manila was inadequately fortified, and Guam and the Aleutian Islands not at all, this arrangement placed them, in case of war, virtually at the mercy of Japan. Naturally such an expression of confidence in Japan produced a favorable impression.

Capital ships were to be limited to 35,000 tons displacement and their guns to 16-inch. Guns on other ships were to be limited to 8-inch. Battle cruisers being classed as capital ships, those that the United States had laid down were to be scrapped—except two for which there was the stipulation that they should be converted into aircraft carriers.

Measures were also discussed for the limitation of other types of warships, especially the submarine. But in this little progress was made save that no cruisers beyond 10,000 tons were to be built, and the size of aircraft carriers was restricted.

This agreement, known as the Treaty for the Limitation of Naval Armament was later ratified by the five powers concerned, and is to continue until the end of 1936, after which it may terminate when any of the powers has given two years' notice.

Of not less significance in fostering peace was a second

---

[3] The total tonnage of new capital ships to be scrapped (in various stages of completion, but not including paper programs) was as follows: United States 618,000 tons; Great Britain 172,000 tons; Japan 289,100 tons. *67th Congress, 2d Session: Senate Documents,* vol. x, p. 797.

compact between the United States, the British Empire, France, and Japan, known as the Four-Power Treaty, in which they covenanted each to respect the others' rights in their insular possessions in the Pacific, and agreed further that, if there should arise a question concerning them which could not be settled by diplomacy, they should invite the four powers to a conference and refer the question to them for consideration and adjustment.

Also of great importance to the United States was the Nine-Power Treaty relating to China—which the conference framed and which was later ratified. In this the powers agreed "to respect the sovereignty, the independence, and the territorial and administrative integrity of China;" also to apply "more effectually the principle of the Open Door or equality of opportunity in China for the trade and industry of all nations."[4] Thus England gave up Wei-Hai-Wei and Japan agreed to yield Shantung if China would reimburse her for what she had spent on its railways.

Undeniably the United States had made this conference a success by coming forward and, without pressure, offering such large concessions. Many people grieved for the battleships and battle cruisers that we thus surrendered, and others were indignant that we had denied ourselves the means of protecting our possessions in the East. But, as certain ones who took the opposite view pointed out, by this conference the two-power treaty between Great Britain and Japan was ended; suspicion between the United States and Japan was at least for the time being largely removed; and the principle of the Open Door in China was accepted by nine of the great

---

[4] For the text of these treaties, see *67th Congress, 2d Session: Senate Documents*, vol. x.

nations. The price was large, but the return, it is hoped, will be commensurate.

THE NAVY IN THE ORIENT

The history of China during the last forty years is increasingly complex, on account of the politics injected by the western powers and the quick changes in the Chinese themselves.

That China is a part now of the modern world is shown by the fact that the unrest and unsettled conditions which, with Russia as a nucleus, spread through all Europe, touching America and gaining a foothold in Japan and the Philippines, should have gripped eastern China with a terrific intensity. Chinese students to the number of hundreds of thousands have become tremendously interested in politics and they are closely following the affairs of western nations. Merchants have developed a new solidarity and are uniting in chambers of commerce. There has been an enormous increase in the number of newspapers, magazines, and periodicals of all kinds, and some of them are exercising sane and constructive leadership.[5] A single spoken as well as written language is being taught in private schools throughout the country.[6] Young men are showing a disposition to arrange their own marriages, being guided by love instead of allowing their parents to negotiate the affair. This radical tendency has shocked conservative parents and implies a wide departure from age-old tradition. Millions imbued with an idea of nationalism have resented the slowness of the powers in reforming the tariff (to which the powers had pledged themselves in one of the treaties drawn up at the

---

[5] Article in Peking *Leader*, quoted in the *Living Age*, February 15, 1927.

[6] *Ibid.*

Washington Conference); they have been an easy prey for the Soviet emissaries busily working among them; and they have openly attacked the exploitation of China by Japan and the western powers.

What the outcome may be is uncertain; how far it has extended into central and western China is a matter of conjecture; but it seems to be scarcely less than revolution for the people whom it has affected.

In consequence banditry has been widespread, and the most important provinces have all suffered from spasmodic outbreaks, at times rising to the proportions of civil war.

The United States might withdraw but this would plunge the people deeper in misery, and as other powers would not follow, China would become indeed a prey. Since she has great fertility of soil, rich mineral and coal resources, and a vast population inured to labor, there are untold possibilities in China.

If the United States does not withdraw there is work for her navy in carrying out the traditional policy, lately reaffirmed in the Nine-Power Treaty.

The navy has ever been active in humanitarian service. Thus when Japan in 1923 was visited with a destructive earthquake, an American destroyer division rushed hospital supplies and every possible relief to Tokyo, Yokohama, and Kobe. When Chinese forces in their foolish fighting were about to shell a large and populous city, the commander of an American gunboat on the Yangtze brought the leaders of the opposing forces together under a truce, and prevented the disaster.[7] Many times on the occasion of famine or floods the navy has given aid.

The Yangtze Patrol has received especial attention of late, and is so important that in 1921 a flag-officer was

---

[7] *Report of the Secretary of the Navy*, 1923, p. 15.

given command of it.[8] It is based on Hankow, 700 miles from the mouth of the Yangtze. This great river, navigable for 1750 miles, floats about 59 per cent. of China's commerce, and reaches over one-half of the population of 159,000,000 included in the provinces bordering upon it. When one considers that in 1920 the United States exported to China merchandise to the extent of $119,000,000 and imported $227,000,000, and that at least one-half of this was handled via the Yangtze, one will realize how important are the little American gunboats that patrol up and down its long course.[9]

But what of the Nationalist uprising of the spring of 1927 that in the brief interval since the preceding pages were written, has spread so swiftly? It is difficult to appraise the events of yesterday and still more to announce those of to-morrow. Merchants and missionaries have been obliged to flee from the provinces bordering on the Yangtze and also from the country to the south and to the north. It is to be noted, however, that when they have come within the reach of American gunboats and destroyers safety has been assured. The outlook for American interests in China is uncertain, but it is already plain that the presence of our naval forces and marines, with those of the European powers, tends to exert a stabilizing influence and has saved thousands of lives.

THE NAVY AND LATIN AMERICA

Although as early as colonial times the West Indies attracted American traders by rum, molasses, and slaves, not until after the Spanish-American War was Latin

---

[8] *Report of the Secretary of the Navy,* 1922, p. 5.
[9] *Ibid.*

The Navy and Latin America 527

America, with all her richness, known to more than a small proportion of our people. The departure of Spain from Cuba and Porto Rico was the signal for a rush of investors to those islands. To a lesser degree the same has in later years been going on in neighboring islands; the guarantee of good order resulting from a treaty and temporary occupation by the United States has greatly stimulated confidence in the countries concerned.[10]

An area two and three-fifths times that of the United States has less than two-thirds her population. Lying much of it in the tropics and being unusually fertile, it promises to become one of the greatest food granaries in the world. Trade of Latin America with the United States has increased enormously so that now it absorbs 18.5 per cent. of the total yearly exports of this country. During the last twenty years, people of the United States have invested in Latin America no less than $4,210,000,000.[11]

In our relations with Latin America three large policies have been followed, and they have governed the operations of the Department of the Navy as well as of State:

1. *Monroe Doctrine.*—"The Americas are controlled politically by Americans only—Americans north and south in the large meaning of the term."

2. *Caribbean Policy.*—"The policing of that important region, keeping the peace, encouraging the maintenance of order, and seeking constructively to build up higher standards in those matters that make national life worth while."

3. *Pan-Americanism.*—"The fraternal relationship

---

[10] Jones, *Caribbean Interests of the United States*, p. 11.

[11] Barreda, "Latin America's Opposition to the New Monroeism," *Current History*, vol. xxv, p. 810.

of all American nations from Cape Horn to the
North Pole." [12]

All of these have been greatly stimulated by the construction of the Panama Canal. Indeed no other one event has had so great an influence in bringing the United States into close relations with Latin America. The Canal has developed a great trade route for us through the Caribbean, which now has become more important than it has been at any time since the palmy days of the Spanish Empire. This sea is second only to the Mediterranean, with which in position it closely corresponds. The Canal is the center of traffic in the American tropics, and in connection with safeguarding it the United States is vitally interested in the welfare of the islands and the countries of Central and northern South America. Thus their health and sanitation have a new significance, and the avoidance of troubles that might invite foreign occupation is essential. European powers are still interested, and competition for their markets is likely to become keener and keener.[13] Furthermore, Washington recognizes a certain responsibility in protecting American commercial enterprise which, following the trade route, has entered these countries.

We will consider how these three policies have been applied in the twentieth century.

The Monroe Doctrine only once during this period has been more than remotely threatened. This was in 1902, when Germany making an occasion out of the financial obligations of a bad debtor was about to resort to military occupation in Venezuela. Roosevelt promptly informed the Kaiser through the German ambassador that the whole American Atlantic Fleet under Admiral Dewey would sail for Venezuela to prevent the landing

---

[12] Dealey, *Foreign Policies of the United States*, p. 360.
[13] Jones, *Caribbean Interests of the United States*, p. 7.

The Navy and Latin America 529

of his forces unless Germany agreed within forty-eight hours to arbitrate the dispute over the debts—the course already urged by our State Department. The Kaiser thereupon offered to arbitrate, and Roosevelt tactfully praised him for his peaceful intentions.[14]

Policing the Caribbean has involved us in many perplexities. Regularly, some factions in the country concerned have felt that their independence was not respected, and other countries have regarded us with suspicion. The Dominican Republic, becoming more and more involved financially and feeling the pressure of several leading European powers, finally in 1905 turned to the United States for assistance. Roosevelt at once drew up a "protocol" by which the United States should send an officer to take charge of their customs. This officer administering their finances was to reserve 55 per cent. for the funding of the public debt and turn over to the people 45 per cent. for their government. When the United States Senate regarded this as a treaty and refused to ratify it, the determined President still held to the arrangement, calling it a *modus vivendi*. Within two years the public debt had been considerably diminished, and the Dominican government, profiting from honesty and stability in its finances, had more money for public purposes than ever before. Then the Senate, persuaded of the practicability of the plan, sanctioned it. All went well until a revolution was imminent, when the United States to carry out the provision for preventing the customs houses from being looted and the finances wrecked landed blue jackets and marines (1916). The Dominican government, such as there was, objecting to this, there followed a military administration by Captain Harry

---

[14] Adams, *A History of the Foreign Policy of the United States*, p. 292.

S. Knapp, U. S. Navy, which continued under him and others for eight years. It brought progress such as the Dominicans had never known before. It built 500 miles of macadamized national highways, modernized the port of Santo Domingo and improved others, taught sanitation, constructed hospitals, established schools and provided means of securing educated teachers (increasing within four years the enrolment of school children from 18,000 to over 100,000), encouraged industries of all kinds, and finally led the way to the election and placing in power of a native government.[15] When this had been accomplished, the American troops were withdrawn (1924). The financial supervision still continues.

What happened in the Dominican Republic has its counterpart in Haiti, the western end of the island. In 1915 internal affairs in that country were such that European intervention for some time had been imminent. The president after having murdered over 100 political prisoners was himself put to death in a shocking manner before the French legation, where he had fled for refuge. To rescue the country from chaos, Rear-Admiral Caperton landed at Port au Prince with a force of seamen and marines. A new president on being elected coöperated with the United States in the establishing of peace. He negotiated a treaty, ratified in 1916, that makes that country for twenty years a political and fiscal protectorate of the United States.[16] Although he organized a military government he was quick to coöperate with the civil government. As soon as conditions warranted it, more and more authority was given to the

---

[15] See report of military governor Admiral Thomas Snowden, included in the *Report of the Secretary of the Navy*, 1920, pp. 321-342.

[16] Latane, *The United States and Latin America*, p. 289.

latter, until now the marines are concentrated at two points—Port au Prince and Cape Haytien, where they are available to protect the government and to insure the continuance of the financial supervision.

In Nicaragua the United States similarly landed marines at a time of revolution to protect important American interests. In 1916 there was concluded the Bryan-Chamorro Treaty, according to which in return for $3,000,000 Nicaragua gave to the United States the right to the San Juan River as a canal route and permission for establishing a naval base in the Gulf of Fonseca to protect the western end of the canal when constructed. Conditions in Nicaragua have not been stable and a guard of marines has been kept at the capital, Managua, and a warship at Corinto, almost continuously since 1912.

In attempting to adhere to her third policy, Pan-Americanism, the United States has not had an easy course. The Central American Union (comprising the five republics of Central America) our country has held to with some resolution, but revolutions coming often break its members apart. There is no railway running the length of Central America and communications are for the most part lacking.[17]

Various nations have at times questioned the motives of the United States in assuming responsibility for the peace and good order of the Caribbean. There is always a liability connected with such a rôle, and what other government in the western hemisphere could or would look out for the small countries when involved in difficulties among their own people or with the strong powers of Europe?

Some other method may in time be found, but at

---

[17] Adams, *A History of the Foreign Policy of the United States*, p. 305.

present it would seem that the United States must keep the Caribbean in order, or the Monroe Doctrine goes by the board and the islands and Central American republics are open for exploitation.[18]

To return, however, to Pan-Americanism, the United States has persistently advocated the principle, both in Washington and elsewhere contributing generously to its work. In recent years our country has coöperated with Brazil and Peru by sending a naval mission to each, not to urge those countries to build more ships, but to show them the highest standards of naval efficiency and to point the way towards getting the most from what they have. Perhaps our fleets in the future may visit more often the ports of Argentine, Brazil, Chile, and Peru.

---

[18] The following solution, remote though its realization may appear, breathes a lofty idealism:

"In the great movement for world peace, the special duty of the United States would therefore seem to be this most difficult, though inspiring, task of helping to bring into harmony the Pan-American nations. If we labor whole-heartedly to foster like conceptions of rights and duties, and identic economic interests and ·sympathies, then may we decide in common those large questions of mutual concern which are now left to the separate diplomatic negotiations and agreements of the several American nations. Then may we constitute a genuine American legislative assembly. Then may we lay the solid foundations of unity, on the sound basis of law. Then may we look forward with justifiable optimism to the speedy establishment of an American International Supreme Court of Justice, maintained by an adequate sanction and thus worthy of all respect. But these magnificent projects will not be accomplished merely through a realization of their desirability or of their feasibility. 'The substitution of law for war' is a painfully slow process. It is to be done by 'doing the work that's nearest,' and the 'work that's nearest' for us is the splendid task of converting Pan-American Union into Pan-American Unity, based on positive law and true justice." Brown, *International Realities*, pp. 172, 173.

Where our warships have carried the flag, respect for our government has followed, American commerce has been stimulated, and new bonds of friendship have been cemented. The officers of our navy have been guided by the traditions of the service, and, though not themselves formulating American policy, have rendered indispensable service in intelligently interpreting it and humanely carrying it out.

AUTHORITIES

This list includes the most important sources consulted, together with some general works that will be found of special help to the student who wishes to pursue the subject further.

BIBLIOGRAPHIES

R. W. NEESER, *Statistical and Chronological History of the United States Navy, 1775–1907*. 1909 to date (in progress). Vols. I–II.

C. T. HARBECK, *A Contribution to the Bibliography of the History of the United States Navy.* 1906.

J. N. LARNED, *History for Ready Reference.* 1894–1901. 6 v.

Excellent bibliographies of a general character will be found in the several volumes of *The American Nation*, edited by A. B. Hart.

GENERAL

W. O. STEVENS and A. WESTCOTT, *A History of Sea Power.* 1920.

H. F. KRAFFT and W. B. NORRIS, *Sea Power in American History.* 1920.

E. S. MACLAY, *A History of the United States Navy.* 1901. 3 v.

J. R. SPEARS, *The History of Our Navy.* 1897–99. 5 v.

J. F. COOPER, *The History of the Navy of the United States of America.* 1839. 2 v.

G. F. EMMONS, *The Navy of the United States, 1775–1853.* 1852. A careful compilation of statistics.

The American Nation: a History. Edited by A. B. Hart. 1904–18. 28 v.

THE REVOLUTION

The Annual Register (*Dodsley's Annual Register*), 1758 to date (in progress). Published in London; state papers of various kinds.

FRANCIS WHARTON, *The Revolutionary Diplomatic Correspondence of the United States.* 1889. 6 v.

C. O. PAULLIN, *The Navy of the American Revolution.* 1906. Deals largely with the administrative side of the early navy.

MRS. REGINALD DE KOVEN, *Life and Letters of John Paul Jones.* 2v. 1913. An intensely interesting biography of the great leader.

John Paul Jones Commemoration. Edited by C. W. Stewart. 1907.

J. H. SHERBURNE, *Life and Character of the Chevalier John Paul Jones.* 1825.

JOHN FISKE, *The American Revolution.* 1898. 2v.

WARS WITH FRANCE AND THE BARBARY STATES

The United States' Naval Chronicle. Edited by C. W. Goldsborough. 1824. 2 v. Contains official reports and letters relating to the navy between the Revolution and the War of 1812.

G. W. ALLEN, *Our Naval War with France.* 1909.

G. W. ALLEN, *Our Navy and the Barbary Corsairs.* 1905.

The Autobiography of Commodore Charles Morris. 1880.

A. S. MACKENZIE, *Life of Stephen Decatur.* 1846.

D. D. PORTER, *Memoir of Commodore David Porter.* 1875.

WAR OF 1812

Niles's Weekly Register, 1811–1849. 75 v. A weekly, published in Baltimore, containing official reports and other contemporary matter.

The Naval Chronicle, 1799–1818 (London). 40 v. Contains British reports, court-martial proceedings, etc.

The Naval Monument. Edited by Abel Bowen. 1816. Also contains official reports.

WILLIAM JAMES, *The Naval History of Great Britain.* 1878. 6 v. (Originally published 1822–24.)

WILLIAM JAMES, *Naval Occurrences in the Late War Between Great Britain and the United States of America.* 1817. "Seriously marred by the bitterest controversial and partisan spirit." (Babcock.)

A. T. MAHAN, *Sea Power in its Relations to the War of 1812.* 1905. 2 v. Unquestionably the best work on the war.

THEODORE ROOSEVELT, *The Naval War of 1812.* 1882. Next to Mahan's, the most reliable and scientific treatment of this subject.

The Royal Navy. Edited by W. L. Clowes. 1897. 7 v. A

valuable collection of articles on the history of the British Navy. Among the American contributors are Mahan and Roosevelt.

I. N. HOLLIS, *The Frigate Constitution.* 1900.

SAMUEL LEECH, *Thirty Years from Home.* 1843. Contains a vivid narrative of the battle between the *United States* and the *Macedonian*, the author being an English lad in the *Macedonian's* crew.

ALBERT GLEAVES, *James Lawrence.* 1904. The work which exposed the myths surrounding the loss of the *Chesapeake*.

J. F. COOPER, *Lives of Distinguished American Naval Officers.* 1846. 2 v.

See also biographies of Decatur, Morris, and Porter, already mentioned, and the biography of Farragut mentioned in connection with the Civil War.

SUPPRESSION OF WEST INDIAN PIRACY, SLAVE TRADE, MUTINY ON THE SOMERS, ETC.

A. H. FOOTE, *Africa and the American Flag.* 1854.

J. R. SPEARS, *The American Slave Trade.* 1900.

Proceedings of the Naval Court-Martial in the Case of A. S. Mackenzie, etc. Edited by J. F. Cooper. 1844. A complete record of the court-martial, to which is added the criticisms of the editor on the conduct of Commander Mackenzie.

PARK BENJAMIN, *The United States Naval Academy.* 1900. This contains also an excellent treatment of the mutiny on the *Somers*.

See also biographies of Farragut and Porter.

MEXICAN WAR

Annual Reports of the Secretary of the Navy.

H. H. BANCROFT, *History of California.* 1884-90. 7 v.

See biographies of Farragut and David D. Porter.

PERRY'S EXPEDITION TO JAPAN

Narrative of the Expedition of an American Squadron to the China Seas and Japan. 1856. 3 v. This was published by order of Congress and was compiled from original notes and journals of Commodore Perry and his officers, under his supervision. The first volume, by Francis L. Hawks, contains the material of chief interest.

W. E. GRIFFIS, *Matthew Calbraith Perry.* 1887.

C. O. PAULLIN, *Diplomatic Negotiations of American Naval Officers, 1778–1883.* 1912. Contains an excellent account not only of the service of Commodore Perry in Japan but also of Commodore Kearney in China, and Commodore Shufeldt in Korea.

CIVIL WAR

Of the first importance, together with the *Reports of the Secretary of the Navy*, are the two following works:

Official Records of the Union and Confederate Navies in the War of the Rebellion. 1894–1922. Vols. 1–30.

Official Records of the Union and Confederate Armies. 1880–1902. 128 v.

Battles and Leaders of the Civil War. 4 v. 1884–87. Narratives by the Union and Confederate officers, of great interest and value.

Also of importance are many of the papers read before the Loyal Legion and various other societies of veterans.

D. D. PORTER, *The Naval History of the Civil War.* 1886.

J. T. SCHARF, *History of the Confederate States Navy.* 1887.

Rear Admiral Du Pont, Official Dispatches and Letters of. 1883.

LOYALL FARRAGUT, *The Life of David Glasgow Farragut.* 1879.

A. T. MAHAN, *Admiral Farragut.* 1892.

J. R. SOLEY, *Admiral Porter.* 1903.

W. C. CHURCH, *The Life of John Ericsson.* 1891. 2 v.

J. M. HOPPIN, *Life of Andrew Hull Foote.* 1874

GIDEON WELLES, *The Diary of.* 3 v. 1911.

J. G. NICOLAY and JOHN HAY, *Abraham Lincoln, a History.* 1890. 10 v.

J. M. ELLICOTT, *The Life of John Ancrum Winslow.* 1902.

RAPHAEL SEMMES, *Memoirs of Service Afloat.* 1869.

ARTHUR SINCLAIR, *Two Years on the Alabama.* 1896.

U. S. GRANT, *Personal Memoirs.* 1885–86. 2 v. Chapters 20–22 and 31–39 relate to the combined movements of the army and navy against Forts Henry and Donelson and against Vicksburg.

HENRY WALKE, *Naval Scenes and Reminiscences of the Civil War.* 1877. As commander of the *Carondelet*, the author had part in the most stirring scenes on the Western rivers.

C. S. ALDEN, *George Hamilton Perkins, Commodore, U. S. N., His Life and Letters.* 1914. The letters by a young officer who took a distinguished part in the battles of New Orleans and Mobile Bay give a vivid picture of those engagements.

J. WILKINSON, *The Narrative of a Blockade-Runner.* 1877. The account of a captain in the Confederate Navy, highly successful in eluding the blockade.

W. H. PARKER, *Recollections of a Naval Officer, 1841–1865.* 1883.

DANIEL AMMEN, *The Atlantic Coast.* 1883.

A. T. MAHAN, *The Gulf and Inland Waters.* 1883.

A. T. MAHAN, *From Sail to Steam.* 1907.

J. R. SOLEY, *The Blockade and the Cruisers.* 1883.

H. W. WILSON, *Ironclads in Action.* 1896. 2 v.

J. S. BARNES, *Submarine Warfare.* 1869. An account by a Union officer of the torpedoes, torpedo-boats, and submarines used during the war.

J. F. RHODES, *History of the United States from 1850.* 1893–1906. 7 v.

B. J. LOSSING, *Pictorial History of the Civil War.* 1866. 3 v.

T. L. HARRIS, *The Trent Affair.* 1896. A careful and exhaustive study.

MOUNTAGUE BERNARD, *A Historical Account of the Neutrality of Great Britain During the American Civil War.* 1870.

J. W. H. PORTER, *A Record of Events in Norfolk County.* 1892. Interesting data on the construction of the ironclad *Merrimac.*

F. M. BENNETT, *The Monitor and the Navy Under Steam.* 1900.

D. B. PHILLIPS, *The Career of the Ironclad Virginia.* (In *Virginia Historical Collection,* vol. 6.)

CHARLES MARTIN, *Personal Reminiscences of the Monitor and Merrimac Engagement.* 1886.

T. O. SELFRIDGE, JR., *The Story of the Cumberland.* (Published for the Military Historical Society of Massachusetts. 1902.)

I. N. STILES, *The Merrimac and the Monitor.* (In *Military Essays and Recollections.* 1891.)

Senate Report, No. 37, 37th Cong., 2d Sess. By Sen. Hale on the surrender of the navy yards at Pensacola and Norfolk.

House Report, No. 1725, 48th Cong., 1st Sess. (in vol. 6). Relating to the U. S. S. *Monitor.*

F. A. PARKER, *The Battle of Mobile Bay.* 1878.

THE NAVY AFTER THE CIVIL WAR

Annual Reports of the Secretary of the Navy.

CHARLES MORRIS, *The Nation's Navy.* 1898.

J. D. LONG, *The New American Navy.* 1903. 2 v.

Authorities

G. W. MELVILLE, *In the Lena Delta*. 1885. A personal narrative of the chief engineer of the *Jeannette* Expedition.
The Voyage of the Jeannette. 1884. 2 v. DeLong's journal, edited by his wife, Emma DeLong.
A. W. GREELY, *Handbook of Polar Discoveries*. 1906.
W. S. SCHLEY and J. R. SOLEY, *The Rescue of Greely*. 1885.
R. E. PEARY, *Nearest the Pole*. 1907.
R. E. PEARY, *The North Pole*. 1910.
FRANKLIN MATTHEWS, *With the Battle Fleet*. 1908.
FRANKLIN MATTHEWS, *Back to Hampton Roads*. 1909.

THE WAR WITH SPAIN

Annual Reports of the Secretary of the Navy.
F. E. CHADWICK, *The Relations of the United States and Spain*. 2 v. 1911. The most authoritative work on the Spanish-American War.
J. F. RHODES, *The McKinley and Roosevelt Administrations*. 1923. A scholarly work.
W. A. M. GOODE, *With Sampson Through the War*. 1899.
A. T. MAHAN, *Lessons of the War with Spain and Other Articles*. 1899.
The Naval Annual. Edited by F. A. Brassey. 1893 to date (in progress). A reliable authority on naval statistics.
H. W. WILSON, *The Downfall of Spain*. 1900. An able work, non-partisan in character, written by an Englishman.
R. H. TITHERINGTON, *A History of the Spanish-American War of 1898*. 1900.
Office of Naval Intelligence. Notes on the Spanish-American War. 1900. Contains comments by Spanish, German, and American officers on the war.

THE WORLD WAR

Annual Reports of the Secretary of the Navy
W. S. SIMS and B. J. HENDRICK, *The Victory at Sea*. 1920. A general account of the war. Admiral Sims, directing American naval affairs from the London office, was most intimately in touch with the large operations.
ALBERT GLEAVES, *A History of the Transport Service*. 1921. An authoritative account by the one in charge of the transport service.

C. S. ALDEN and RALPH EARLE, *Makers of Naval Tradition.* 1925. Chap. XIV, on the World War, by Admiral Earle, is significant as written by the Chief of the Bureau of Ordnance, who was responsible for the Northern Mine Barrage and the Mounted Naval Railway Batteries.

E. V. IZAC, *The Prisoner of the U-90.* 1919. A vivid account of the experience of an American lieutenant who was on the President Lincoln when torpedoed. Unfortunately out of print.

REINHARD SCHEER, *Germany's High Sea Fleet in the World War.* 1920. Gives the other side.

A. P. F. VON TIRPITZ, *My Memories.* 2 v. 1919.

THE NAVY AND FOREIGN AFFAIRS

R. G. ADAMS, *A History of the Foreign Policy of the United States.* 1924.

J. Q. DEALEY, *Foreign Policies of the United States.* 1926.

C. L. JONES, *Caribbean Interests of the United States.* 1916.

J. H. LATANE, *United States and Latin America.* 1920.

C. A. HERRICK, *History of Commerce and Industry.* 1920.

P. M. BROWN, *International Realities.* 1917.

Senate Documents, 67th Congress, 2d Session, 1921–1922. v. 10. Official report of the Washington Conference.

INDEX

A

Act for the Better Government of the Navy, 60
Adams, Capt., 230, 231
Adams, Minister, 371
Adams, 68
Aeolus, 102, 106
Aeroplane, early beginnings, 481; trans-Atlantic flight, 515 ff.
Africa, 102
Agrippina, 371, 374
Aguinaldo, 434.
AL-boats, 501–503.
Alabama, hunted by the *Wyoming*, 365; cruise of, 371 ff.; map of cruise, 373; engages the *Kearsarge*, 376 ff.; diagram of action, 381; the controversy, 383 ff.; claims, 387.
Albatross passes Port Hudson, 327.
Albatross and the Fisheries Commission, 425
Albemarle, 350 ff.
Albemarle Sound, operations on, 348 ff.; and Pamlico Sound, map of, 349.
Alden, James, sent to Norfolk, 257; battle of Mobile Bay, 334, 336.
Alert, captures the *Lexington*, 19; taken by Barry, 30.
Alert, in Polar expedition, 418.
Alert, in Central American waters, 423.
Alfred, 13, 24.
Algiers, treaty with Spain, 42; treaty with Portugal, 43; treaty with United States, 61; Dey of, makes use of the *George Washington*, 61; encouraged by Great Britain, 203; war with United States, 203–206; treaty with United States, 206.
Alleghany, 203, 204.
Allen, W. H., on the *Chesapeake*, 96; defeated by Maples, 151, 152.
Allen, W. H., Jr., 151, 152.
Alliance, in Jones's fleet, 31 ff.; under Barry, 40; sold, 42.
Almirante Oquendo, 447 ff.
Alphonso XII, 428.
Alwyn, Lt., 114, 131.
America, 39, 42.
Amphitrite, 411, 449.
Amy, 422.
Anderson, Thomas O., 77.
Andrea Doria, 13.
Aquia Creek, 243.
Arbuthnot, James, 158.
Arctic Regions, map of, 417.
Argus, in the Tripolitan War, 84, 88, 89, 91; in Rodgers' squadron, 102, 118; captured by the *Pelican*, 151, 152; injures British commerce, 160.
Ariel, 166, 169.
Arkansas, 324, 325.
Arkansas Post, 326.
Armada, 157.
Arnold, Benedict, 15 ff.
Aroostook, 287.
Arthur, Pres., 409.
Atlanta, British brig, 158.
Atlanta, Confederate ram, 396, 397.
Atlanta, U. S. Crusier, 410.

Atlantic, 177.
Augustin, Gen., 434, 440, 443.
Avon, 157, 158.

B

Bagley, Worth, 459.
Bahama, 371, 372.
Bailey, Capt, 314, 320.
Bainbridge, Joseph, 76.
Bainbridge, Wm., surrenders the *Retaliation*, 53, 54; commands the *George Washington*, 61, 62; commands the *Essex*, 64; loses the *Philadelphia*, 69 ff.; plan for destroying the *Philadelphia*, 76; report of the *Intrepid* disaster, 90; captures the *Java*, 126 ff.; career of, 132; commands squadron for Algiers, 204, 206.
Ballard, Acting Lt., 135.
Baltimore, 435 ff.
Baltimore affair, 53, 54.
Bancroft, George, 218, 219.
Bankhead, J. P., 287.
Banks, Gen., 327.
Barbary States, map of, 63.
Barclay, Robert H., defeated by Perry, 165 ff.
Barclay, Thomas, 43.
Barclay, 177, 178.
Barnard, John G., 243.
Barney, Joshua, 50.
Barron, James, commands the *President*, 64; commands the *Chesapeake*, 96; court-marial of Porter, 209.
Barron, Samuel, commands the *Philadelphia*, 64, 66; courtmarial of Morris, 69; supersedes Preble, 87; relieved, 90.
Barron, Samuel (2d), 244, 377.

Barry, John, commands the *Lexington*, 29, 30, the *Alliance*, 40; appointed captain, 50; commands the *United States*, 51.
Bastard, Capt., 102.
Battle Fleet, cruise of, 473 ff.
Battleships, development of, 478, 479; service in World War, 496 ff.
Bayly, Lewis, 487.
Beagle, 209.
Bear, 416.
Beatty, David, 509.
Belknap, R. R., 505.
Bell, H. H., 313, 314.
Belmont, battle of, 292.
Belvidera, 102.
Benham, A. E. K., 422 ff.
Benson, William S., 500.
Benton, 290.
Berceau, 59.
Beresford, Capt., 149.
Berkeley, Vice-Admiral, 94, 95.
Beauregard, Gen., 393, 394.
Biddle, James, in the *Hornet*, 134; boards the *Frolic*, 147; captures the *Penguin*, 158, 159; service in West Indies, 208; goes to Japan, 226.
Biddle, Nicholas, 13, 29.
Bienville, 247.
Black Rock, 162.
Black Warrior, 426.
Blakely, Johnston, captures the *Reindeer*, 154 ff; captures the *Mary*, 157; sinks the *Avon*, 157 ff.; captures the *Atlanta*, 158.
Blanco, Gen., 427, 434.
Blockade of Southern ports, 241, 242, 388 ff., 404.

Blockade-runner, 390 ff.
Blue, Victor, 498.
Blyth, Samuel, 153.
Board of Admiralty, 12.
Bombshell, 352.
Bonhomme Richard, cruise of, map, 28; captures the *Serapis*, 30 ff.
Bonne Citoyenne, 127, 133, 149.
Boston, frigate, 59, 68.
Boston, cruiser, 375, 410, 435 ff.
Boxer, capture of, 152, 153.
Boxer trouble, 468–471.
Bragg, Gen., 401.
Breaking the line, explanation of the term, 172.
Breese, Lt.-Comdr., 403.
Brilliante, 212.
Bristol, Mark L., 512, 513.
British Navy, during the Revolution, 13; in the War of 1812, 101.
Broke, J. M., 262, 264.
Broke, Philip B. V., chases the *Constitution*, 102 ff.; captures the *Chesapeake*, 135 ff.
Brooklyn, steam sloop, battle below New Orleans, 315 ff.; below Vicksburg, 324; battle of Mobile Bay, 330 ff.
Brooklyn, cruiser, battle of Santiago, 452 ff.
Brown, Surgeon, 385.
Browne, Ralph A., 505.
Brumby, Thomas M., 463.
Buchanan, Franklin, in expedition to Japan, 230, 231; battle of Hampton Roads, 266 ff.; Battle of Mobile Bay, 338 ff.
Buchanan, Pres., 239.
Buckner, Gen., 296.
Budd, Lt., 140, 142.

Buford, Col., 301.
Burgoyne, Gen., 18.
Burnside, Gen., 348, 349.
Burrows Wm. 152 153.
Bush Lt., 113.
Bushnell, David, 355.
Bustamente, Capt., 457.
Butler, Benjamin F., at Hatteras Inlet, 244; New Orleans, 312, 319; Fort Fisher, 399, 400.
Butt., Lt., 281.
Byrd, Richard E., 517.
Byron, Capt., 102.

C

Cabot, 13.
Cairo, 290.
Caldwell, Lt., 87.
Caledonia, captured by Elliott, 162, 164; battle of Lake Erie, 166 ff.
Camara, Admiral, 459.
Cambon, Ambassador, 461.
Campos, Gen., 426.
Cand, Jack, 119.
Canonicus, 399.
Caperton, W. B., 530.
Carden, John S., 118 ff.
Carleton, Guy, 15.
Carleton, Thomas, 17.
Carolina, 198.
Carondelet, building of, 290; attacks Fort Donelson, 297, 298; passes Island No. 10, 303–6; engages the *Arkansas*, 325.
Carronades, explanation of the term, 46.
Casembroot, Capt., 367, 370.
Cassin, Lt., 196.
Castilla, 442.
Catalana, Salvatore, 77.
Cayuga, 314 ff.

Celia, 70, 71.
Ceres, 352.
Cerf, 31 ff:
Cervera, Admiral, 430, 433, 446 ff.
Chads, Lt., 129.
Chandler, Sec., 416.
Charleston, naval operations before, 393–7.
Charleston, building of, 411; sent to Philippines, 444; lost, 464.
Chase, Samuel, 12.
Chauncey, Isaac, 162, 165, 173, 189.
Cherub, engagement with the *Essex*, 178 ff.
Chesapeake, building of, 50; sent to Tripoli, 68; encounter with the *Leopard*, 94, 95; captured by the *Shannon*, 133 ff.; diagram of action, 138.
Chicago, 410.
Chickamauga, 375.
Chickasaw, battle of Mobile Bay, 334, 337, 343–5.
Chicora, 394.
China and the Boxer trouble, 468–471; Nationalist uprising, 524–526.
Chipp, Lt., 415.
Chippewa, 166, 170.
Chub, 192 ff.
Cincinnati, building of, 290; attacks Fort Henry, 294; attacked at Fort Pillow, 308.
Civil War, 238 ff.
Clark, Charles E., 430.
Cleveland, Pres., 421.
Collins, Pilot, 336.
Colonel Lloyd Aspinwall, 426.
Colonial Navy, 9 ff.
Colorado, 399.
Columbia, 259.

Columbiads, 259.
Columbus, in Esek Hopkins' fleet, 13.
Columbus, goes to Japan, 226; destroyed at Norfolk, 259.
Commerce, restrictions on, 96 ff.; growth, 519.
Commodore Hull, 352,
Concas, Capt., 457.
Cone, H. I., 504.
Concord, 435.
Conestoga, building of, 292; goes up the Tennessee, 296; attacks Fort Donelson, 297.
Confiance, captured by Macdonough, 191 ff.
Conger, E. H., 469.
Congress, on Lake Champlain, 17.
Congress, building of, 50; in Rodgers' squadron, 102, 118; sails from Boston, 134; blockaded in Portsmouth, 144.
Congress, destroyed by the *Merrimac*, 265, 268 ff.
Connecticut, 471.
Conner, David, in the action with the *Peacock*, 150; in the Mexican War, 222.
Constellation, building of, 50, 51; captures the *Insurgente*, 55, 56; engages the *Vengeance*, 57, 58; sent to Tripoli. 68, 90; blockaded, 144; sent to Algiers, 204, 205.
Constitution, building of, 50, 51; in the Tripolitan War, 69, 84, 88; chased by British squadron, 102 ff.; captures the *Guerrière*, 109 ff.; diagram of action, 111; captures the *Java*, 126; diagram of action, 128;

blockaded in Boston, 134, 143; captures the *Cyane* and *Levant*, 198, 200, 201; in 1881, 408.
Contee, Lt., 229.
Continental Navy, 15.
Convoy room, 494.
Conyngham, Gustavus, 19 ff.
Cooke, Capt., 350-4.
Cornwallis, Lord, 41.
Corvette, explanation of the term, 46.
Cottineau, Capt., 32.
Cotton Plant, 352.
Countess of Scarborough, captured, 32, 38.
Couronne, 377, 378.
Cox, Acting Lt., 135, 142, 143.
Cox, Capt., 105.
Crane, Lt., 107.
Craney, Lt., 217.
Craven, T. A. M., battle of Mobile Bay, 334 ff.
Craven, T. T., in command of Potomac Flotilla, 243; battle below New Orleans, 315-7.
Craven, T. T., World War, 504.
Cristobal Colon, 447 ff.
Cromwell, Boatswain's Mate, 215, 216.
Croyable, captured, 53.
Cuba, insurrection in, 426 ff.; blockade of, 432, 434, 445, 446; Platt amendment, 475, 476.
Cumberland, saved at Norfolk, 257, 258; sunk by the *Merrimac*, 264-8.
Curtiss, G. H., 481.
Cushing, Wm. B., 354 ff.; diagram of his launch, 357.
Cyane, captured by the *Constitution*, 198, 200, 201.

D

Dacres, James, commands the *Guerrière*, 102; defeated by Hull, 110 ff.; challenge to Rodgers, 116.
Dahlgren, Rear-Admiral, commands South Atlantic squadron, 390; operations before Charleston, 397.
Dahlgren gun, 260.
Dale, Richard, in Mill prison, 19; in engagement with the *Serapis*, 31 ff.; appointed captain, 50; commands the *Ganges*, 52; sent to Tripoli, 64, 66.
Daniel Webster, 368 ff.
Daniels, Josephus, 500.
Dauphin, 42.
Davids. *See* Submarines.
Davidson, Lt., 278, 284.
Davis, Charles H., member of board of operations, 243; at Port Royal, 245; member of board on ironclads, 274; engages fleet at Fort Pillow, 308; moves down the Mississippi, 322.
Davis, John, 77.
Davis, Pres., 388, 389.
Davis, Rear-Admiral, 425.
Davison, Trubee, 503.
Deane, 42.
Dearborn, Gen., 161, 162, 165.
Decatur, James, 86.
Decatur, Stephen (Sr.), 52.
Decatur, Stephen, in the Mediterranean, 69; burns the *Philadelphia*, 76 ff.; gunboat attack on Tripoli, 84 ff.; captures the *Macedonian*, 117 ff.; loses the *President*, 199, 200; expedition to Algiers, 204-6.
Decatur, 110.

Deerhound, 378, 382 ff.
De Grasse, Count, 41.
De Haven, E. J., 413.
Delaware, takes the *Croyable*, 52, 53.
Delaware, destroyed at Norfolk, 259.
Delaware, in World War, 498, 499.
De Long, G. W., 414 ff.
De Sartine, Minister, 30.
Destroyers, American in World War, 486 ff.
Detroit, 115, 162, 174.
Detroit, British brig, destroyed, 162, 164.
Detroit, Barclay's flagship, 166 ff.
Detroit, U. S. cruiser, 423.
Dewey, George, services after battle of Manila, 424; battle of Manila Bay, 435 ff.; prevents German interference, 462, 463; Venezuelan affair, 528.
Dickinson, Capt., 159.
Dolphin, brig, destroyed at Norfolk, 257, 259.
Dolphin, cruiser, 410.
Dominican Republic, 529, 530.
Don Antonio de Ulloa, 441, 442.
Don Juan de Austria, 442.
Dorsey, Midn., 87.
Douglas, Charles, 17.
Downes, Capt., 396.
Downes, John, 178, 182, 186, 205.
Downie, Capt., 191 ff.
Dragon, 280.
Drake, captured by the *Ranger*, 27 ff.
Drayton, Percival, 334, 338, 339, 342.
Dreadnoughts, 478, 479.

Du Pont, Samuel, member of board of operations, 243; captures Port Royal, 244 ff.; commands South Atlantic squadron, 390; operations before Charleston, 393-7.

E

Eads, J. B., 288.
Eagle, sloop, 191.
Eagle, brig, 191 ff.
Earle, Ralph, 505, 507.
Eastport, 296.
Eaton, Wm., 66-8, 91, 92.
Edsall, N. E., 466.
Edward, 29.
Edwin, 204.
Effingham, 29.
Ellet, Lt.-Col., 324, 325.
Elliott, Gilbert, 350.
Elliott, Jesse D., work on Lake Erie, 162 ff.; battle of Lake Erie, 167 ff.; controversy, 169, 171, 172.
Ellis. 354.
Embargoes, in War of 1812, 96-98.
Endymion, 199, 200.
Enlistment, term of, 57, 67.
Enterprise, on Lake Champlain, 17.
Enterprise (2d), cruise in West Indies, 59; sent to Tripoli, 64; captures the *Tripoli*, 65; in second squadron before Tripoli, 68, 69; burning of the *Philadelphia*, 76; bombardment of Tripoli, 84; captures the *Boxer*, 152, 153.
Epervier, captured by the *Peacock*, 153; sent to Algiers, 204; engages the *Mashuda*, 205.

Ericsson, John, 274, 453, 455.
Erie, 223.
Espiegle, 150.
Essex, frigate, sent to Tripoli, 64, 68; in Bainbridge's squadron, 126; cruise of, under Porter, 175 ff.; map of cruise, 181.
Essex, gunboat, attacks Ft. Henry, 294; engages the *Arkansas*, 325.
Essex case, 96, 97.
Essex Junior, 178 ff.
Everard, Capt., 191.
Experiment, 30.

F

Fairfax, D. M., 252.
Fajardo affair, 209, 210.
Fanning, 489, 490.
Farragut, David G., commands the *Barclay*, 178; account of the loss of the *Essex*, 180 ff.; service in West Indies, 208; in Mexican War, 222, 223; joins Davis, 308, 309; captures New Orleans, 310 ff.; at Vicksburg, 322 ff.; passes Port Hudson, 327; victorious at Mobile Bay, 330 ff.; subsequent honors, 347.
Farrand, Comdr., 404.
Finch, 192 ff.
Finnis, Capt., 170.
Firefly, 204.
Flambeau, 204.
Fleet in being, defined, 450.
Florida, 371, 375, 387.
Florida, World War, 498, 499.
Floyd, Gen., 296.
Flusser, Lt., 351, 352.
Fly, 13.

Foote, A. H., and the slave trade, 213; construction of river gunboats, 290; takes Ft. Henry, 293 ff.; attacks Ft. Donelson, 296 ff.; attacks Island No. 10, 299 ff.; moves on Ft. Pillow, 307; relieved by Davis, 308.
Fort Beauregard, 246 ff.
Fort Clark, 244.
Fort Donelson, 296 ff.
Fort Fisher, 398 ff.; plan of second assault, 402.
Fort Gaines, 331 ff.
Fort George, 165.
Fort Hatteras, 244.
Fort Henry, 293 ff.
Fort Jackson, 312 ff.
Fort McAllister, 394, 395.
Fort Morgan, 331 ff.
Fort Pillow, 307, 308.
Fort Powell, 331 ff.
Fort St. Philip, 312 ff.
Fort Walker, 246 ff.
Forton prison, 22.
Foster, Paul F., 502.
Four-Power Treaty, 523.
Fox, Gustavus, made Ass't Secc. of the Navy, 240, 241; plans New Orleans expedition, 310; faith in monitors, 393.
France, alliance with the U. S., 30; war with the U. S., 51 ff.; map of scene of war, 55; treaty of peace with the U. S., 59; World War, 484 ff.
Franklin, Benj., goes to France, 19; commissions Conyngham, 20.
Franklin, Sir John, 412.
Franklin, 68.
Freeman, A. H., 466.

Index

French, assistance of, 41.
French floating batteries, 261.
Frigate, explanation of the term, 46; illustration, 47.
Frigate and sloop actions in War of 1812 (map), 145.
Frolic, defeated by the *Wasp*, 146 ff.
Frolic (2d), 153.
Fullam, Master's Mate, 372, 383.
Fullinwider, S. P., 505.
Fulton, Robt., 355.
Fulton, 261.
Furor, 447, 449, 454.

G

Gaines, 334, 339.
Galena, gunboat, 339.
Galena, ironclad, 274, 387.
Gamble, Lt., 179.
Ganges, 52, 137.
Garfield, Pres., 408, 409.
Gates, Gen., 17.
General Lezo, 442.
General Monk, 40, 41.
General Pike, 192.
George Washington, 61, 68.
Georgia, 371, 375.
Georgiana, 178.
Germantown, 256 ff.
Ghent, treaty of, 198, 201, 202.
Gilmer, J. F., 293, 299.
Gilmore, 304.
Gilmore, Gen., 396.
Glasgow, 14.
Gleaves, Albert, 496.
Gloucester, 453 ff.
Glynn, Comdr., 227.
Goldsborough, Flag-Officer, 348, 349.
Governor Moore, 317, 318.
Grampus, 306.

Granger, Gen., 305.
Grand Fleet, 496 ff.
Grant, U. S., at Belmont, 292, 293; captures Ft. Henry, 293 ff.; captures Ft. Donalson, 296 ff.; at Pittsburgh Landing, 306, 307; at Vicksburg, 326 ff.; at Ft. Fisher, 400.
Graves, Admiral, 10.
Great Lakes, importance in 1812-15, 161 ff.; map of campaigns on, 163.
Greeley, A. W., 416 ff.
Green, Chas., 334.
Greene, S. D., executive officer of the *Monitor*, 277 ff.; commands *Monitor*, 283.
Greenwich, 178.
Greer, J. A., 252.
Gridley, Capt., 439.
Growler (Lake Ontario), 189
Growler (Lake Champlain), 191.
Guanabora, 423.
Guerrière, boards the *Spitfire*, 99; in Broke's squadron, 102; captured by the *Constitution*, 109 ff.
Guerrière (2d), sent against Algiers, 204; captures the *Mashuda*, 205.
Gunnery, at end of 18th century, 48; recent improvement in, 479.
Guns, development after 1812, 259, 260; recent developments in, 479.

H

Haiti, 530, 531.
Halifax, 94, 95.
Halleck, Gen., 293, 307, 324.
Hamet Karamauli, 91 ff.
Hampton Roads, battle of, 255 ff.; map of, 265.

Index 549

Hancock, John, 12.
Hancock, 40.
Hanrahan, David C., 504.
Hardee, Gen., 397.
Harrison, Gen., 171.
Hartford, type of ship, 260; at New Orleans, 312 ff.; up the Mississippi, 323; passes Port Hudson, 327; at Mobile Bay, 330 ff.
Harvard, 447, 449, 455.
Hatteras, 374.
Hatteras Inlet, 243, 244.
Hay, John, 468, 470.
Hayes, Capt., 199.
Hayes, Pres., 407.
Hebert, Gen., 354.
Henley, Midn., 86.
Hermann, Lewis, 76.
Higgins, Samuel, 360, 364.
High Seas Fleet, surrender of, 508, 509.
Higgins, Samuel, 360, 364.
Hillyar, Capt., 181 ff.
Hist, 453, 455.
Hobson, Naval Constructor, 451.
Hoel, Master, 304.
Hoke, Gen., 351, 352.
Holland, John P., 480, 481.
Hope, David, 118, 123, 125.
Hopkins, Esek, 13, 14.
Hopkins, J. B., 13.
Hornet, sloop in Revolutionary Navy, 13.
Hornet, in war with Tripoli, 91; in Rodgers' squadron, 102; in Bainbridge's squadron, 126 ff., 175; blockades the *Bonne Citoyenne*, 133; captures the *Peacock*, 149, 150; captures the *Penguin*, 158, 159, 198; leaves the Mediterranean (1807), 203.

Hotchkiss, 411.
Housatonic, 356.
Howe, Gen., 18.
Howell, Commodore, 446.
Huger, Maj., 250.
Hughes, Charles E., 521.
Hughes, C. F., 498.
Hull, Gen., 161, 162.
Hull, Isaac, exploit at Port Plate, 59; before Tripoli, 69; escapes Broke's squadron, 103 ff.; takes prizes, 109; captures the *Guerrière*, 109 ff.; superiority to Carden in maneuvering, 124.
Humphreys, Joshua, 44.
Hunter, 166 ff.
Hurlbut, Gen., 306.
Hyder Ali, 41.
Hyslop, Gen., 131.

I

Impressment, 53, 54, 93 ff.
Indiana, 411, 433, 452 ff.
Indianola, 328.
Indian troubles and the War of 1812, 98, 99.
Ingram, Lt., 187.
Insurgente, takes the *Retaliation*, 54; captured by the *Constellation*, 55 ff.; loss of, 59, 60.
Intrepid, attack on the *Philadelphia*, 77 ff.; blowing up of, 88 ff.
Iowa, 433, 452 ff.
Iris, 40.
Ironclads, introduction of, 261 ff.
Isherwood, Engineer, 256, 409.
Isla de Cuba, 440 ff.
Isla de Luzon, 441.
Isla de Mindanao, 442.

Island No. 10, captured, 299 ff.; map, 300.
Israel, Lt., 88.
Itasca, 318, 319.
Izard, Gen., 192.
Izard, Ralph, 76.

J

James, Reuben, 86.
Jamestown, 269, 271, 278.
Japan, Perry's expedition to, 225 ff:; map of, 228; treaty with, 236, 365; civil war in, 365 ff.
Jarvis, Midn., 58.
Java, captured by the *Constitution*, 126 ff.
Jeannette expedition, 413 ff.
Jeff Davis, 375.
Jefferson, Pres., 97.
Jersey, 22.
John Adams, 68, 87, 90, 218.
Johnson, Pres., 404.
Johnston, A. S., 298, 306.
Johnston, J. D., 343, 344.
Jones, Catesby, 270 ff.
Jones, Jacob, 146 ff.
Jones, J. P., commissioned lieutenant, 13; early career, 24 ff.; captures the *Drake*, 27 ff.; captures the *Serapis*, 30 ff.; later career, 39, 43; letter to Marine Committee, 419.
Jouett, J. E., 334, 338.

K

Katahdin, 324.
Kate, 393.
Kearny, Brig.-Gen., 221.
Kearny, Lawrence, 226.
Kearsarge, action with the *Alabama*., 376 ff.; diagram, 381.

Kell, Lt., 383, 385, 386.
Kempff, Admiral, 469.
Kennebec, 318, 319, 324.
Kennon, Beverly, 318.
Keokuk, 395.
Keystone State, 394.
Kineo, 319.
Knapp, H. S., 530.
Knowles, Quartermaster, 342.

L

Lackawanna, 338, 342–4.
Lady Prevost, 166, 168.
Lafittes, 207.
Lake Champlain, first battle of, 15 ff.; map, 16; second battle of, 190 ff.; plan of battle, 194.
Lake Erie, battle of, 168 ff.; plan of battle, 169.
Lake Ontario, operations on, 189, 190.
Lamb, Col., 398 ff.
Lambert, Capt., 129 ff.
Lancefield, 368 ff.
Landais, Pierre, 31 ff.
Lang, Jack, 147.
Langdon, John, 26.
Lanrick, 368 ff.
Lansdale, P. V., 466.
Latin America and the United States, 526 ff.
Lawrence, James, at Tripoli, 76 ff.; commands the *Hornet*, 102, 126; commands the *Chesapeake*, 133 ff.; action with the Shannon, 137 ff.; captures the *Peacock*, 149, 150.
Lawrence, 166 ff.
Laws, Alex., 76, 77.
Lay, Engineer, 356.
Lear, Tobias, 90, 91, 203, 204.
Lee, Admiral, 398.

Index 551

Lee, Consul-Gen., 427.
Lee, R. E., 398, 404.
Lee, 10.
Lee, (blockade runner), 392.
Leech, Samuel, 122.
Leopard, 94, 95.
Levant, 198, 200, 201.
Lexington, 19, 29.
Lexington, gunboat, 292, 293,-296, 306, 307.
Lincoln, Pres., and *Trent* affair, 253; election in 1864, 346.
Lindsay, 328, 329.
Linnet, 192 ff.
Little Belt, 99.
Little Belt (sloop), 166, 170.
Llewellyn, Asst. Surg., 372.
Lockwood, Lt., 418.
Long, Sec., 447.
Long guns, explanation of the term, 46.
Loring, Commodore, 53, 54.
Los Angeles, 516.
Louisiana, 198.
Louisiana, Confederate ironclad, 321.
Louisiana, gunboat, 400.
Louisville, construction, 290; drawing of, 291; attacks Ft. Donelson, 297, 298.
Lovell, Gen., 320.
Low, Lt., 372.
Luckenback, 488.
Ludlow, Lt., 135.
Lundy's Lane, 190.
Lusitania, 483.
Lyman, Midn., 187.
Lynch, Cap., 348.

M

McCall, Ed. R., 153.
McCalla, B. H., 464, 469.

McCauley, C. S., 255 ff.
McClellan, Gen., 309, 310.
McClernand, Gen., 292, 326.
McCulloch, 435.
Macdonough, Thomas, takes part in burning the *Philadelphia*, 76; defeats the British on Lake Champlain, 191 ff.
McDougal, David, action at Shimonoséki, 365 ff.
Macedonian, captured by the *United States*, 117 ff.; blockaded in New London, 144; sent to Algiers, 204.
Mackenzie, A. S., mutiny on *Somers*, 214–8.
Mackinac, 162.
McKinley, Pres., 423 ff.
McKnight, Lt., 182, 187.
Macomb, Comdr., 364.
Macomb, Gen., 192.
Madison, Pres., 100.
Mahan, A. T., 424, 425.
Mahopac, 399.
Maine, 427–9.
Majestic, 199.
Mallory, Sec., 262.
Manassas, 316, 317, 321.
Manhattan, 334, 339, 343.
Manila, battle of, 437, ff.; diagram, 438; the city taken, 459, 463.
Manila, 442.
Manly, John, 11.
Manners, Wm., 155 ff.
Maples, Capt., 151, 152.
Marblehead, 451, 452.
Maria, 42.
Maria Teresa, 447 ff.
Marine Committee, 11 ff.
Marine Corps, established, **52**; in World War, 508.

552   Index

Marques del Duero, 442.
Marston, Capt., 278.
Mary Ann, 203.
Mashuda, 205.
Mason, James M., 251 ff.
Mastico, 76.
Massachusetts, 411, 433, 451 ff.
Mattabesett, 352, 353.
Maury, Matthew Fontaine, 425.
Mease, Purser, 35.
Mayo, Henry T., 500.
Medusa, 367.
Melampus, 95.
Mellish, 24.
Melville, G. W., with *Jeannette* expedition, 414 ff.; in Greely relief party, 418.
Memphis captured, 308.
Mercedita, 394.
Merchant marine disappearance of, after the Civil War, 387; growth during World War, 518–520.
Merrimac, burned at Norfolk, 256–9, 262; a new type, 260; rebuilding of, 262–4; destroys the *Cumberland*, 264–8; destroys the *Congress*, 268–272; engages the *Monitor*, 278 ff.; later career, 286; attempt to break the blockade, 390.
Merrimac (collier), 451, 457.
Merritt, Gen., 444.
Metacomet, 334, 337–9.
Metcalf, Sec., 473.
Mexican War, 220 ff.
Mexico refuses to sell California, 220; treaty with, 225.
Miami, 351–3.
Miantonomah, 411.
Miles, Gen., 458, 459.
Milford, 24.

Mill prison, 19, 22.
Miller, Rear-Admiral, 423.
Minneapolis, 449.
Minnesota, at Hampton Roads, 265, 270; attacked by the *Merrimac*, 278 ff.; at Fort Fisher, 399.
Mississippi, in Perry's expedition to Japan, 227 ff.; the battle below New Orleans, 317; burned, 327.
Mississippi (Confederate ironclad), 321.
Mississippi and tributaries, map of, 289.
Mobile captured, 404.
Mobile Bay, battle of, 330 ff.; diagram of, 333.
Monadnock, 399, 411, 444.
Monaghan, Ensign, 466.
Monitor, contract for, 273, 274; transverse section (drawing), 275; trip to Hampton Roads, 272, 277; engages the *Merrimac*, 278 ff.; later career, 286, 287.
Monocacy, 435.
Monongahela, 338, 340, 344.
Montague, 149, 175.
Montauk, 394, 395.
Monterey, 411, 444.
Montezuma, 54.
Montgomery, Capt., 220.
Montojo, Admiral, 436 ff.
Morgan, 334, 339.
Morocco, 61, 71.
Morris, Charles, in the Tripolitan War, 76; the burning of the *Philadelphia*, 77 ff.; the chase of the *Constitution* 103 ff.; battle of the *Constitution* and the *Guerrière*, 113.

Morris, G. U., 264.
Morris, Richard V., 68, 69.
Morris, Robert, 12.
Morrison, 226.
Mound City, 290.
Mounted Naval Railway Batteries, 507.

N

Nahant, 396, 397.
Nanshan, 435.
Napoleon, decrees of, 96.
Napoleon, Louis, 328, 329.
Napoleon, 211.
Nashville, 375, 394.
Naugatuck, 287.
Nautilus, 69, 84, 88, 89, 91, 102.
Naval Academy, 218, 219.
Naval Boards, in the Revolution, 12.
Naval Committee, in the Revolution, 11 ff.
Navy, in the Revolution, size of, 15; building of a new, 44; at outbreak of the Civil War, 238 ff.; changes in, after 1850, 406; decay of, after the Civil War, 406 ff.; rehabilitation of, 409 ff.; in Polar exploration, 412 ff.; diplomatic and special services of 419 ff.; in Spanish-American War, 433; humanitarian service, 512, 525.
Nelson, C. P., 491.
Newark, 411, 466, 469.
New Ironsides, contracted for, 274; torpedo attack on, 356; description of, 395; at Ft. Fisher, 399, 401.
New Orleans, battle of, 198.
New Orleans, expedition against, 310 ff.

New York, frigate, 68.
New York, Ship-of-the-line, 259.
New York, cruiser, 452 ff.
New York, battleship, 498, 499.
Nicaragua, 531.
Niagara, 166 ff.
Nicholson, Capt., 40, 50, 51.
Nicholson, 489, 490.
Nields, H. C., 338.
Nine-Power Treaty, 523.
Nissen, Consul, 74, 206.
Non-Intercourse Act, 98.
Norfolk, 54.
Norfolk Navy Yard, abandoned, 255 ff.
North Carolina, 217.
North Dakota, 50, 473.
North Pole, 418, 517.
Northern Mine Barrage, 504–506.

O

O'Brien, 9, 10.
Octorora, 334, 337, 338.
Ohio, 166, 171.
Olympia, 435 ff.
Oneida, 317, 318, 338, 339.
Ontario, 204.
Open Door, 468.
Orders in Council, 97 ff.
Oregon, 411, 430, 451 ff.
Ossipee, 344, 345.
Ottawa, 250.

P

Page, Octavius, 135.
Pallas, 31 ff., 38.
Palmer, Surgeon, 340.
Palmetto State, 394.
Pamlico and Albemarle Sounds (map), 349.
Panama Canal, 528.
Pan-Americanism, 532.

Paris, Declaration of, 388.
Parrott guns, 260.
Patrick Henry, 269, 271, 278.
Patterson, Master-Comdt., 207.
Paulding, Hiram, sent to Norfolk, 257, 258, 262; member of board on ironclads, 274.
Pawnee, 257, 258.
Peacock, captured by the *Hornet*, 149, 150.
Peacock (2d), takes the *Epervier,*, 153, 154; attack on British commerce, 160.
Peake, Wm., 150.
Pearson, Capt., 32 ff.
Peary, Robt. E., 418, 419.
Pelican, captures the *Argus*, 151, 152.
Pembroke, 366, 367.
Pendergrast, Lt., 269.
Penguin, taken by the *Hornet*, 158, 159.
Pennsylvania, 257, 259.
Pensacola, 312 ff.
Pensacola, surrender of yard, 258.
Perkins, G. H., at New Orleans, 317, 318; Mobile Bay, 343.
Perry, M. C., in West Indies, 208; the slave trade, 213; Mexican War, 224–5; commands expedition to Japan, 225 ff.; as a diplomat, 419.
Perry, O. H., Lake Erie, 164 ff.; West Indies, 208.
Petrel, 411, 435.
Phelps, Lt.-Comdr., 295.
Philadelphia, sent to Tripoli, 64, 68; blockade duty, 66, 70; under Preble, 69; loss of, 71 ff.; burning of, 77 ff.
Philadelphia, cruiser, 423.

Philippines, war in, 434 ff., 462–465.
Phillips, Capt., 53, 54.
Phoebe, 178, 180 ff.
Pillow, Gen., 296.
Pillsbury, Rear-Admiral, 425.
Piracy, in West Indies, 207–11.
Pittsburg, building of, 290; attacks Ft. Donelson, 297, 298; passes Island No. 10, 305, 306.
Pittsburg Landing, battle of, 306, 307.
Platt, Lt., 209.
Plunkett, C. P., 507.
Pluton, 447, 454.
Plymouth, 227, 257, 259.
Poictiers, 149.
Polar explorations, the navy in, 412 ff., 517.
Polk, Pres., 220.
Pomone, 199, 200.
Pope, Gen., at Island No. 10, 301–6; Ft. Pillow, 307.
Porcupine, 166.
Porter, David, in action with the *Insurgente*, 56; with a prize crew, 57; first lt. of the *Philadelphia*, 72; commands *Essex*, 126; cruise of the *Essex*, 175 ff.; in West Indies, 208–11; court-martial of, 210.
Porter, David D., in Mexican War, 222–5; plans for capture of New Orleans, 310; commands mortar boats, 312, 319; suggests tactics, 321; attacks Vicksburg, 323; commands river squadron, 326; attacks Arkansas Post, 326; coöperates with Grant, 326–8;

ordered against Ft. Fisher, 347; captures Ft. Fisher, 398 ff.
Porter, J. L., 262.
Porter, W. D., 294, 325.
Port Hudson, 327.
Porto Rico, 449, 458, 459.
Port Royal, capture of, 244 ff.; diagram of battle, 246.
Port Royal, 287.
Post captain, explanation of the term, 136.
Potomac flotilla, 242, 243.
Powhatan, 236, 408.
Preble, Edward, commands squadron before Tripoli, 69; disciplinarian, 70; loss of the *Philadelphia*, 74, 75; plans to destroy the *Philadelphia*, 76; blockade and bombardment of Tripoli, 84 ff.; *Intrepid* disaster, 88 ff.; returns, 90; comments on treaty with Tripoli, 91; services in the war, 92; rounds Cape of Good Hope, 176.
Preble, battle of Lake Champlain, 191 ff.
Preble goes to Japan, 227.
President, building of, 50; sent to Tripoli, 64; under Barron, 90; action with the *Little Belt*, 99; cruise under Rodgers, 99, 102, 118; chase of the *Belvidera*, 102; runs the blockade, 134; captured, 198–200.
Pressqu'isle (Erie), naval base, 164, 166.
Provost, Geo., 191-2, 194, 198.
Prince of Orange, 20.
Princeton, 261, 274.
Pring, Capt., 191.

Prisoners, in the Revolution, 22, 23; in the Civil War, 389, 390.
Privateering, during the Revolution, 10, 40, 41; War of 1812, 201; Civil War, 388, 389.
Providence, 13, 24.

Q

Queen Charlotte, 166 ff.
Queen of the West, 328.

R

Raccoon, 178, 180.
Radford, Wm., 265, 268.
Rais Hammida, 205.
Raleigh, in the Revolution, 29.
Raleigh, Confederate ram, 354.
Raleigh, battle of Manila, 435.
Randolph, 29.
Ranger, cruise of, under Jones, 24 ff.; map of cruise, 28; engagement with the *Drake*, 27 ff.
Ranks, relative, in army and navy, 14.
Raritan, 259.
Razee, explanation of the term, 46.
Read, A. C., 515.
Reina Cristina, 439 ff.
Reina Mercedes, 451.
Reindeer, 154–7.
Reprisal, 19.
Resolution, 149.
Retaliation, 53, 54.
Retribution, 375.
Revenge, 21.
Rhode Island, 287.
Richmond, 330 ff.
Rifled cannon, 260.
River Defense Fleet, at Fort Pillow, 307, 308; engages Farragut, 321.

Roanoke, 265, 270.
Roanoke Island, capture of, 348, 349.
Roberts, Col., 302.
Robertson, Lt., 197.
Robinson, Lt., 69.
Robion, Capt., 441.
Rodgers, John, commands prize crew of the *Insurgente*, 57; in the Tripolitan War, 90; the *Little Belt* affair, 99; chases the *Belvidera*, 102.
Rodgers, John, at Port Royal, 250; begins construction of Mississippi River flotilla, 290, 292; commands the *Weehawken*, 396, 397.
Rodgers, John, flight to Hawaii, 516.
Rodgers, T. S., 497.
Rodman, Hugh, 498.
Roe, Capt., 353.
Rogers, Midn., 215.
Ronckendorff, Comdr., 374.
Roosevelt, Theodore, Russian-Japanese War, 471; Moroccan affair, 472; cruise of the Battle Fleet, 473; and Latin America, 528, 529.
Roosevelt, 418.
Rowan, Comdr., 348, 349.
Rowe, John, 76.
Russell, Lord, 371.

S

Sagasta, Prime Minister, 427, 428.
St. Lawrence, 265, 270.
St. Louis, building of, 290; attacks Ft. Donelson, 297, 298; attacks Island No. 10, 301.
St. Louis, scout cruiser, in Spanish-American War, 447.
St. Mary's Isle, 27.
St. Paul, 449.
Sallie, 375.
Saltonstall, Dudley, 13.
Samoan affair, 465–468.
Sampson. Wm. T., commands North Atlantic squadron, 432; blockades Cuba, 445 ff.; battle of Santiago, 452 ff.
San Diego, 500.
San. Jacinto and the *Trent*, 251 ff.; seeks the *Alabama*, 374, 377.
San Juan de Ulloa, Vera Cruz, 223, 224.
San Juan, Porto Rico, bombardment of, 449.
Santiago, battle of, 452 ff.
Saranac, 446.
Saratoga, battle of Lake Champlain, 191 ff.
Saratoga, in Perry's expedition to Japan, 227.
Sassacus, 352, 353.
Saugus, 399.
Savannah, 389, 390.
Sawyer, Vice-Admiral, 102.
Scales, Archibald H., 498, 499.
Scapa Flow, 497 ff.
Schley, W. S., conducts relief of Greeley party, 418; commands Flying Squadron, 446; blockades Cienfuegos, 449; blockades Santiago, 450; at battle of Santiago, 454, 455.
Schofield, Gen., 403.
Schools for officers and enlisted men, 518. *See also* Naval Academy.
Scorpion, 166, 169, 170.

Index

Scott, Winfield, 190, 222, 255.
Scourge, 84.
Screw propellers, 260.
Secretary of the Navy, office created, 52.
Selkirk, Earl of, 27.
Selma, 334, 339.
Semmes, Raphael, 371 ff.
Serapis, battle with the Bonhomme Richard, 30 ff.
Sever, James, 50.
Seymour, Vice-Admiral, 467.
Shafter, Gen., 452, 458.
Shannon, flagship of Broke's squadron, 102; captures the Chesapeake, 137 ff.
Shark, 208.
Shaw, John, 59.
Shenandoah, cruiser, 371, 375, 387.
Shenandoah, dirigible, 516.
Sheridan, Gen., 346.
Sherman, Thomas W., 244.
Sherman, Wm. T., captures Atlanta, 346; captures Savannah and Charleston, 397.
Ship-of-the-line, illustration, 45; explanation of the term, 46.
Ships, development, 1812–1861, 260–2; recent developments, 478, 479.
Shot, comparative weight of American and British, 117.
Shufeldt, Robert W., 237.
Sibylle, 40.
Sicard, Rear-Admiral, 432.
Simms, Charles, 266.
Sims, W. S., 485.
Sinclair, Lt., commands the Argus, 102.
Sinclair, Lt., of the Alabama, account of the action with the

Kearsarge, 378 ff.; testimony in the Alabama-Kearsarge controversy, 384, 386.
Siren, 69, 77, 78, 84.
Sixth Battle Squadron, 498–500, 509.
Slave trade, 211–4.
Slidell, John, 251 ff.
Sloat, Commodore, 220, 221.
Sloop actions in the War of 1812, 144 ff.; map, 145.
Sloop of war, explanation of the term, 46; illustration, 49.
Small, Seaman, 215, 216.
Smith, John, in the Tripolitan War, 69, 102.
Smith, Joseph, on board to investigate building of armorclads, 274.
Smith, Joseph B., commands the Congress in the Civil War, 268, 269.
Smith, Melancton, 352.
Solebay, 24.
Somers, Richard, 69, 85, 88 ff.
Somers, battle of Lake Erie, 166 ff.
Somers, mutiny on, 214–8; loss of, 372.
Southfield, 351, 352, 358.
Spain, alliance with the United States, 30.
Spanish-American War, causes, 426 ff.; comparison of navies, 433; campaign in the West Indies (map), 448; losses, 459, 460; treaty of peace, 460, 461.
Spark, 204.
Spences, J. M., 335.
Spencer, Philip, 214–8.
Sperry, Rear-Admiral, 425.
Spitfire, 99, 224, 225.

Springs, explanation of the term, 184.
Stack, Lt., 35.
State navies in the Revolution, 41.
Stembel, Comdr., 292.
Sterrett, Andrew, 64 ff.
Stewart, Charles, commands the *Siren*, 69, 76; captures the *Cyane* and the *Levant*, 200, 201.
Stimers, Chief Engineer, 279.
Stockton, Commodore, 220 ff.
Stodder, Master, 279.
Stoddert, Benj., 52.
Stonewall Jackson, 318.
Stringham, Silas H., 244.
Strauss, Joseph, 505.
Subchasers, 491, 492.
Submarines, early forms of, 355, 356; recent developments in, 480, 481; World War, 485, 501 ff.; later developments, 514.
Sumter, 372, 375.
Surprise, 20.
Susquehanna, in Perry's expedition, 227 ff.; at Port Royal, 245.

T

Talbot, Silas, 50.
Tallahassee, 375.
Tattnall, Josiah, in the Mexican War, 224; at Port Royal, 248, 249; destroys the *Merrimac*, 286.
Taussig, J. K., 486, 487.
Taylor, Capt., 224.
Taylor, Gen., 222.
Tecumseh, 98, 174.
Tecumseh, 334–8, 345.

Tenedos, 134, 136, 199, 200.
Tennessee, captured by Farragut, 331 ff.; illustration, 341.
Terror, monitor, 441, 449.
Terror, Spanish torpedo-boat destroyer, 447.
Terry, Gen., 400 ff.
Texas, 452 ff.
Thames, battle of, 174.
Thetis, 416.
Thorn, Jonathan, 76.
Thornton, Lt.-Comdr., 384.
Thurot, 21.
Ticonderoga, 191 ff.
Tigress, 166 ff.
Tilghman, Gen., 295, 296.
Tingey, Capt., 137.
Torpedo, invention of, 355 ff.
Torpedo-boat, early forms of, 355 ff.; recent development of, 480.
Torpedo-boat destroyer, 480.
Torpedo bureau, in the Confederate Navy Dept., 356.
Toucey, Sec., 239.
Townsend, Capt., 102.
Trajano, 423.
Transport service, World War, 492 ff.
Treaty, with France, 23, 59; with Algiers, 50, 51, 206; with Great Britain, 52, 93, 201; with Morocco, 61; with Tunis, 61, 206; with Tripoli, 61, 91, 206; with Mexico, 225; with Japan, 236, 365; with Spain, 460; Limitation of Naval Armament, 521, 522; Four-Power Treaty, 523; Nine-Power Treaty, 523.
Trent affair, 251 ff.

Index

Tripoli, treaty with, 61, 91, 206; war with, 64 ff.; harbor of (map), 79; bombardment of, 84 ff.
Tripoli, action with the *Enterprise*, 65.
Trippe, Lt., 86.
Trippe, 166, 170.
Trumbull, 40.
Truxtun, Thomas, promoted to captaincy, 50; commands the *Constellation*, 51, 52; captures *Insurgente*, 55, 56; commands squadron against Tripoli, 67; resigns, 68.
Tunis, treaty with, 61, 206.
Tyler, 292, 293, 296, 297, 325.

U

U-58, 489, 490.
UB-65, 503.
Unicorn, 30.
United States, building of, 50, 51; in Rodgers' squadron, 102; captures the *Macedonian*, 117 ff.; plan of engagement with the *Macedonian*, 120; blockaded at New London, 144, 199; destroyed, 259.

V

Valley City, 363, 364.
Van Brunt, Capt., 280, 284.
Vanderbilt, 377.
Varuna, 317, 318.
Vengeance, brig., 31 ff.
Vengeance, frigate, 57, 58.
Venezuela Affair, 528.
Vera Cruz., naval operations before, 221 ff.
Vicksburg, attacked by the ships, 322 ff.

Vincennes, 226.
Virginia. See *Merrimac*.
Virginius affair, 409, 426.
Vixen, schooner, blockades Tripoli, 69-71; at bombardment of Tripoli, 84, 86; in the *Intrepid* disaster, 88, 89.
Vixen, steamer, 224.
Vixen, gunboat, 453, 455, 456.
Vizcaya, battle of Santiago, 447 ff.
Volontier, 54.
von Ketteler, Baron, 470.

W

Wabash, at Port Royal, 245 ff.; at Ft. Fisher, 399.
Wadsworth, Lt., 88.
Wainwright, Lt.-Comdr., 453.
Wales, Capt., 153.
Walke, Henry, 292, 302-6.
War of 1812, causes of, 93 ff., 100; declared, 100; preparation for by Congress, 100; comparison of naval forces, 101; results of, 201.
Ward, J. H., 242, 243.
Warley, Lt., 354 ff.
Warrington, Lewis, 153.
Washington, Geo., fits out a fleet, 10, 11; assisted by De Grasse, 41.
Washington, Thomas, 498.
Washington, 42.
Washington Conference, 520-524.
Wasp, schooner in Revolutionary Navy, 13.
Wasp, sloop of war (1st), defeats the *Frolic*, 146-9.
Wasp, sloop of war (2d), building of, 153; captures the *Reindeer*, 154-7; captures the

560 Index

Avon, 157, 158; success against British commerce, 160; loss of, 187.
Wasp, British sloop on Lake Champlain, 191.
Waterbury, Gen., 18.
Watson, Lt., 209.
Watson, J. C., 342.
Watson, W. H., 151, 152..
Watts, Lt., 140.
Weather-gage, explanation of the term, 119.
Weehawken, 396, 397.
Welles, Gideon, 240, 241, 376.
Wessells, Gen., 352.
Weyler, Gen., 426, 427.
Whinyates, Thomas, 146 ff.
Whipple, Abraham, 13.
Whipple, Wm., 26.
White Squadron, 410 ff.
Whitehaven, 27.
Whitehead, 352.
Whiting, J. W., 336.
Wickes, Lambert, 19.
Wiley, H. A., 498.
Wilkes, Charles, and the Trent affair, 251 ff.; commands Antarctic expedition, 412.
Wilkinson, Capt., 392.
Wilkinson, T. S., 505.
Williams, Col., 322, 324.
Williamson, W. P., 262.
Wilson, Seaman, 304.
Wilson, Joseph, 385.
Wilson, Henry P., 496.

Winnebago, 334, 337, 343.
Winona, 318, 319.
Winslow Comdr., 376 ff.
Winslow, 459.
Wise, Gen., 348.
Wissahickon, 319.
Wood, E. P., 441.
Wood, J. T., 268.
Wood, W. C., 464.
Woodford, Minister, 429, 432.
Woodman, Acting Master's Mate, 361, 364.
Worden, J. L., commands the Monitor, 277 ff.; destroys the Nashville, 394, 395.
World War, 483 ff.
Wright brothers, 481.
Wyalusing, 352.
Wyoming, at Shimonoséki, 365 ff.; search for the Alabama, 374, 377.

Y

Yale, 447.
Yangtze Patrol, 525, 526.
Yankee, 452.
Yantic, 416.
Yarmouth, 29.
Yeo, James Lucas, 165, 173, 189.
Yezaiman, Kayama, 232, 233.
York, capture of, 165.
Yorktown, 411.

Z

Zafiro, 435.
Zouave, 269.

www.ingramcontent.com/pod-product-compliance
Lightning Source LLC
Chambersburg PA
CBHW052042290426
44111CB00011B/1589